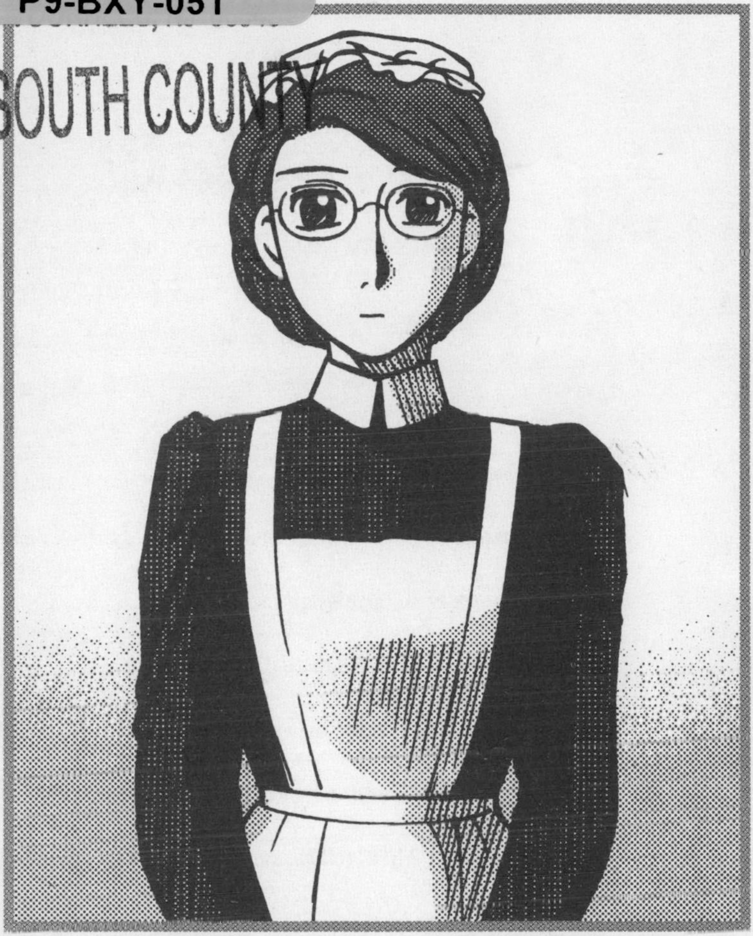

EMMA

Volume 3

By Kaoru Mori

-Contents-

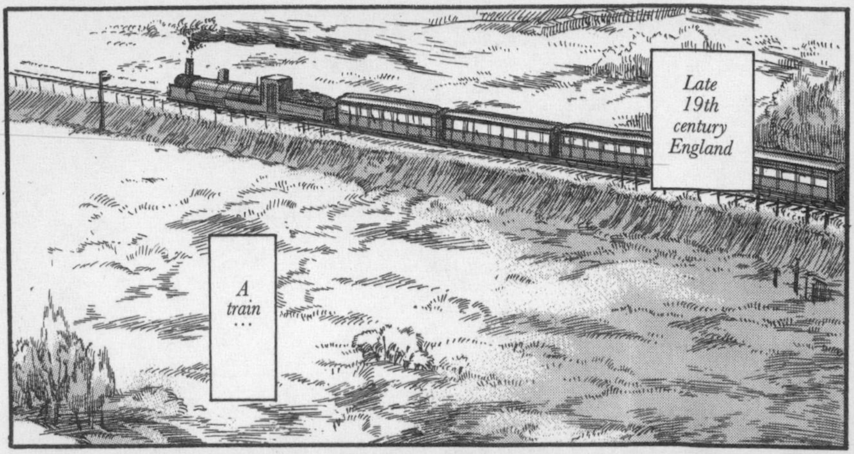
Late 19th century England
A train…
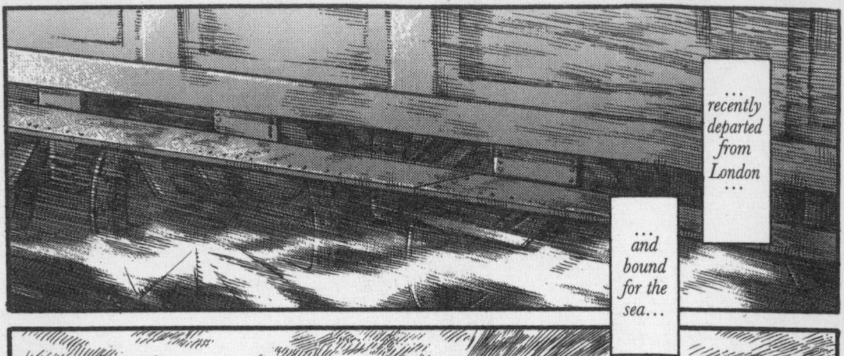
…recently departed from London…
…and bound for the sea…
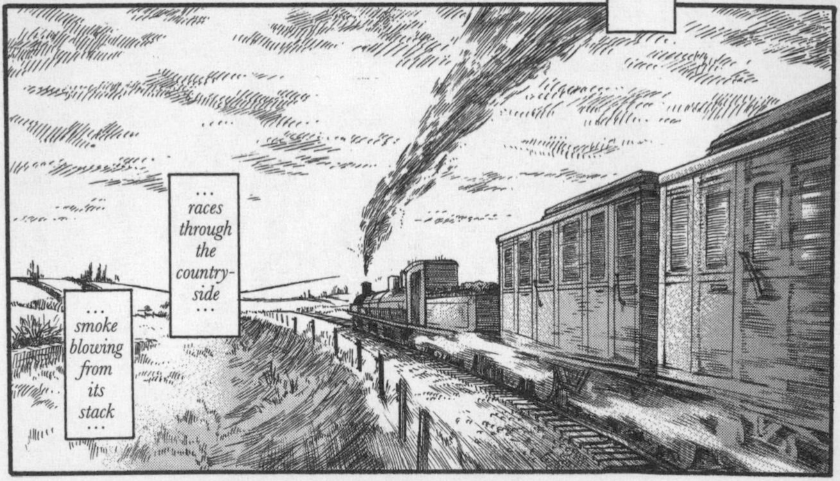
…races through the country-side…
…smoke blowing from its stack…

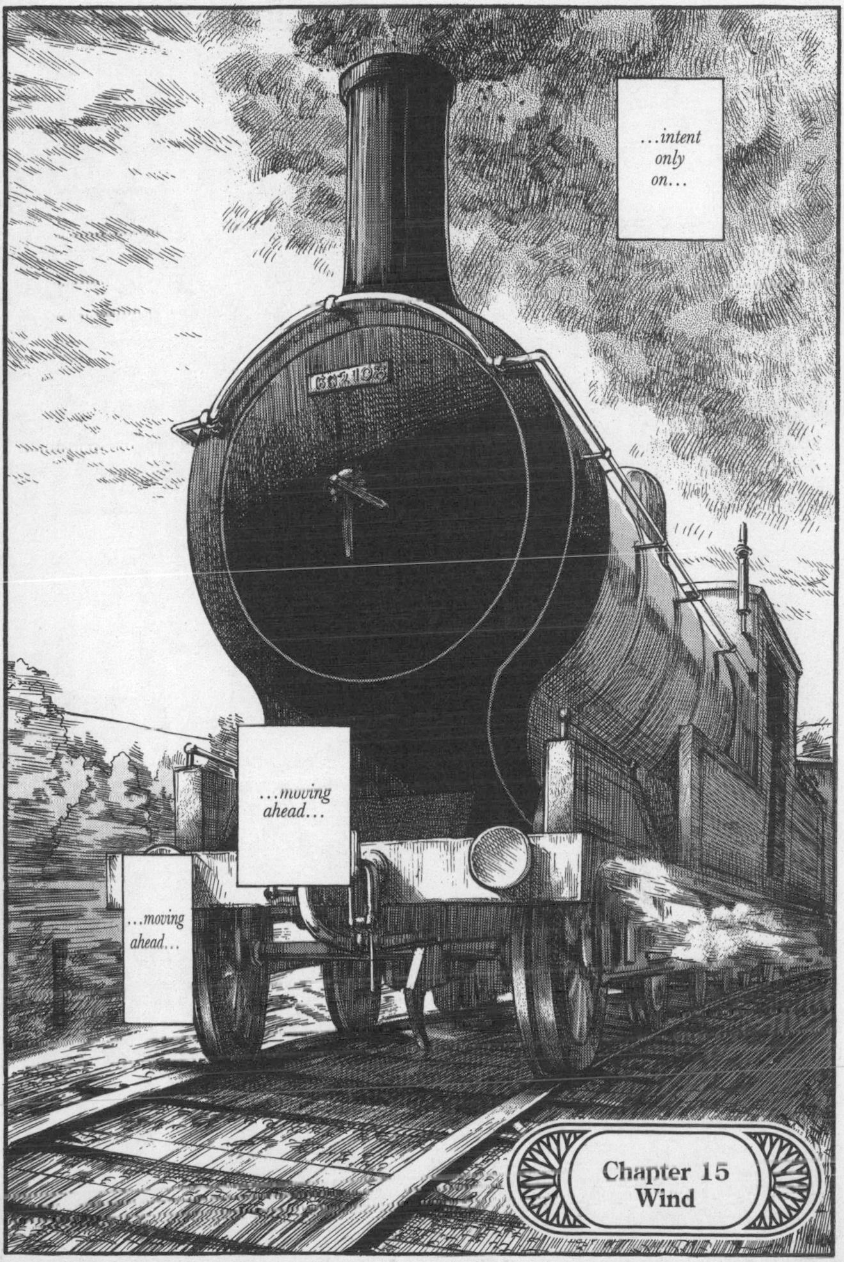

...intent only on...
...moving ahead...
...moving ahead...
Chapter 15 Wind

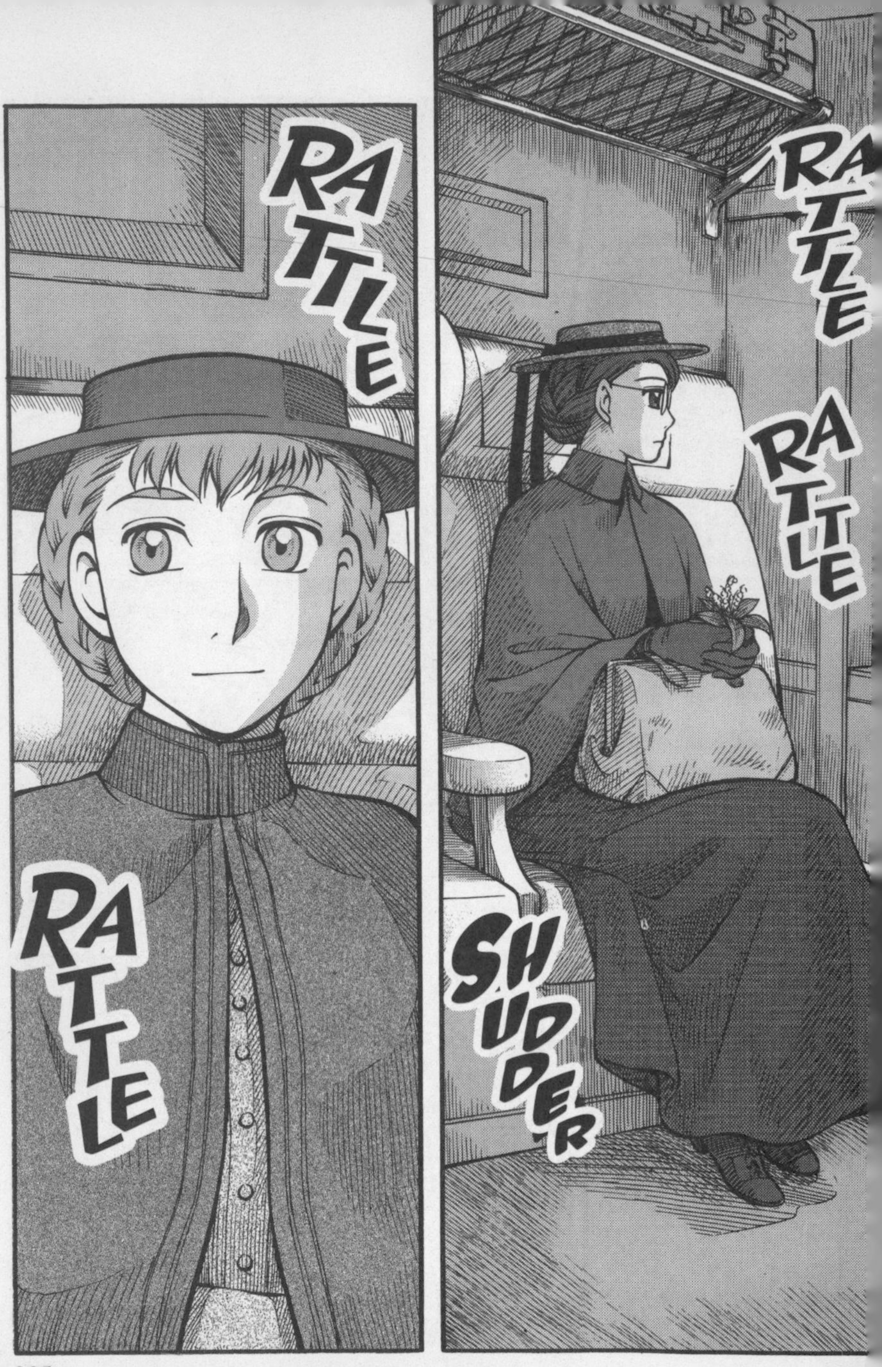
RATTLE
RATTLE
SHUDDER
RATTLE
RATTLE

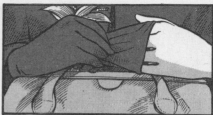

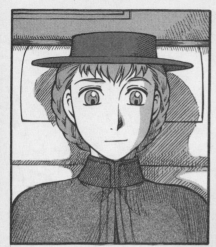

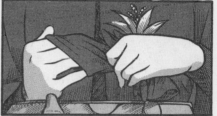

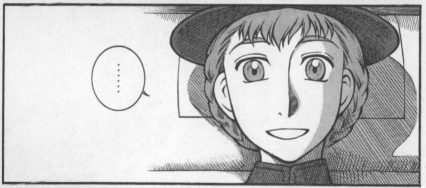

……

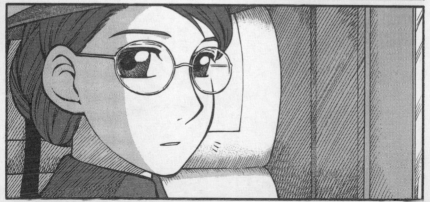

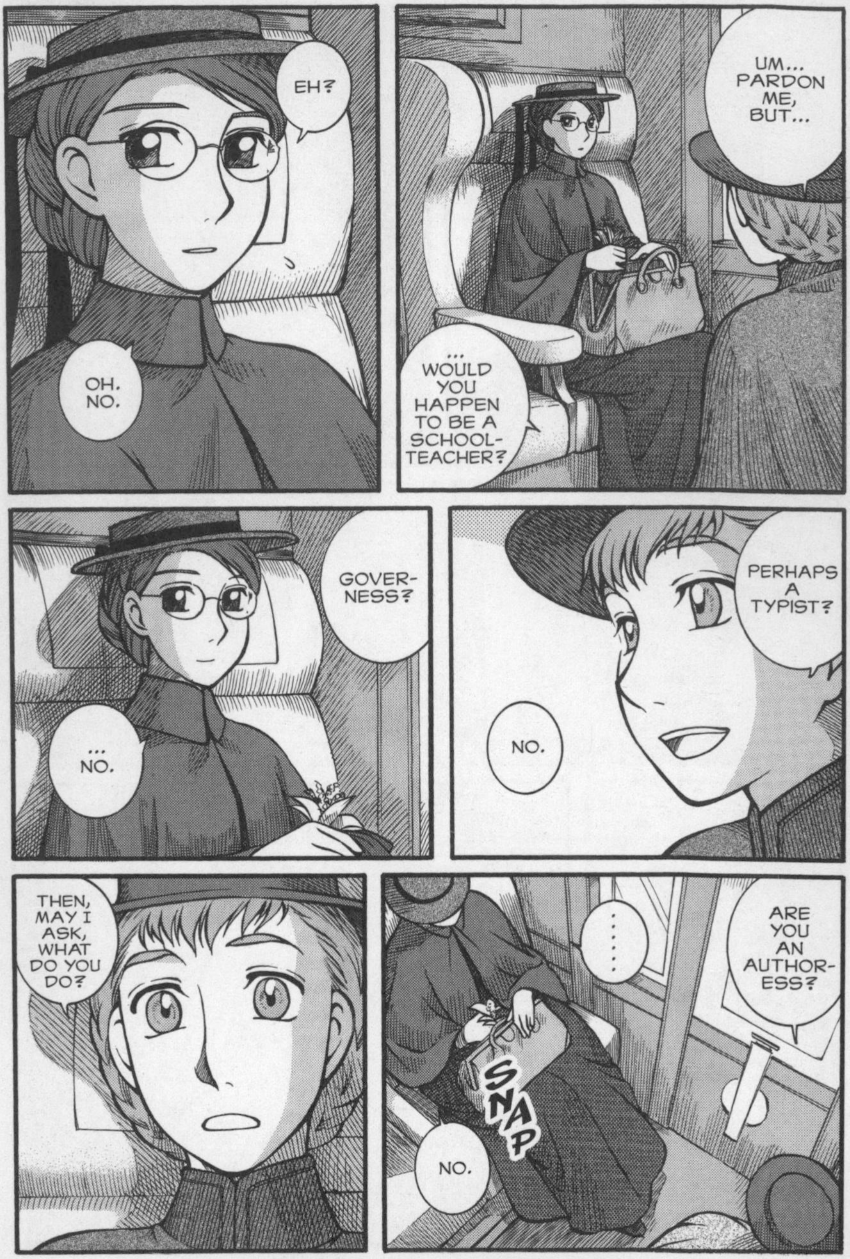
UM... PARDON ME, BUT...
...WOULD YOU HAPPEN TO BE A SCHOOL-TEACHER?
EH?
OH. NO.
PERHAPS A TYPIST?
NO.
GOVER-NESS?
... NO.
ARE YOU AN AUTHOR-ESS?
......
SNAP
NO.
THEN, MAY I ASK, WHAT DO YOU DO?

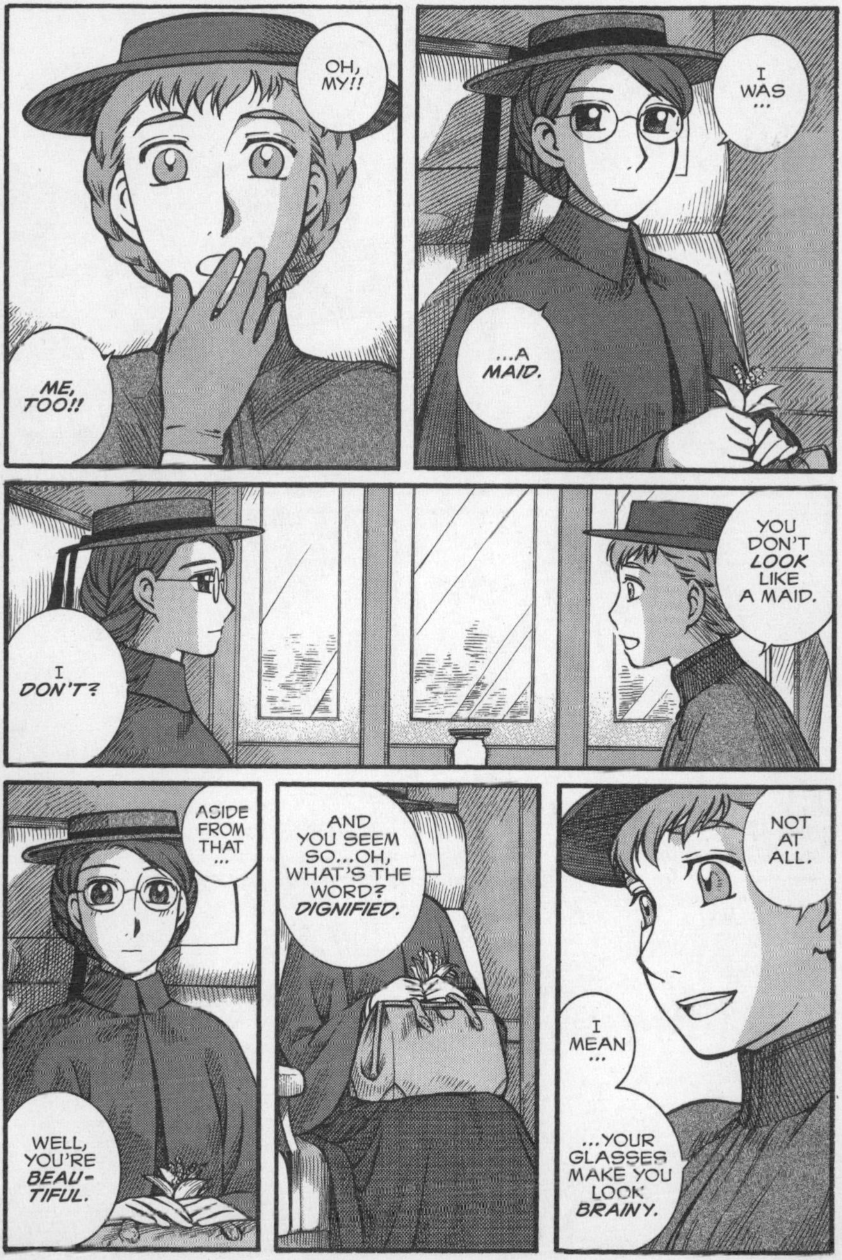
I WAS ...
...A *MAID.*
OH, MY!!
ME, TOO!!
YOU DON'T *LOOK* LIKE A MAID.
I *DON'T?*
NOT AT ALL.
I MEAN ...
...YOUR GLASSES MAKE YOU LOOK *BRAINY.*
AND YOU SEEM SO...OH, WHAT'S THE WORD? *DIGNIFIED.*
ASIDE FROM THAT ...
WELL, YOU'RE *BEAU-TIFUL.*

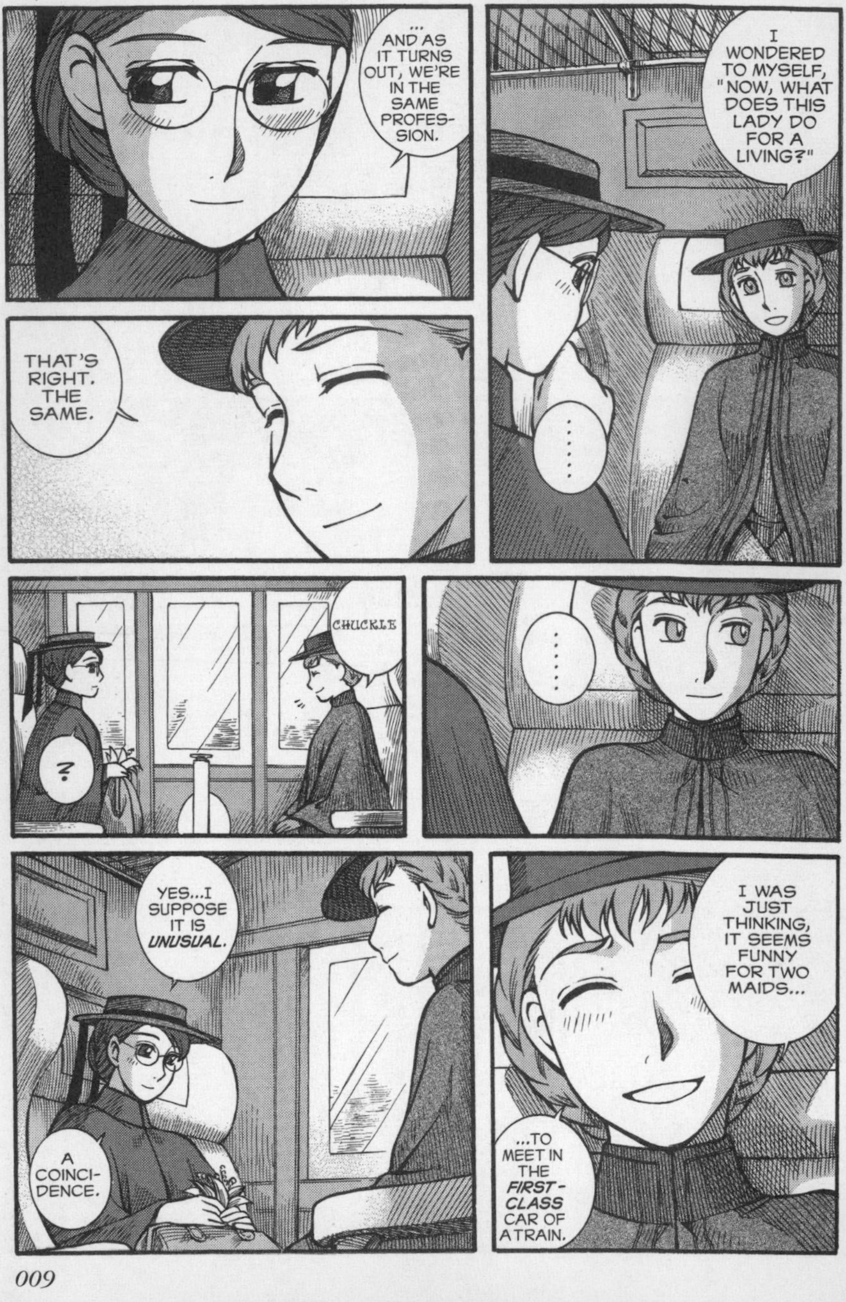
I WONDERED TO MYSELF, "NOW, WHAT DOES THIS LADY DO FOR A LIVING?"
......
...AND AS IT TURNS OUT, WE'RE IN THE SAME PROFES-SION.
THAT'S RIGHT. THE SAME.
......
CHUCKLE
?
I WAS JUST THINKING, IT SEEMS FUNNY FOR TWO MAIDS...
...TO MEET IN THE *FIRST-CLASS* CAR OF A TRAIN.
YES...I SUPPOSE IT IS *UNUSUAL*.
A COINCI-DENCE.

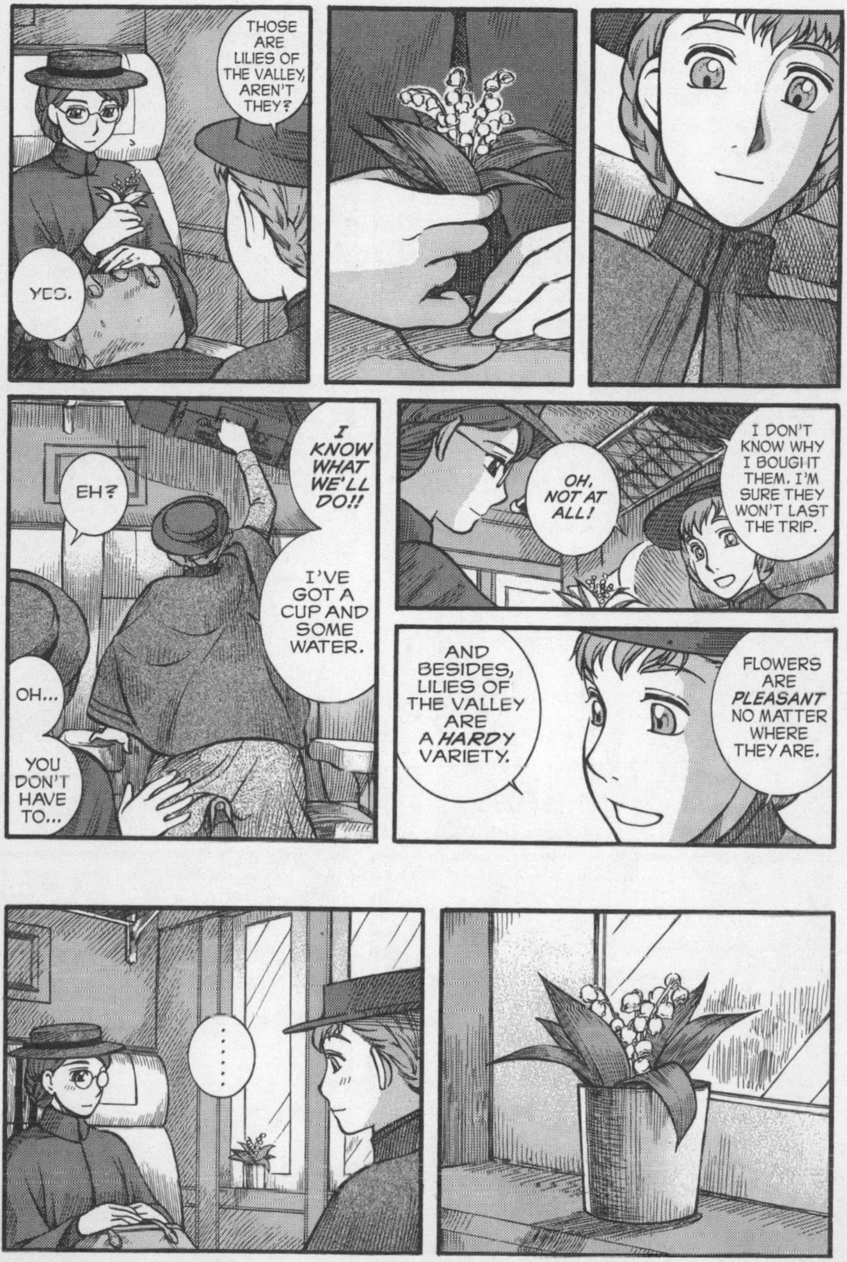
THOSE ARE LILIES OF THE VALLEY, AREN'T THEY?
YES.
I DON'T KNOW WHY I BOUGHT THEM. I'M SURE THEY WON'T LAST THE TRIP.
OH, NOT AT ALL!
FLOWERS ARE PLEASANT NO MATTER WHERE THEY ARE.
AND BESIDES, LILIES OF THE VALLEY ARE A HARDY VARIETY.
I KNOW WHAT WE'LL DO!!
I'VE GOT A CUP AND SOME WATER.
EH?
OH...
YOU DON'T HAVE TO...
......

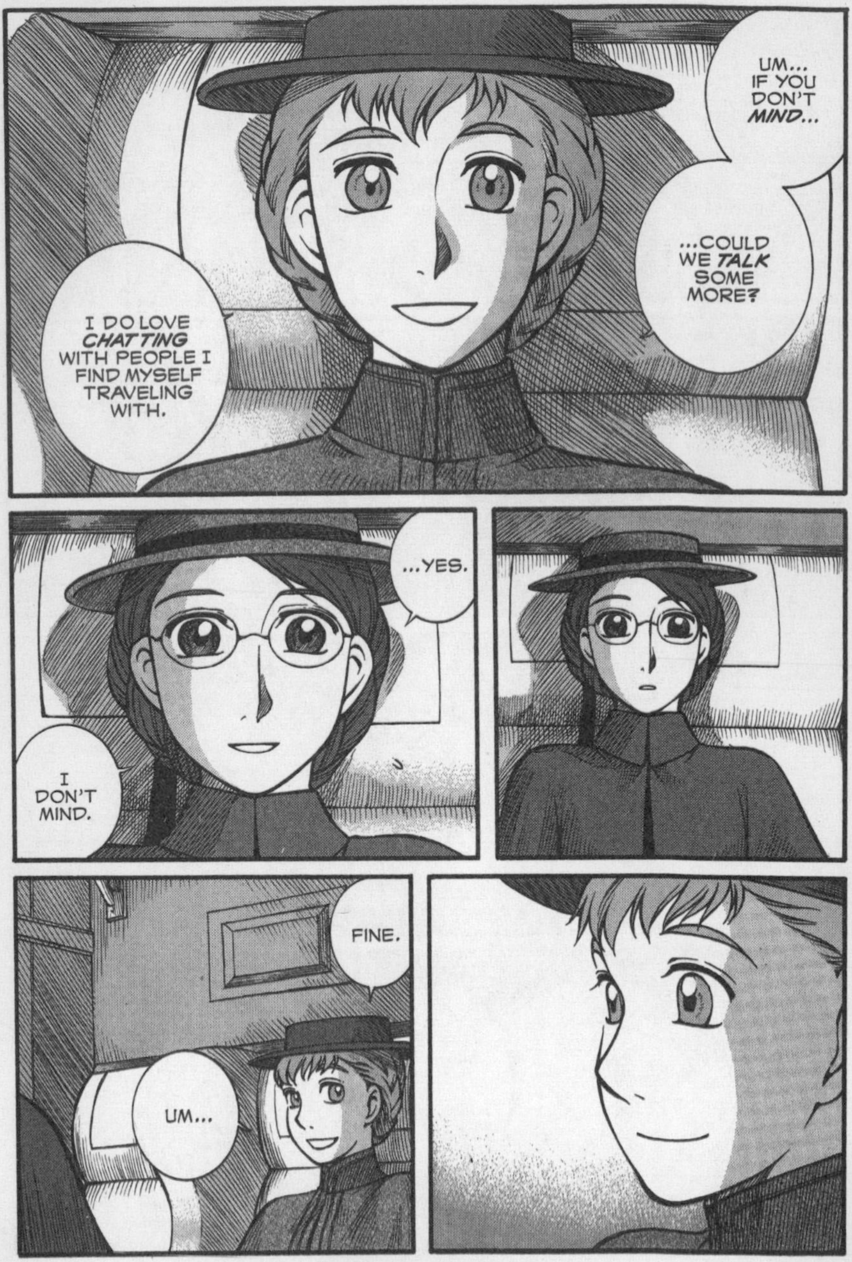
UM... IF YOU DON'T MIND...
...COULD WE TALK SOME MORE?
I DO LOVE CHATTING WITH PEOPLE I FIND MYSELF TRAVELING WITH.
...YES.
I DON'T MIND.
FINE.
UM...

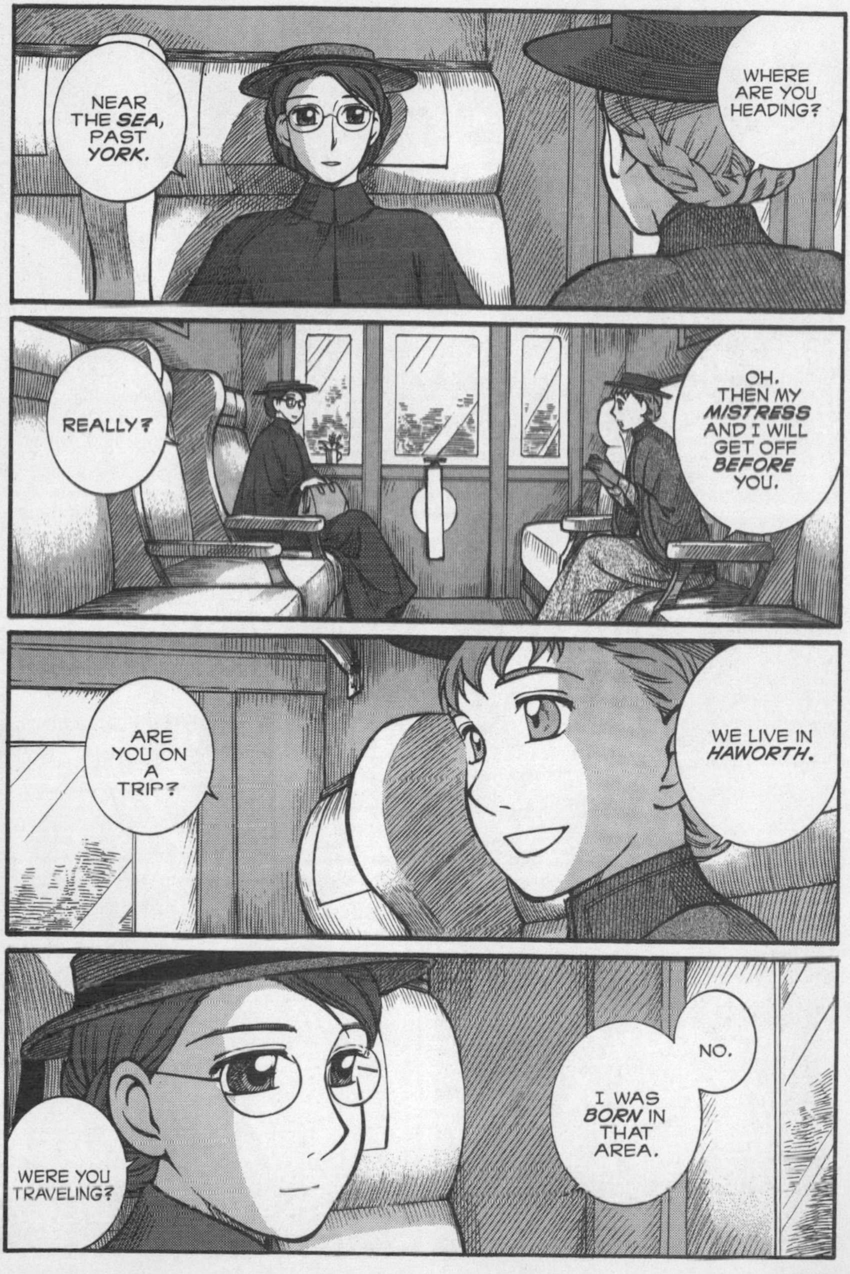
WHERE ARE YOU HEADING?
NEAR THE SEA, PAST YORK.
OH. THEN MY MISTRESS AND I WILL GET OFF BEFORE YOU.
REALLY?
WE LIVE IN HAWORTH.
ARE YOU ON A TRIP?
NO.
I WAS BORN IN THAT AREA.
WERE YOU TRAVELING?

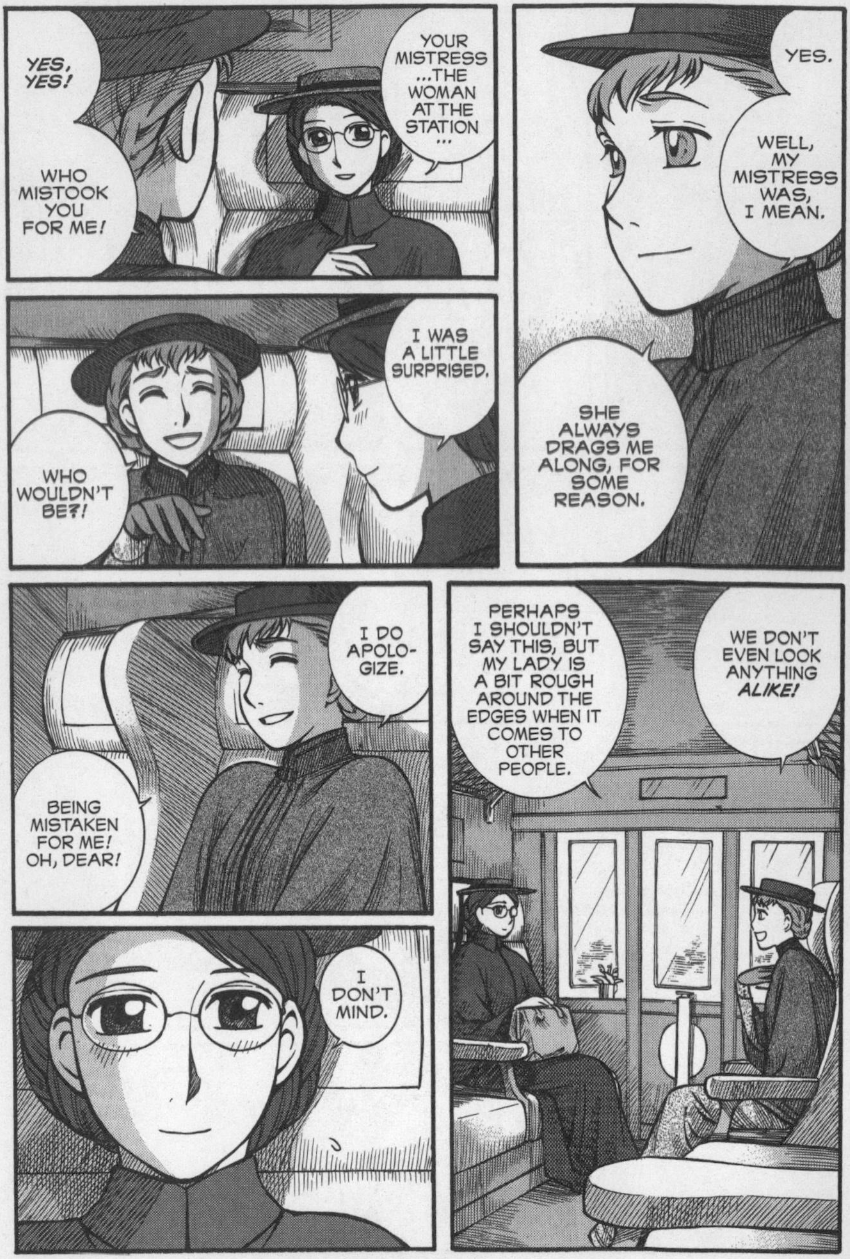
YES.
WELL, MY MISTRESS WAS, I MEAN.
SHE ALWAYS DRAGS ME ALONG, FOR SOME REASON.
YOUR MISTRESS ...THE WOMAN AT THE STATION ...
YES, YES!
WHO MISTOOK YOU FOR ME!
I WAS A LITTLE SURPRISED.
WHO WOULDN'T BE?!
WE DON'T EVEN LOOK ANYTHING *ALIKE!*
PERHAPS I SHOULDN'T SAY THIS, BUT MY LADY IS A BIT ROUGH AROUND THE EDGES WHEN IT COMES TO OTHER PEOPLE.
I DO APOLO-GIZE.
BEING MISTAKEN FOR ME! OH, DEAR!
I DON'T MIND.

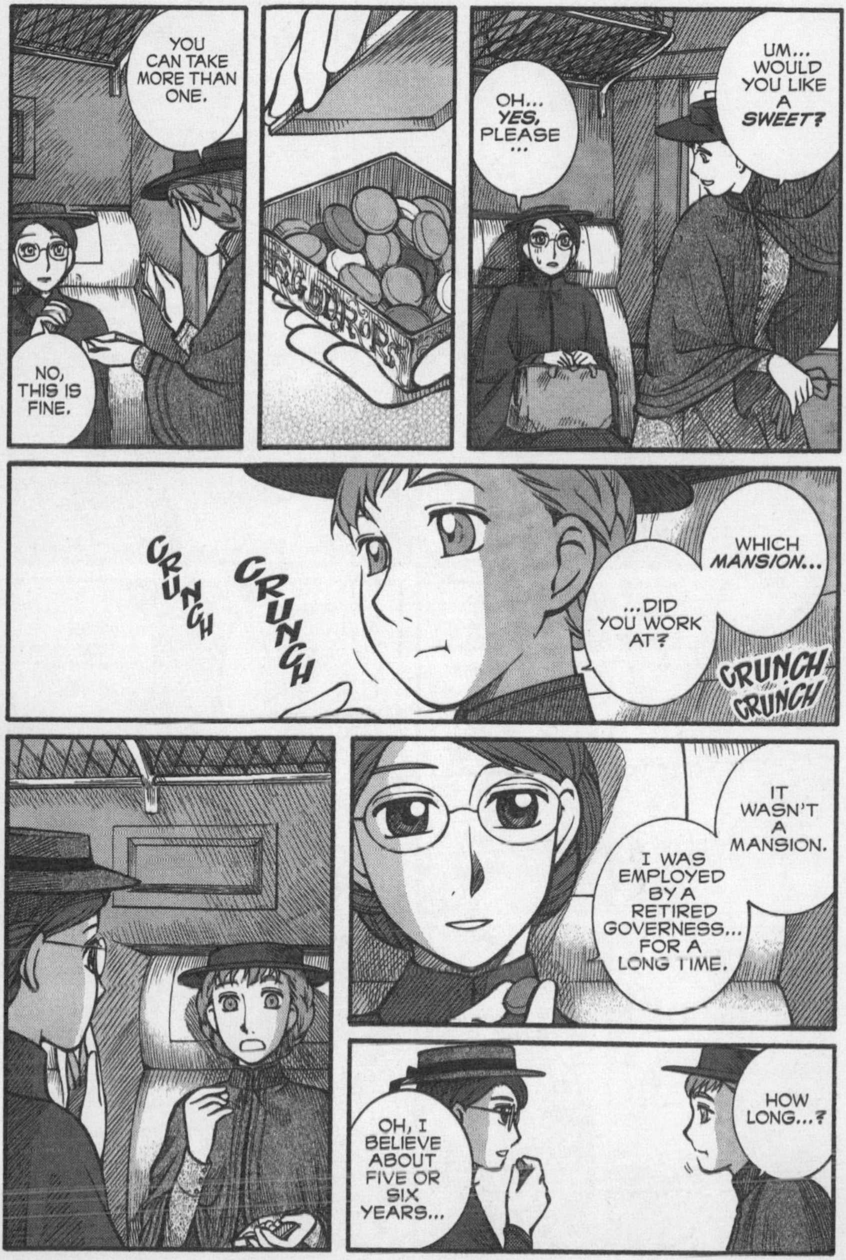

UM... WOULD YOU LIKE A *SWEET?*
OH... *YES,* PLEASE ...
YOU CAN TAKE MORE THAN ONE.
NO, THIS IS FINE.
WHICH *MANSION...*
...DID YOU WORK AT?
CRUNCH CRUNCH
CRUNCH
CRUNCH
IT WASN'T A MANSION.
I WAS EMPLOYED BY A RETIRED GOVERNESS... FOR A LONG TIME.
HOW LONG...?
OH, I BELIEVE ABOUT FIVE OR SIX YEARS...

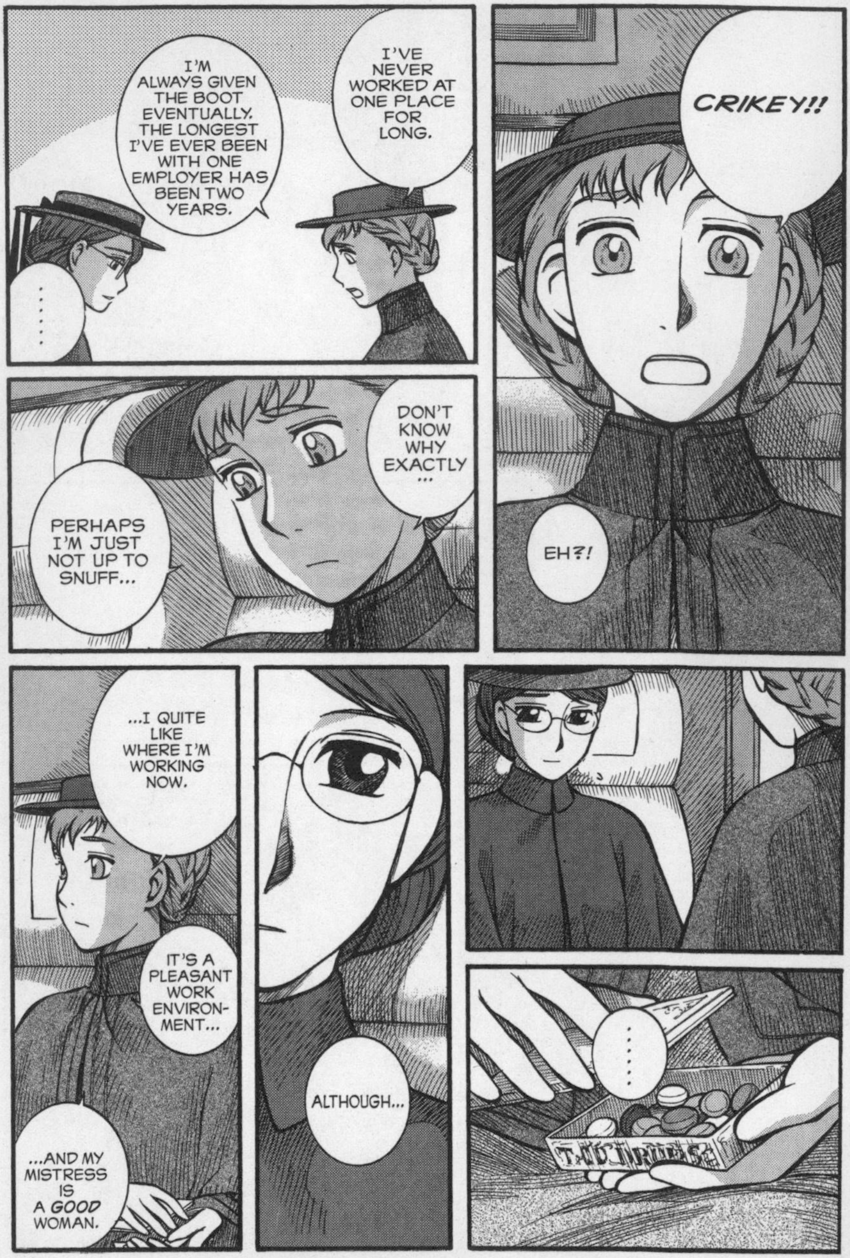
CRIKEY!!
EH?!
I'VE NEVER WORKED AT ONE PLACE FOR LONG.
I'M ALWAYS GIVEN THE BOOT EVENTUALLY. THE LONGEST I'VE EVER BEEN WITH ONE EMPLOYER HAS BEEN TWO YEARS.
......
DON'T KNOW WHY EXACTLY...
PERHAPS I'M JUST NOT UP TO SNUFF...
......
ALTHOUGH...
...I QUITE LIKE WHERE I'M WORKING NOW.
IT'S A PLEASANT WORK ENVIRONMENT...
...AND MY MISTRESS IS A *GOOD* WOMAN.

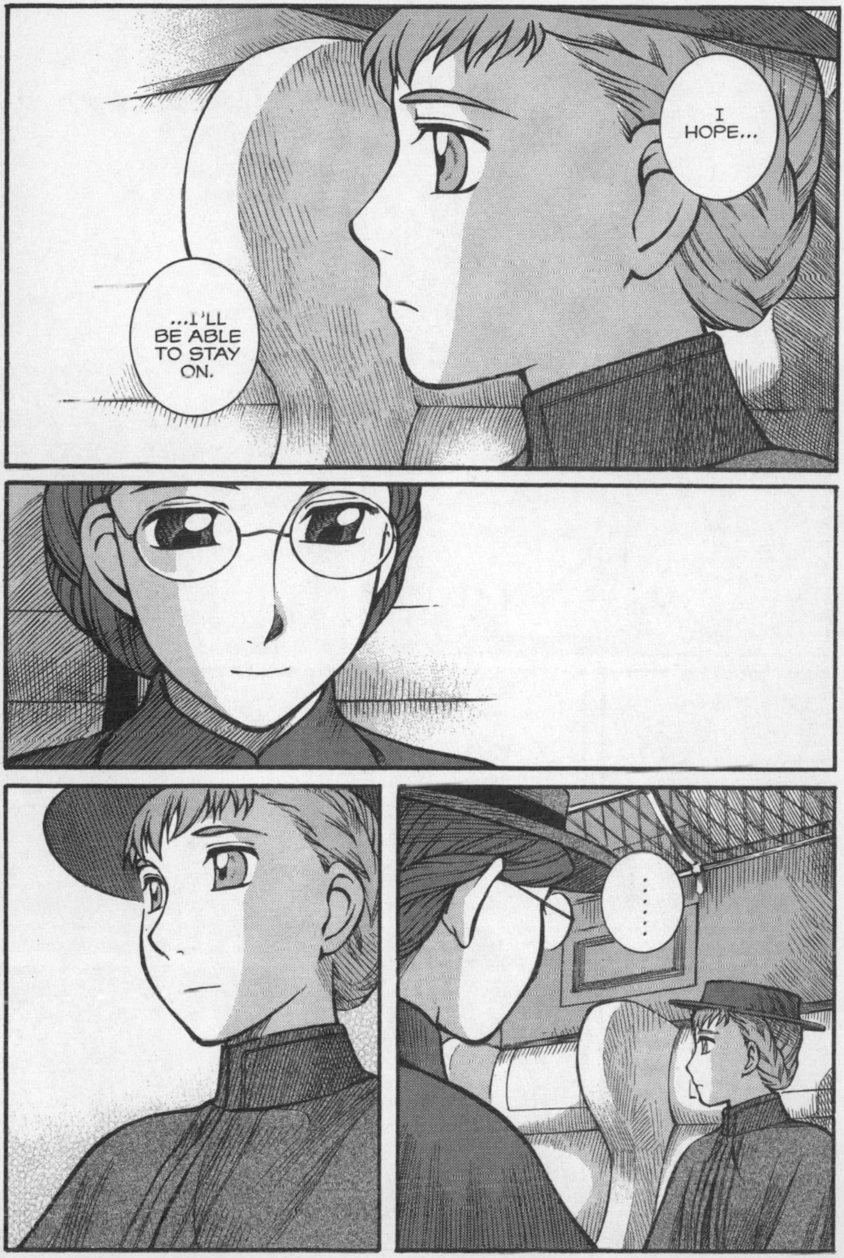
I HOPE...
...I'LL BE ABLE TO STAY ON.
......

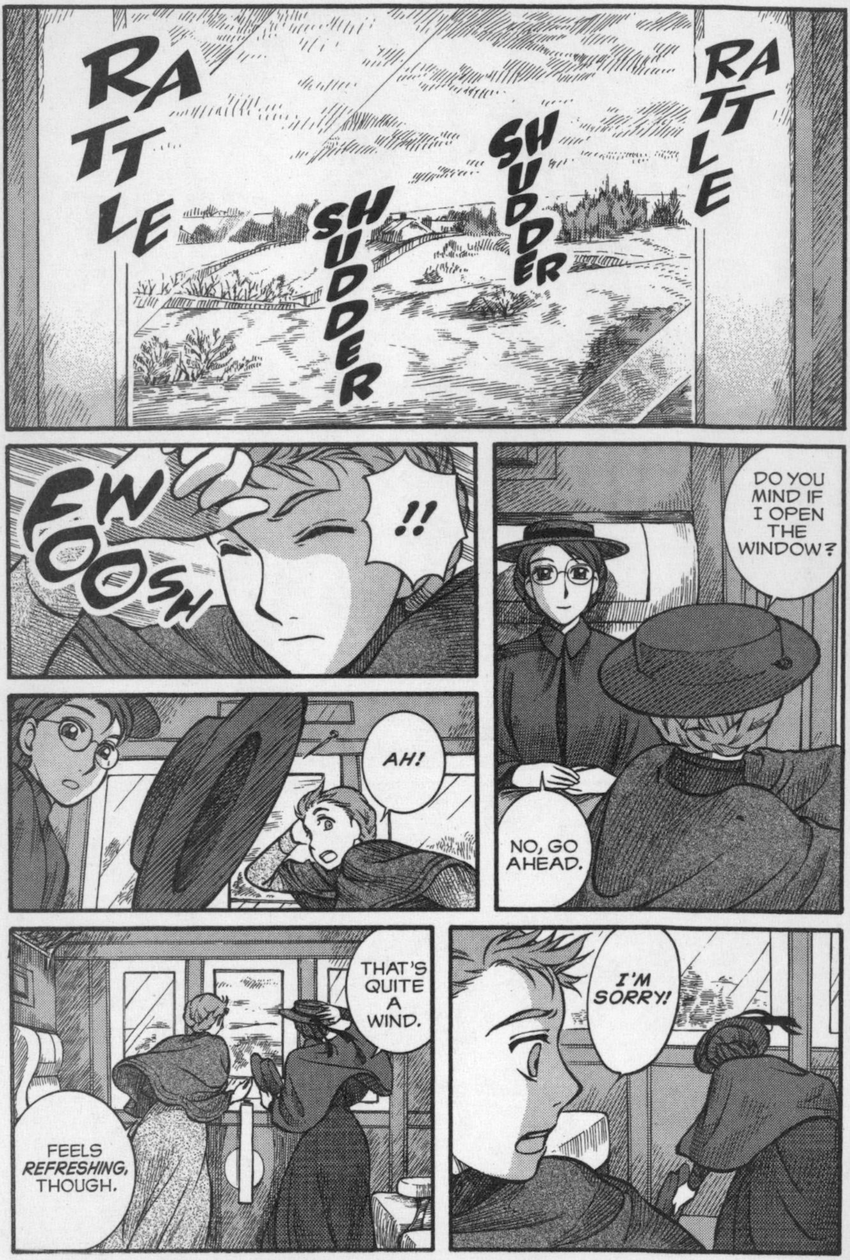
RATTLE
SHUDDER
SHUDDER
RATTLE
DO YOU MIND IF I OPEN THE WINDOW?
NO, GO AHEAD.
!!
FWOOSH
AH!
I'M SORRY!
THAT'S QUITE A WIND.
FEELS REFRESHING, THOUGH.

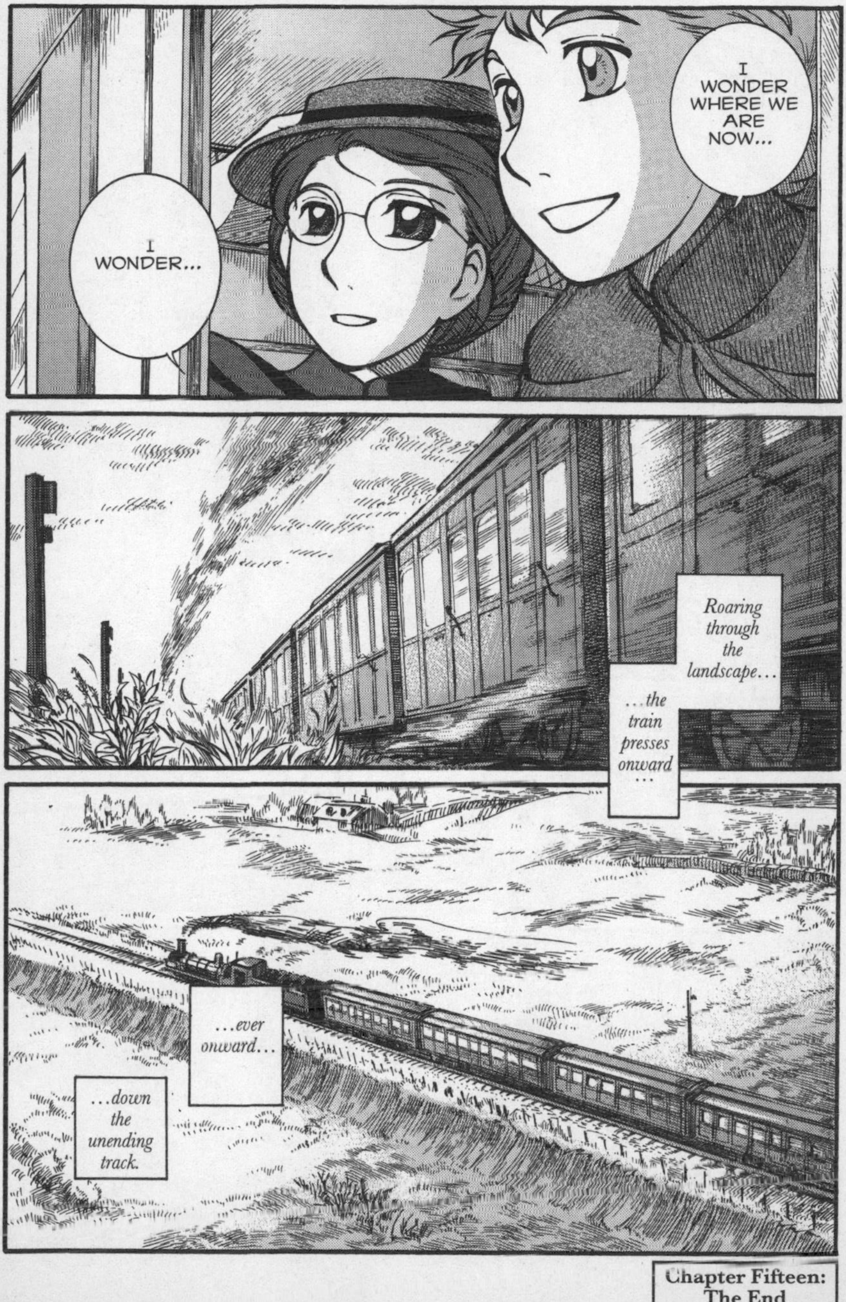
I WONDER WHERE WE ARE NOW...
I WONDER...
Roaring through the landscape...
...the train presses onward...
...ever onward...
...down the unending track.

Chapter Fifteen:
The End

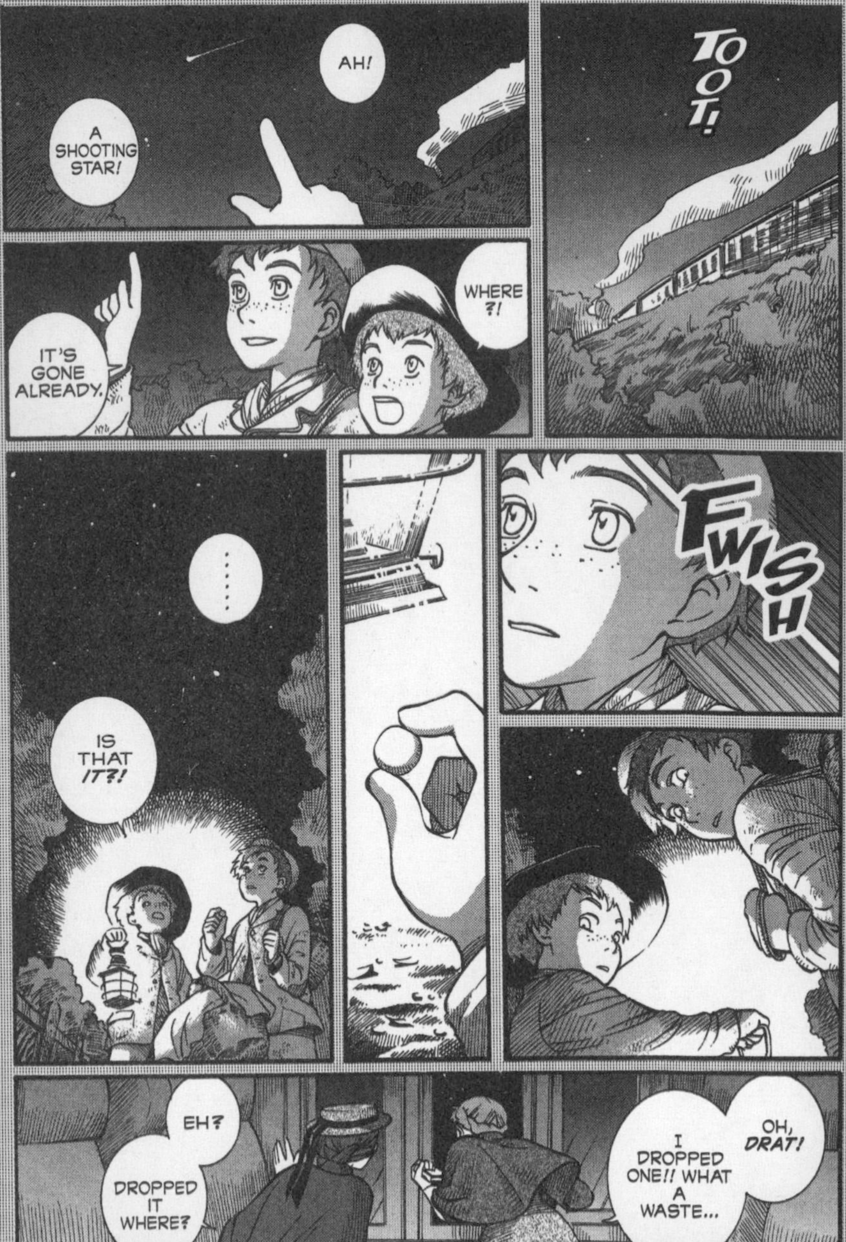
TOOT!
AH!
A SHOOTING STAR!
WHERE?!
IT'S GONE ALREADY.
FWISH
......
IS THAT IT?!
OH, DRAT!
I DROPPED ONE!! WHAT A WASTE...
EH?
DROPPED IT WHERE?

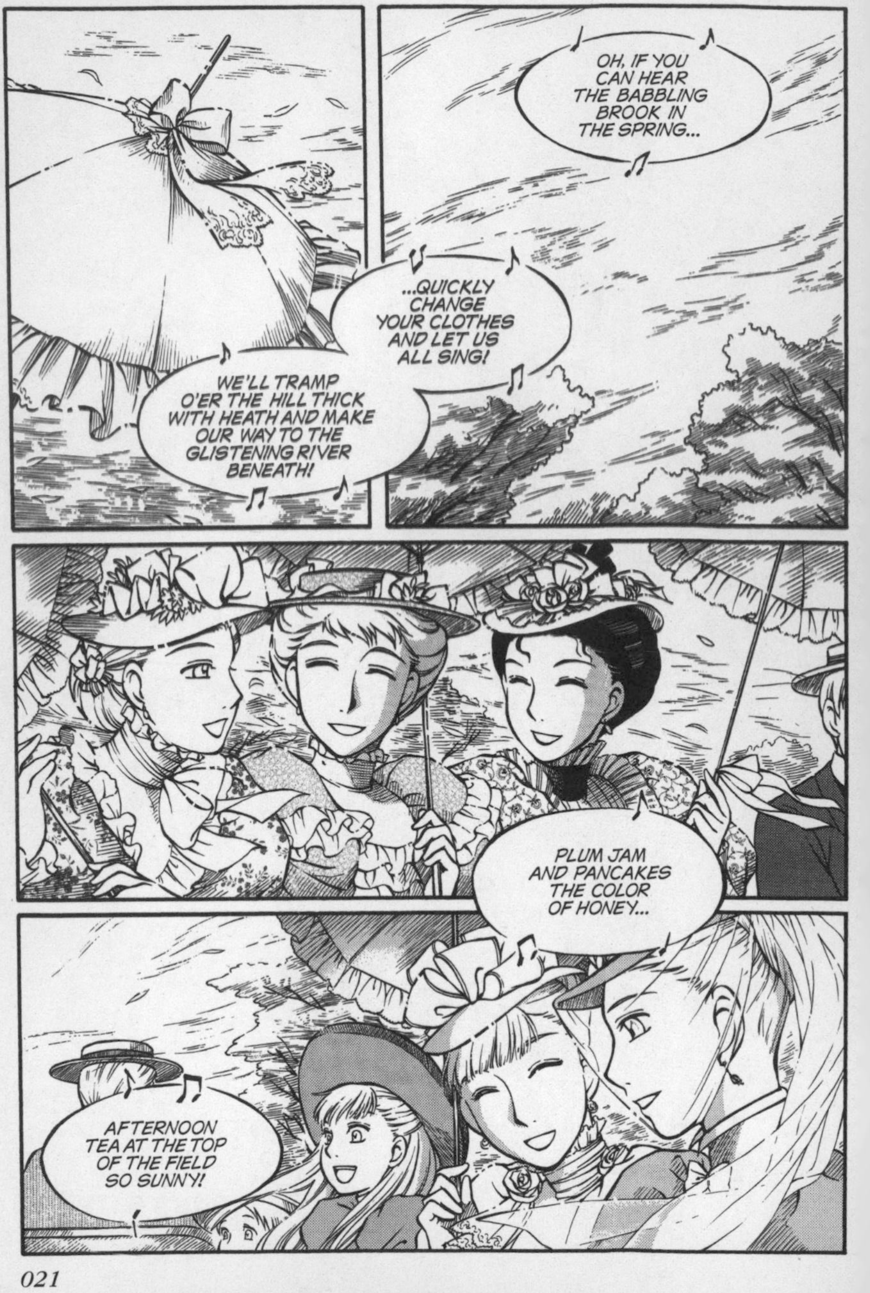
OH, IF YOU CAN HEAR THE BABBLING BROOK IN THE SPRING...
...QUICKLY CHANGE YOUR CLOTHES AND LET US ALL SING!
WE'LL TRAMP O'ER THE HILL THICK WITH HEATH AND MAKE OUR WAY TO THE GLISTENING RIVER BENEATH!
PLUM JAM AND PANCAKES THE COLOR OF HONEY...
AFTERNOON TEA AT THE TOP OF THE FIELD SO SUNNY!

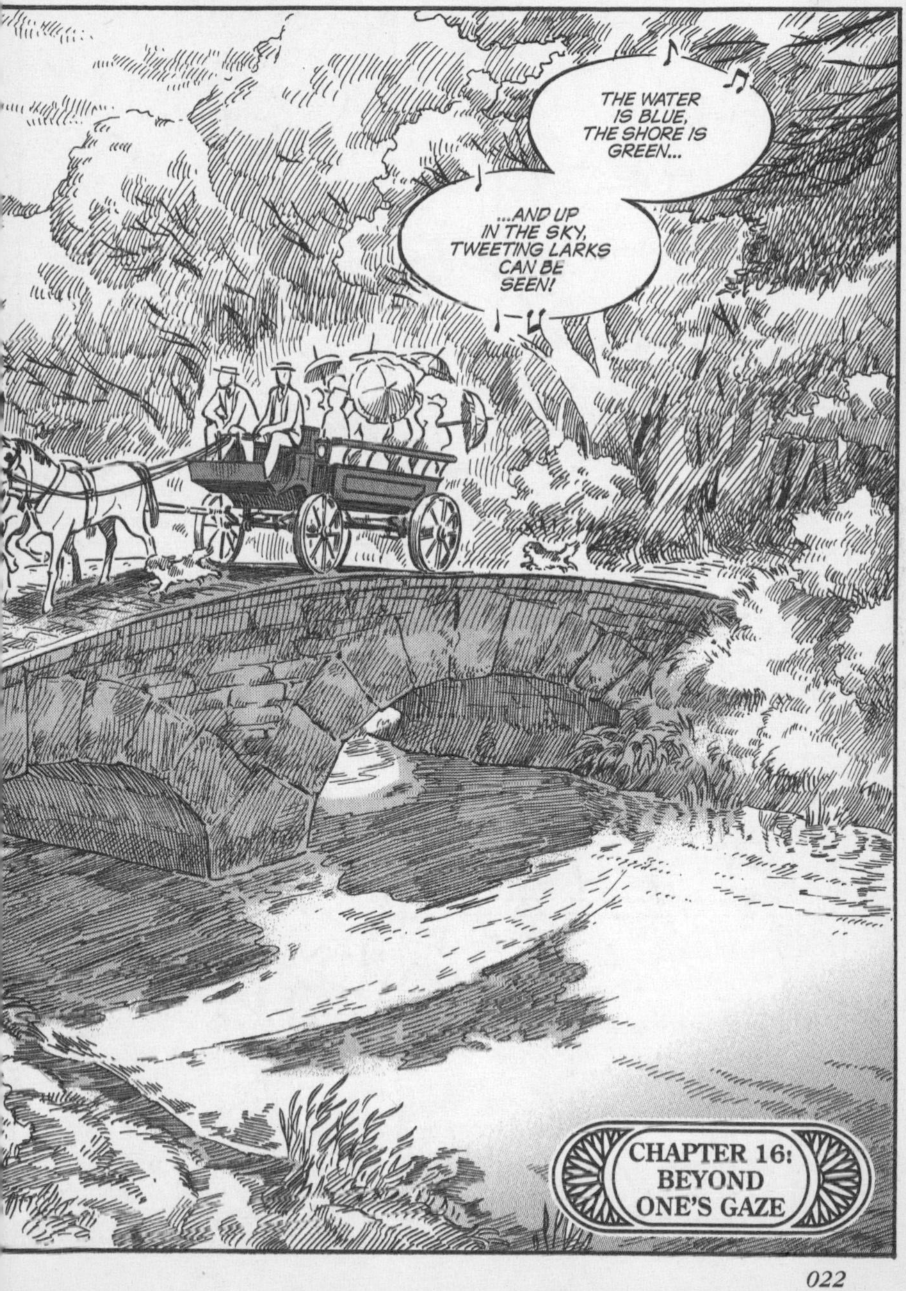
THE WATER IS BLUE, THE SHORE IS GREEN...
...AND UP IN THE SKY, TWEETING LARKS CAN BE SEEN!
CHAPTER 16: BEYOND ONE'S GAZE

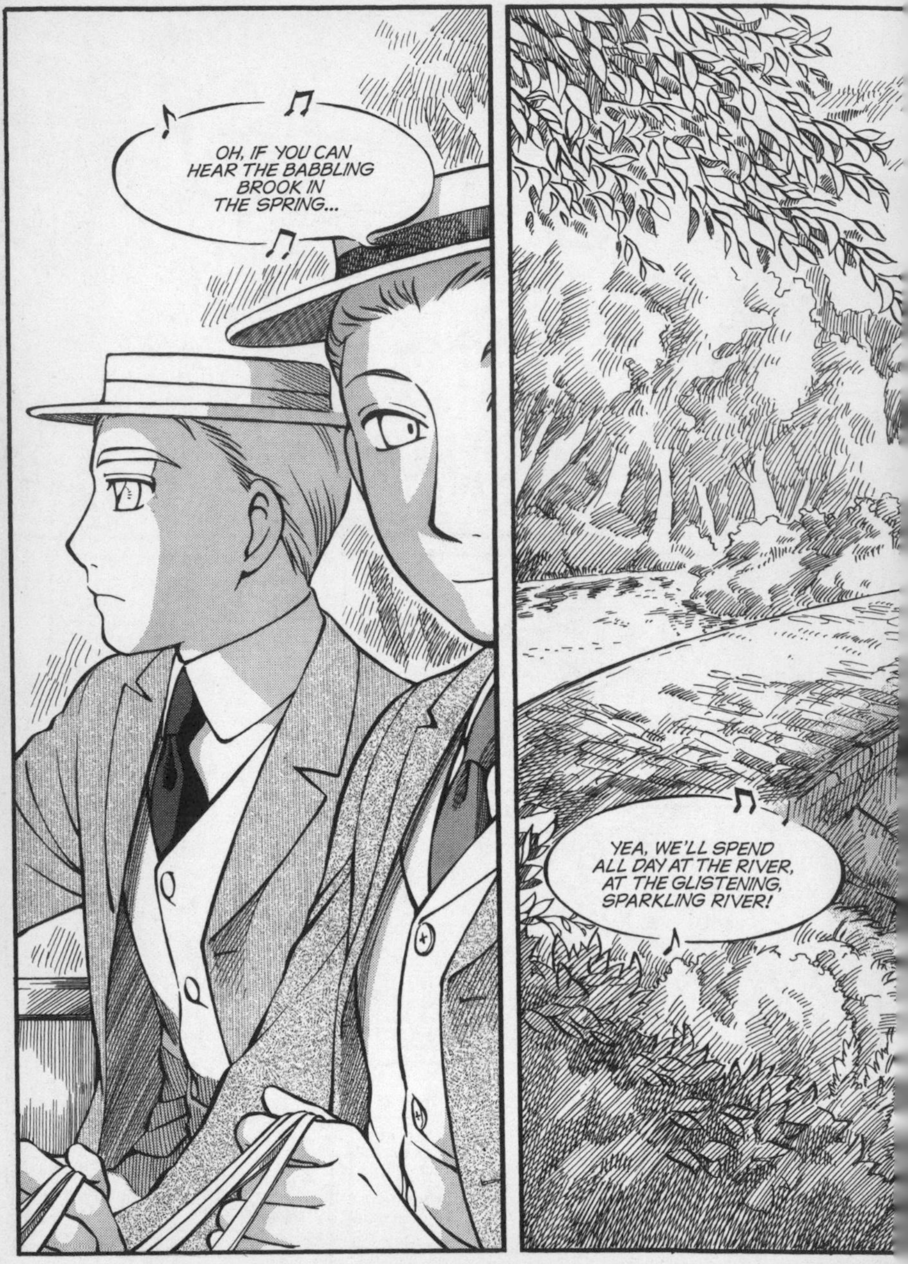
YEA, WE'LL SPEND ALL DAY AT THE RIVER, AT THE GLISTENING, SPARKLING RIVER!
OH, IF YOU CAN HEAR THE BABBLING BROOK IN THE SPRING...

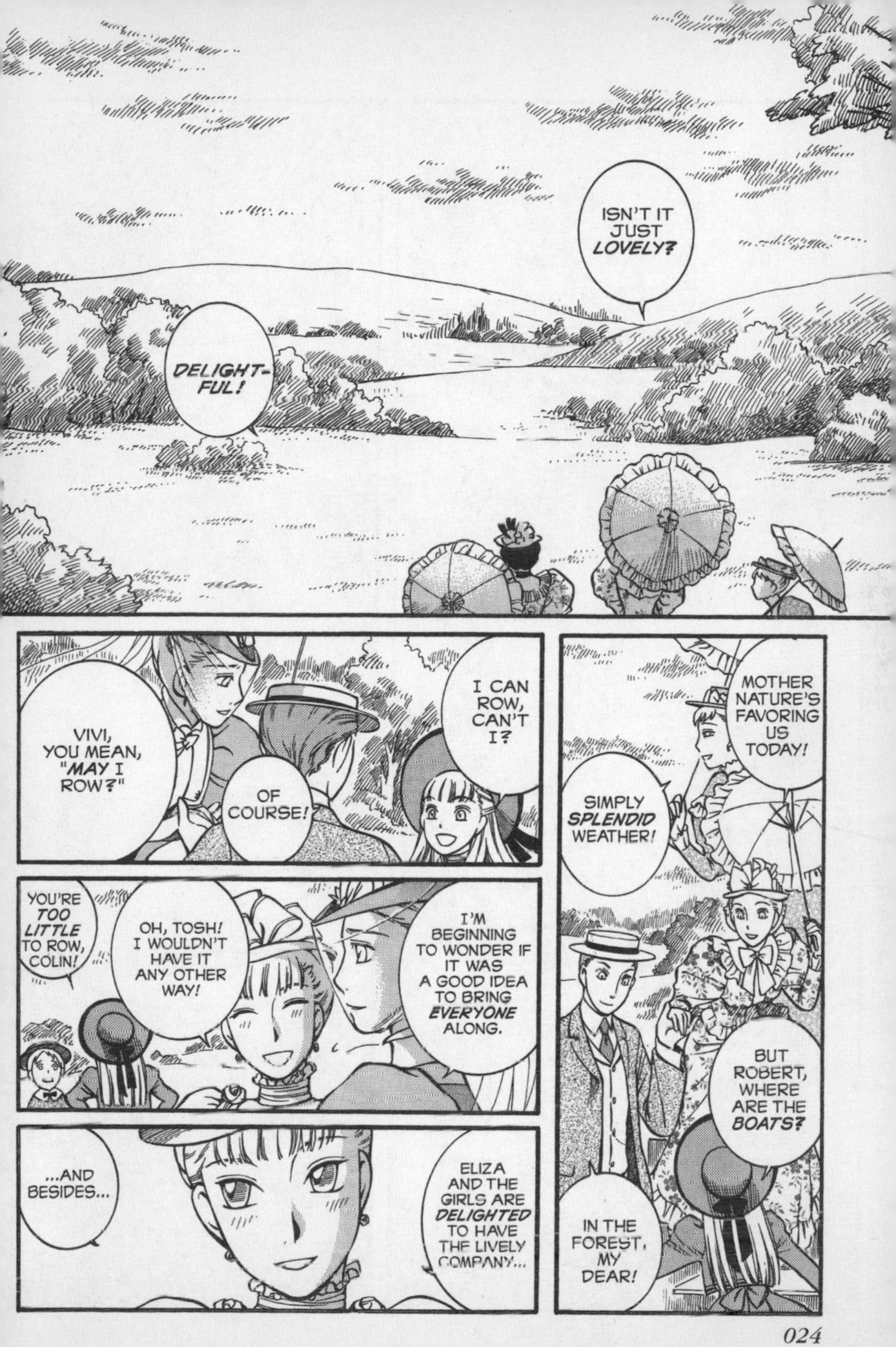
ISN'T IT JUST LOVELY?
DELIGHTFUL!
MOTHER NATURE'S FAVORING US TODAY!
SIMPLY SPLENDID WEATHER!
BUT ROBERT, WHERE ARE THE BOATS?
IN THE FOREST, MY DEAR!
I CAN ROW, CAN'T I?
OF COURSE!
VIVI, YOU MEAN, "MAY I ROW?"
I'M BEGINNING TO WONDER IF IT WAS A GOOD IDEA TO BRING EVERYONE ALONG.
OH, TOSH! I WOULDN'T HAVE IT ANY OTHER WAY!
YOU'RE TOO LITTLE TO ROW, COLIN!
ELIZA AND THE GIRLS ARE DELIGHTED TO HAVE THE LIVELY COMPANY...
...AND BESIDES...

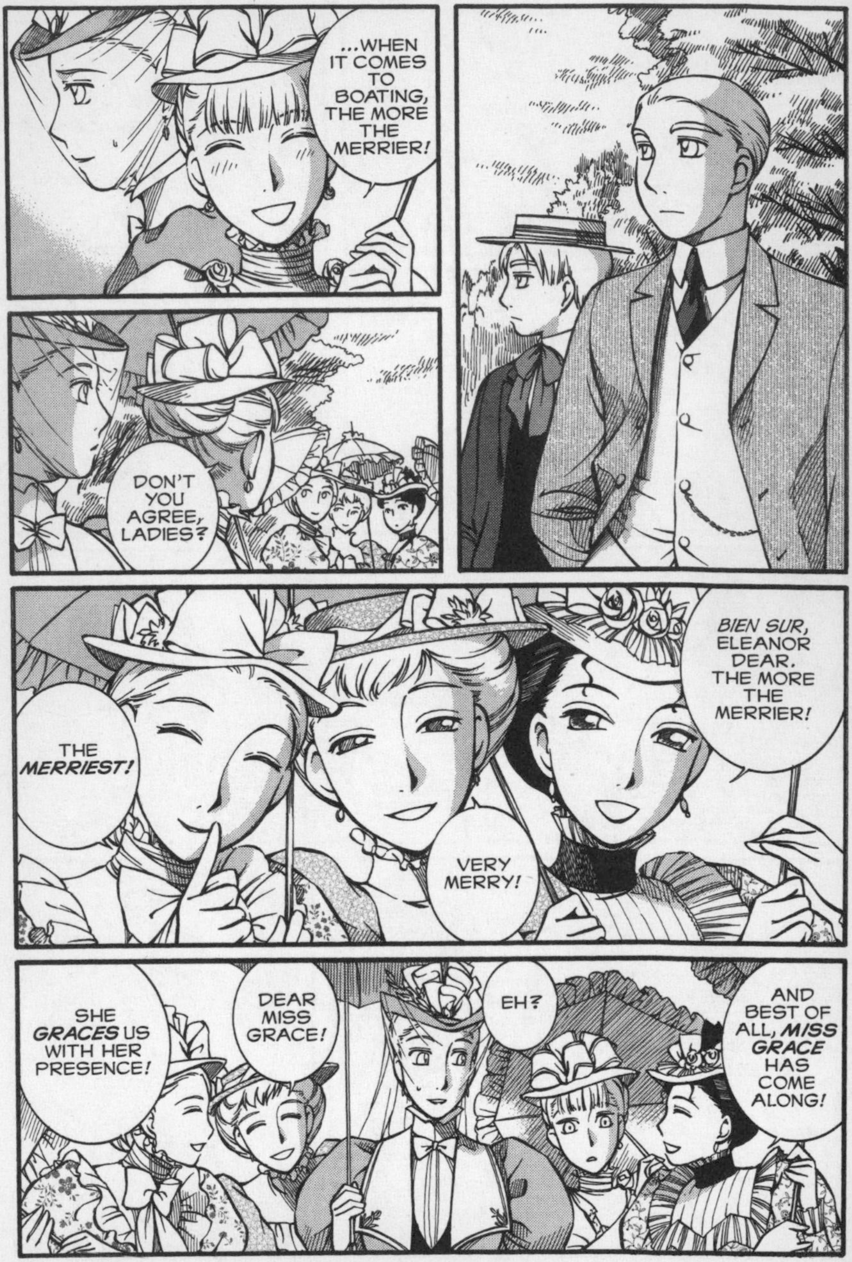
...WHEN IT COMES TO BOATING, THE MORE THE MERRIER!
DON'T YOU AGREE, LADIES?
BIEN SUR, ELEANOR DEAR. THE MORE THE MERRIER!
VERY MERRY!
THE ***MERRIEST!***
AND BEST OF ALL, ***MISS GRACE*** HAS COME ALONG!
EH?
DEAR MISS GRACE!
SHE ***GRACES*** US WITH HER PRESENCE!

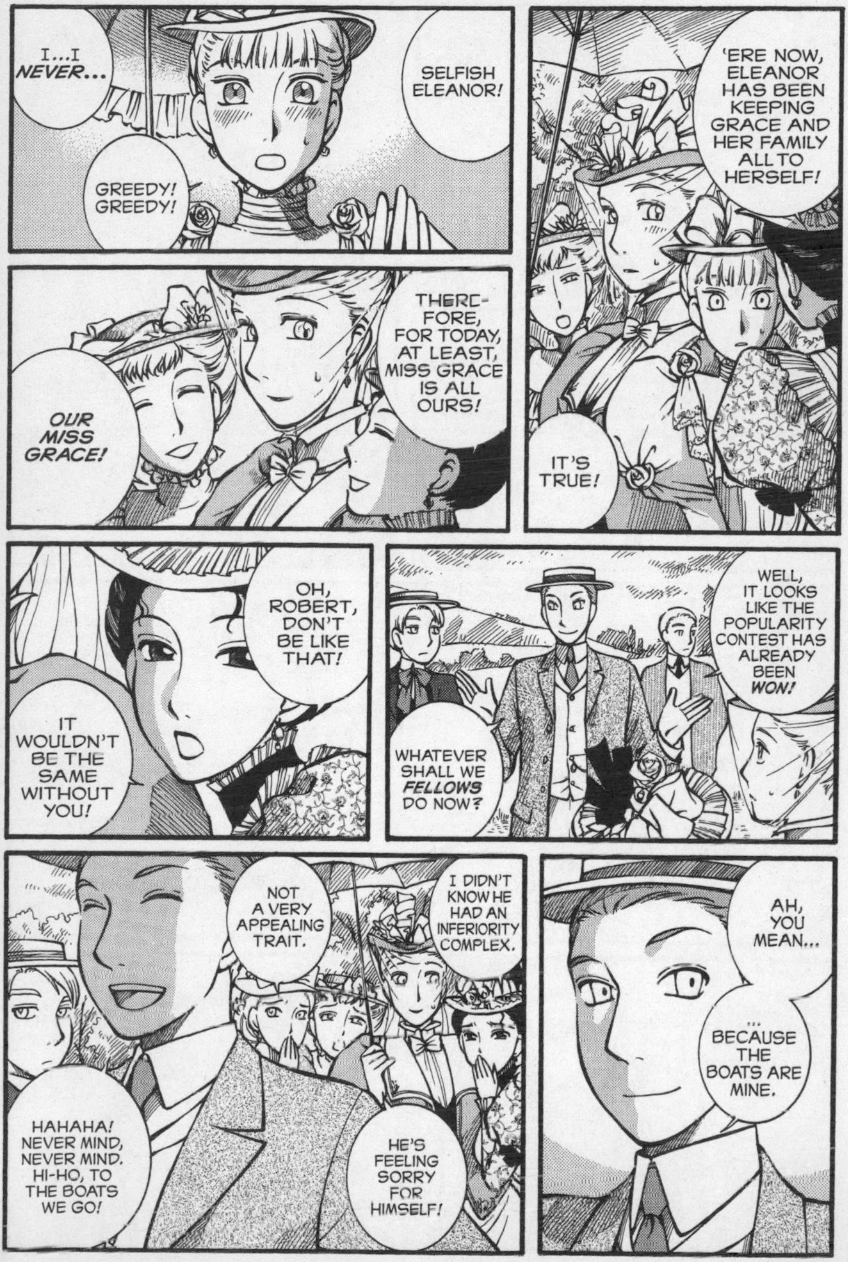
'ERE NOW, ELEANOR HAS BEEN KEEPING GRACE AND HER FAMILY ALL TO HERSELF!
IT'S TRUE!
SELFISH ELEANOR!
I...I NEVER...
GREEDY! GREEDY!
THEREFORE, FOR TODAY, AT LEAST, MISS GRACE IS ALL OURS!
OUR MISS GRACE!
WELL, IT LOOKS LIKE THE POPULARITY CONTEST HAS ALREADY BEEN WON!
WHATEVER SHALL WE FELLOWS DO NOW?
OH, ROBERT, DON'T BE LIKE THAT!
IT WOULDN'T BE THE SAME WITHOUT YOU!
AH, YOU MEAN...
...BECAUSE THE BOATS ARE MINE.
I DIDN'T KNOW HE HAD AN INFERIORITY COMPLEX.
NOT A VERY APPEALING TRAIT.
HE'S FEELING SORRY FOR HIMSELF!
HAHAHA! NEVER MIND, NEVER MIND. HI-HO, TO THE BOATS WE GO!

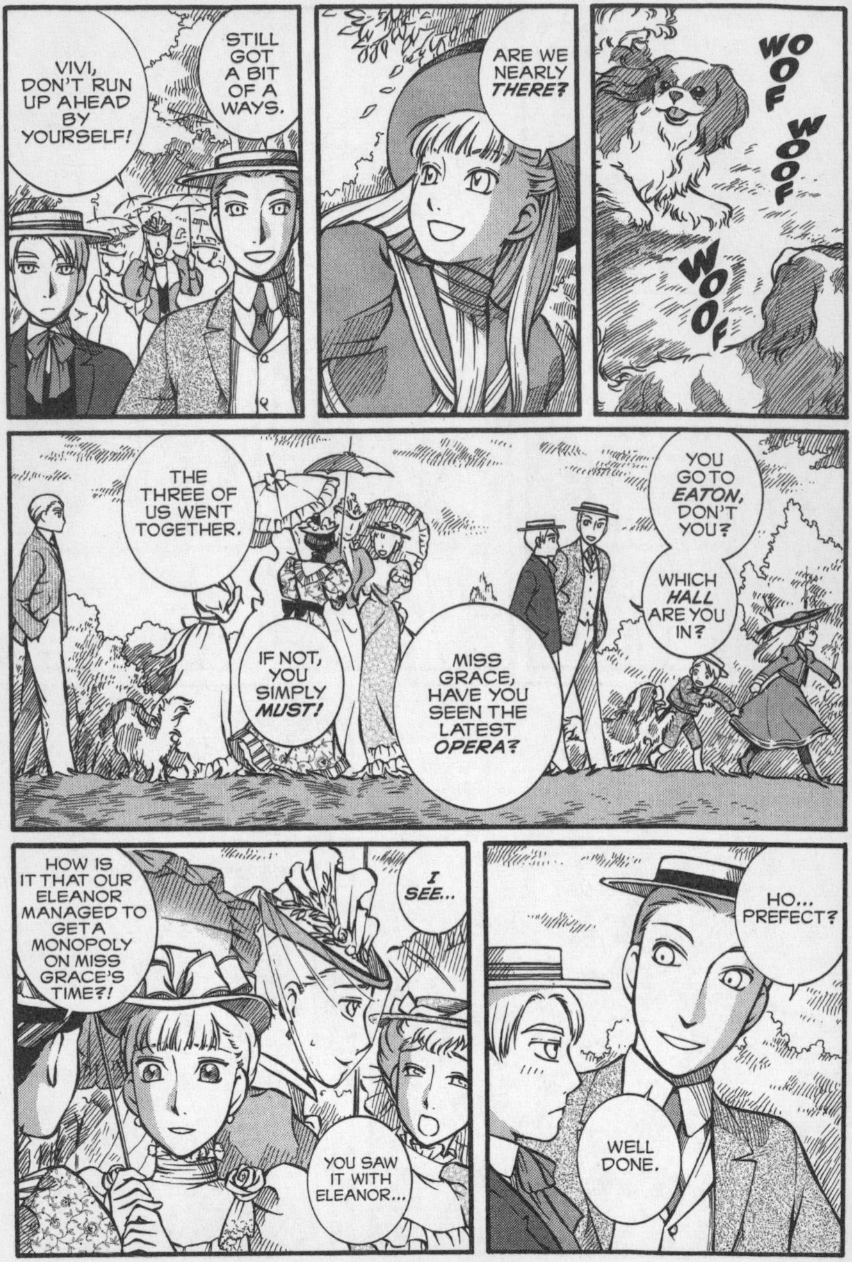
WOOF WOOF
WOOF WOOF
WOOF WOOF
ARE WE NEARLY *THERE?*
STILL GOT A BIT OF A WAYS.
VIVI, DON'T RUN UP AHEAD BY YOURSELF!
YOU GO TO *EATON,* DON'T YOU?
WHICH *HALL* ARE YOU IN?
MISS GRACE, HAVE YOU SEEN THE LATEST *OPERA?*
THE THREE OF US WENT TOGETHER.
IF NOT, YOU SIMPLY *MUST!*
HO... PREFECT?
WELL DONE.
I SEE...
HOW IS IT THAT OUR ELEANOR MANAGED TO GET A MONOPOLY ON MISS GRACE'S TIME?!
YOU SAW IT WITH ELEANOR...

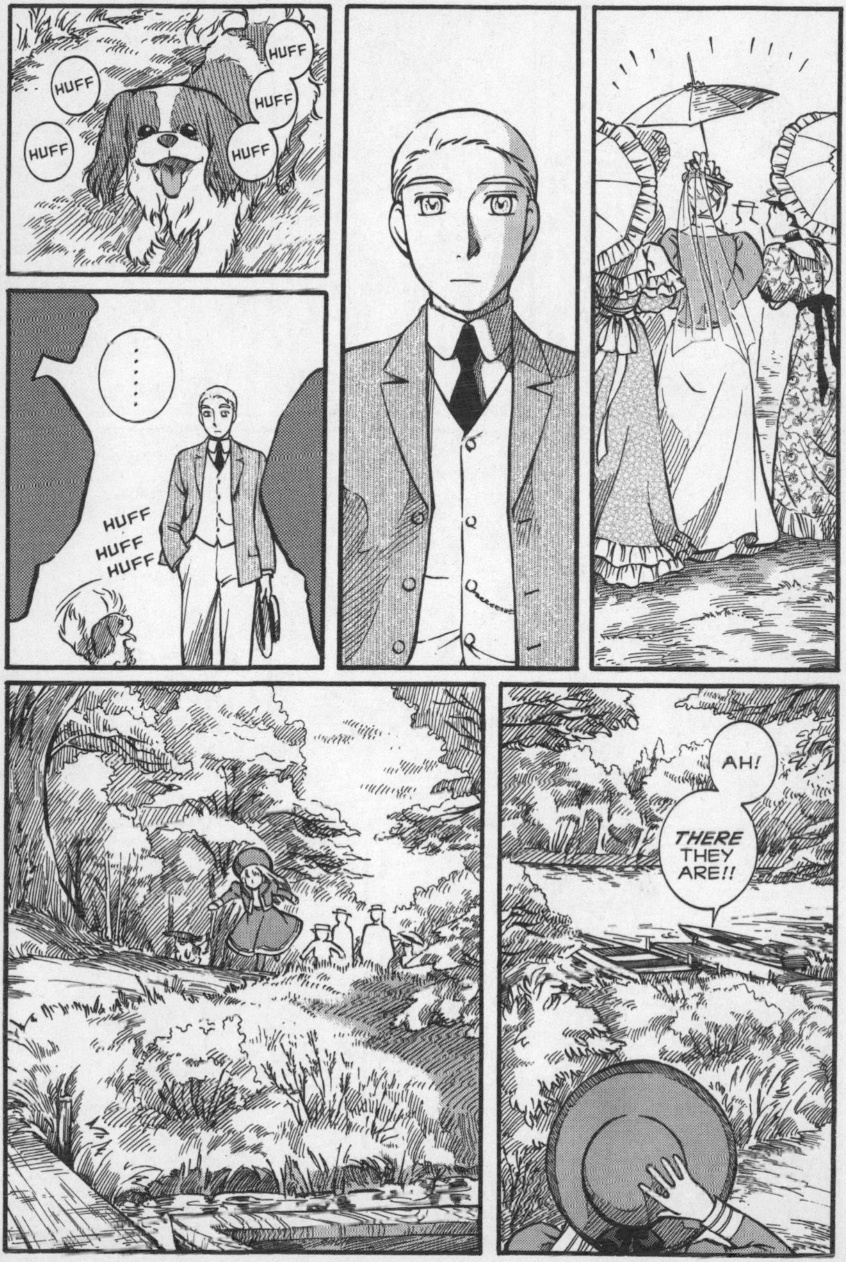
HUFF
HUFF
HUFF
HUFF
HUFF
......
HUFF
HUFF
HUFF
AH!
THERE THEY ARE!!

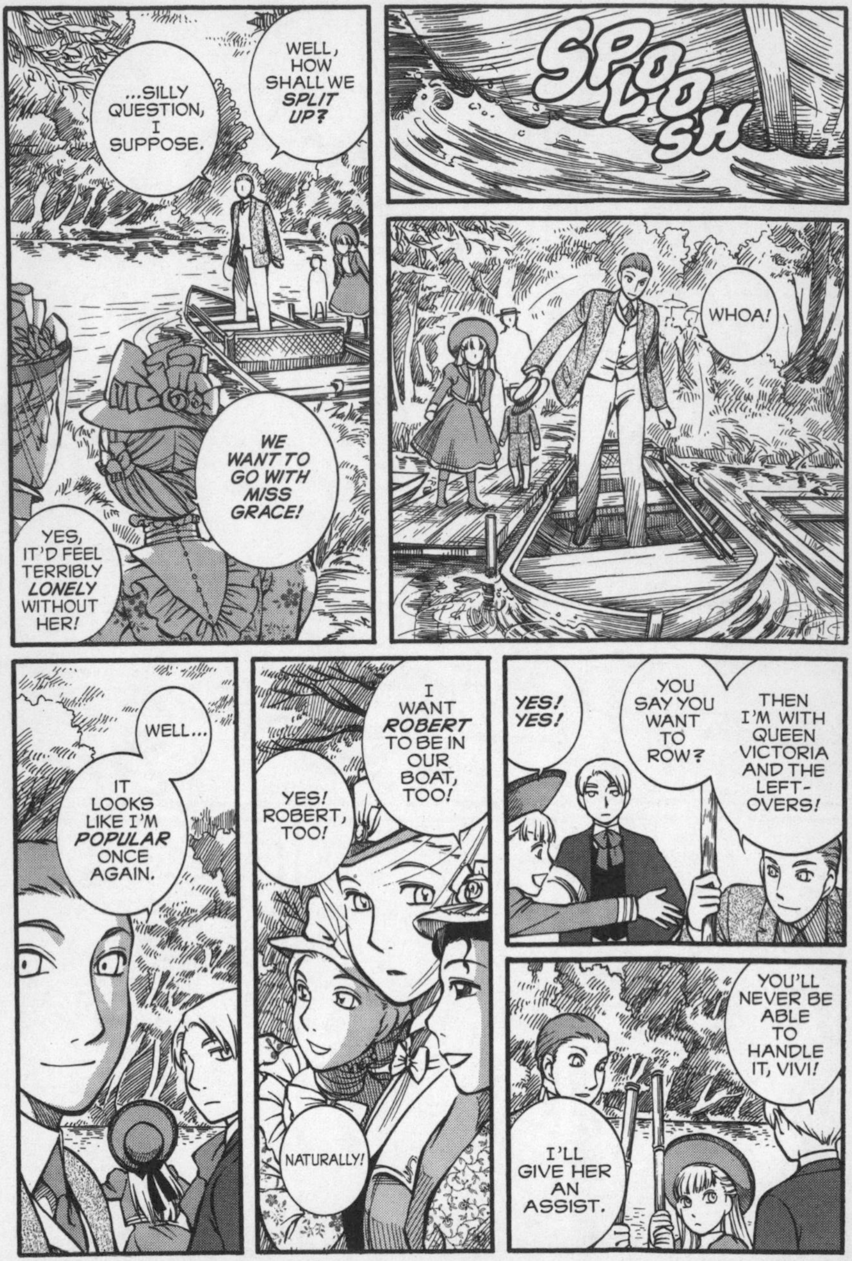
SPLOOSH
WHOA!
WELL, HOW SHALL WE SPLIT UP?
...SILLY QUESTION, I SUPPOSE.
WE WANT TO GO WITH MISS GRACE!
YES, IT'D FEEL TERRIBLY LONELY WITHOUT HER!
THEN I'M WITH QUEEN VICTORIA AND THE LEFT-OVERS!
YOU SAY YOU WANT TO ROW?
YES! YES!
YOU'LL NEVER BE ABLE TO HANDLE IT, VIVI!
I'LL GIVE HER AN ASSIST.
I WANT ROBERT TO BE IN OUR BOAT, TOO!
YES! ROBERT, TOO!
NATURALLY!
WELL...
IT LOOKS LIKE I'M POPULAR ONCE AGAIN.

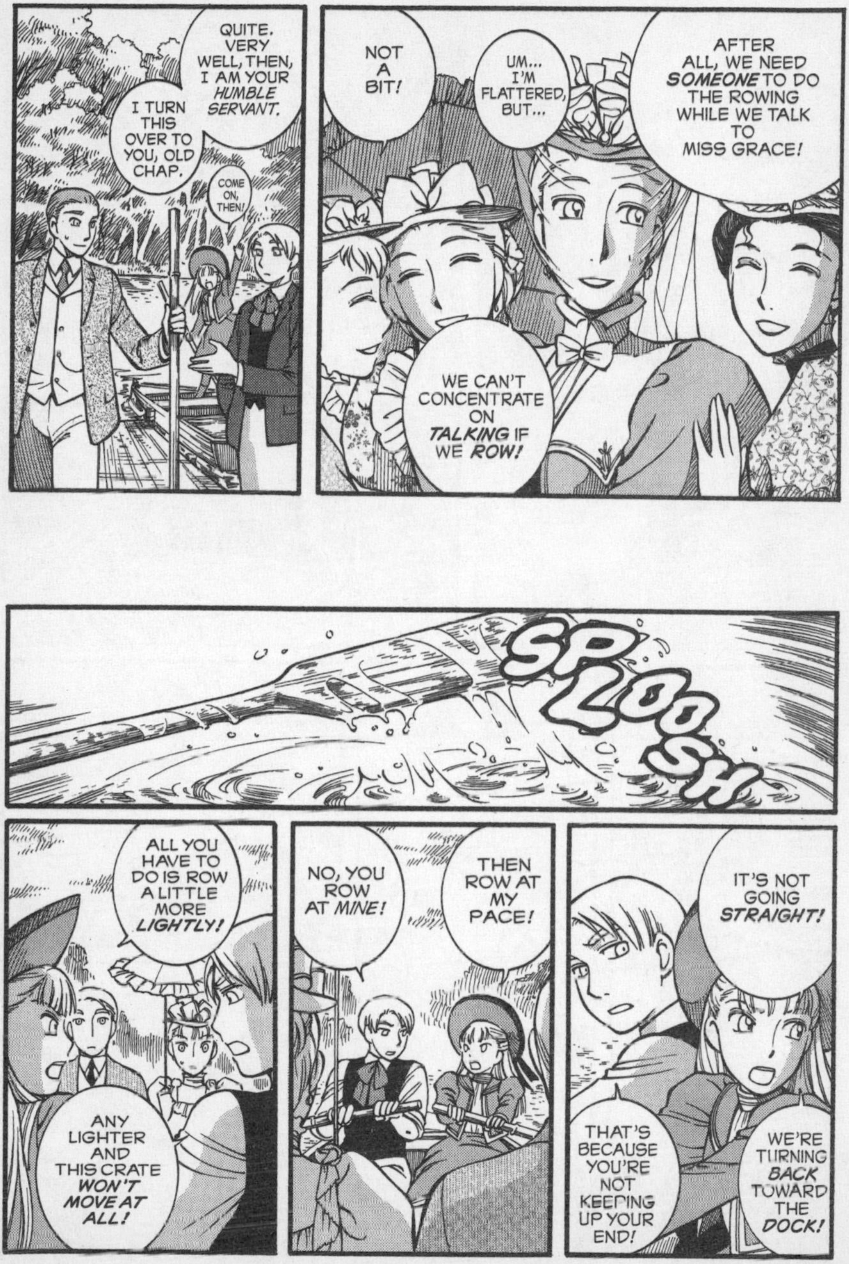
AFTER ALL, WE NEED SOMEONE TO DO THE ROWING WHILE WE TALK TO MISS GRACE!
UM... I'M FLATTERED, BUT...
NOT A BIT!
WE CAN'T CONCENTRATE ON TALKING IF WE ROW!
QUITE. VERY WELL, THEN, I AM YOUR HUMBLE SERVANT.
I TURN THIS OVER TO YOU, OLD CHAP.
COME ON, THEN!
SPLOOSH
IT'S NOT GOING STRAIGHT!
WE'RE TURNING BACK TOWARD THE DOCK!
THAT'S BECAUSE YOU'RE NOT KEEPING UP YOUR END!
THEN ROW AT MY PACE!
NO, YOU ROW AT MINE!
ALL YOU HAVE TO DO IS ROW A LITTLE MORE LIGHTLY!
ANY LIGHTER AND THIS CRATE WON'T MOVE AT ALL!

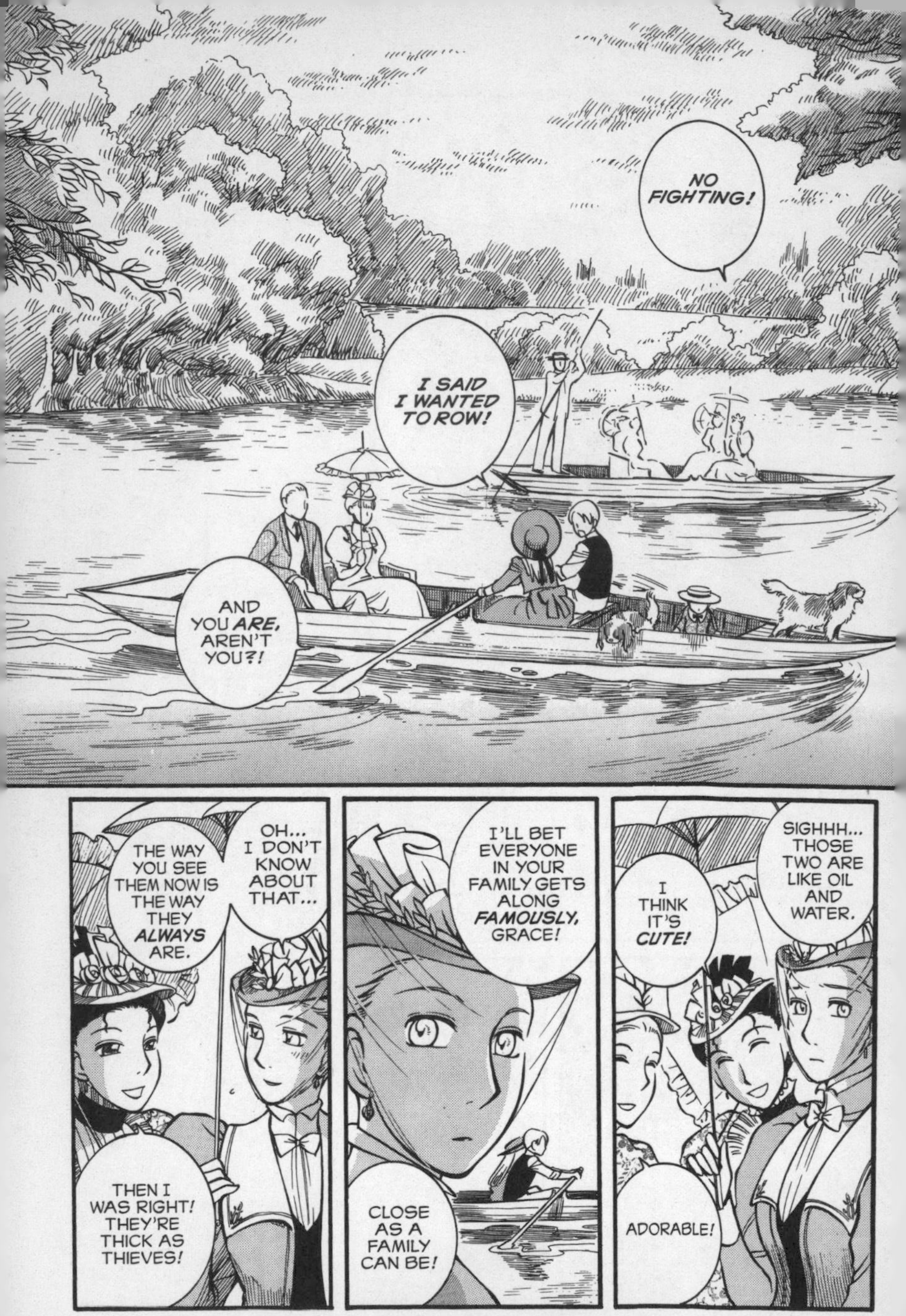
NO FIGHTING!
I SAID I WANTED TO ROW!
AND YOU ARE, AREN'T YOU?!
SIGHHH... THOSE TWO ARE LIKE OIL AND WATER.
I THINK IT'S CUTE!
ADORABLE!
I'LL BET EVERYONE IN YOUR FAMILY GETS ALONG FAMOUSLY, GRACE!
CLOSE AS A FAMILY CAN BE!
OH... I DON'T KNOW ABOUT THAT...
THE WAY YOU SEE THEM NOW IS THE WAY THEY ALWAYS ARE.
THEN I WAS RIGHT! THEY'RE THICK AS THIEVES!

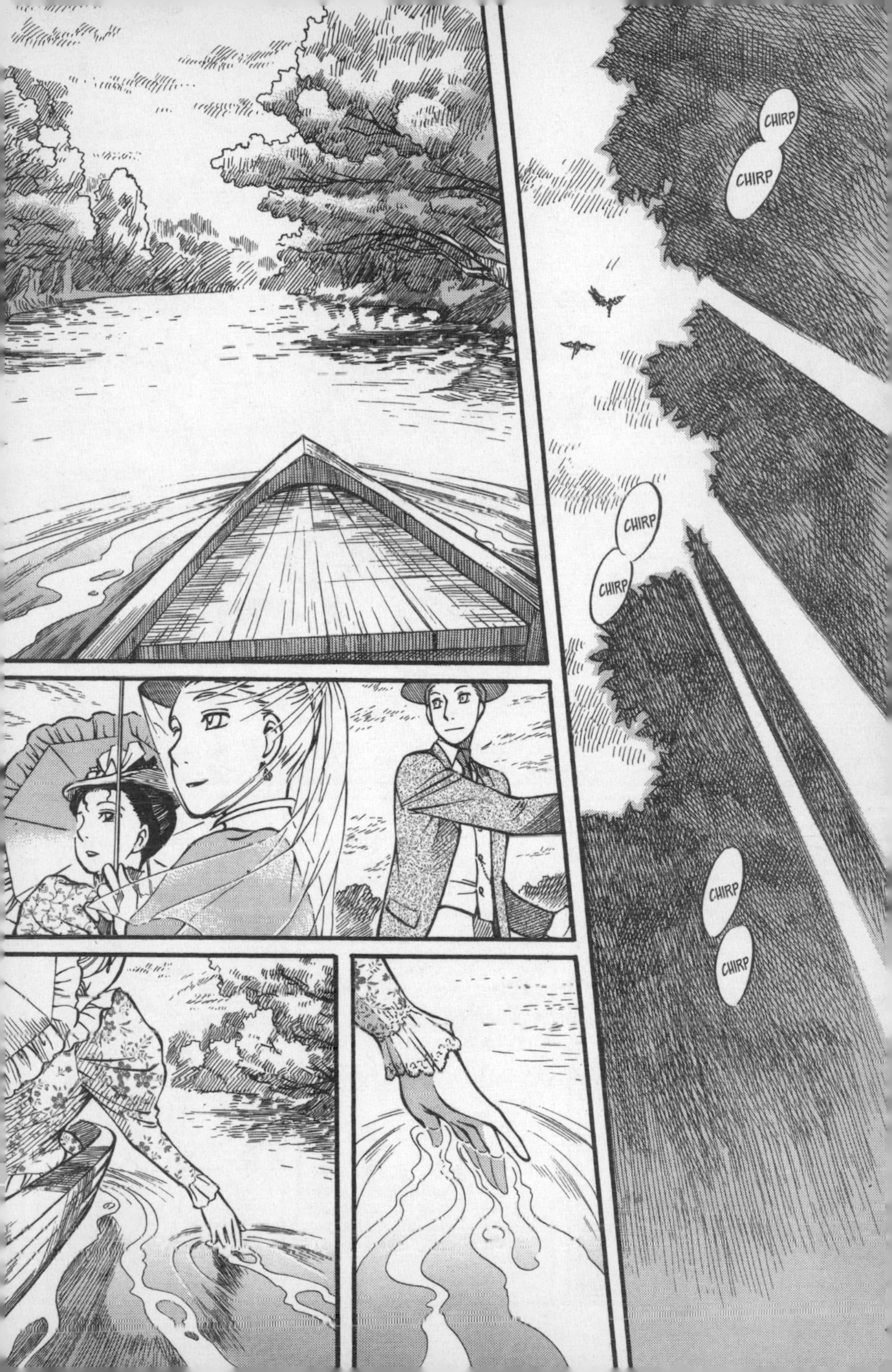
CHIRP
CHIRP
CHIRP
CHIRP
CHIRP
CHIRP

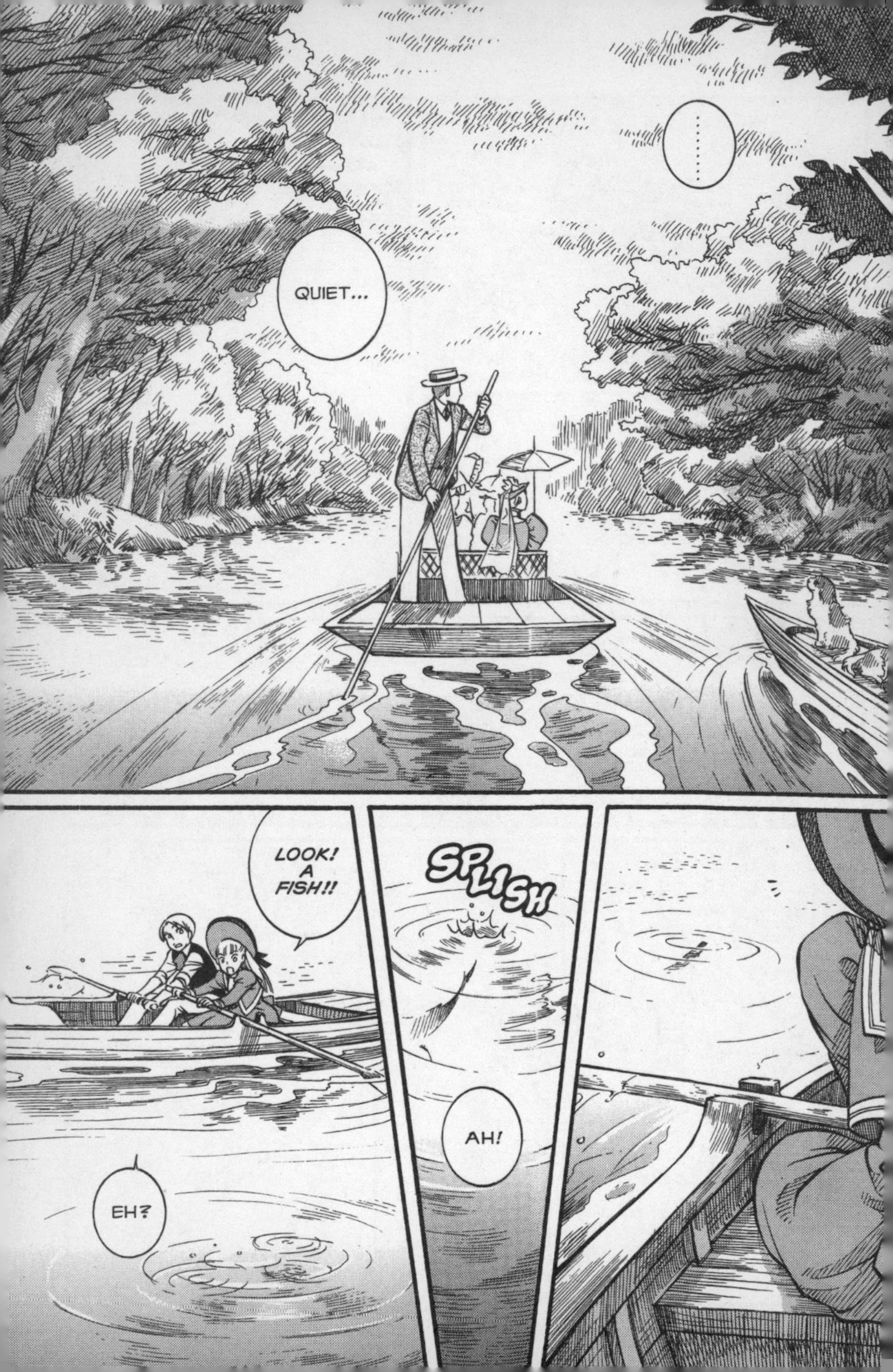
......
QUIET...
SPLISH
AH!
LOOK! A FISH!!
EH?

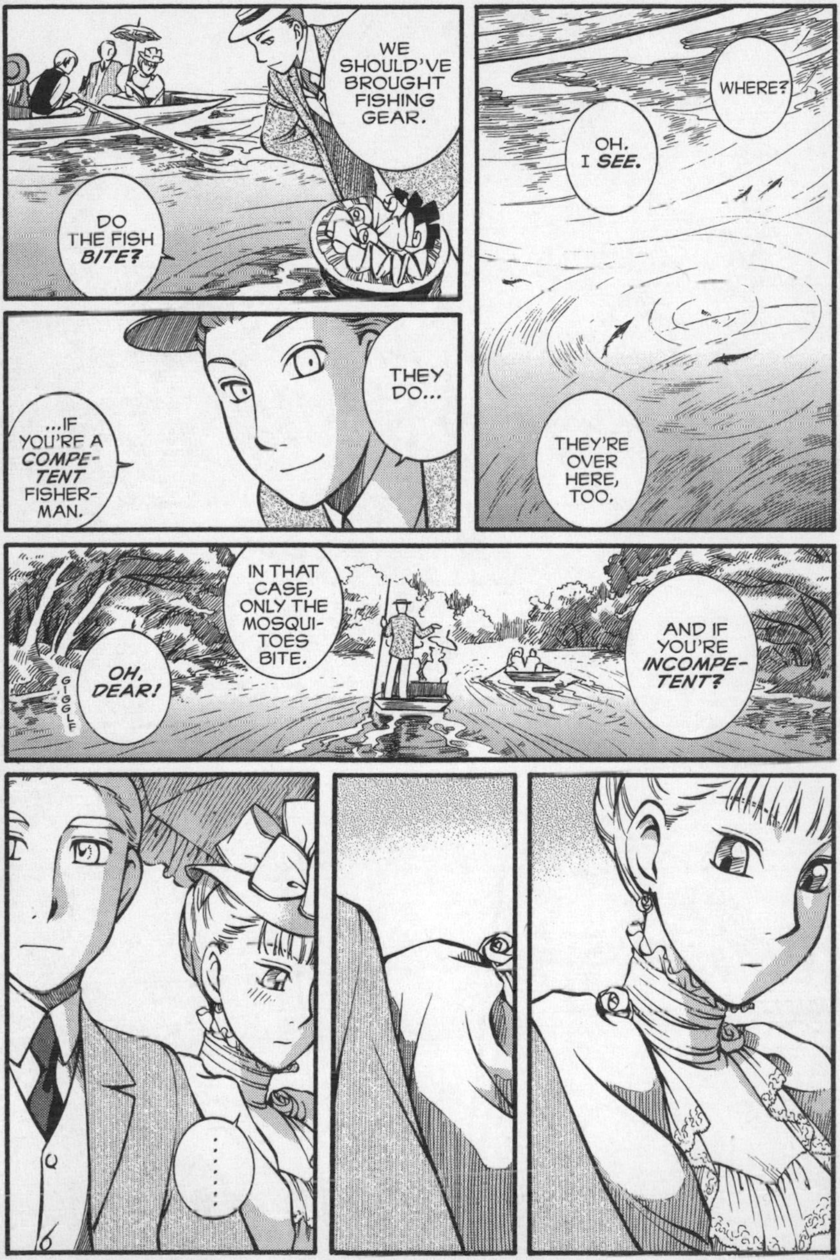

WHERE?
OH. I *SEE.*
THEY'RE OVER HERE, TOO.
WE SHOULD'VE BROUGHT FISHING GEAR.
DO THE FISH *BITE?*
THEY DO...
...IF YOU'RF A *COMPETENT* FISHERMAN.
AND IF YOU'RE *INCOMPETENT?*
IN THAT CASE, ONLY THE MOSQUITOES BITE.
OH, DEAR!
GIGGLF
......

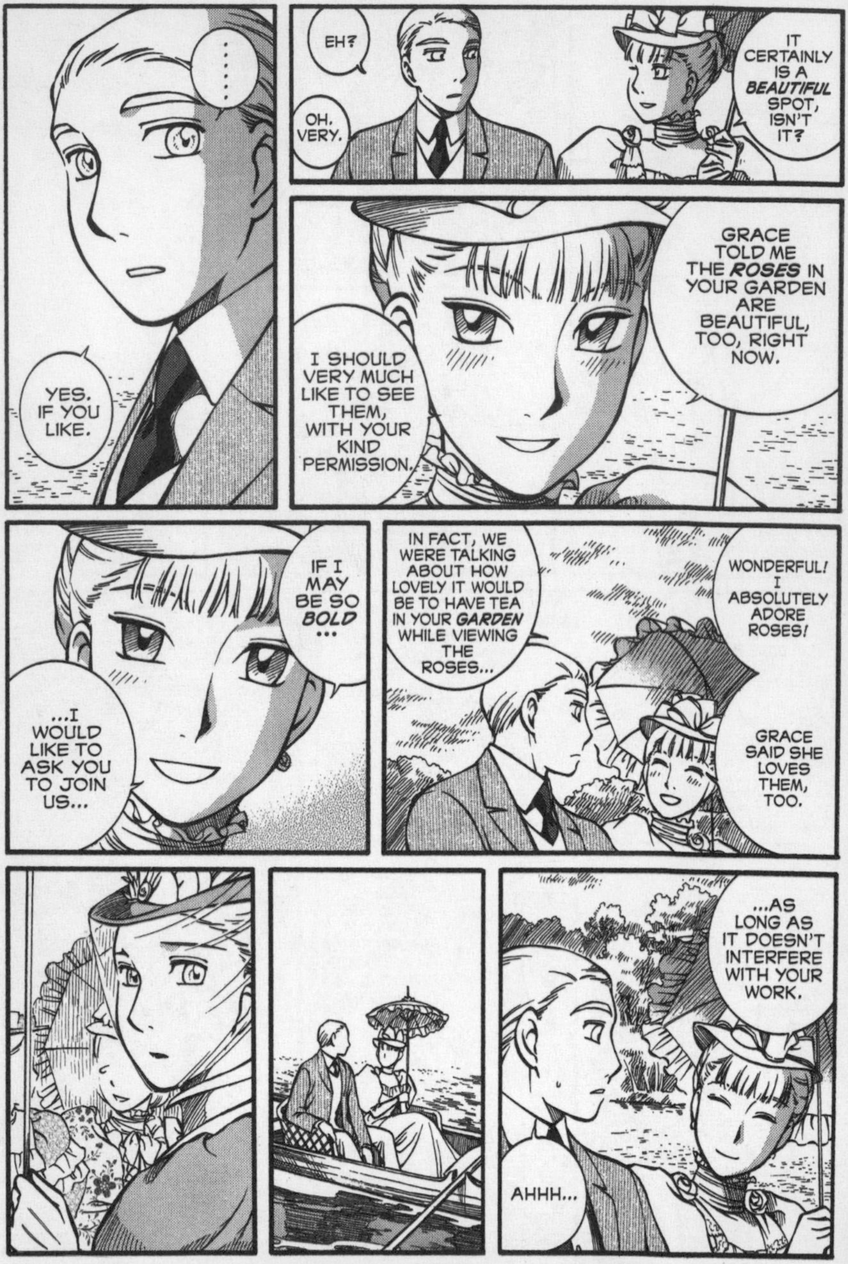
IT CERTAINLY IS A *BEAUTIFUL* SPOT, ISN'T IT?
EH?
OH. VERY.
GRACE TOLD ME THE *ROSES* IN YOUR GARDEN ARE BEAUTIFUL, TOO, RIGHT NOW.
I SHOULD VERY MUCH LIKE TO SEE THEM, WITH YOUR KIND PERMISSION.
......
YES. IF YOU LIKE.
WONDERFUL! I ABSOLUTELY ADORE ROSES!
GRACE SAID SHE LOVES THEM, TOO.
IN FACT, WE WERE TALKING ABOUT HOW LOVELY IT WOULD BE TO HAVE TEA IN YOUR *GARDEN* WHILE VIEWING THE ROSES...
IF I MAY BE SO *BOLD*...
...I WOULD LIKE TO ASK YOU TO JOIN US...
...AS LONG AS IT DOESN'T INTERFERE WITH YOUR WORK.
AHHH...

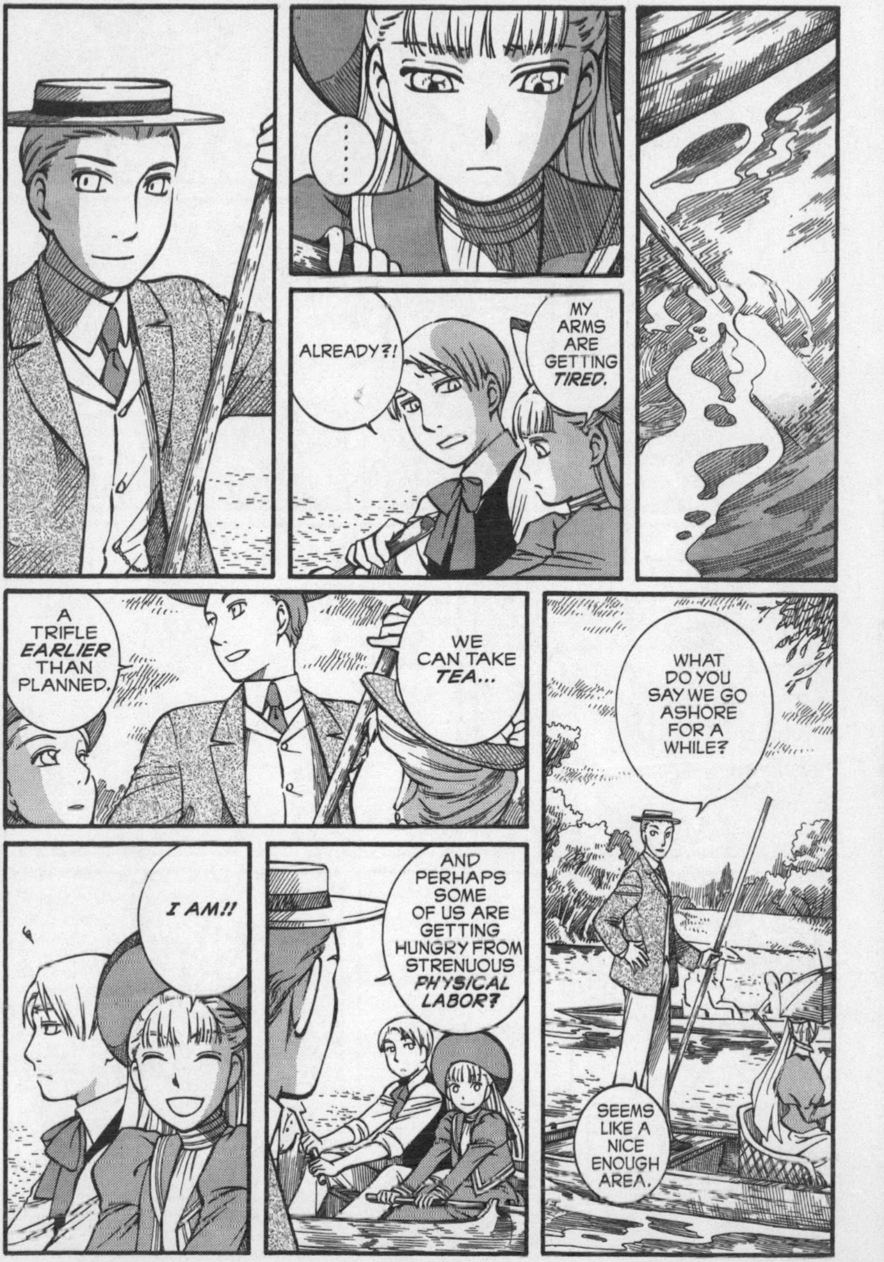
......
MY ARMS ARE GETTING TIRED.
ALREADY?!
WHAT DO YOU SAY WE GO ASHORE FOR A WHILE?
SEEMS LIKE A NICE ENOUGH AREA.
WE CAN TAKE TEA...
A TRIFLE EARLIER THAN PLANNED.
AND PERHAPS SOME OF US ARE GETTING HUNGRY FROM STRENUOUS PHYSICAL LABOR?
I AM!!

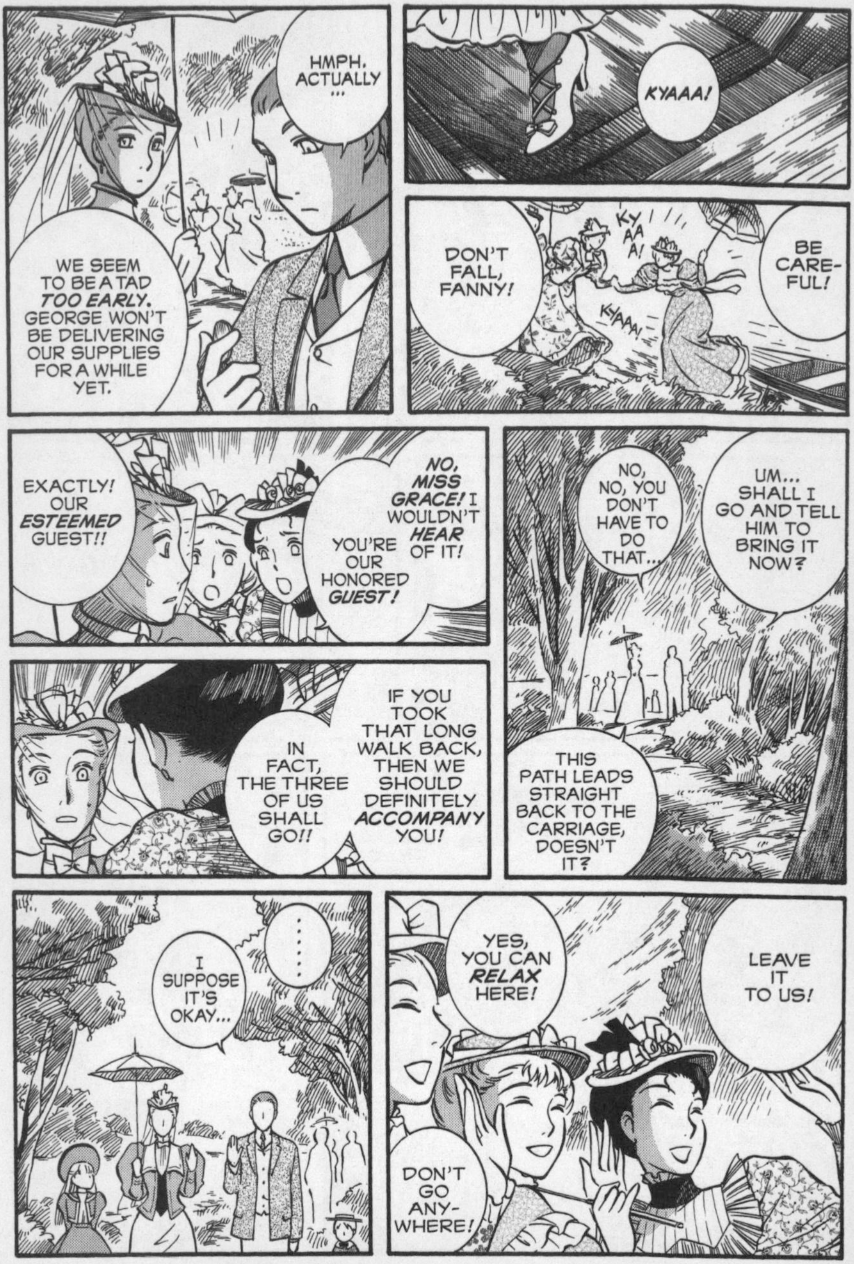
KYAAA!
BE CAREFUL!
KY AA A!
KYAAA!
DON'T FALL, FANNY!
HMPH. ACTUALLY ...
WE SEEM TO BE A TAD TOO EARLY. GEORGE WON'T BE DELIVERING OUR SUPPLIES FOR A WHILE YET.
UM... SHALL I GO AND TELL HIM TO BRING IT NOW?
NO, NO, YOU DON'T HAVE TO DO THAT...
THIS PATH LEADS STRAIGHT BACK TO THE CARRIAGE, DOESN'T IT?
NO, MISS GRACE! I WOULDN'T HEAR OF IT!
YOU'RE OUR HONORED GUEST!
EXACTLY! OUR ESTEEMED GUEST!!
IF YOU TOOK THAT LONG WALK BACK, THEN WE SHOULD DEFINITELY ACCOMPANY YOU!
IN FACT, THE THREE OF US SHALL GO!!
LEAVE IT TO US!
YES, YOU CAN RELAX HERE!
DON'T GO ANYWHERE!
......
I SUPPOSE IT'S OKAY...

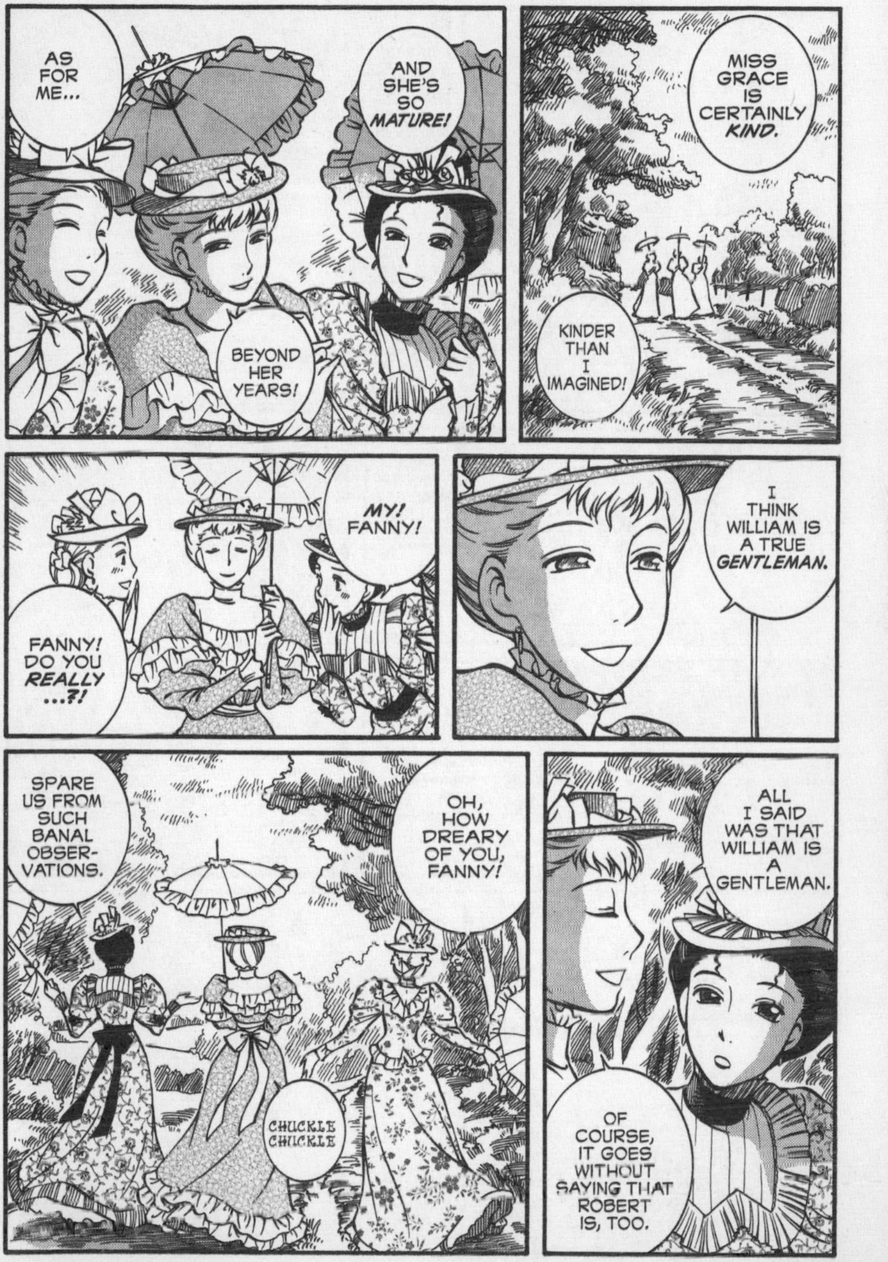

MISS GRACE IS CERTAINLY *KIND.*
KINDER THAN I IMAGINED!
AND SHE'S SO *MATURE!*
AS FOR ME...
BEYOND HER YEARS!
I THINK WILLIAM IS A TRUE *GENTLEMAN.*
MY! FANNY!
FANNY! DO YOU *REALLY* ...?!
ALL I SAID WAS THAT WILLIAM IS A GENTLEMAN.
OF COURSE, IT GOES WITHOUT SAYING THAT ROBERT IS, TOO.
OH, HOW DREARY OF YOU, FANNY!
SPARE US FROM SUCH BANAL OBSER-VATIONS.
CHUCKLE CHUCKLE

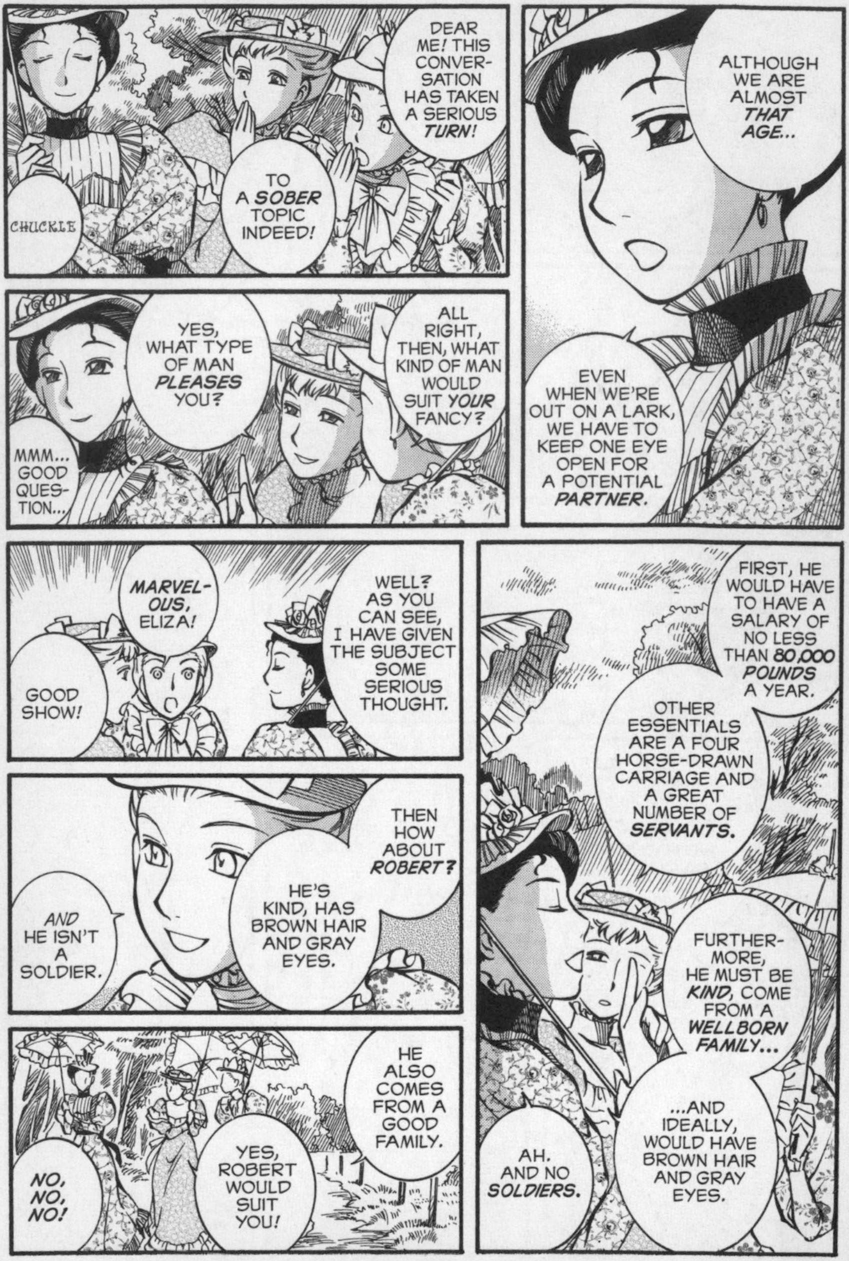
ALTHOUGH WE ARE ALMOST *THAT AGE...*
EVEN WHEN WE'RE OUT ON A LARK, WE HAVE TO KEEP ONE EYE OPEN FOR A POTENTIAL *PARTNER*.
DEAR ME! THIS CONVERSATION HAS TAKEN A SERIOUS *TURN*!
TO A *SOBER* TOPIC INDEED!
CHUCKLE
ALL RIGHT, THEN, WHAT KIND OF MAN WOULD SUIT *YOUR* FANCY?
YES, WHAT TYPE OF MAN *PLEASES* YOU?
MMM... GOOD QUESTION...
FIRST, HE WOULD HAVE TO HAVE A SALARY OF NO LESS THAN *80,000 POUNDS* A YEAR.
OTHER ESSENTIALS ARE A FOUR HORSE-DRAWN CARRIAGE AND A GREAT NUMBER OF *SERVANTS*.
FURTHERMORE, HE MUST BE *KIND*, COME FROM A *WELLBORN FAMILY...*
...AND IDEALLY, WOULD HAVE BROWN HAIR AND GRAY EYES.
AH. AND NO *SOLDIERS*.
WELL? AS YOU CAN SEE, I HAVE GIVEN THE SUBJECT SOME SERIOUS THOUGHT.
MARVELOUS, ELIZA!
GOOD SHOW!
THEN HOW ABOUT *ROBERT*?
HE'S KIND, HAS BROWN HAIR AND GRAY EYES.
AND HE ISN'T A SOLDIER.
HE ALSO COMES FROM A GOOD FAMILY.
YES, ROBERT WOULD SUIT YOU!
NO, NO, NO!

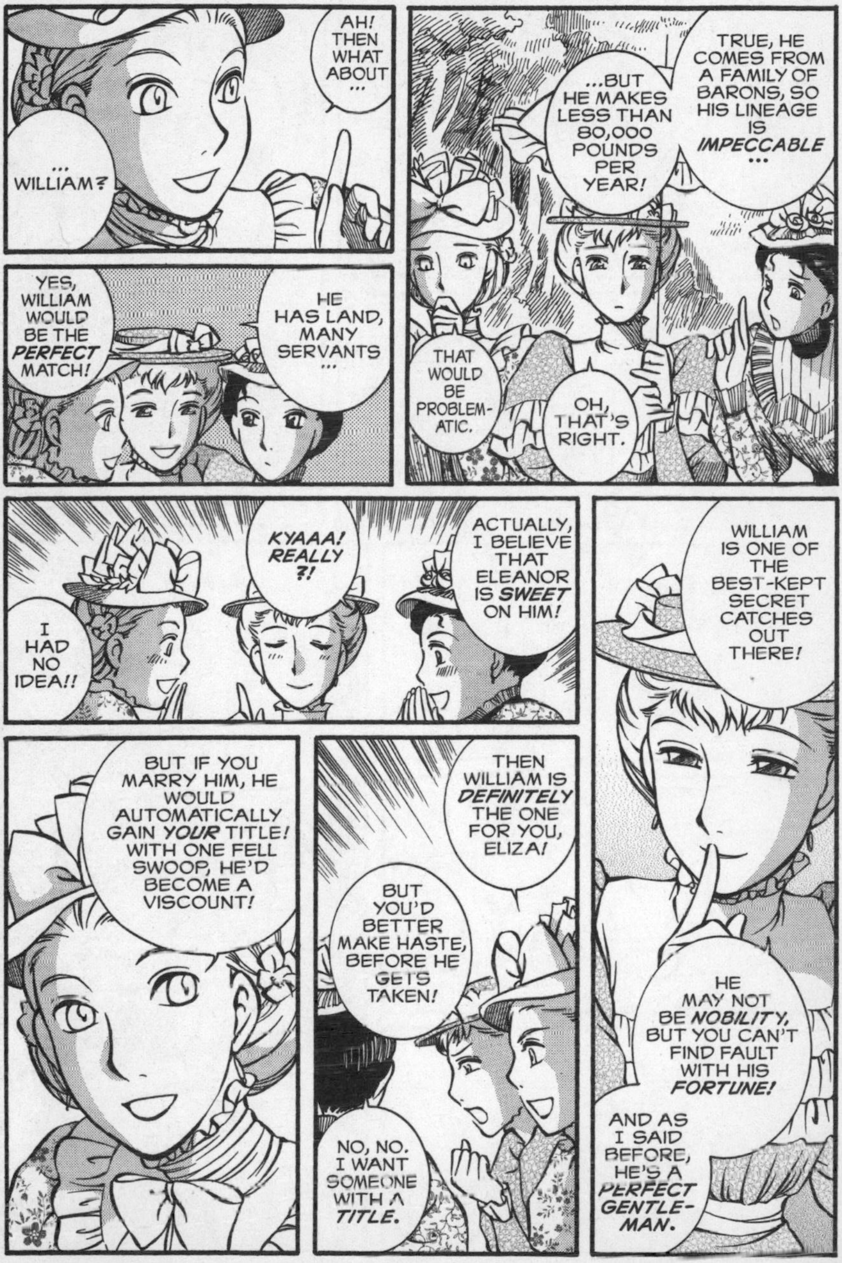
AH! THEN WHAT ABOUT...
...WILLIAM?
YES, WILLIAM WOULD BE THE *PERFECT* MATCH!
HE HAS LAND, MANY SERVANTS...
TRUE, HE COMES FROM A FAMILY OF BARONS, SO HIS LINEAGE IS *IMPECCABLE*...
...BUT HE MAKES LESS THAN 80,000 POUNDS PER YEAR!
THAT WOULD BE PROBLEMATIC.
OH, THAT'S RIGHT.
ACTUALLY, I BELIEVE THAT ELEANOR IS *SWEET* ON HIM!
KYAAA! REALLY?!
I HAD NO IDEA!!
WILLIAM IS ONE OF THE BEST-KEPT SECRET CATCHES OUT THERE!
HE MAY NOT BE *NOBILITY*, BUT YOU CAN'T FIND FAULT WITH HIS *FORTUNE!*
AND AS I SAID BEFORE, HE'S A *PERFECT GENTLEMAN*.
THEN WILLIAM IS *DEFINITELY* THE ONE FOR YOU, ELIZA!
BUT YOU'D BETTER MAKE HASTE, BEFORE HE GETS TAKEN!
NO, NO. I WANT SOMEONE WITH A *TITLE*.
BUT IF YOU MARRY HIM, HE WOULD AUTOMATICALLY GAIN *YOUR* TITLE! WITH ONE FELL SWOOP, HE'D BECOME A VISCOUNT!

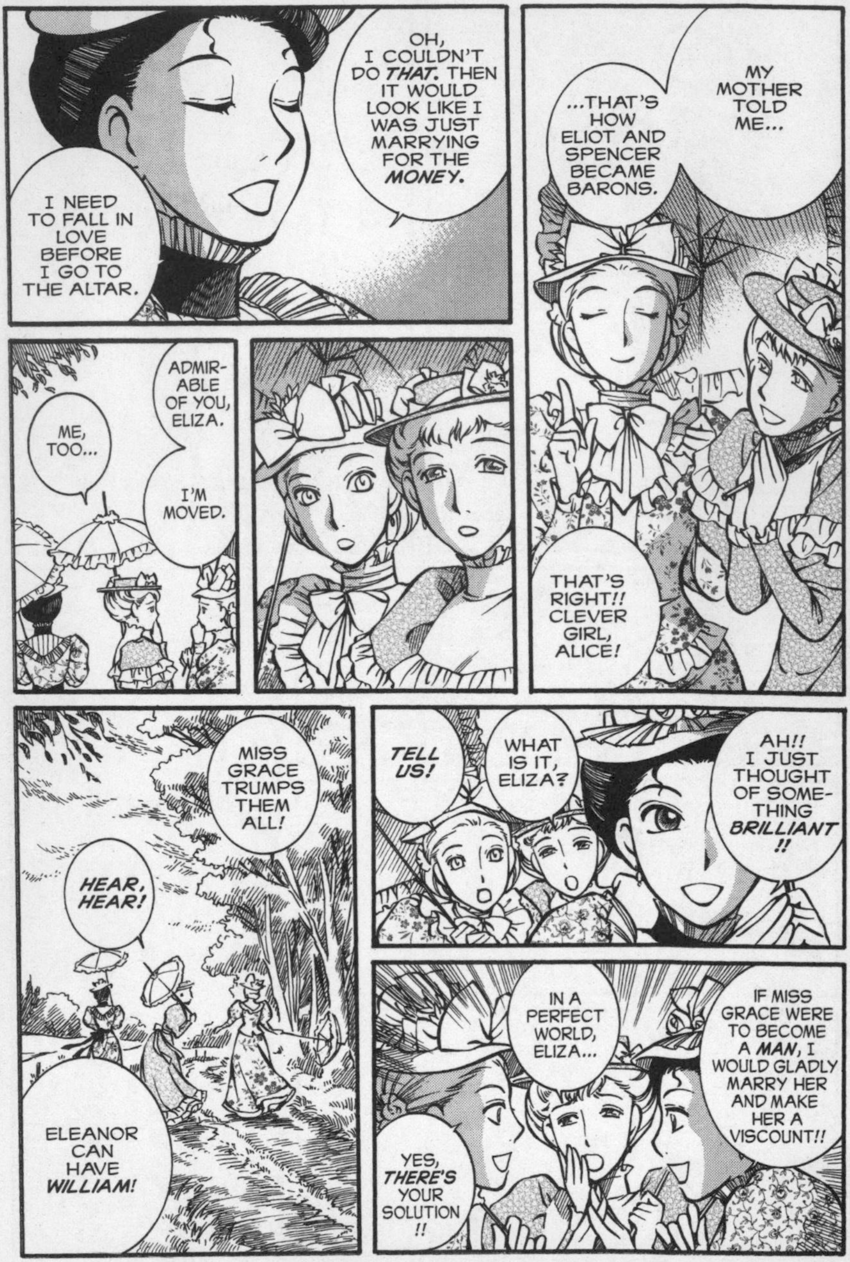
MY MOTHER TOLD ME...
...THAT'S HOW ELIOT AND SPENCER BECAME BARONS.
THAT'S RIGHT!! CLEVER GIRL, ALICE!
OH, I COULDN'T DO *THAT.* THEN IT WOULD LOOK LIKE I WAS JUST MARRYING FOR THE *MONEY.*
I NEED TO FALL IN LOVE BEFORE I GO TO THE ALTAR.
ADMIR-ABLE OF YOU, ELIZA.
I'M MOVED.
ME, TOO...
AH!! I JUST THOUGHT OF SOME-THING *BRILLIANT* !!
WHAT IS IT, ELIZA?
TELL US!
IF MISS GRACE WERE TO BECOME A *MAN*, I WOULD GLADLY MARRY HER AND MAKE HER A VISCOUNT!!
IN A PERFECT WORLD, ELIZA...
YES, *THERE'S* YOUR SOLUTION !!
MISS GRACE TRUMPS THEM ALL!
HEAR, HEAR!
ELEANOR CAN HAVE *WILLIAM!*

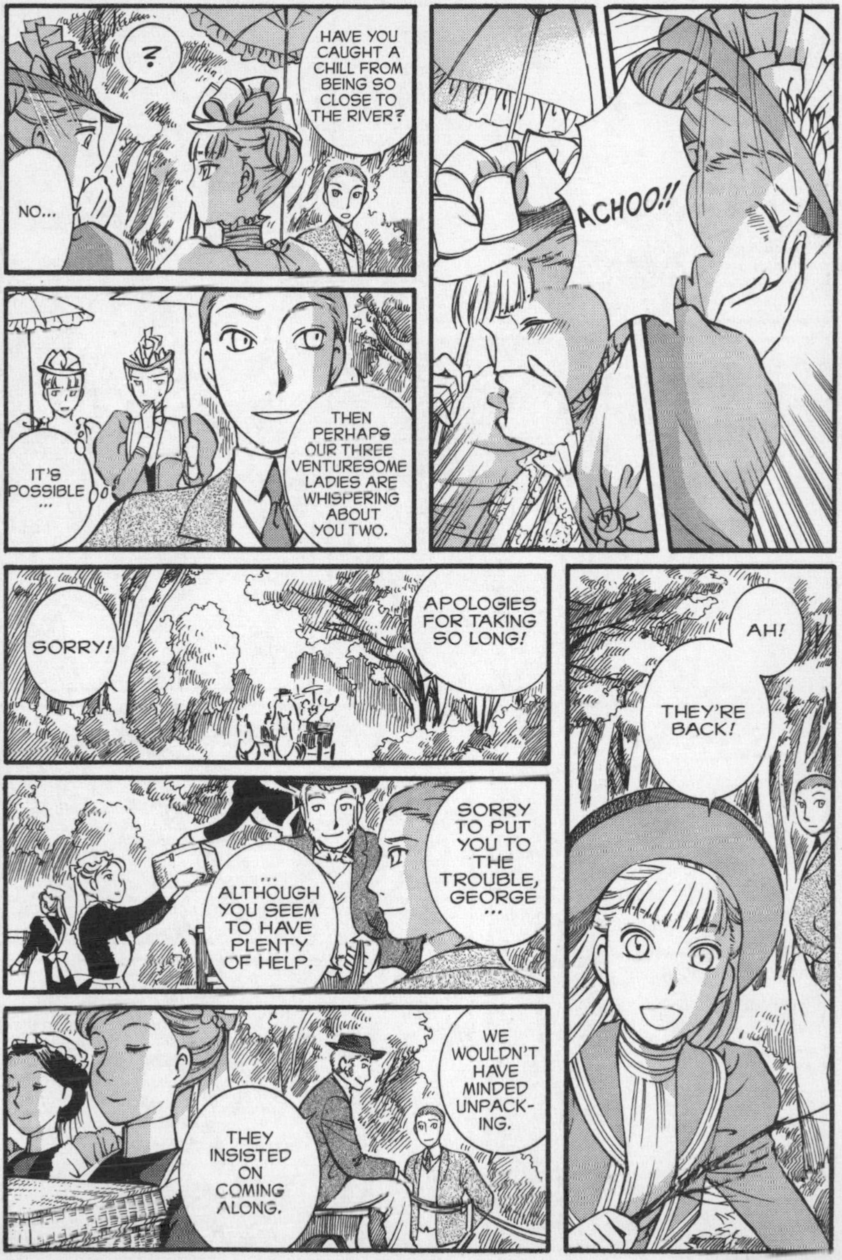
ACHOO!!
HAVE YOU CAUGHT A CHILL FROM BEING SO CLOSE TO THE RIVER?
?
NO...
THEN PERHAPS OUR THREE VENTURESOME LADIES ARE WHISPERING ABOUT YOU TWO.
IT'S POSSIBLE...
AH!
THEY'RE BACK!
APOLOGIES FOR TAKING SO LONG!
SORRY!
SORRY TO PUT YOU TO THE TROUBLE, GEORGE...
...ALTHOUGH YOU SEEM TO HAVE PLENTY OF HELP.
WE WOULDN'T HAVE MINDED UNPACK-ING.
THEY INSISTED ON COMING ALONG.

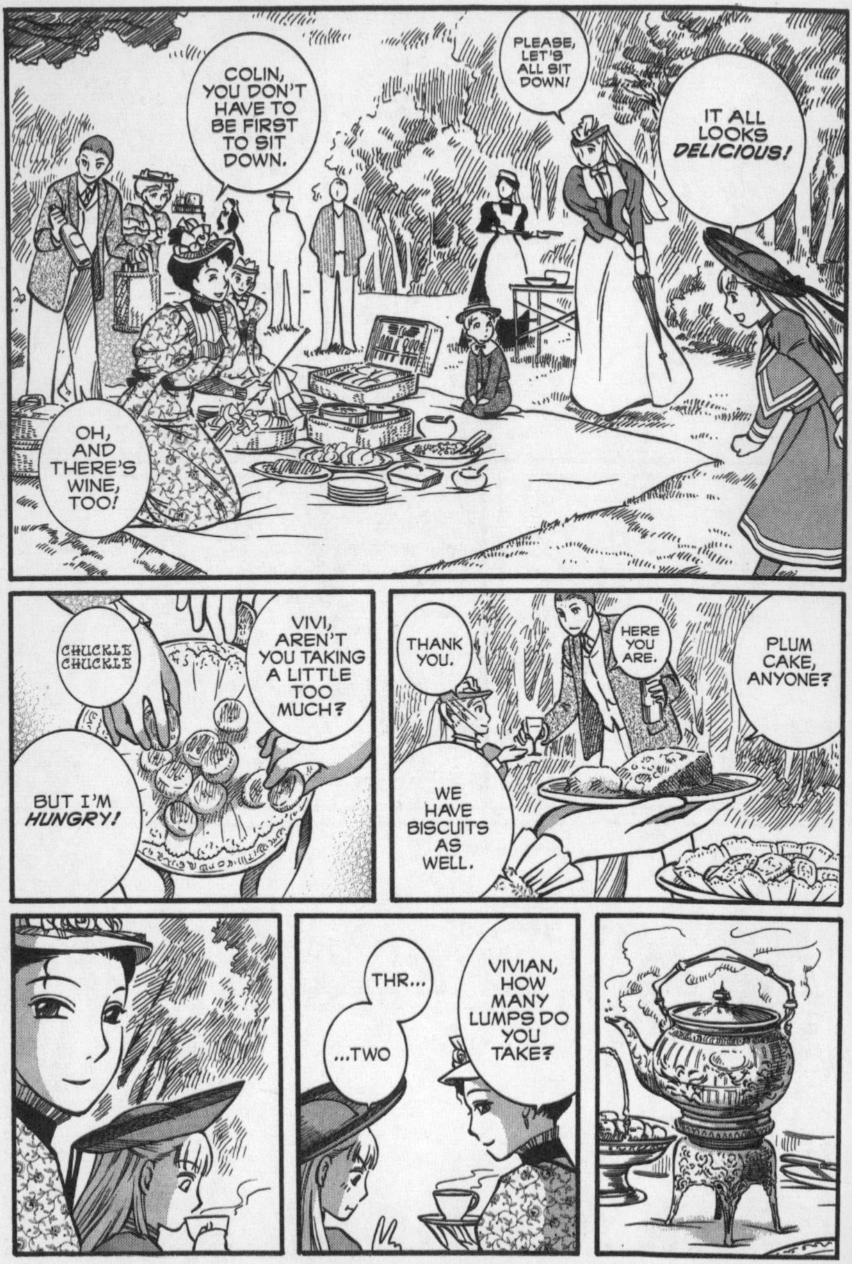
IT ALL LOOKS *DELICIOUS!*
PLEASE, LET'S ALL SIT DOWN!
COLIN, YOU DON'T HAVE TO BE FIRST TO SIT DOWN.
OH, AND THERE'S WINE, TOO!
PLUM CAKE, ANYONE?
HERE YOU ARE.
THANK YOU.
WE HAVE BISCUITS AS WELL.
VIVI, AREN'T YOU TAKING A LITTLE TOO MUCH?
CHUCKLE CHUCKLE
BUT I'M *HUNGRY!*
VIVIAN, HOW MANY LUMPS DO YOU TAKE?
THR...
...TWO

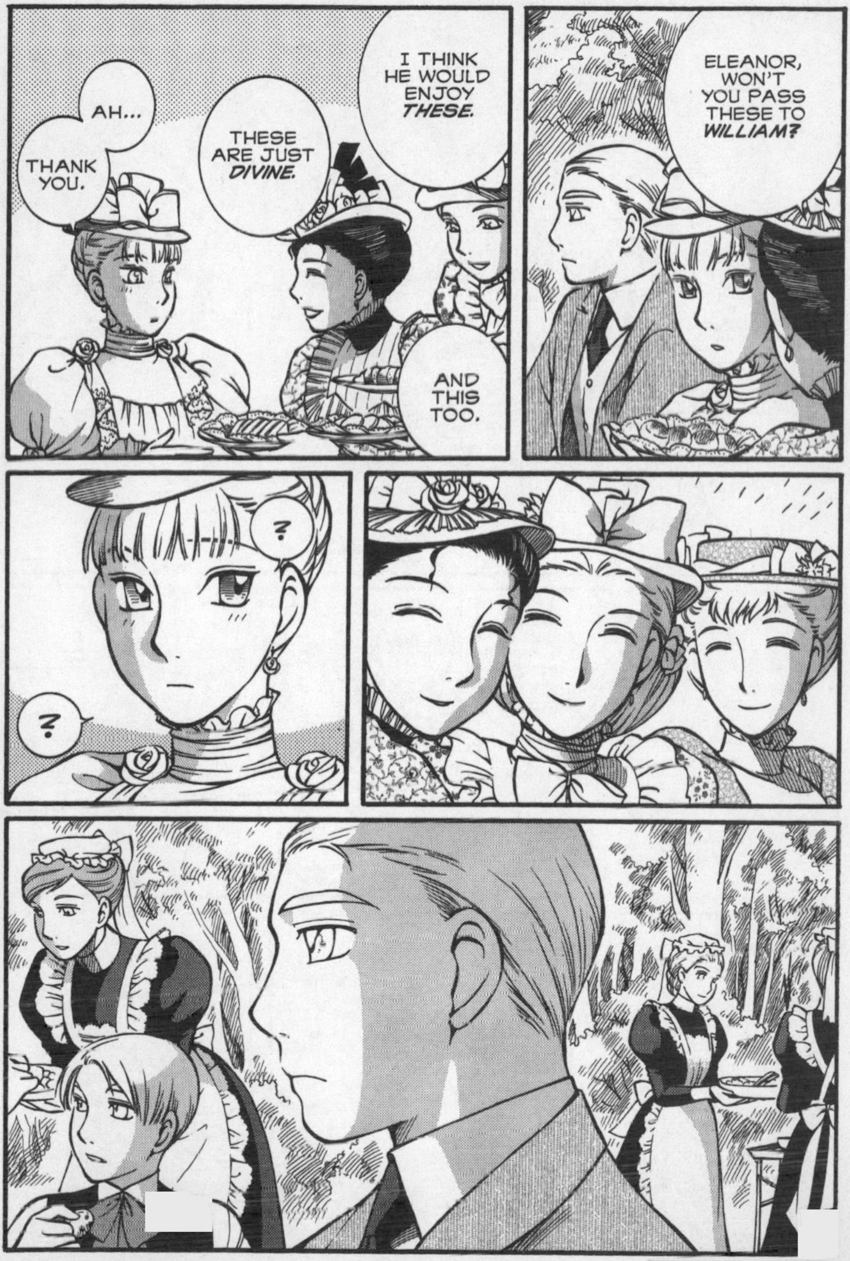
ELEANOR, WON'T YOU PASS THESE TO *WILLIAM?*
I THINK HE WOULD ENJOY *THESE.*
AND THIS TOO.
THESE ARE JUST *DIVINE.*
AH...
THANK YOU.
?
?

Chapter Sixteen: The End

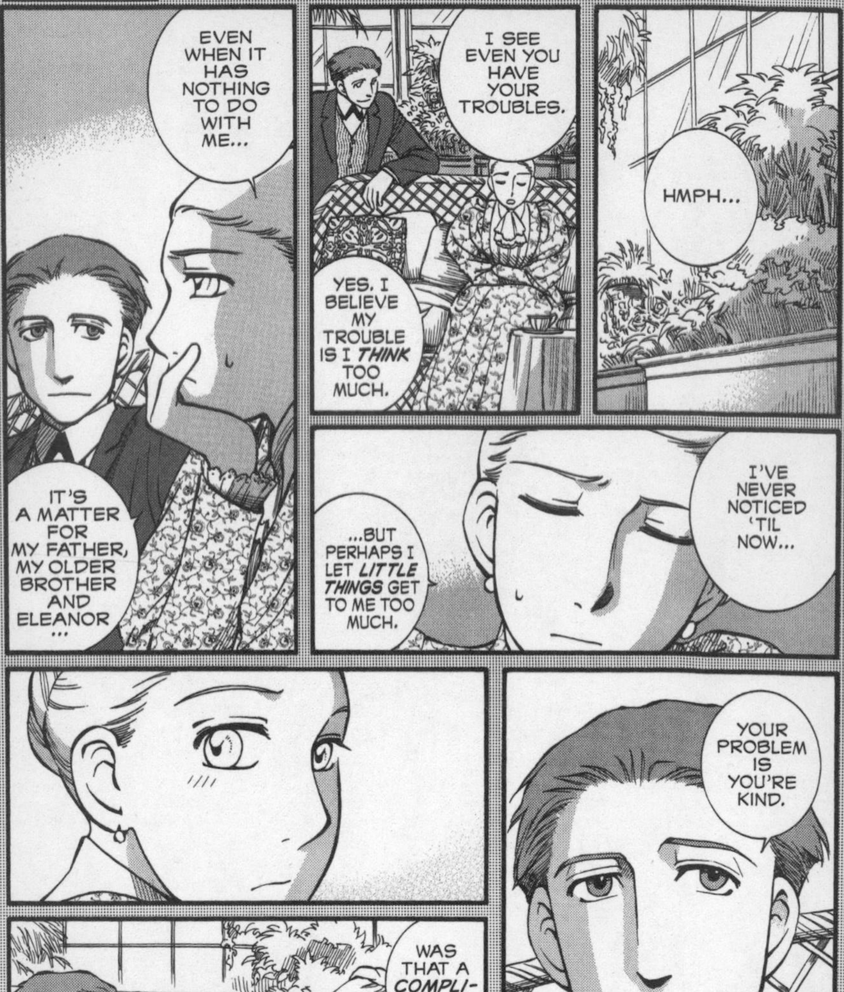
HMPH...
I SEE EVEN YOU HAVE YOUR TROUBLES.
YES. I BELIEVE MY TROUBLE IS I *THINK* TOO MUCH.
I'VE NEVER NOTICED 'TIL NOW...
...BUT PERHAPS I LET *LITTLE THINGS* GET TO ME TOO MUCH.
EVEN WHEN IT HAS NOTHING TO DO WITH ME...
IT'S A MATTER FOR MY FATHER, MY OLDER BROTHER AND ELEANOR ...
YOUR PROBLEM IS YOU'RE KIND.
WAS THAT A *COMPLIMENT*?
TAKE IT AS YOU LIKE.

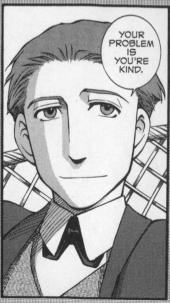

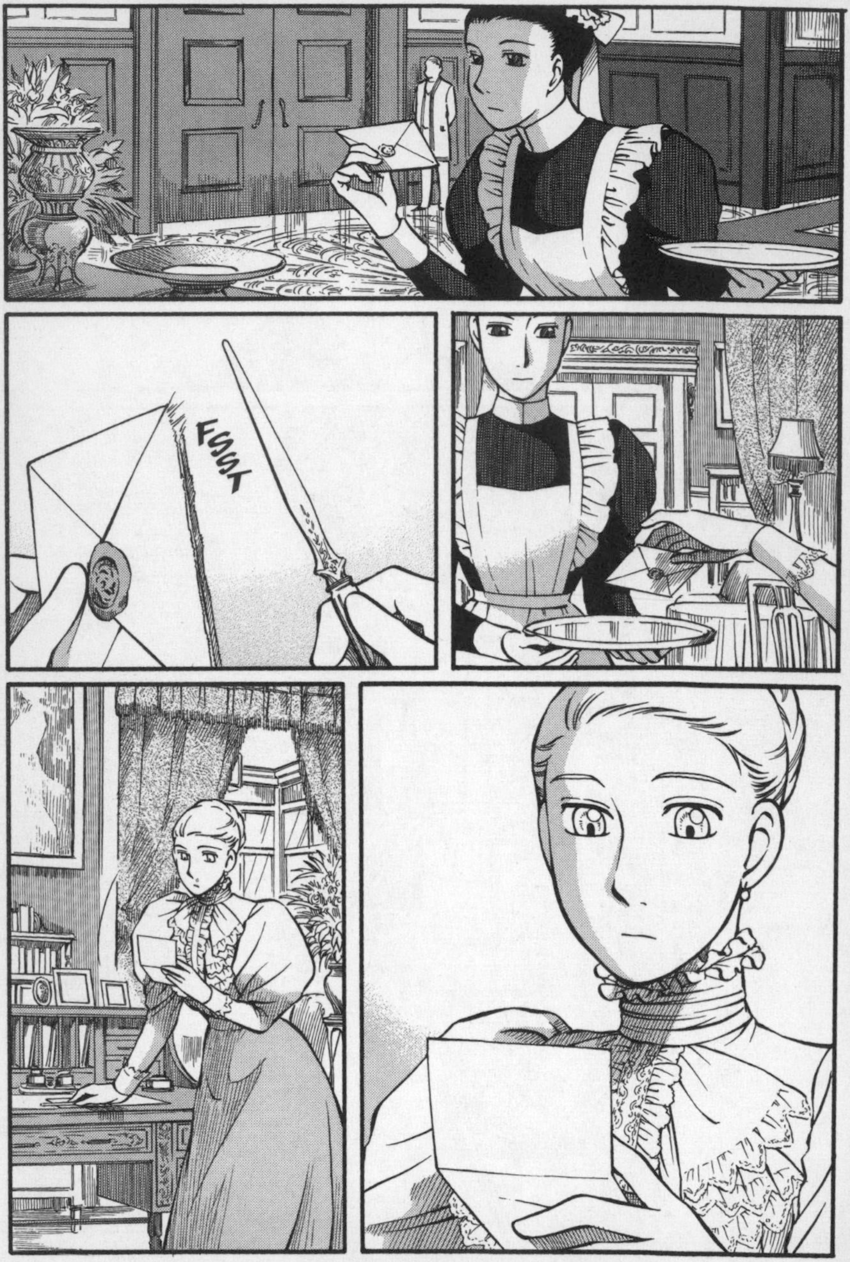
FSST

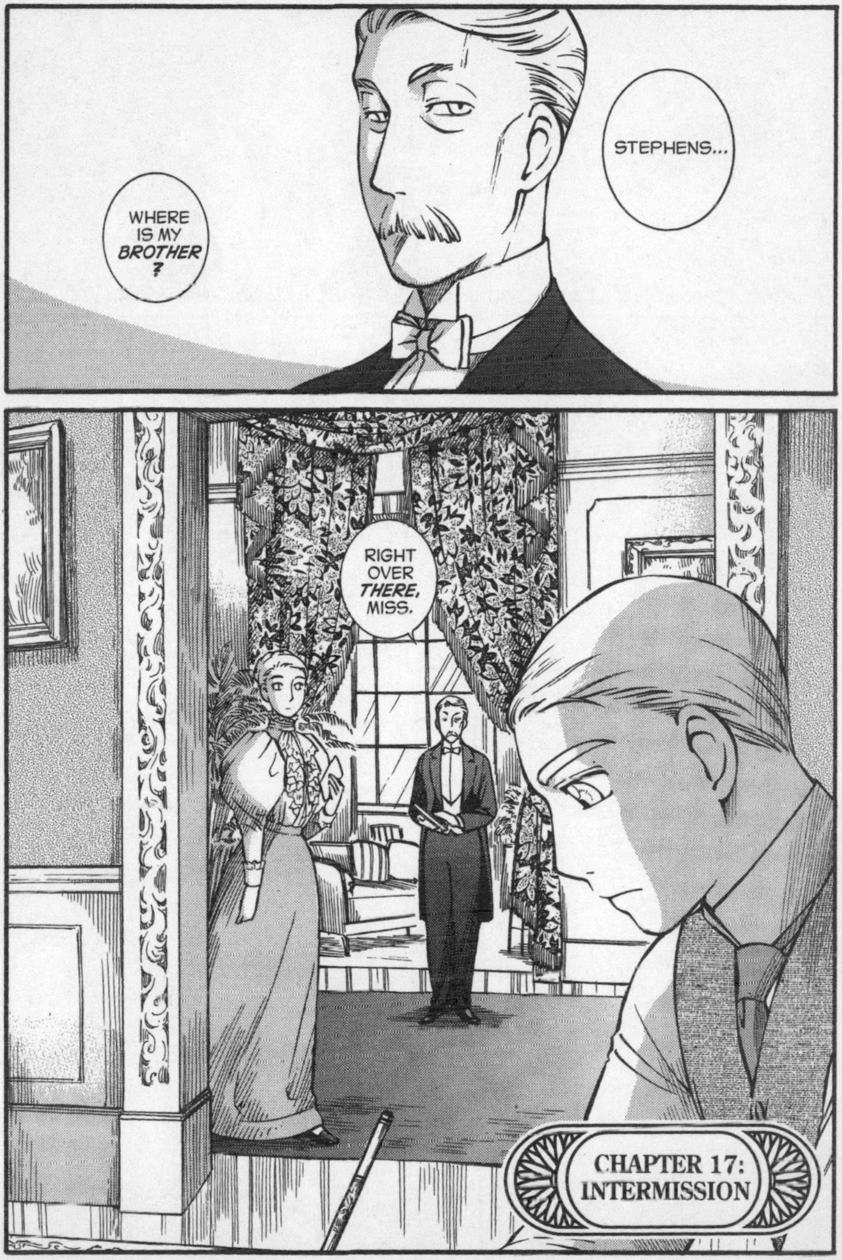
STEPHENS...
WHERE IS MY *BROTHER*?
RIGHT OVER *THERE,* MISS.
CHAPTER 17: INTERMISSION

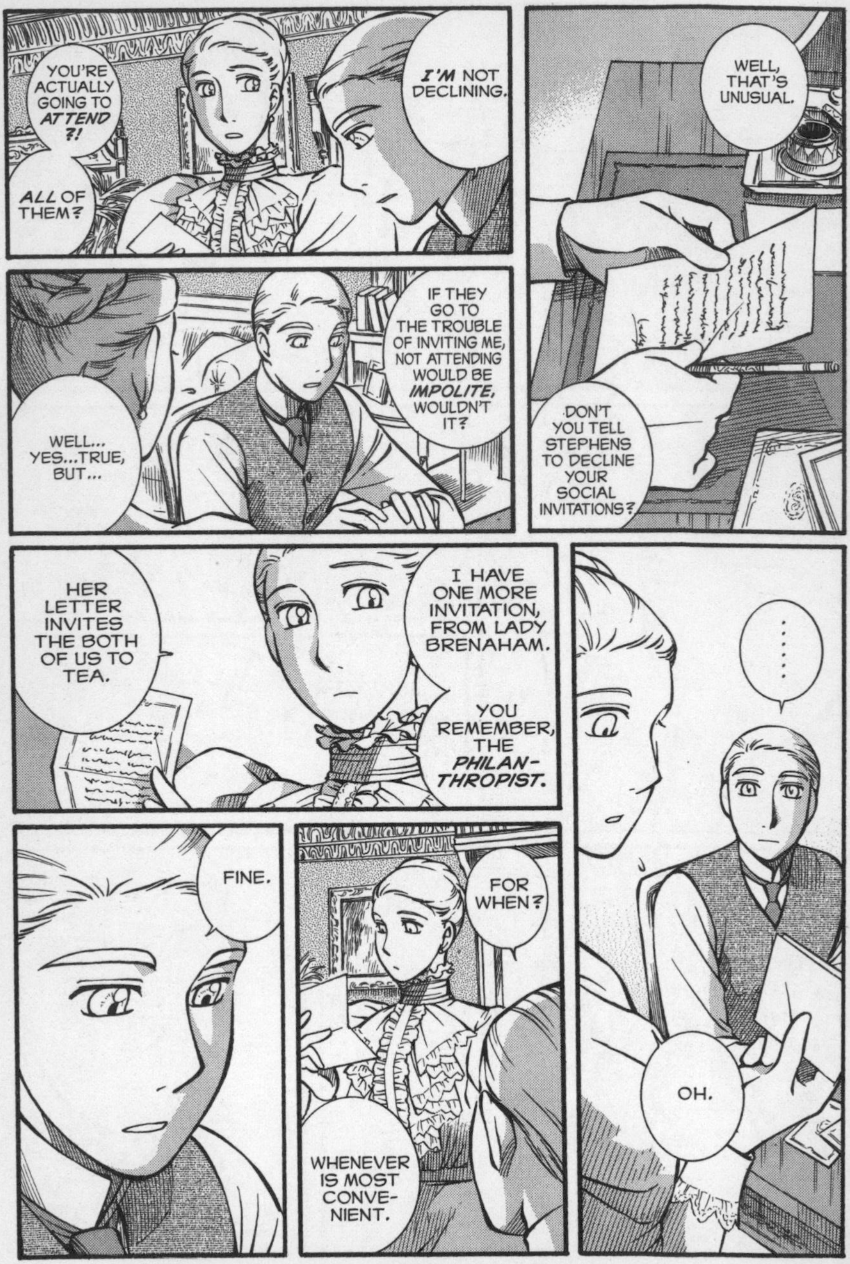
WELL, THAT'S UNUSUAL.
DON'T YOU TELL STEPHENS TO DECLINE YOUR SOCIAL INVITATIONS?
I'M NOT DECLINING.
YOU'RE ACTUALLY GOING TO *ATTEND* ?!
ALL OF THEM?
IF THEY GO TO THE TROUBLE OF INVITING ME, NOT ATTENDING WOULD BE *IMPOLITE,* WOULDN'T IT?
WELL... YES...TRUE, BUT...
......
OH.
I HAVE ONE MORE INVITATION, FROM LADY BRENAHAM.
YOU REMEMBER, THE *PHILAN-THROPIST.*
HER LETTER INVITES THE BOTH OF US TO TEA.
FOR WHEN?
WHENEVER IS MOST CONVE-NIENT.
FINE.

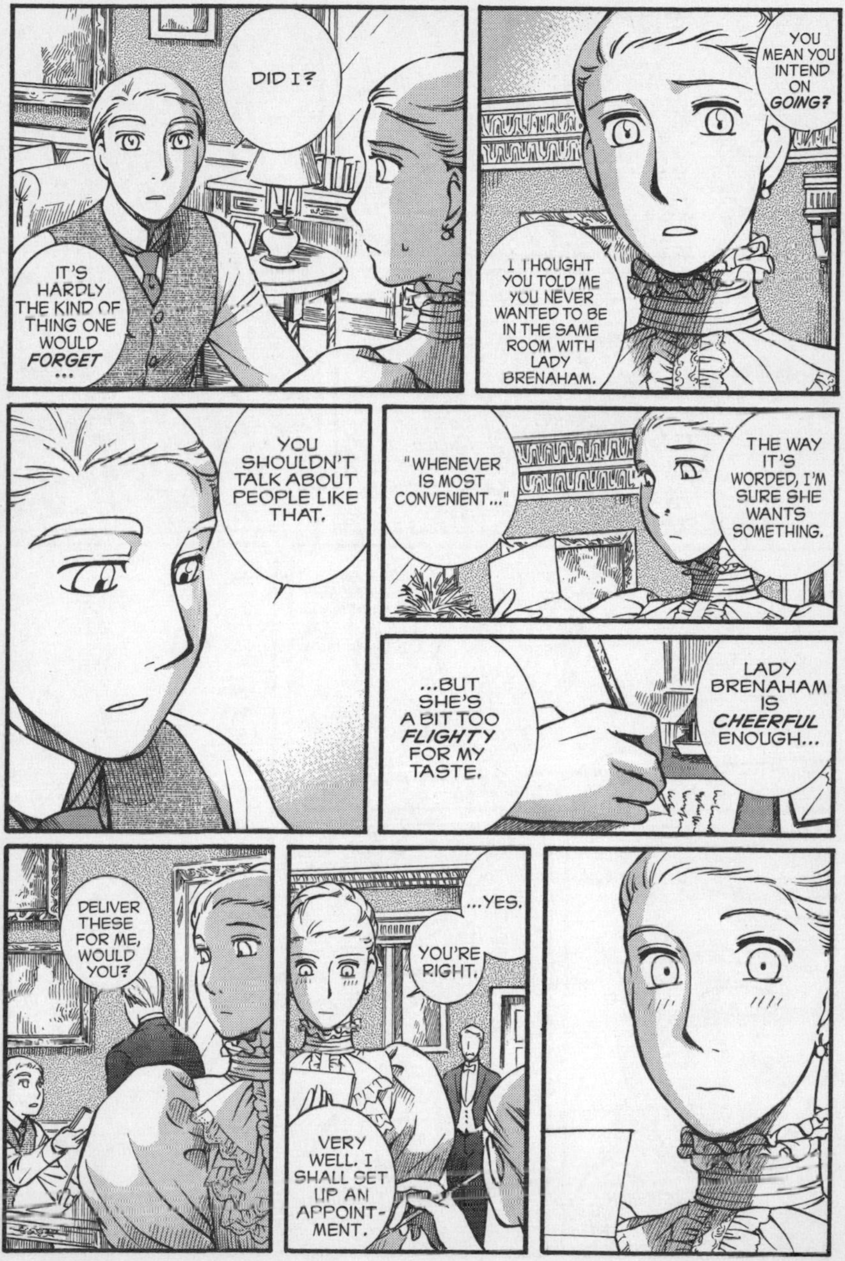
YOU MEAN YOU INTEND ON *GOING?*
I THOUGHT YOU TOLD ME YOU NEVER WANTED TO BE IN THE SAME ROOM WITH LADY BRENAHAM.
DID I?
IT'S HARDLY THE KIND OF THING ONE WOULD *FORGET* ...
"WHENEVER IS MOST CONVENIENT..."
THE WAY IT'S WORDED, I'M SURE SHE WANTS SOMETHING.
LADY BRENAHAM IS *CHEERFUL* ENOUGH...
...BUT SHE'S A BIT TOO *FLIGHTY* FOR MY TASTE.
YOU SHOULDN'T TALK ABOUT PEOPLE LIKE THAT.
...YES.
YOU'RE RIGHT.
VERY WELL. I SHALL SET UP AN APPOINT-MENT.
DELIVER THESE FOR ME, WOULD YOU?

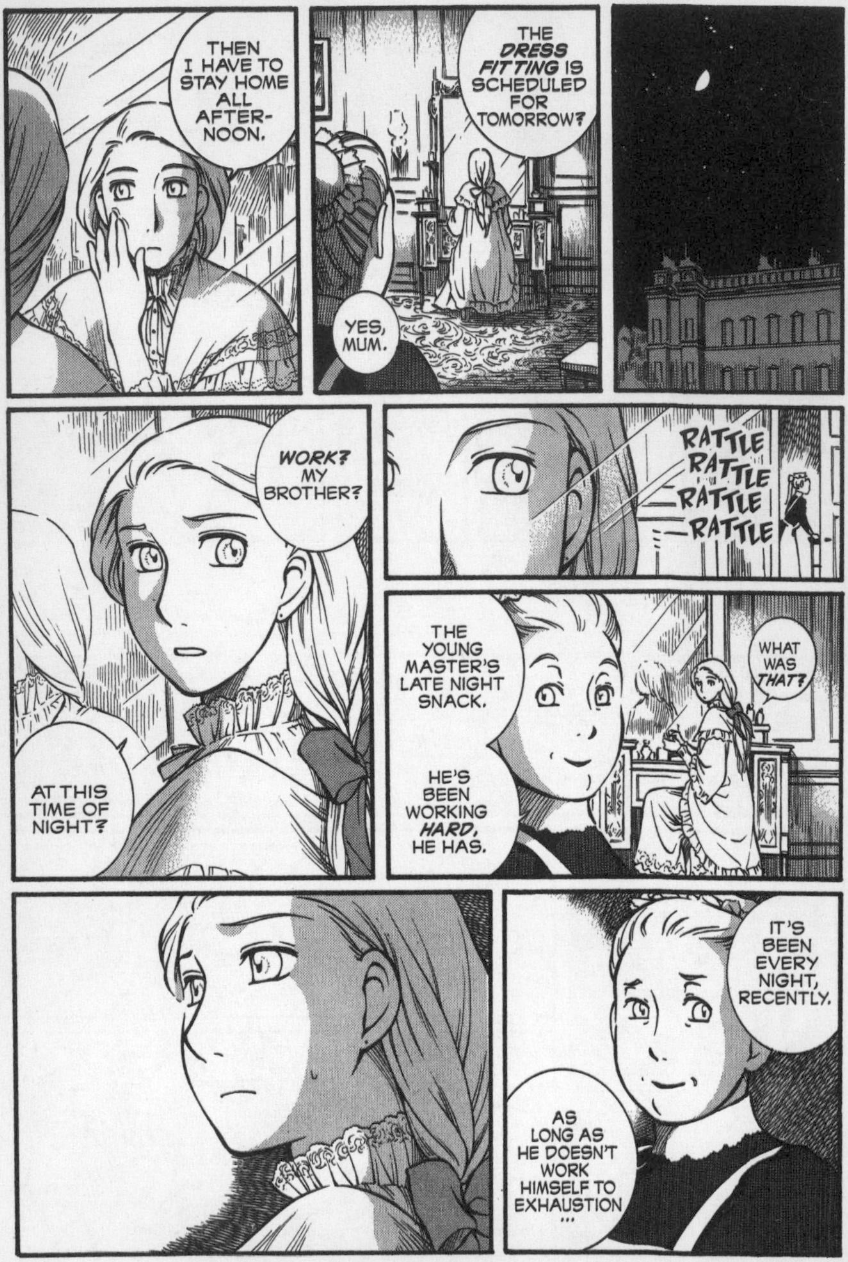

THE DRESS FITTING IS SCHEDULED FOR TOMORROW?
YES, MUM.
THEN I HAVE TO STAY HOME ALL AFTER-NOON.
RATTLE RATTLE RATTLE RATTLE
WHAT WAS THAT?
THE YOUNG MASTER'S LATE NIGHT SNACK.
HE'S BEEN WORKING HARD, HE HAS.
WORK? MY BROTHER?
AT THIS TIME OF NIGHT?
IT'S BEEN EVERY NIGHT, RECENTLY.
AS LONG AS HE DOESN'T WORK HIMSELF TO EXHAUSTION ...

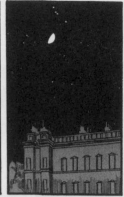

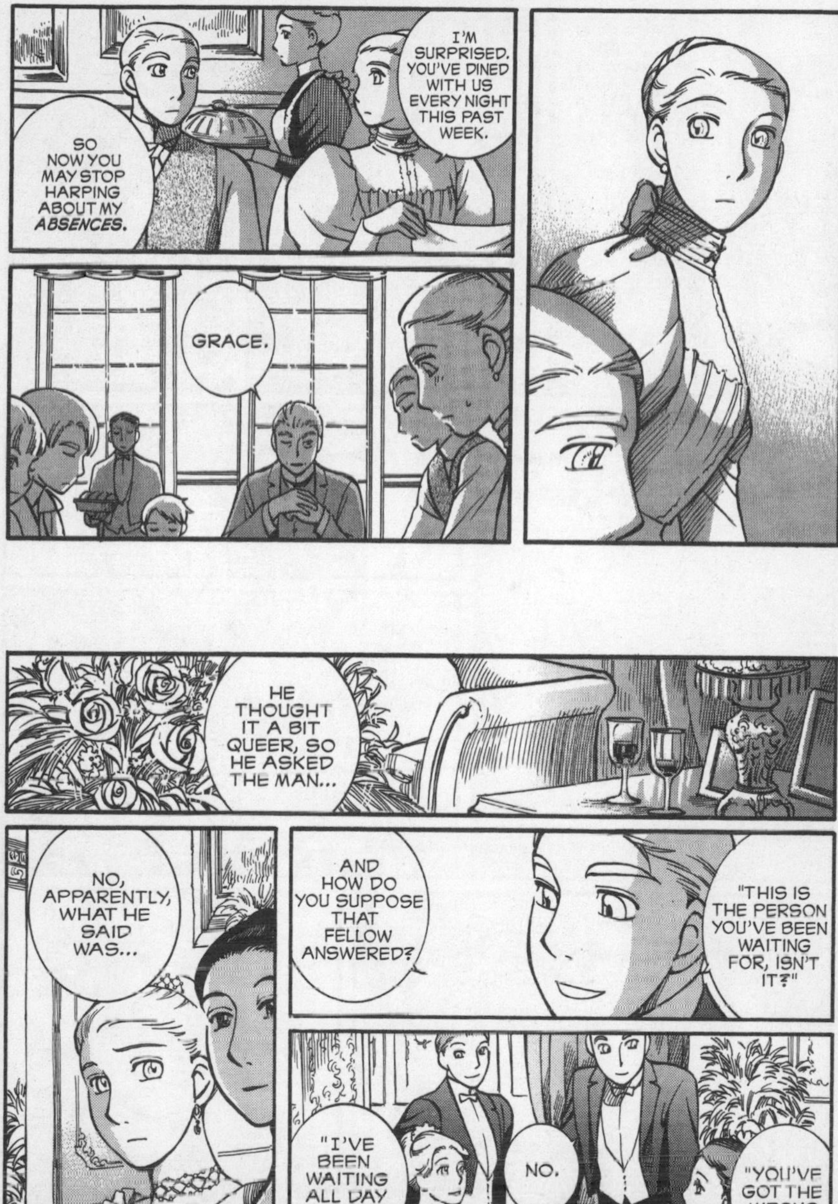
I'M SURPRISED. YOU'VE DINED WITH US EVERY NIGHT THIS PAST WEEK.
SO NOW YOU MAY STOP HARPING ABOUT MY *ABSENCES*.
GRACE.
HE THOUGHT IT A BIT QUEER, SO HE ASKED THE MAN...
"THIS IS THE PERSON YOU'VE BEEN WAITING FOR, ISN'T IT?"
AND HOW DO YOU SUPPOSE THAT FELLOW ANSWERED?
"YOU'VE GOT THE WRONG MAN?"
NO.
"I'VE BEEN WAITING ALL DAY FOR YOU?"
NO, APPARENTLY, WHAT HE SAID WAS...

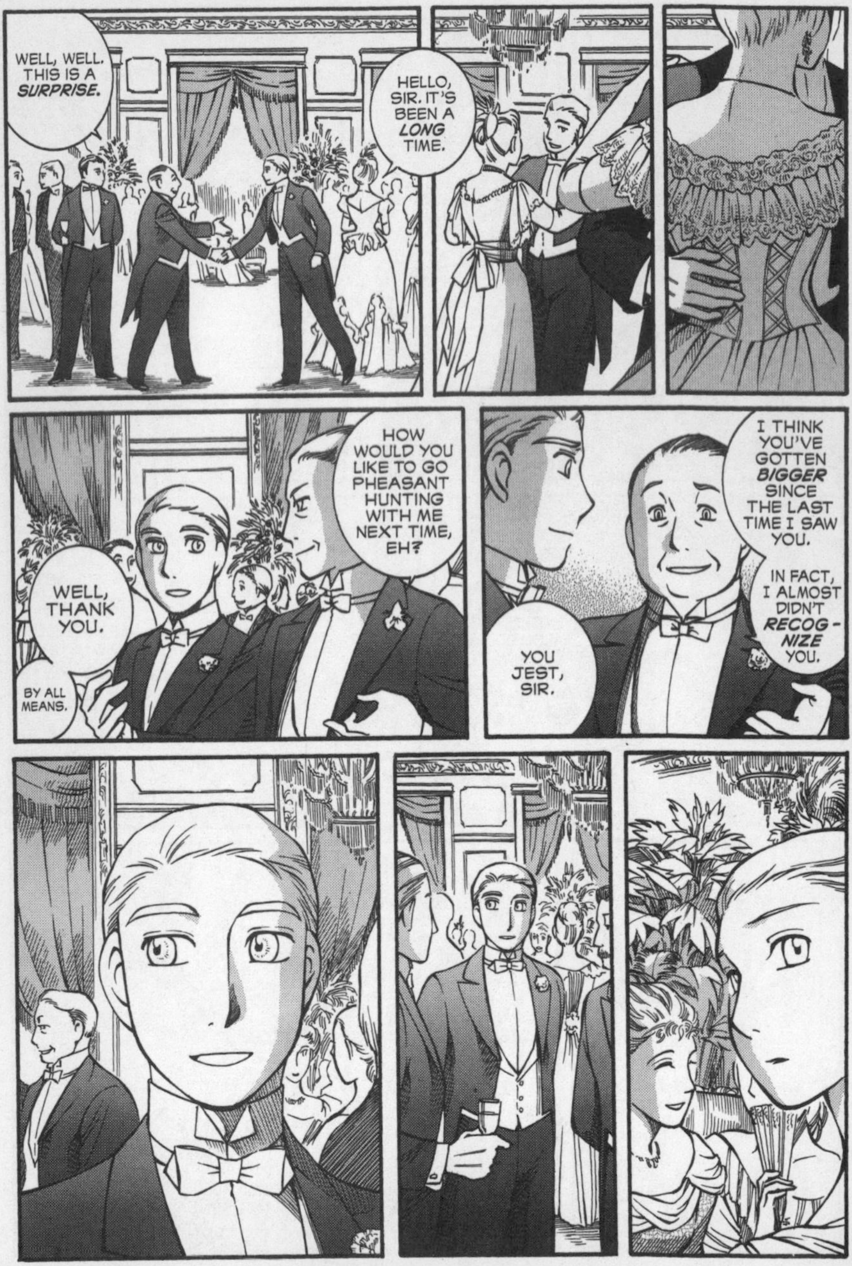
HELLO, SIR. IT'S BEEN A *LONG* TIME.
WELL, WELL. THIS IS A *SURPRISE.*
I THINK YOU'VE GOTTEN *BIGGER* SINCE THE LAST TIME I SAW YOU.
IN FACT, I ALMOST DIDN'T *RECOGNIZE* YOU.
YOU JEST, SIR.
HOW WOULD YOU LIKE TO GO PHEASANT HUNTING WITH ME NEXT TIME, EH?
WELL, THANK YOU.
BY ALL MEANS.

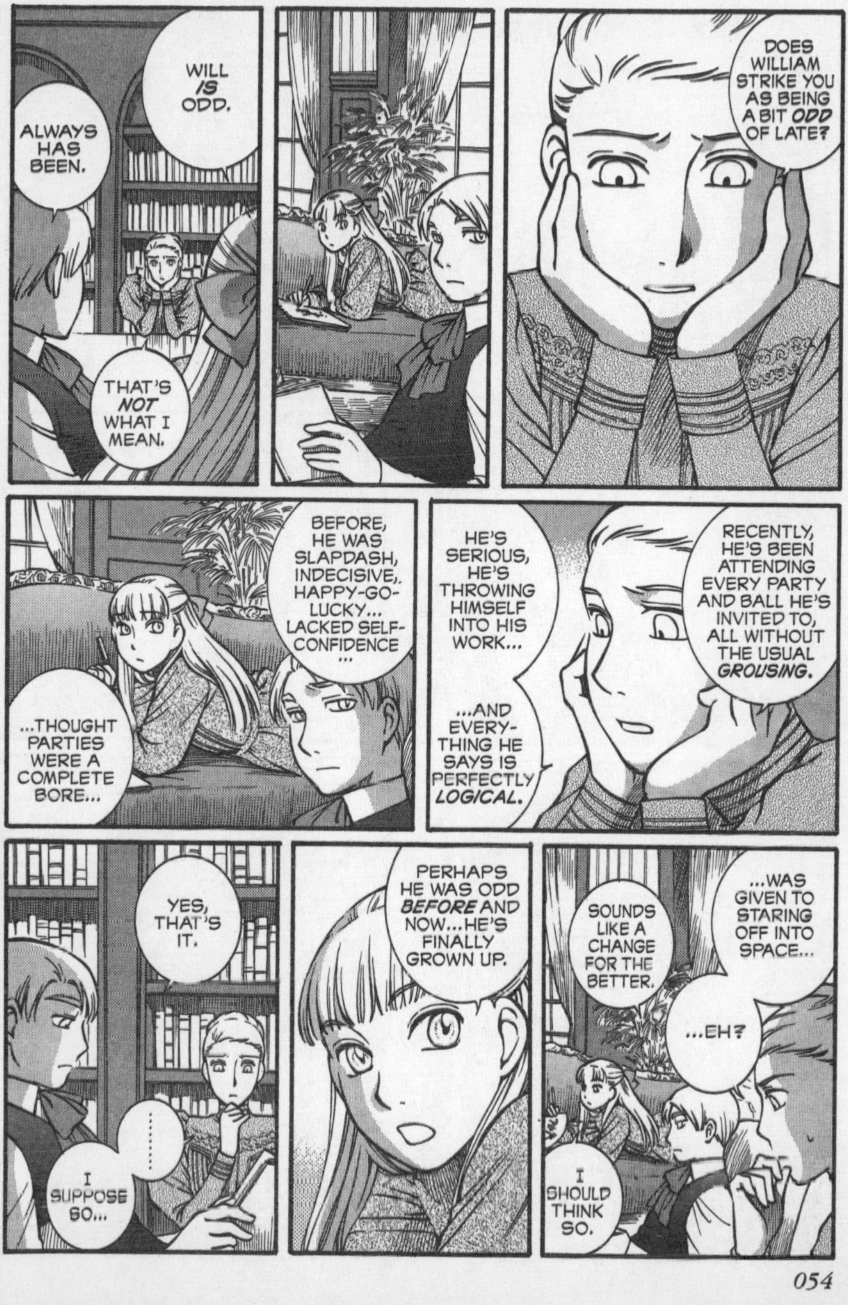
DOES WILLIAM STRIKE YOU AS BEING A BIT *ODD* OF LATE?
WILL *IS* ODD.
ALWAYS HAS BEEN.
THAT'S *NOT* WHAT I MEAN.
RECENTLY, HE'S BEEN ATTENDING EVERY PARTY AND BALL HE'S INVITED TO, ALL WITHOUT THE USUAL *GROUSING*.
HE'S SERIOUS, HE'S THROWING HIMSELF INTO HIS WORK...
...AND EVERYTHING HE SAYS IS PERFECTLY *LOGICAL*.
BEFORE, HE WAS SLAPDASH, INDECISIVE, HAPPY-GO-LUCKY... LACKED SELF-CONFIDENCE...
...THOUGHT PARTIES WERE A COMPLETE BORE...
...WAS GIVEN TO STARING OFF INTO SPACE...
SOUNDS LIKE A CHANGE FOR THE BETTER.
...EH?
I SHOULD THINK SO.
PERHAPS HE WAS ODD *BEFORE* AND NOW... HE'S FINALLY GROWN UP.
YES, THAT'S IT.
......
I SUPPOSE SO...

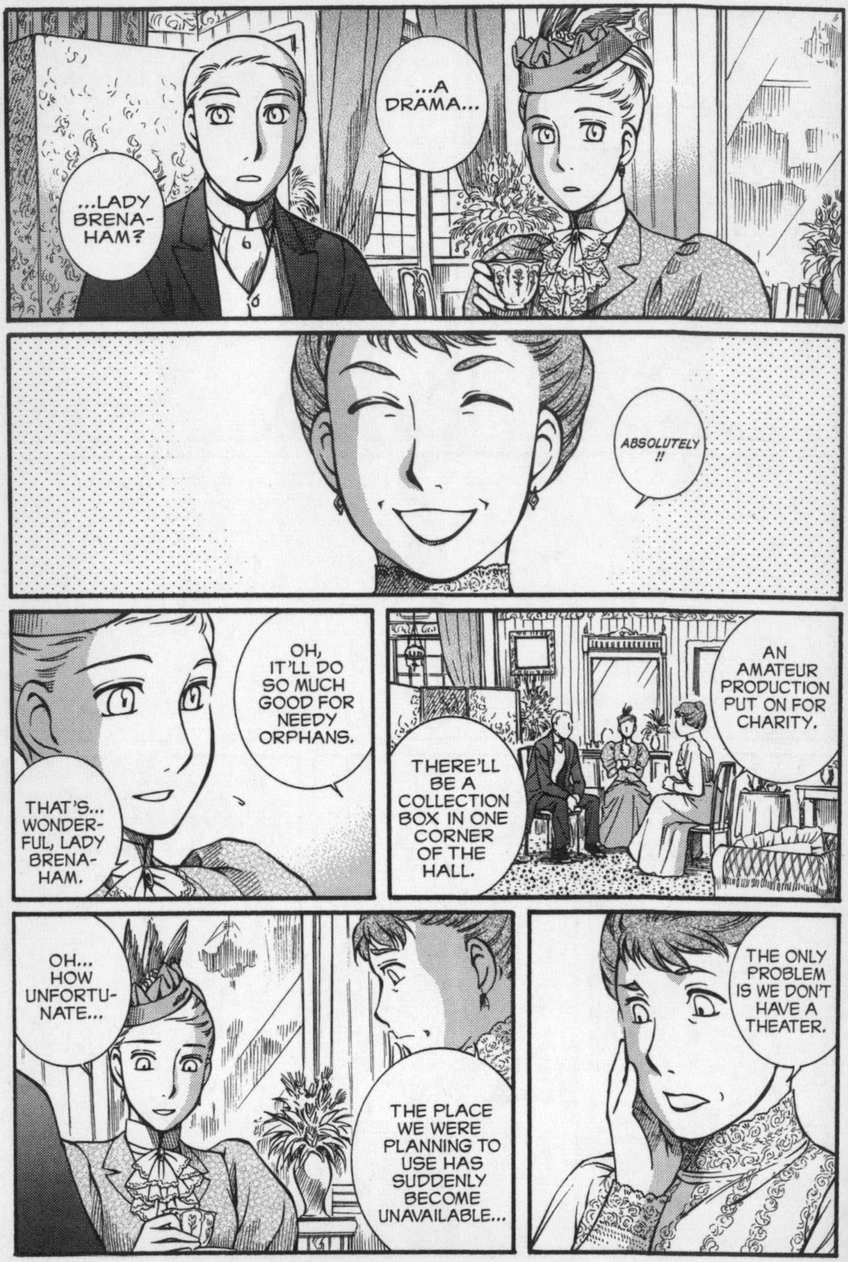
...A DRAMA...
...LADY BRENAHAM?
ABSOLUTELY!!
AN AMATEUR PRODUCTION PUT ON FOR CHARITY.
THERE'LL BE A COLLECTION BOX IN ONE CORNER OF THE HALL.
OH, IT'LL DO SO MUCH GOOD FOR NEEDY ORPHANS.
THAT'S... WONDERFUL, LADY BRENAHAM.
THE ONLY PROBLEM IS WE DON'T HAVE A THEATER.
THE PLACE WE WERE PLANNING TO USE HAS SUDDENLY BECOME UNAVAILABLE...
OH... HOW UNFORTUNATE...

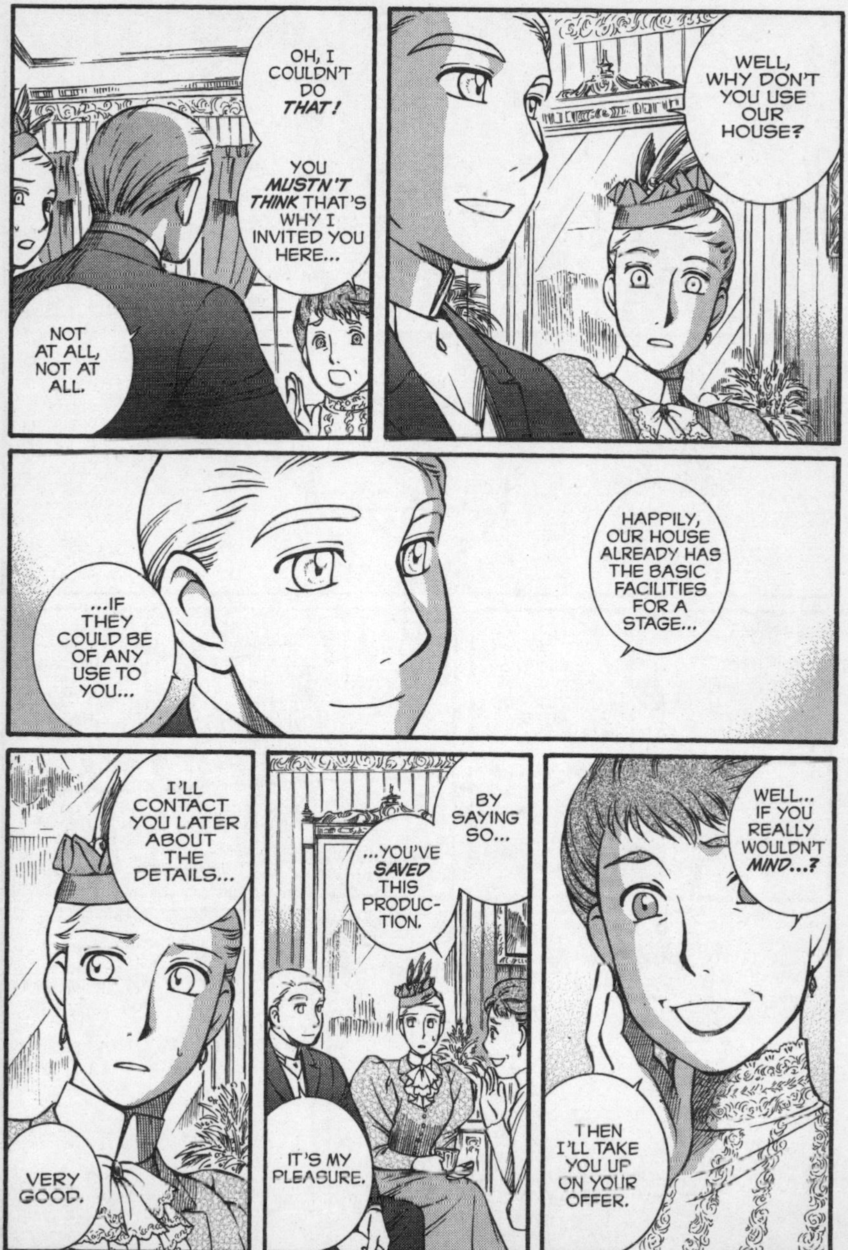
WELL, WHY DON'T YOU USE OUR HOUSE?
OH, I COULDN'T DO *THAT!*
YOU *MUSTN'T THINK* THAT'S WHY I INVITED YOU HERE...
NOT AT ALL, NOT AT ALL.
HAPPILY, OUR HOUSE ALREADY HAS THE BASIC FACILITIES FOR A STAGE...
...IF THEY COULD BE OF ANY USE TO YOU...
WELL... IF YOU REALLY WOULDN'T *MIND...?*
THEN I'LL TAKE YOU UP ON YOUR OFFER.
BY SAYING SO...
...YOU'VE *SAVED* THIS PRODUCTION.
IT'S MY PLEASURE.
I'LL CONTACT YOU LATER ABOUT THE DETAILS...
VERY GOOD.

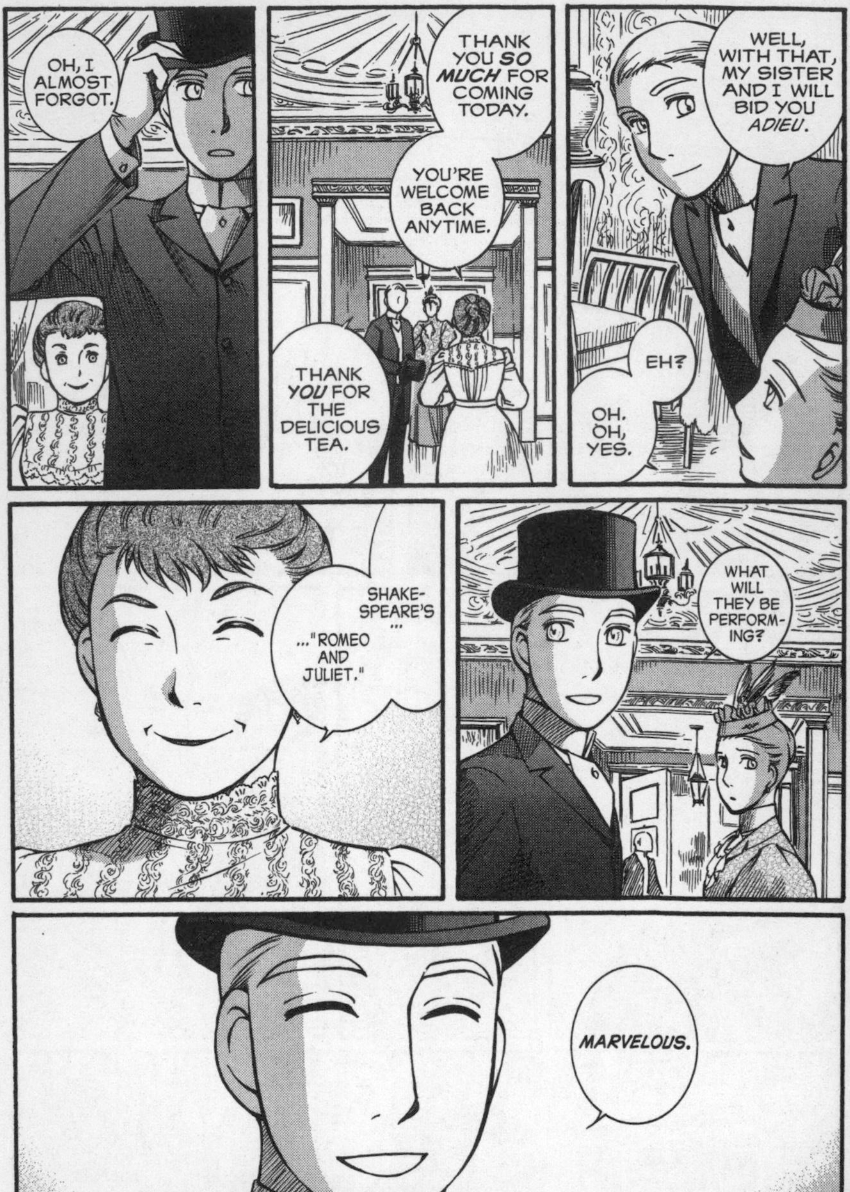
WELL, WITH THAT, MY SISTER AND I WILL BID YOU *ADIEU*.
EH?
OH. OH, YES.
THANK YOU **SO MUCH** FOR COMING TODAY.
YOU'RE WELCOME BACK ANYTIME.
THANK ***YOU*** FOR THE DELICIOUS TEA.
OH, I ALMOST FORGOT.
WHAT WILL THEY BE PERFORMING?
SHAKESPEARE'S...
..."ROMEO AND JULIET."
MARVELOUS.

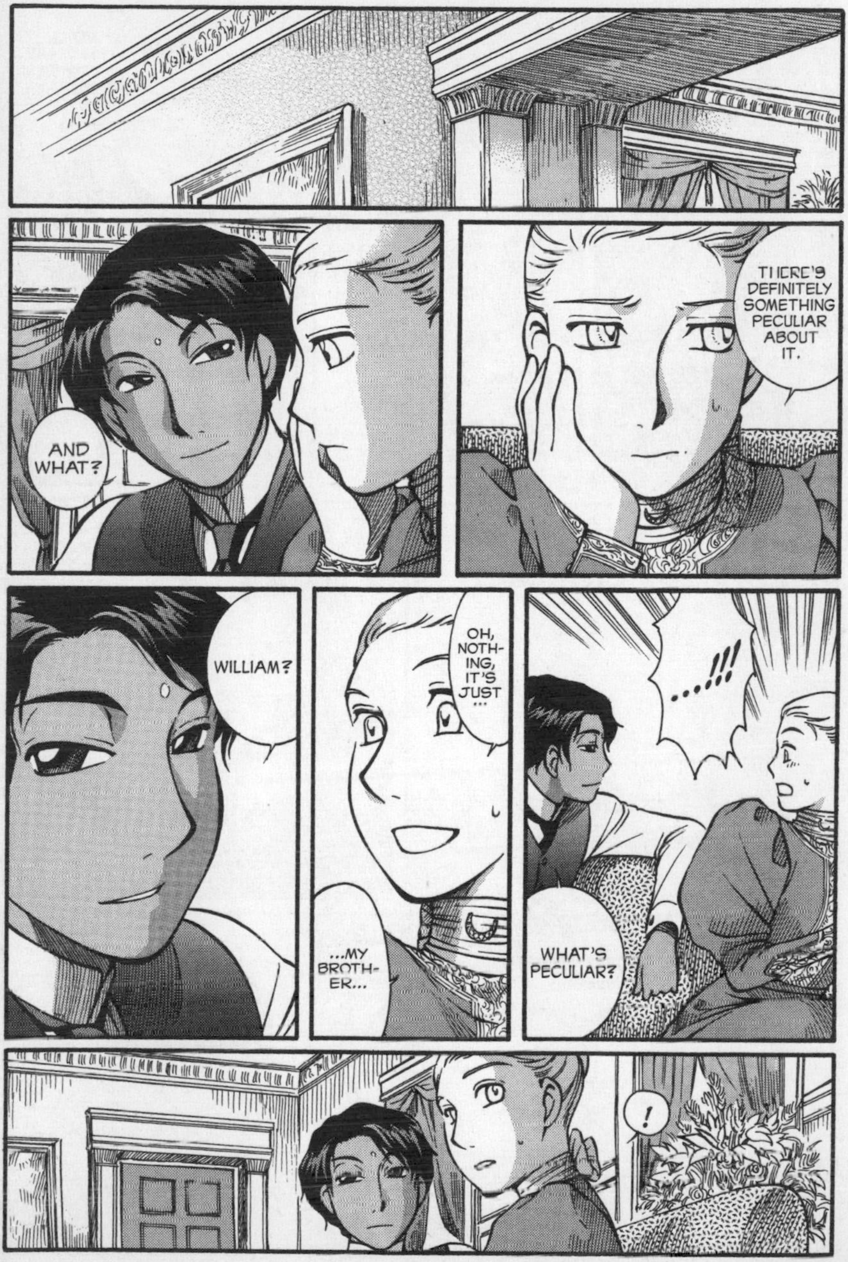
THERE'S DEFINITELY SOMETHING PECULIAR ABOUT IT.
AND WHAT?
...!!!
WHAT'S PECULIAR?
OH, NOTHING, IT'S JUST...
...MY BROTHER...
WILLIAM?
!

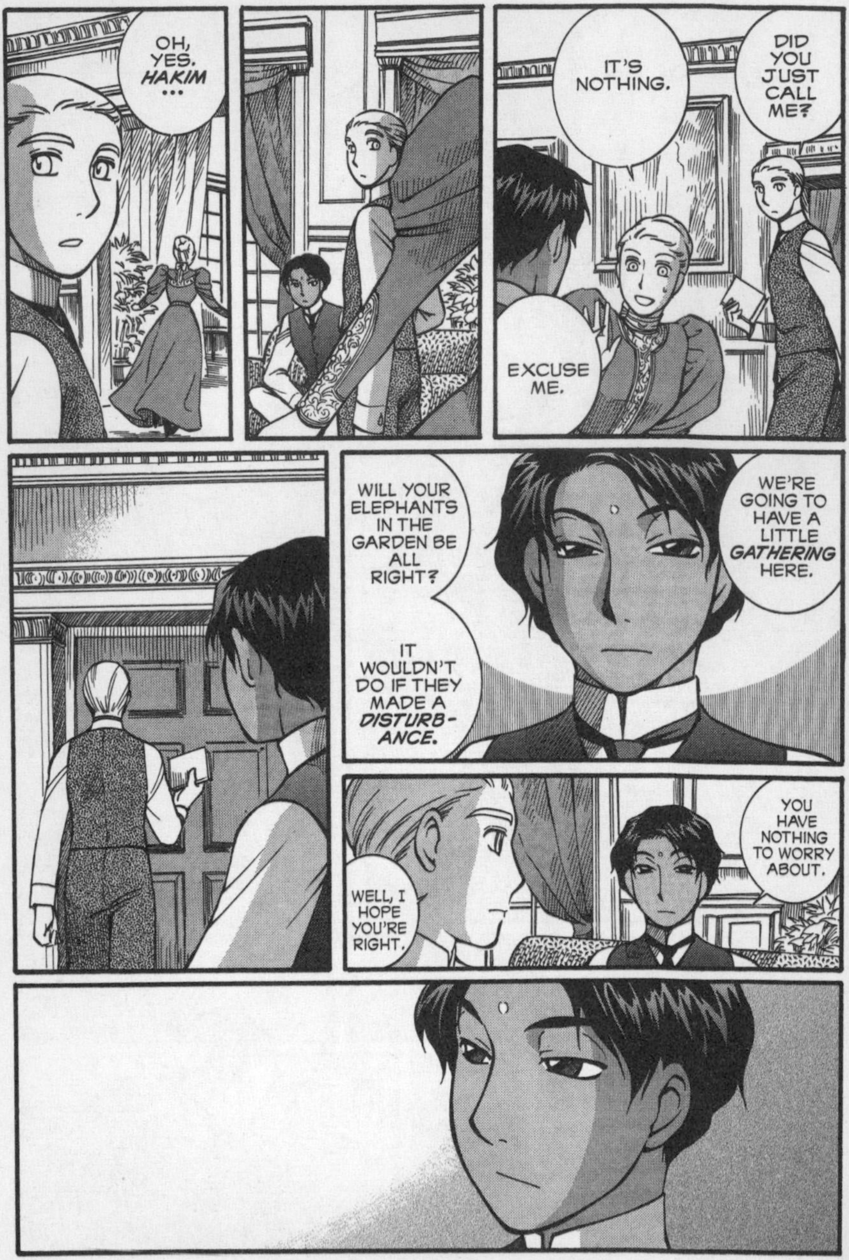
DID YOU JUST CALL ME?
IT'S NOTHING.
EXCUSE ME.
OH, YES. *HAKIM*...
WE'RE GOING TO HAVE A LITTLE *GATHERING* HERE.
WILL YOUR ELEPHANTS IN THE GARDEN BE ALL RIGHT?
IT WOULDN'T DO IF THEY MADE A *DISTURB-ANCE.*
YOU HAVE NOTHING TO WORRY ABOUT.
WELL, I HOPE YOU'RE RIGHT.

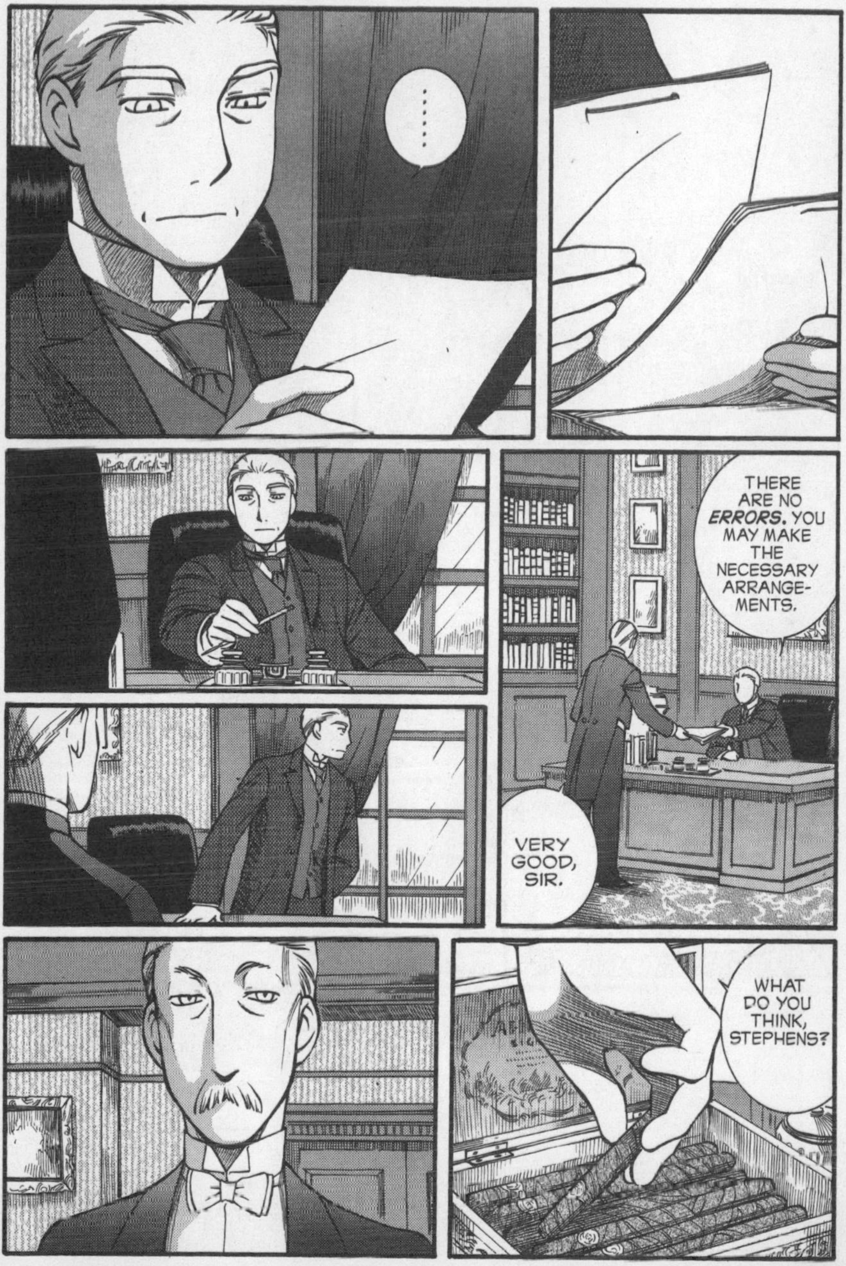
......
THERE ARE NO ERRORS. YOU MAY MAKE THE NECESSARY ARRANGEMENTS.
VERY GOOD, SIR.
WHAT DO YOU THINK, STEPHENS?

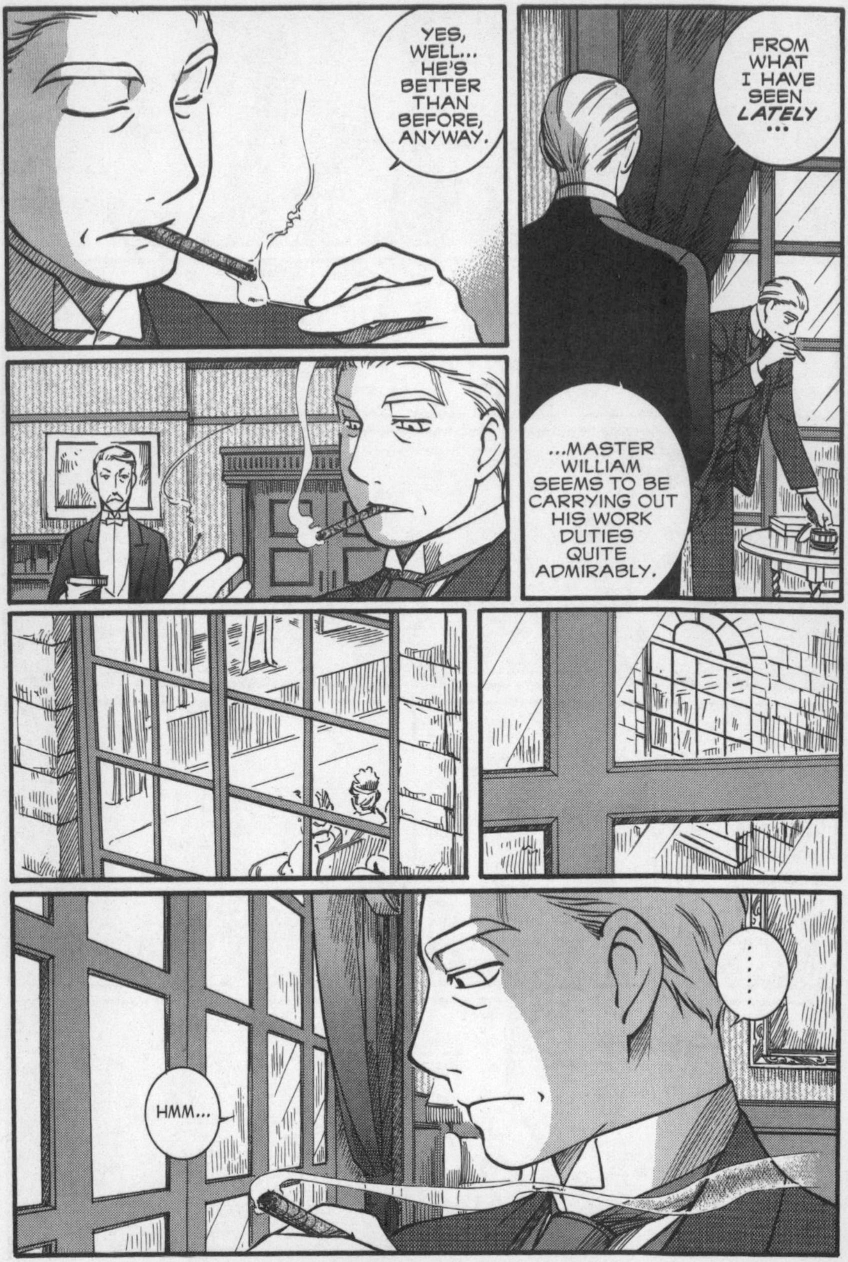
FROM WHAT I HAVE SEEN *LATELY*...
...MASTER WILLIAM SEEMS TO BE CARRYING OUT HIS WORK DUTIES QUITE ADMIRABLY.
YES, WELL... HE'S BETTER THAN BEFORE, ANYWAY.
......
HMM...

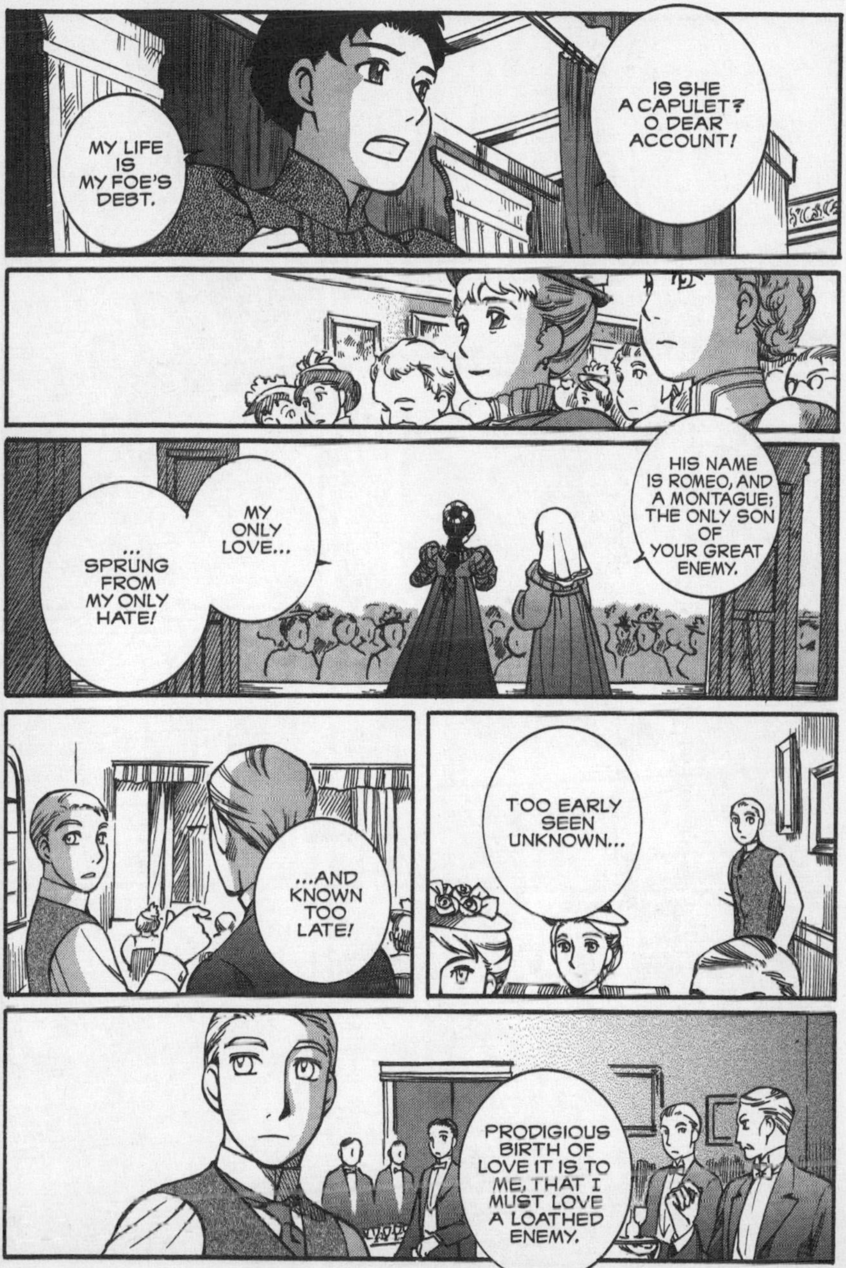
IS SHE A CAPULET? O DEAR ACCOUNT!
MY LIFE IS MY FOE'S DEBT.
HIS NAME IS ROMEO, AND A MONTAGUE; THE ONLY SON OF YOUR GREAT ENEMY.
MY ONLY LOVE...
... SPRUNG FROM MY ONLY HATE!
TOO EARLY SEEN UNKNOWN...
...AND KNOWN TOO LATE!
PRODIGIOUS BIRTH OF LOVE IT IS TO ME, THAT I MUST LOVE A LOATHED ENEMY.

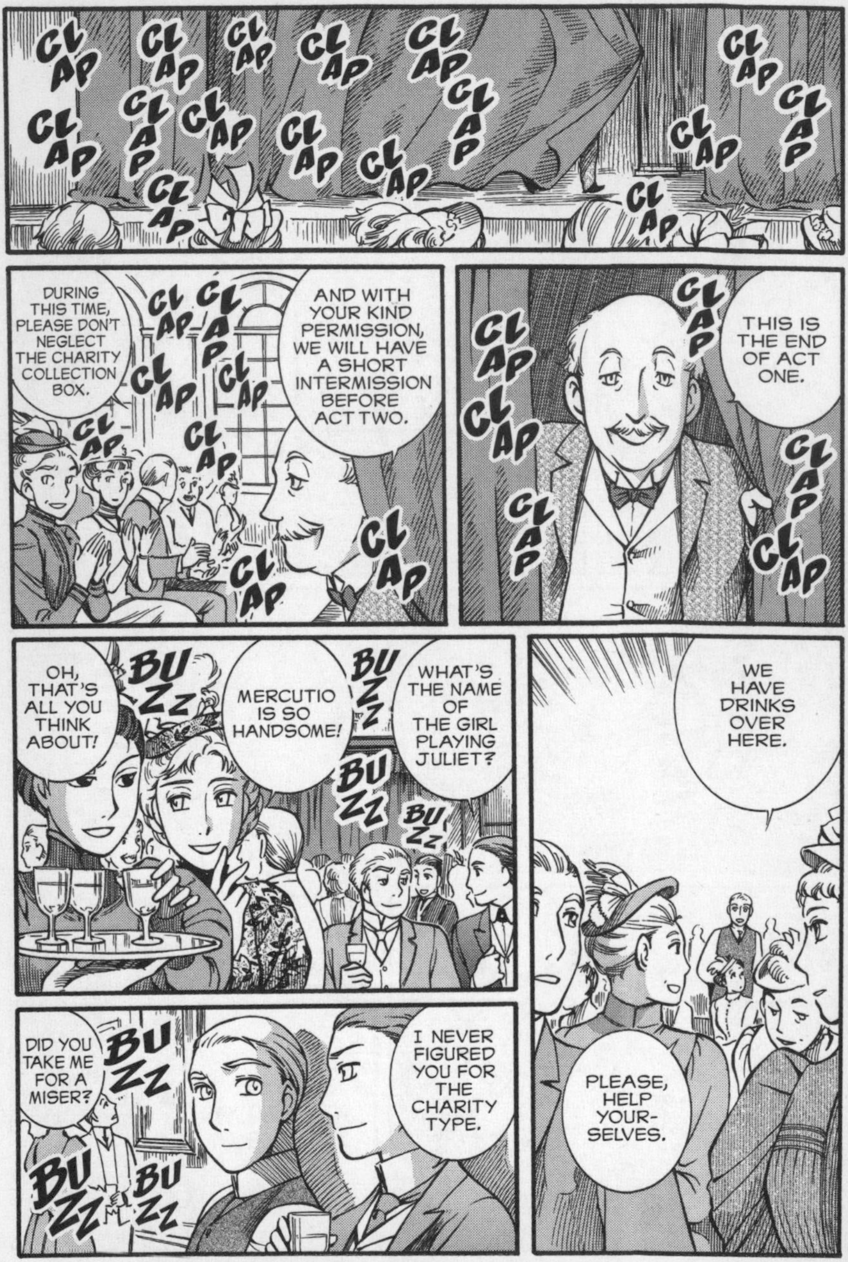
CLAP CLAP CLAP CLAP CLAP CLAP CLAP CLAP CLAP CLAP CLAP CLAP CLAP CLAP CLAP CLAP
CLAP CLAP CLAP CLAP CLAP
THIS IS THE END OF ACT ONE.
CLAP CLAP CLAP CLAP CLAP CLAP CLAP CLAP
AND WITH YOUR KIND PERMISSION, WE WILL HAVE A SHORT INTERMISSION BEFORE ACT TWO.
DURING THIS TIME, PLEASE DON'T NEGLECT THE CHARITY COLLECTION BOX.
WE HAVE DRINKS OVER HERE.
PLEASE, HELP YOURSELVES.
BUZZ BUZZ BUZZ BUZZ
WHAT'S THE NAME OF THE GIRL PLAYING JULIET?
MERCUTIO IS SO HANDSOME!
OH, THAT'S ALL YOU THINK ABOUT!
I NEVER FIGURED YOU FOR THE CHARITY TYPE.
BUZZ BUZZ BUZZ
DID YOU TAKE ME FOR A MISER?

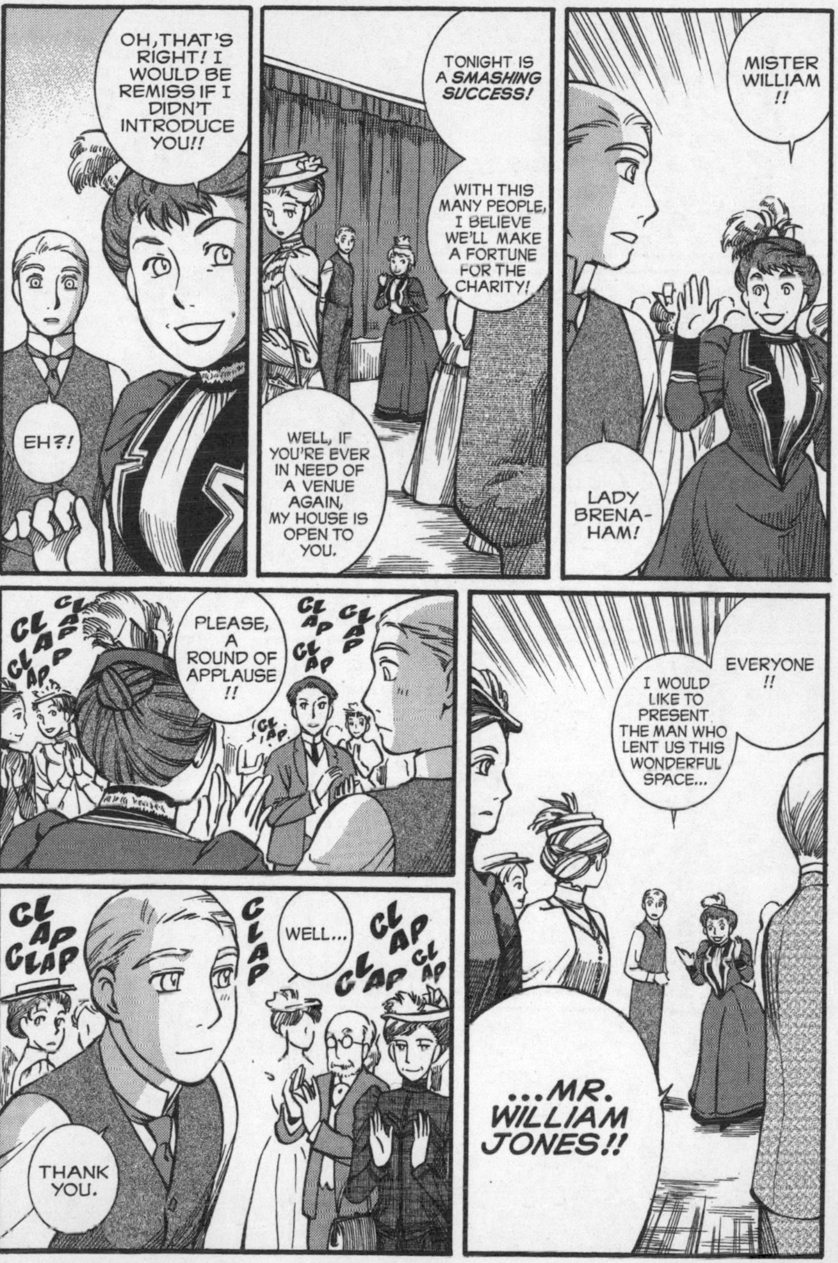
MISTER WILLIAM !!
LADY BRENA-HAM!
TONIGHT IS A SMASHING SUCCESS!
WITH THIS MANY PEOPLE, I BELIEVE WE'LL MAKE A FORTUNE FOR THE CHARITY!
WELL, IF YOU'RE EVER IN NEED OF A VENUE AGAIN, MY HOUSE IS OPEN TO YOU.
OH, THAT'S RIGHT! I WOULD BE REMISS IF I DIDN'T INTRODUCE YOU!!
EH?!
EVERYONE !!
I WOULD LIKE TO PRESENT THE MAN WHO LENT US THIS WONDERFUL SPACE...
...MR. WILLIAM JONES!!
CLAP CLAP
CLAP CLAP
PLEASE, A ROUND OF APPLAUSE !!
CLAP CLAP
CLAP
CLAP
WELL...
CLAP CLAP
CLAP
CLAP CLAP
THANK YOU.

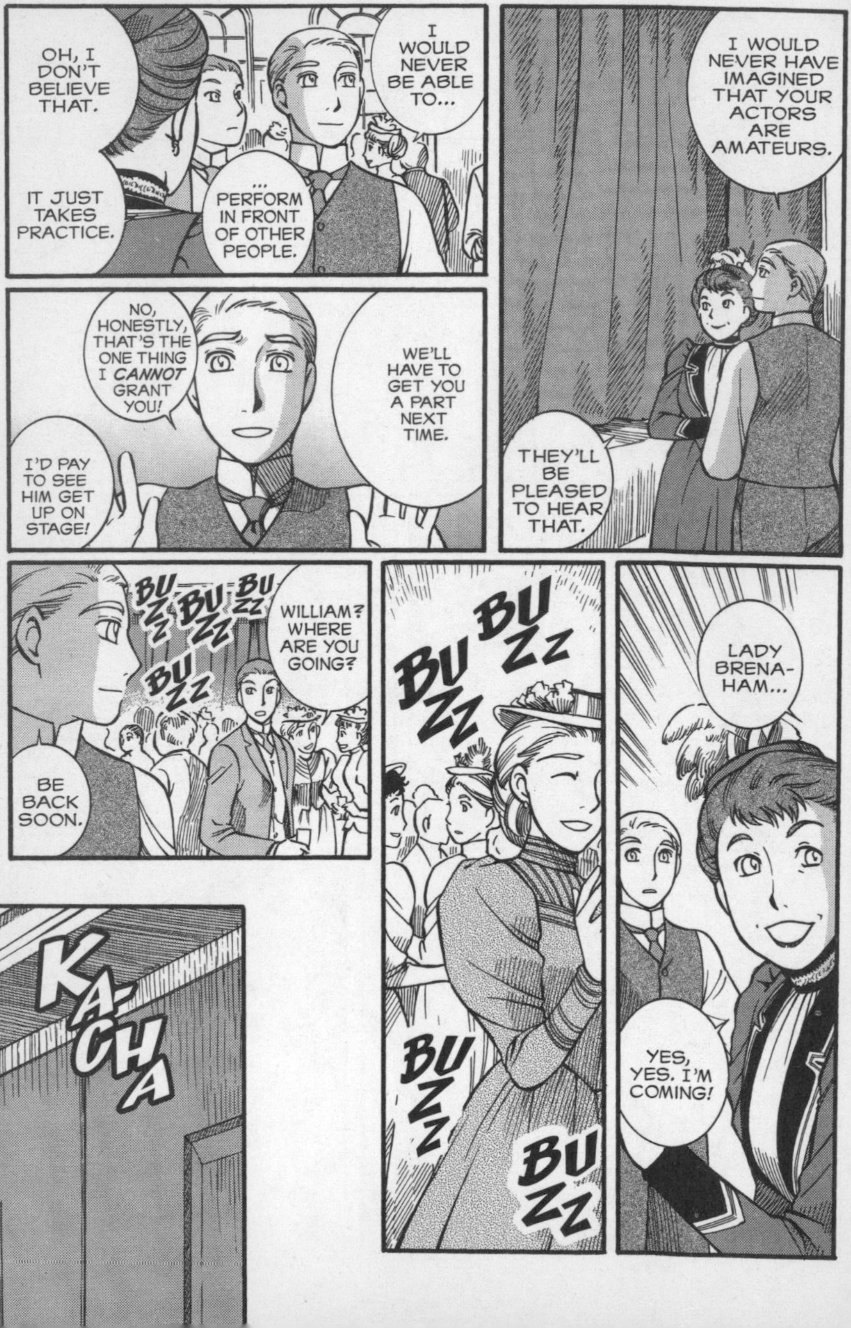
I WOULD NEVER HAVE IMAGINED THAT YOUR ACTORS ARE AMATEURS.
THEY'LL BE PLEASED TO HEAR THAT.
I WOULD NEVER BE ABLE TO...
OH, I DON'T BELIEVE THAT.
...PERFORM IN FRONT OF OTHER PEOPLE.
IT JUST TAKES PRACTICE.
WE'LL HAVE TO GET YOU A PART NEXT TIME.
NO, HONESTLY, THAT'S THE ONE THING I *CANNOT* GRANT YOU!
I'D PAY TO SEE HIM GET UP ON STAGE!
LADY BRENAHAM...
YES, YES. I'M COMING!
BUZZ BUZZ
BUZZ
BUZZ
BUZZ BUZZ BUZZ
BUZZ
WILLIAM? WHERE ARE YOU GOING?
BE BACK SOON.
KA-CHA

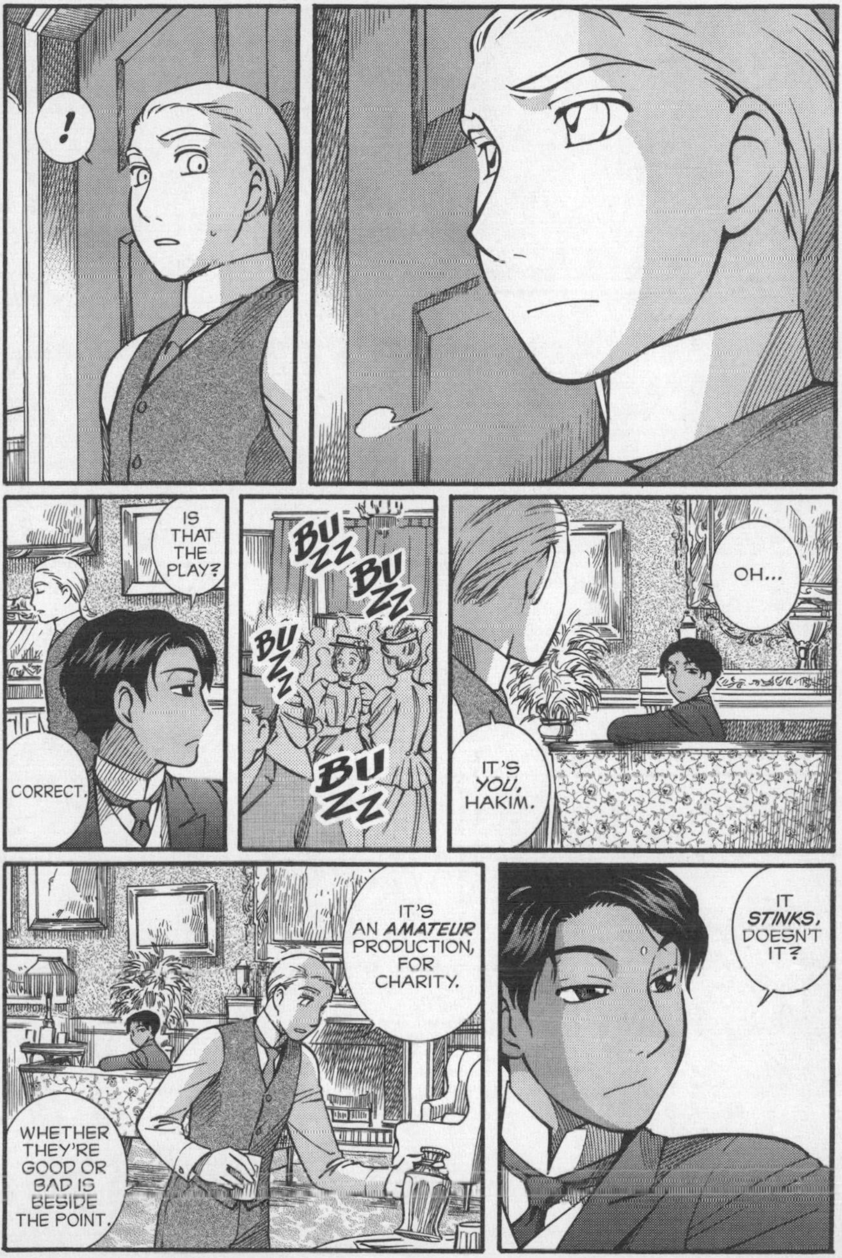
!
OH...
IT'S *YOU*, HAKIM.
BUZZ
BUZZ
BUZZ
BUZZ
IS THAT THE PLAY?
CORRECT.
IT *STINKS*, DOESN'T IT?
IT'S AN *AMATEUR* PRODUCTION, FOR CHARITY.
WHETHER THEY'RE GOOD OR BAD IS BESIDE THE POINT.

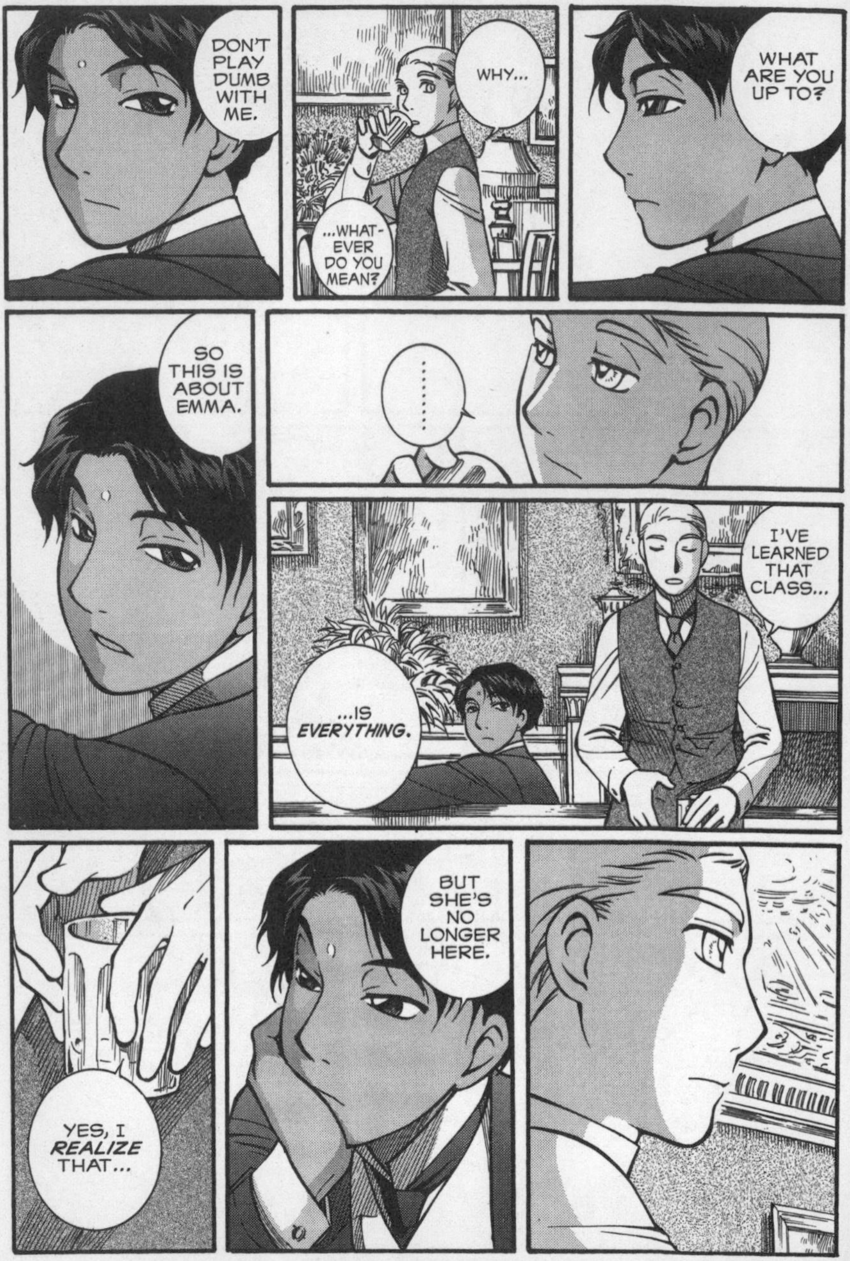
WHAT ARE YOU UP TO?
WHY...
...WHAT-EVER DO YOU MEAN?
DON'T PLAY DUMB WITH ME.
......
I'VE LEARNED THAT CLASS...
...IS *EVERYTHING*.
SO THIS IS ABOUT EMMA.
BUT SHE'S NO LONGER HERE.
YES, I *REALIZE* THAT...

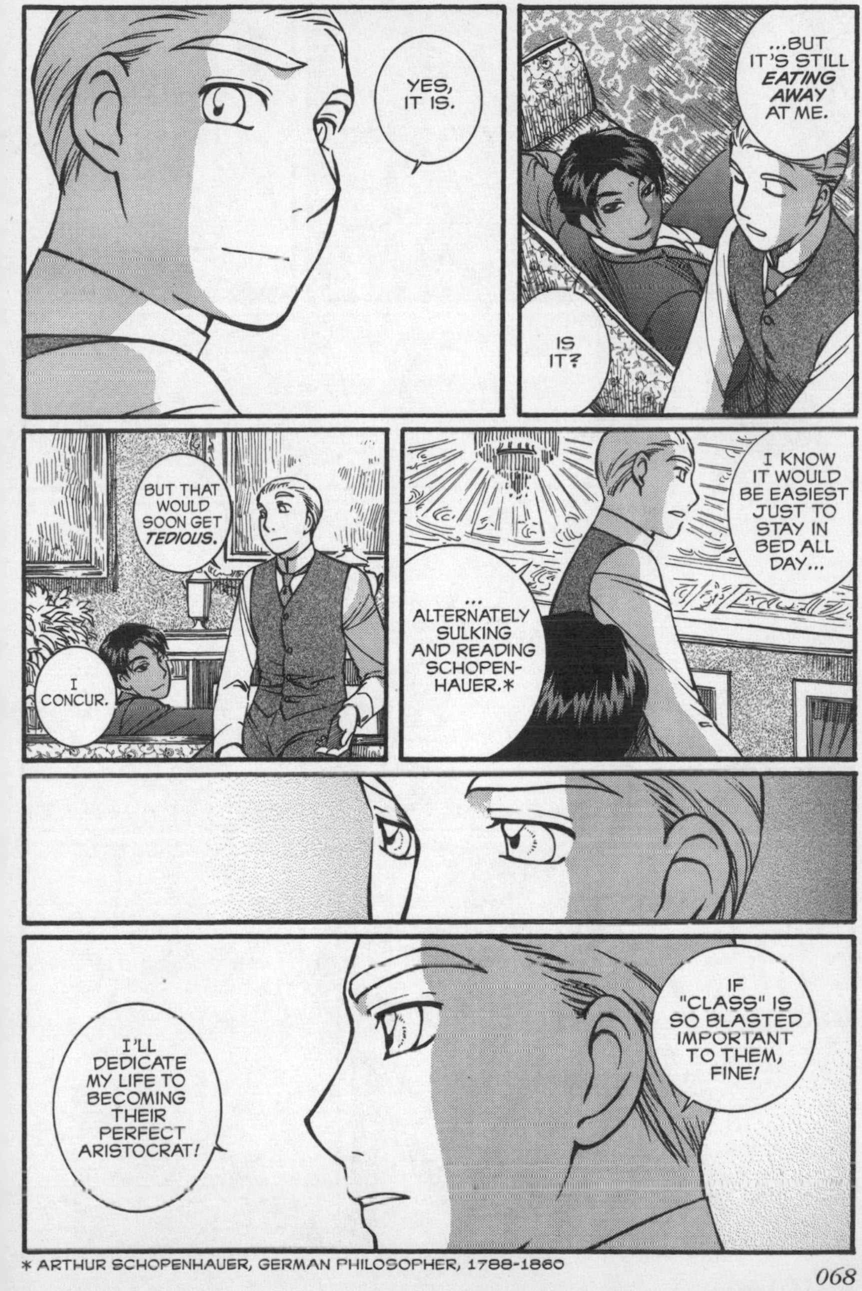
...BUT IT'S STILL *EATING AWAY* AT ME.
IS IT?
YES, IT IS.
I KNOW IT WOULD BE EASIEST JUST TO STAY IN BED ALL DAY...
...ALTERNATELY SULKING AND READING SCHOPENHAUER.*
BUT THAT WOULD SOON GET *TEDIOUS.*
I CONCUR.
IF "CLASS" IS SO BLASTED IMPORTANT TO THEM, FINE!
I'LL DEDICATE MY LIFE TO BECOMING THEIR PERFECT ARISTOCRAT!

* ARTHUR SCHOPENHAUER, GERMAN PHILOSOPHER, 1788-1860

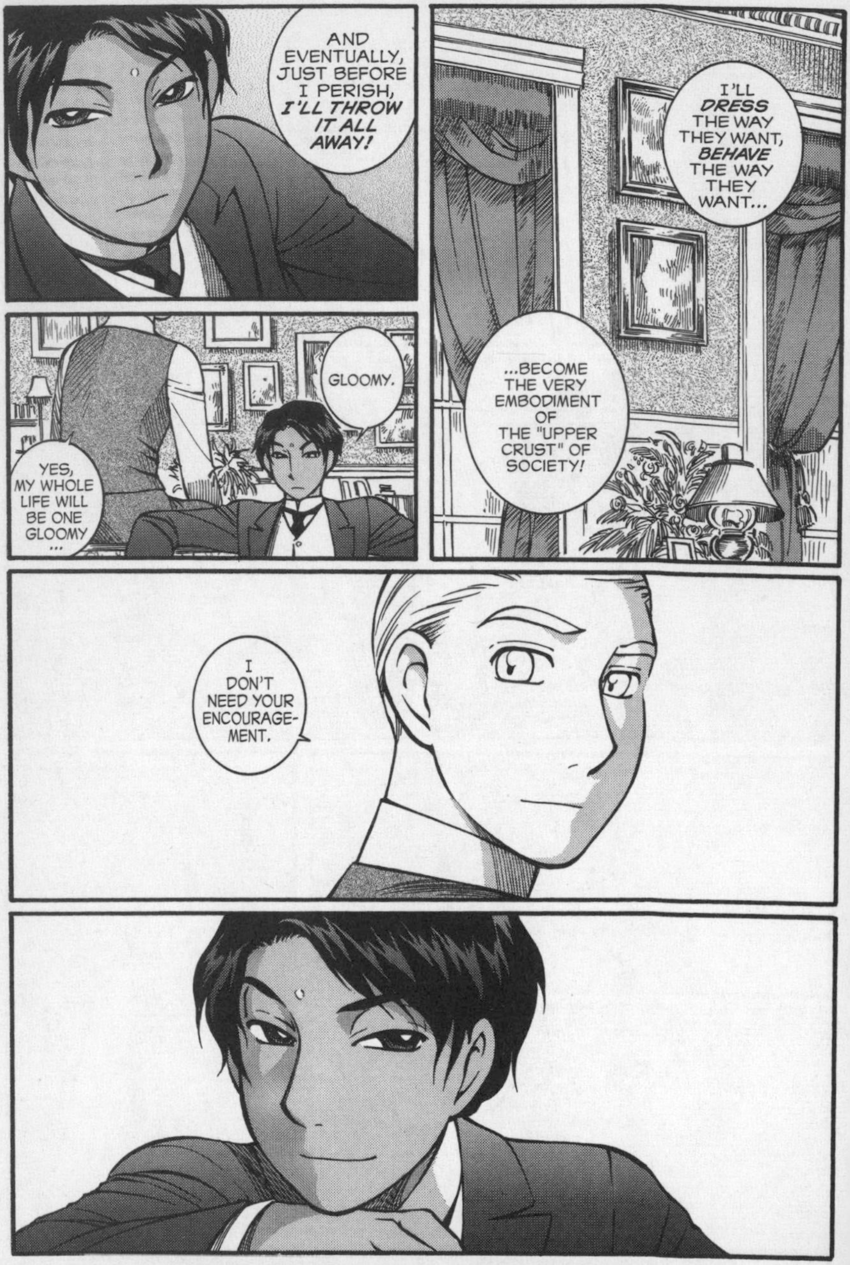
I'LL *DRESS* THE WAY THEY WANT, *BEHAVE* THE WAY THEY WANT...
...BECOME THE VERY EMBODIMENT OF THE "UPPER CRUST" OF SOCIETY!
AND EVENTUALLY, JUST BEFORE I PERISH, *I'LL THROW IT ALL AWAY!*
GLOOMY.
YES, MY WHOLE LIFE WILL BE ONE GLOOMY ...
I DON'T NEED YOUR ENCOURAGE-MENT.

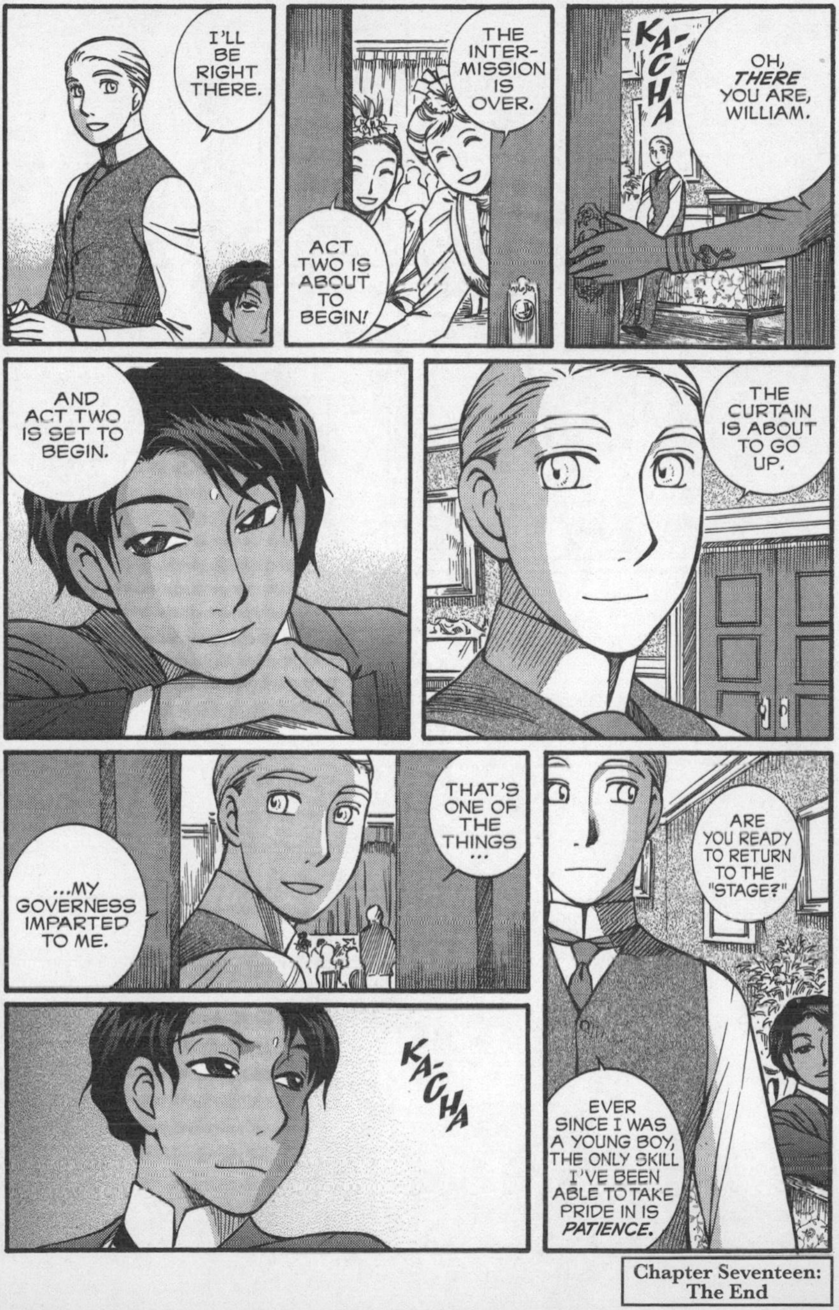
KA-CHA
OH, *THERE* YOU ARE, WILLIAM.
THE INTERMISSION IS OVER.
ACT TWO IS ABOUT TO BEGIN!
I'LL BE RIGHT THERE.
THE CURTAIN IS ABOUT TO GO UP.
AND ACT TWO IS SET TO BEGIN.
ARE YOU READY TO RETURN TO THE "STAGE?"
EVER SINCE I WAS A YOUNG BOY, THE ONLY SKILL I'VE BEEN ABLE TO TAKE PRIDE IN IS *PATIENCE*.
THAT'S ONE OF THE THINGS...
...MY GOVERNESS IMPARTED TO ME.
KA-CHA

Chapter Seventeen: The End

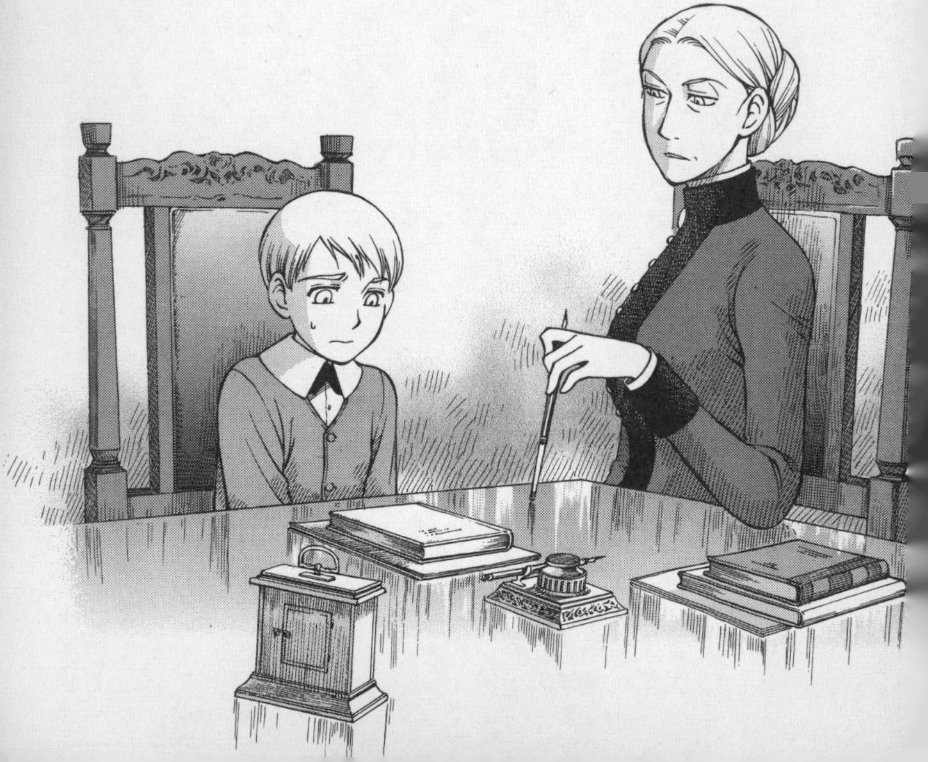

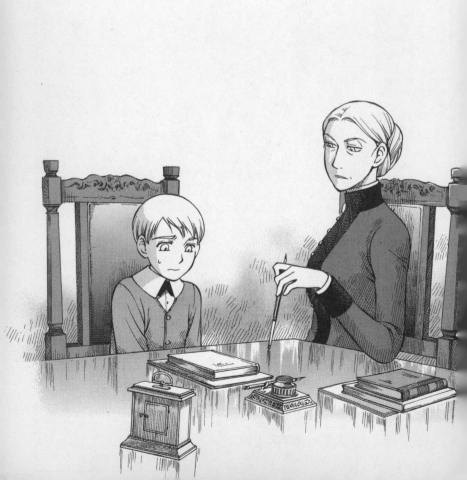

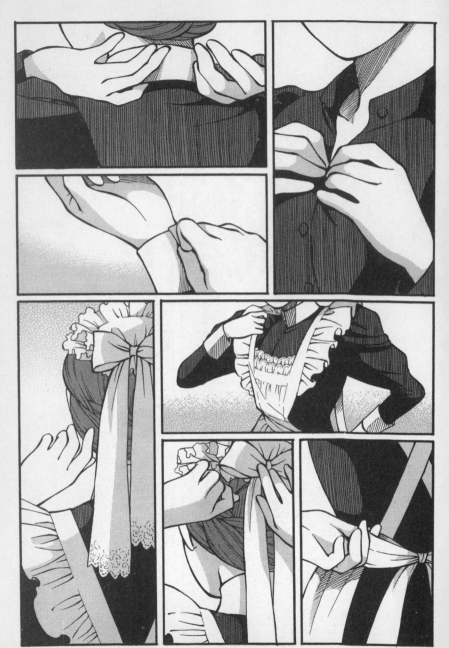

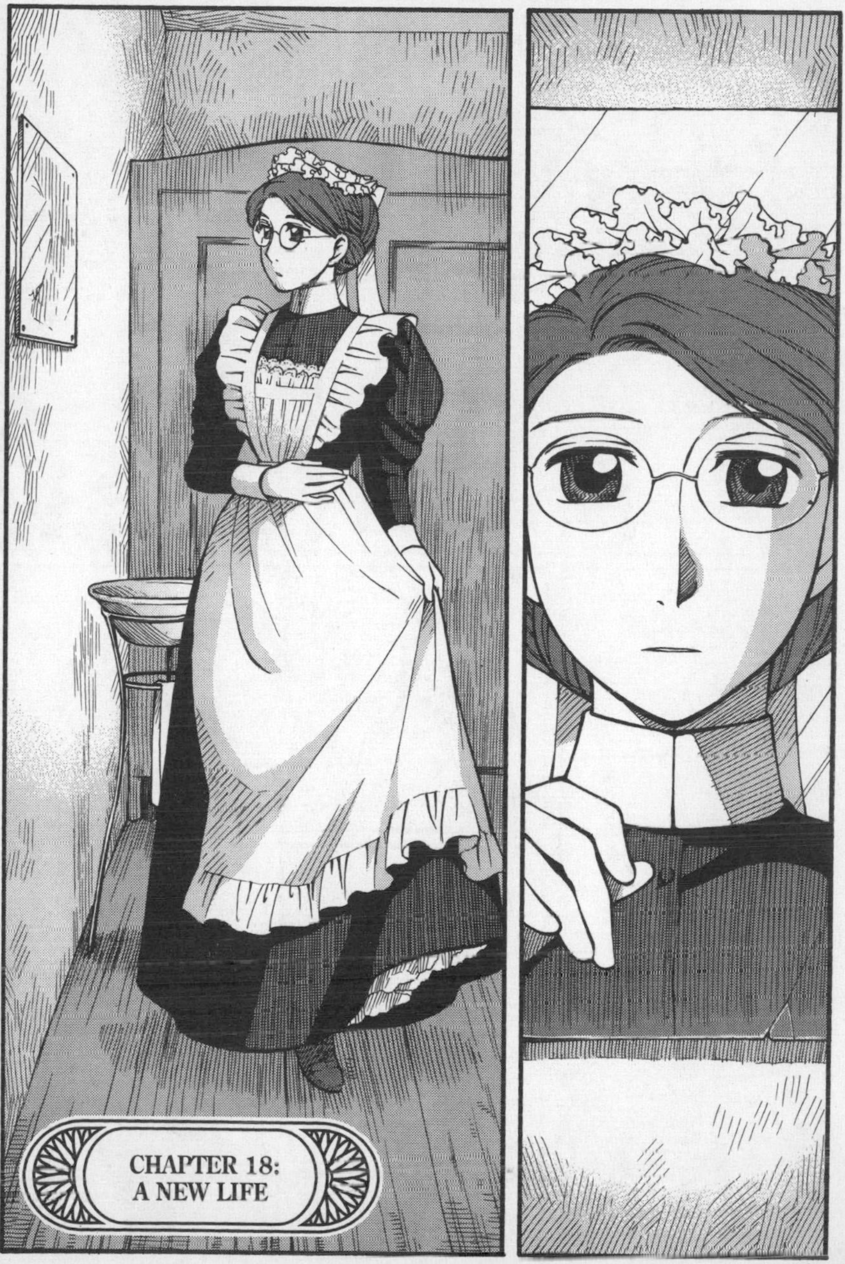
CHAPTER 18:
A NEW LIFE

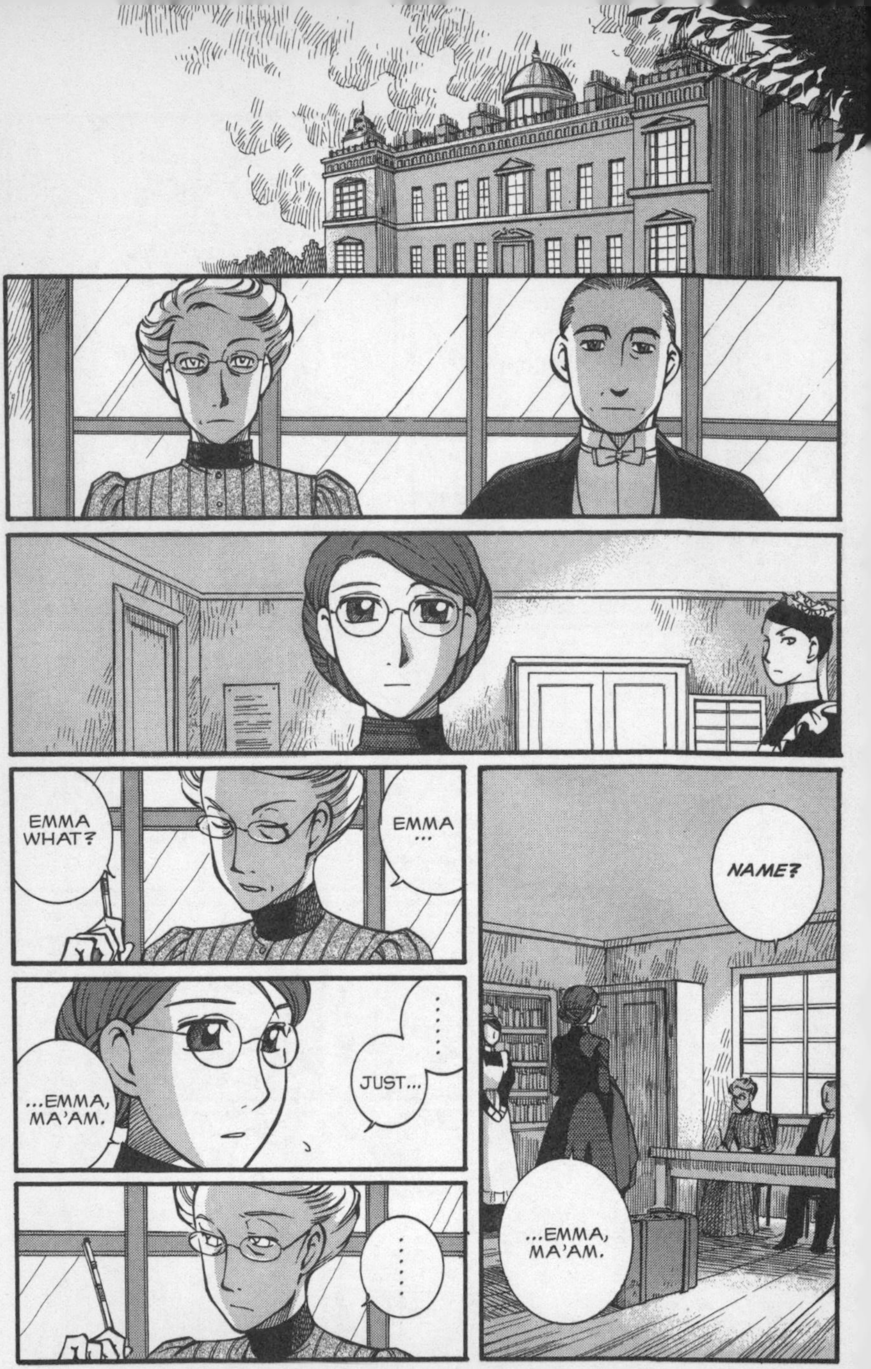
NAME?
...EMMA, MA'AM.
EMMA ...
EMMA WHAT?
......
JUST...
...EMMA, MA'AM.
......

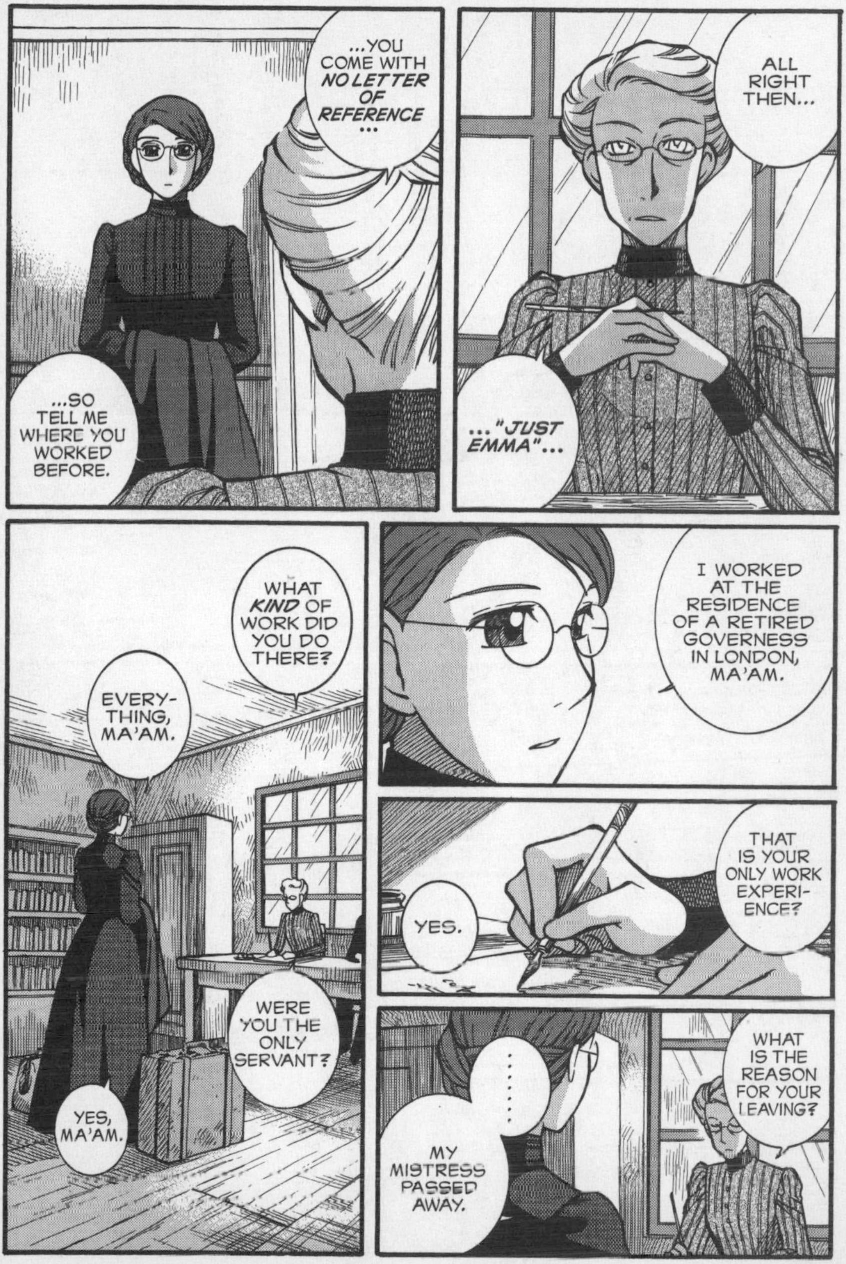
ALL RIGHT THEN...
..."JUST EMMA"...
...YOU COME WITH NO LETTER OF REFERENCE...
...SO TELL ME WHERE YOU WORKED BEFORE.
I WORKED AT THE RESIDENCE OF A RETIRED GOVERNESS IN LONDON, MA'AM.
THAT IS YOUR ONLY WORK EXPERIENCE?
YES.
WHAT IS THE REASON FOR YOUR LEAVING?
......
MY MISTRESS PASSED AWAY.
WHAT KIND OF WORK DID YOU DO THERE?
EVERYTHING, MA'AM.
WERE YOU THE ONLY SERVANT?
YES, MA'AM.

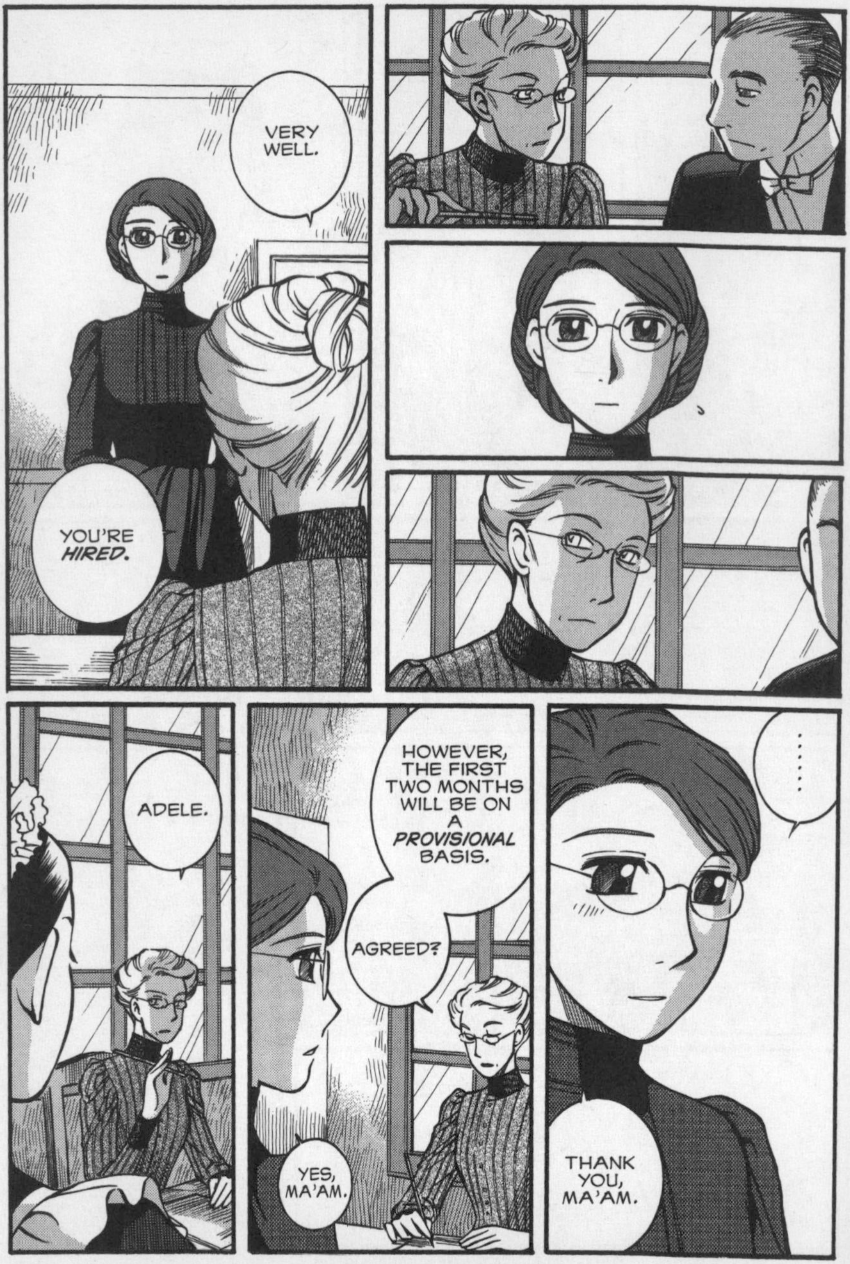
VERY WELL.
YOU'RE *HIRED*.
......
THANK YOU, MA'AM.
HOWEVER, THE FIRST TWO MONTHS WILL BE ON A *PROVISIONAL* BASIS.
AGREED?
YES, MA'AM.
ADELE.

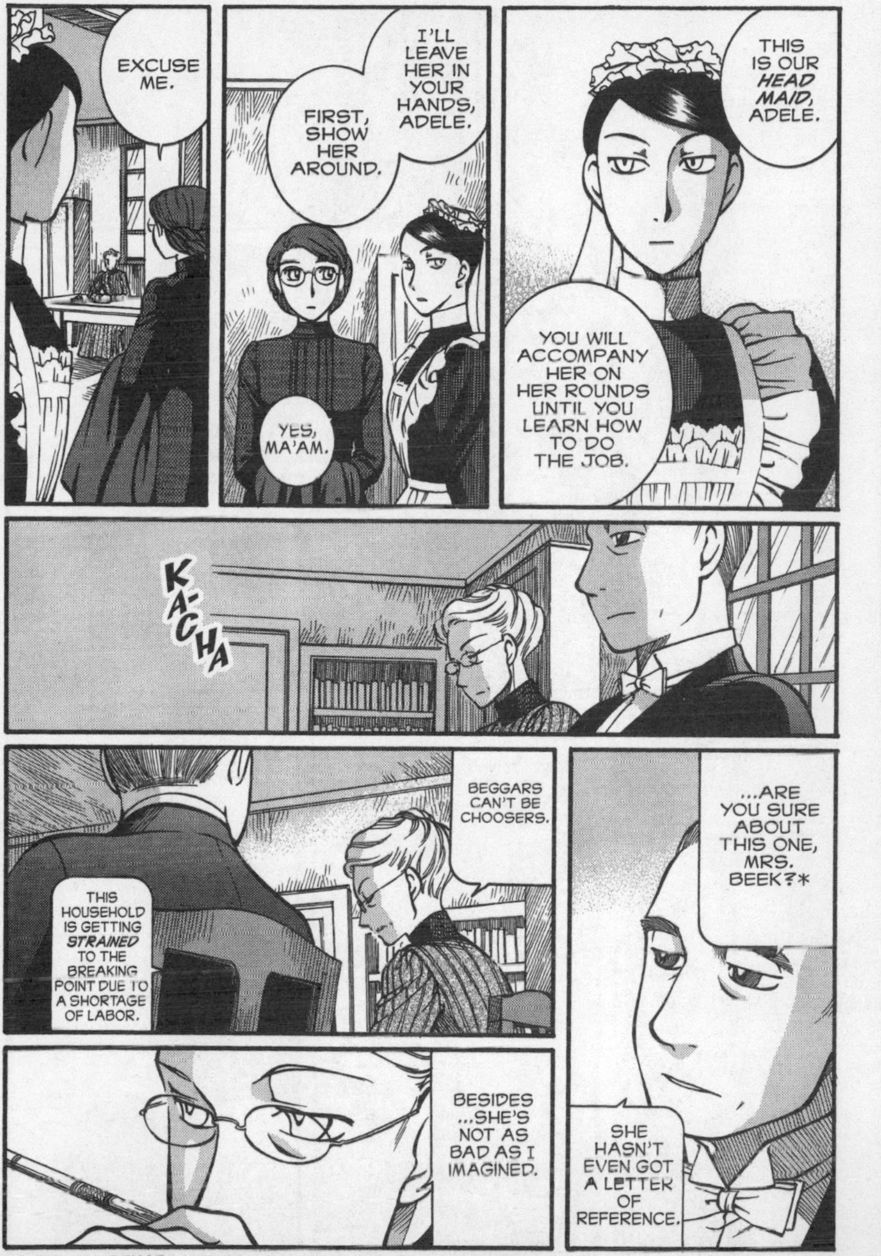

THIS IS OUR *HEAD MAID,* ADELE.
YOU WILL ACCOMPANY HER ON HER ROUNDS UNTIL YOU LEARN HOW TO DO THE JOB.
I'LL LEAVE HER IN YOUR HANDS, ADELE.
FIRST, SHOW HER AROUND.
YES, MA'AM.
EXCUSE ME.
KA-CHA
...ARE YOU SURE ABOUT THIS ONE, MRS. BEEK?*
SHE HASN'T EVEN GOT A LETTER OF REFERENCE.
BEGGARS CAN'T BE CHOOSERS.
THIS HOUSEHOLD IS GETTING *STRAINED* TO THE BREAKING POINT DUE TO A SHORTAGE OF LABOR.
BESIDES ...SHE'S NOT AS BAD AS I IMAGINED.

* NOTE: ALL SQUARE-LIKE BALLOONS DENOTE GERMAN SPEECH.

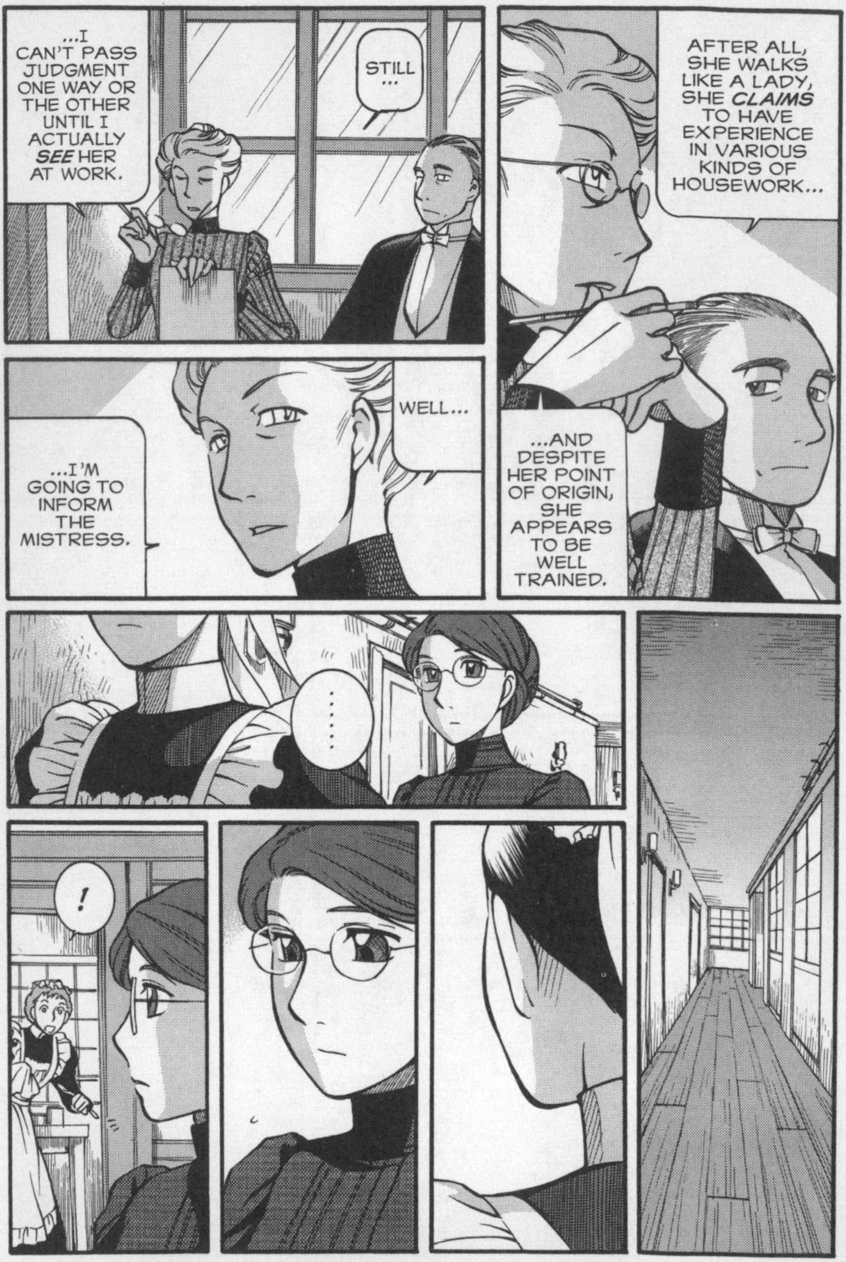
AFTER ALL, SHE WALKS LIKE A LADY, SHE *CLAIMS* TO HAVE EXPERIENCE IN VARIOUS KINDS OF HOUSEWORK...
...AND DESPITE HER POINT OF ORIGIN, SHE APPEARS TO BE WELL TRAINED.
STILL...
...I CAN'T PASS JUDGMENT ONE WAY OR THE OTHER UNTIL I ACTUALLY *SEE* HER AT WORK.
WELL...
...I'M GOING TO INFORM THE MISTRESS.
......
!

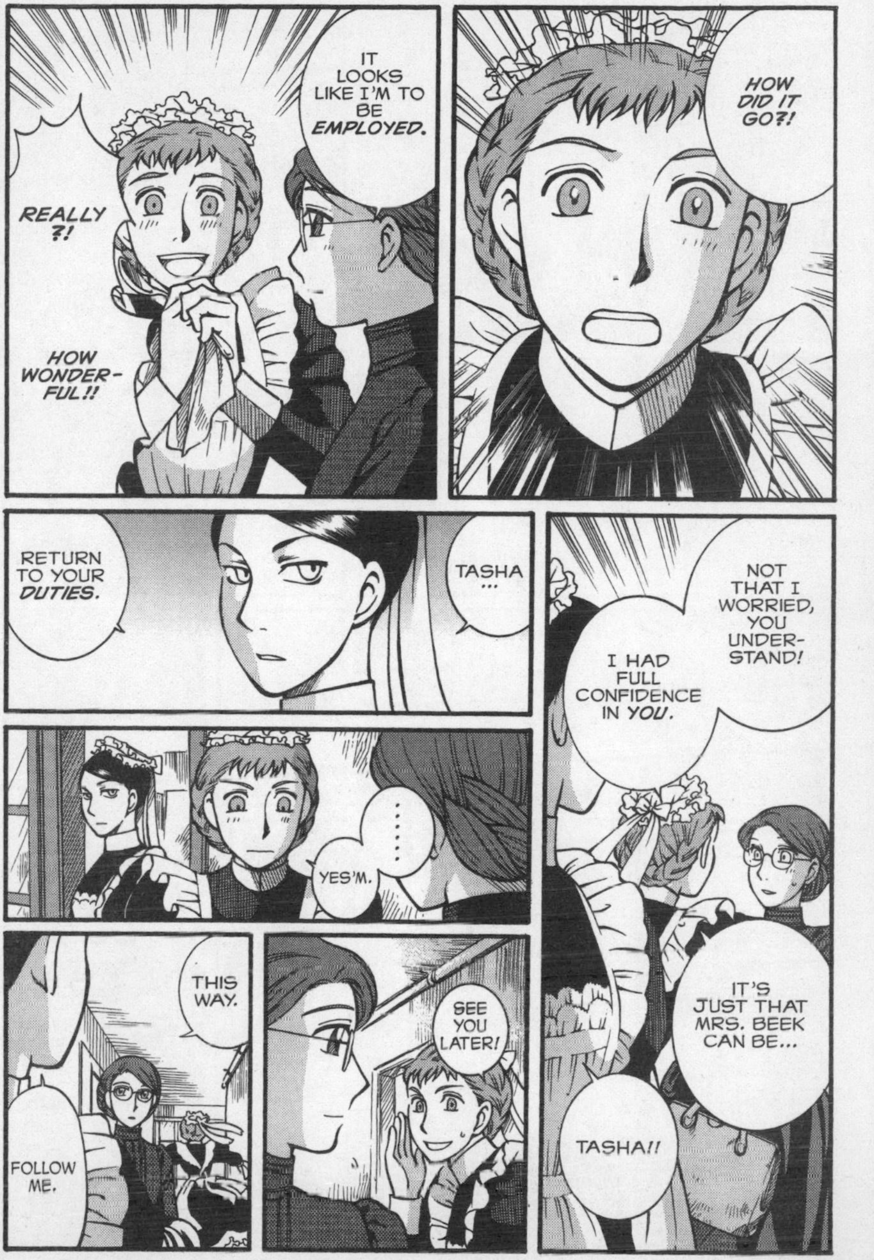
HOW DID IT GO?!
IT LOOKS LIKE I'M TO BE *EMPLOYED*.
REALLY?!
HOW WONDERFUL!!
NOT THAT I WORRIED, YOU UNDERSTAND!
I HAD FULL CONFIDENCE IN *YOU*.
IT'S JUST THAT MRS. BEEK CAN BE...
TASHA!!
TASHA...
RETURN TO YOUR *DUTIES*.
......
YES'M.
SEE YOU LATER!
THIS WAY.
FOLLOW ME.

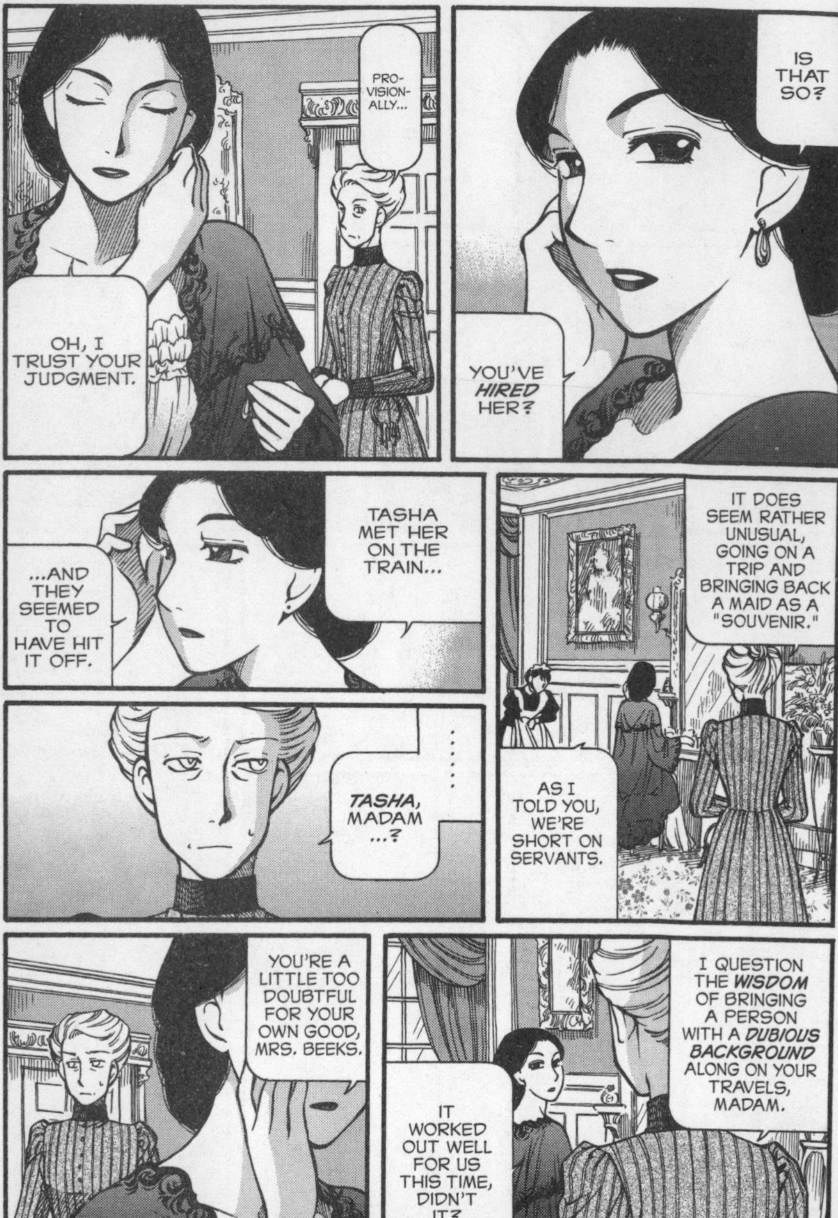
IS THAT SO?
YOU'VE *HIRED* HER?
PRO-VISION-ALLY...
OH, I TRUST YOUR JUDGMENT.
IT DOES SEEM RATHER UNUSUAL, GOING ON A TRIP AND BRINGING BACK A MAID AS A "SOUVENIR."
AS I TOLD YOU, WE'RE SHORT ON SERVANTS.
TASHA MET HER ON THE TRAIN...
...AND THEY SEEMED TO HAVE HIT IT OFF.
......
TASHA, MADAM ...?
I QUESTION THE *WISDOM* OF BRINGING A PERSON WITH A *DUBIOUS BACKGROUND* ALONG ON YOUR TRAVELS, MADAM.
IT WORKED OUT WELL FOR US THIS TIME, DIDN'T IT?
YOU'RE A LITTLE TOO DOUBTFUL FOR YOUR OWN GOOD, MRS. BEEKS.

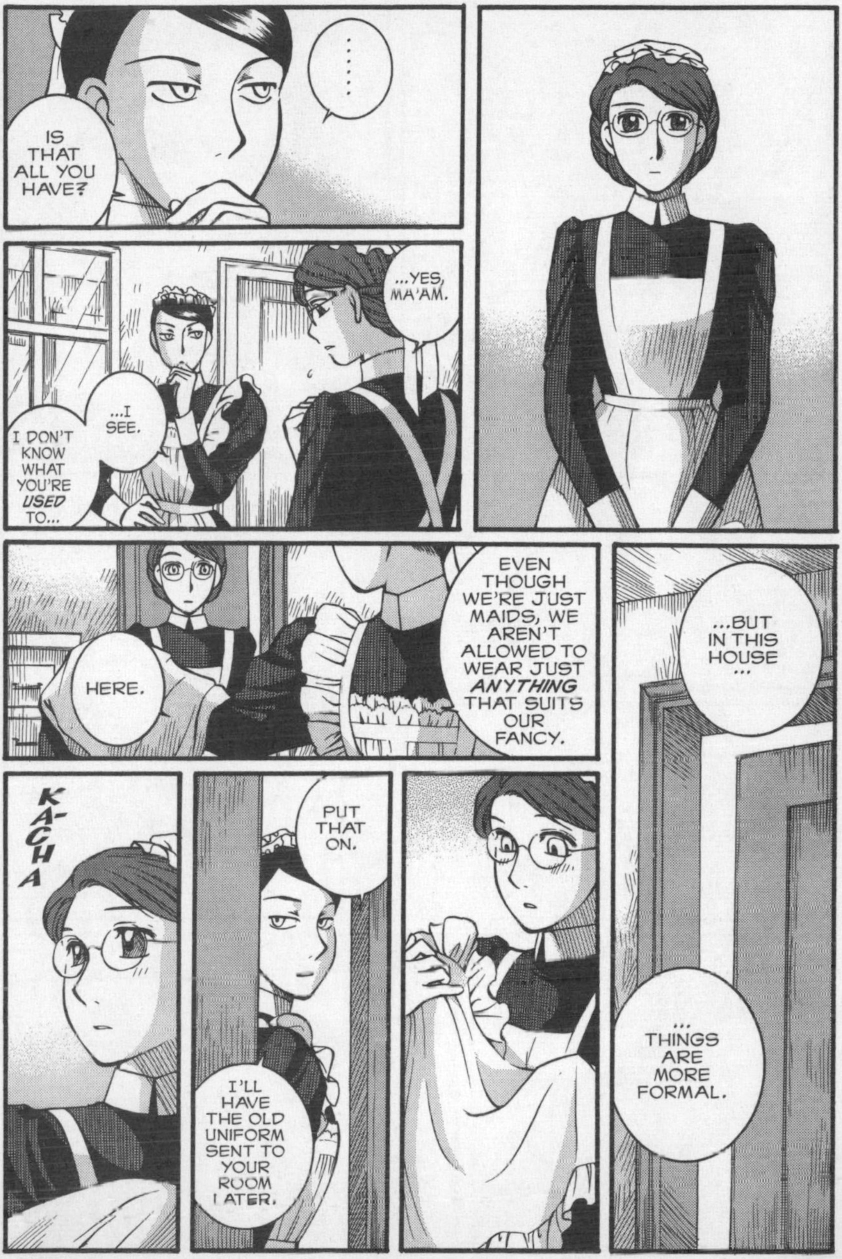
......
IS THAT ALL YOU HAVE?
...YES, MA'AM.
...I SEE.
I DON'T KNOW WHAT YOU'RE *USED* TO...
...BUT IN THIS HOUSE...
...THINGS ARE MORE FORMAL.
EVEN THOUGH WE'RE JUST MAIDS, WE AREN'T ALLOWED TO WEAR JUST *ANYTHING* THAT SUITS OUR FANCY.
HERE.
PUT THAT ON.
I'LL HAVE THE OLD UNIFORM SENT TO YOUR ROOM LATER.
KA-CHA

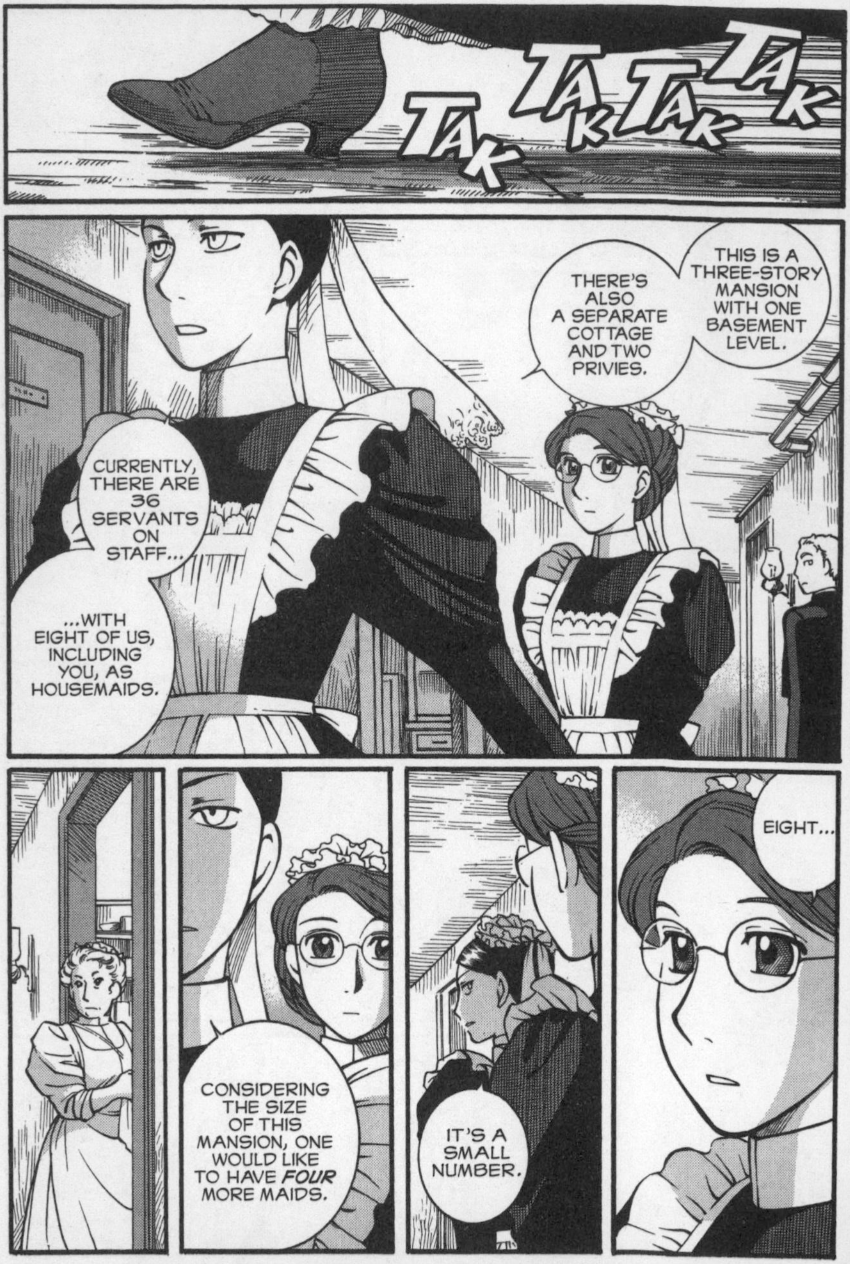
TAK TAK TAK TAK
THIS IS A THREE-STORY MANSION WITH ONE BASEMENT LEVEL.
THERE'S ALSO A SEPARATE COTTAGE AND TWO PRIVIES.
CURRENTLY, THERE ARE 36 SERVANTS ON STAFF...
...WITH EIGHT OF US, INCLUDING YOU, AS HOUSEMAIDS.
EIGHT...
IT'S A SMALL NUMBER.
CONSIDERING THE SIZE OF THIS MANSION, ONE WOULD LIKE TO HAVE *FOUR* MORE MAIDS.

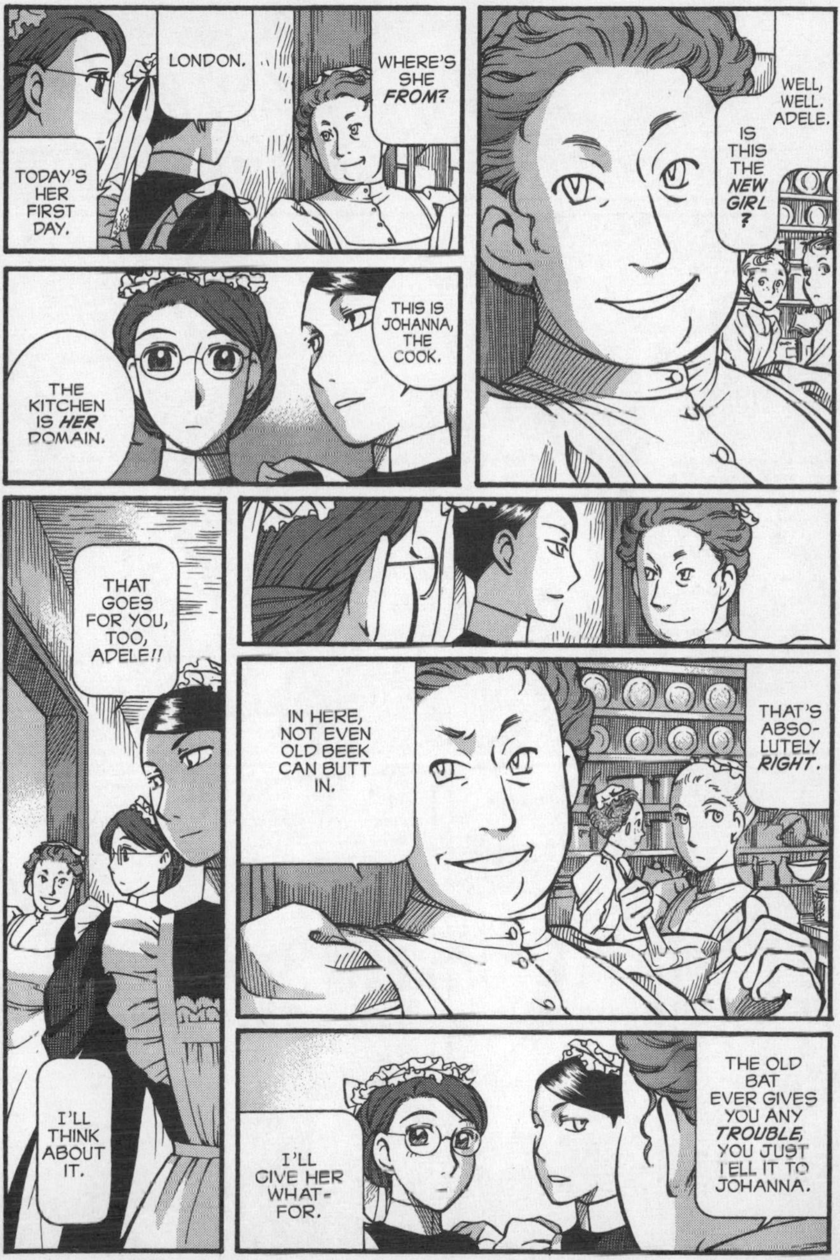
WELL, WELL. ADELE. IS THIS THE *NEW GIRL*?
WHERE'S SHE *FROM*?
LONDON.
TODAY'S HER FIRST DAY.
THIS IS JOHANNA, THE COOK.
THE KITCHEN IS *HER* DOMAIN.
THAT'S ABSO-LUTELY *RIGHT*.
IN HERE, NOT EVEN OLD BEEK CAN BUTT IN.
THE OLD BAT EVER GIVES YOU ANY *TROUBLE*, YOU JUST TELL IT TO JOHANNA.
I'LL GIVE HER WHAT-FOR.
THAT GOES FOR YOU, TOO, ADELE!!
I'LL THINK ABOUT IT.

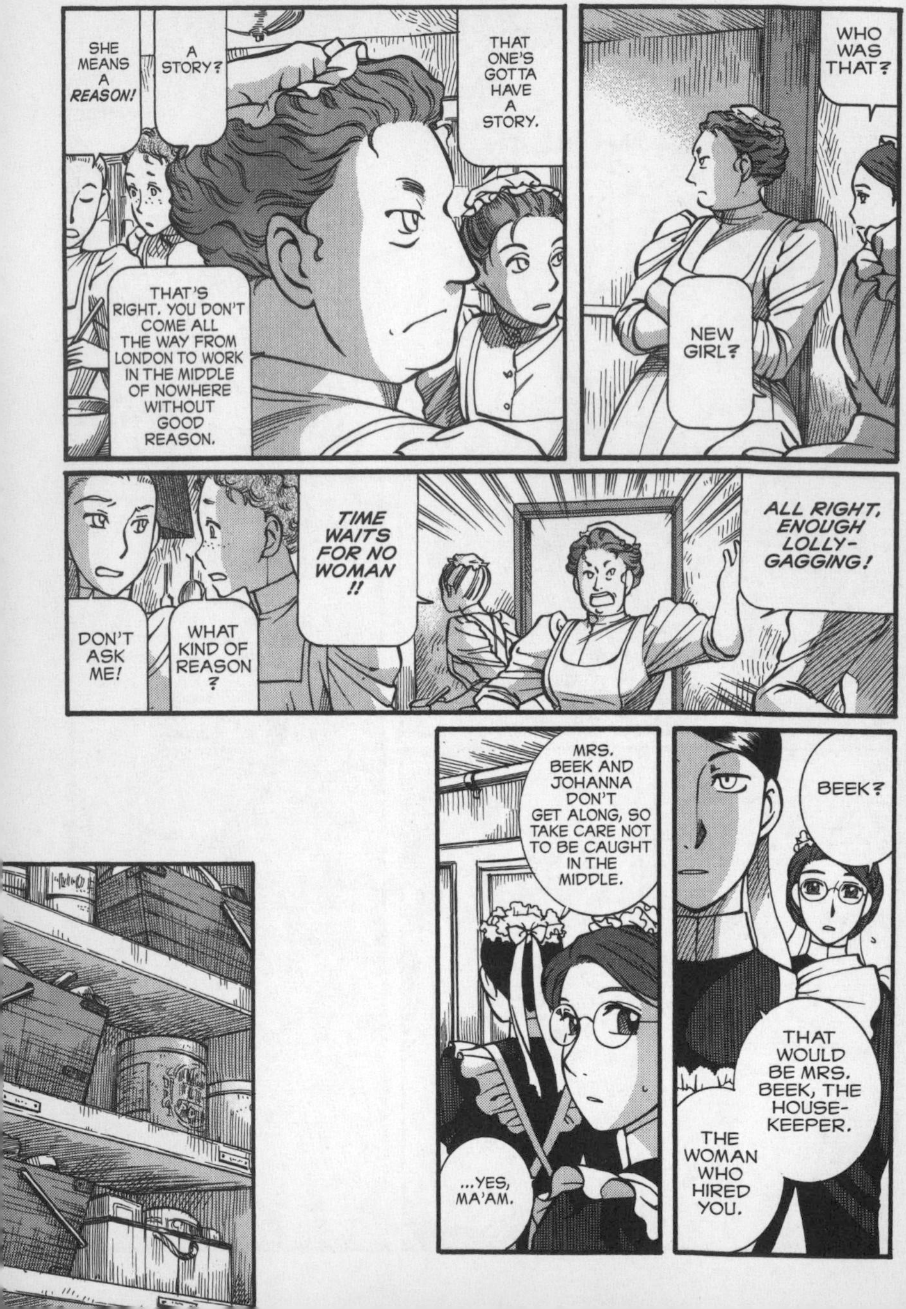
WHO WAS THAT?
NEW GIRL?
THAT ONE'S GOTTA HAVE A STORY.
A STORY?
SHE MEANS A *REASON!*
THAT'S RIGHT. YOU DON'T COME ALL THE WAY FROM LONDON TO WORK IN THE MIDDLE OF NOWHERE WITHOUT GOOD REASON.
ALL RIGHT, ENOUGH LOLLY-GAGGING!
TIME WAITS FOR NO WOMAN!!
WHAT KIND OF REASON?
DON'T ASK ME!
BEEK?
THAT WOULD BE MRS. BEEK, THE HOUSE-KEEPER.
THE WOMAN WHO HIRED YOU.
MRS. BEEK AND JOHANNA DON'T GET ALONG, SO TAKE CARE NOT TO BE CAUGHT IN THE MIDDLE.
...YES, MA'AM.

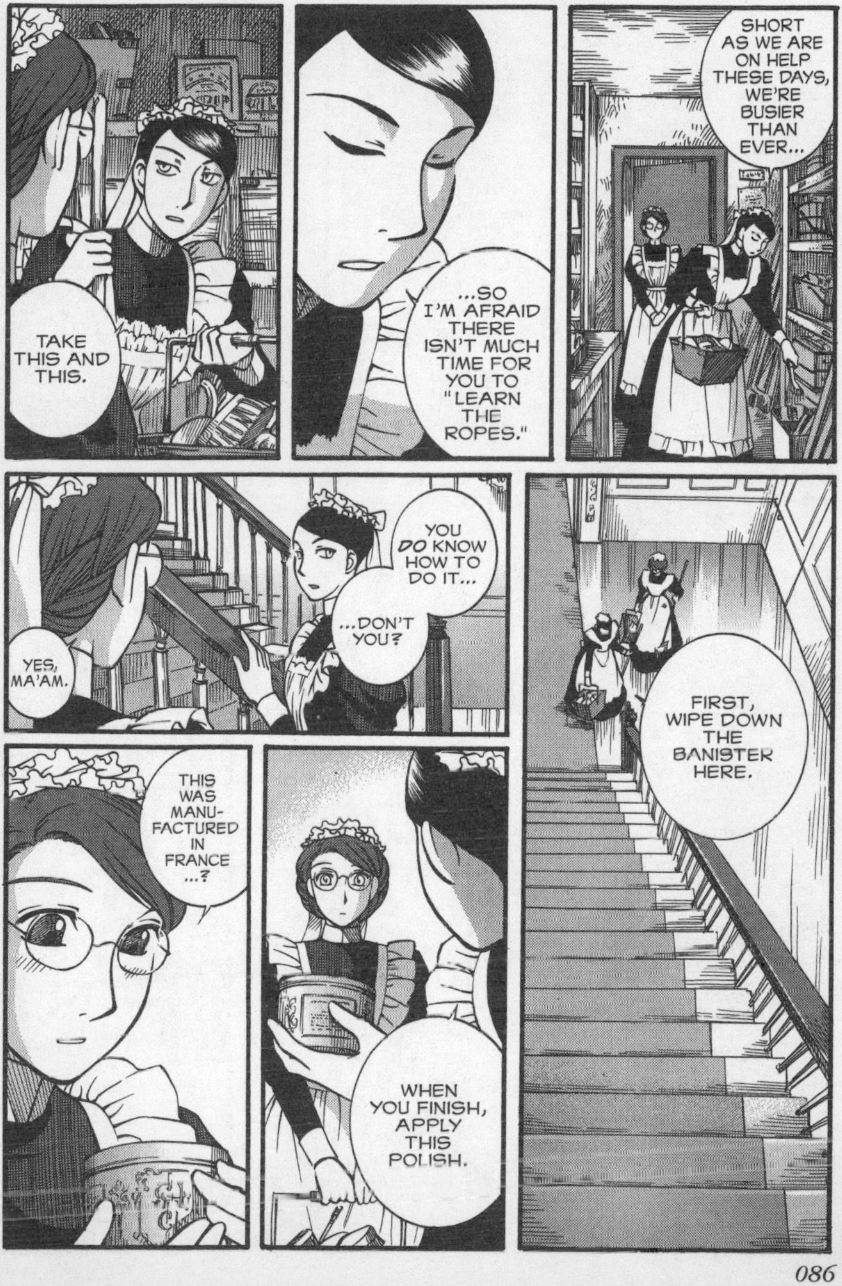
SHORT AS WE ARE ON HELP THESE DAYS, WE'RE BUSIER THAN EVER...
...SO I'M AFRAID THERE ISN'T MUCH TIME FOR YOU TO "LEARN THE ROPES."
TAKE THIS AND THIS.
FIRST, WIPE DOWN THE BANISTER HERE.
YOU *DO* KNOW HOW TO DO IT...
...DON'T YOU?
YES, MA'AM.
WHEN YOU FINISH, APPLY THIS POLISH.
THIS WAS MANU-FACTURED IN FRANCE ...?

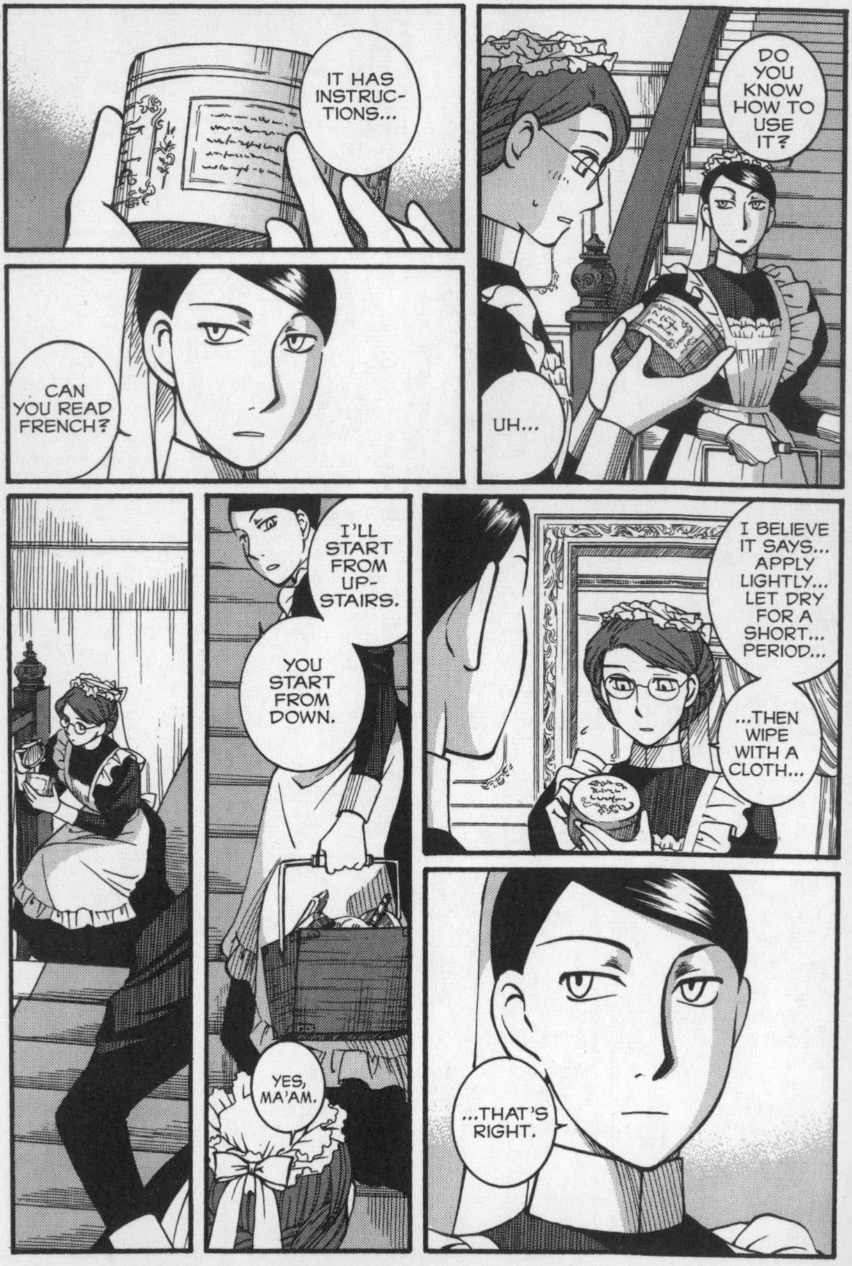
DO YOU KNOW HOW TO USE IT?
IT HAS INSTRUCTIONS...
UH...
CAN YOU READ FRENCH?
I BELIEVE IT SAYS... APPLY LIGHTLY... LET DRY FOR A SHORT... PERIOD...
...THEN WIPE WITH A CLOTH...
...THAT'S RIGHT.
I'LL START FROM UPSTAIRS.
YOU START FROM DOWN.
YES, MA'AM.

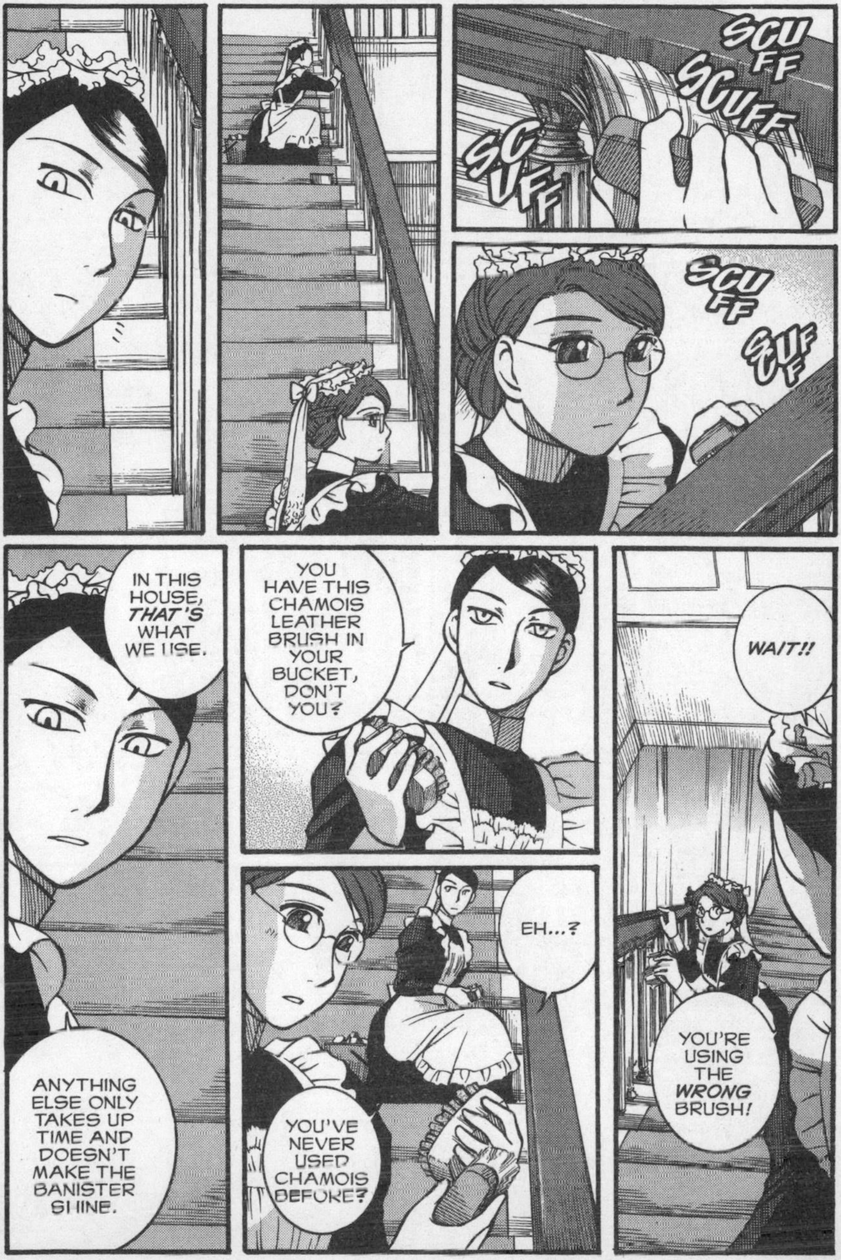

SCUFF SCUFF
SCUFF
SCUFF
SCUFF
WAIT!!
YOU'RE USING THE WRONG BRUSH!
YOU HAVE THIS CHAMOIS LEATHER BRUSH IN YOUR BUCKET, DON'T YOU?
EH...?
YOU'VE NEVER USED CHAMOIS BEFORE?
IN THIS HOUSE, THAT'S WHAT WE USE.
ANYTHING ELSE ONLY TAKES UP TIME AND DOESN'T MAKE THE BANISTER SHINE.

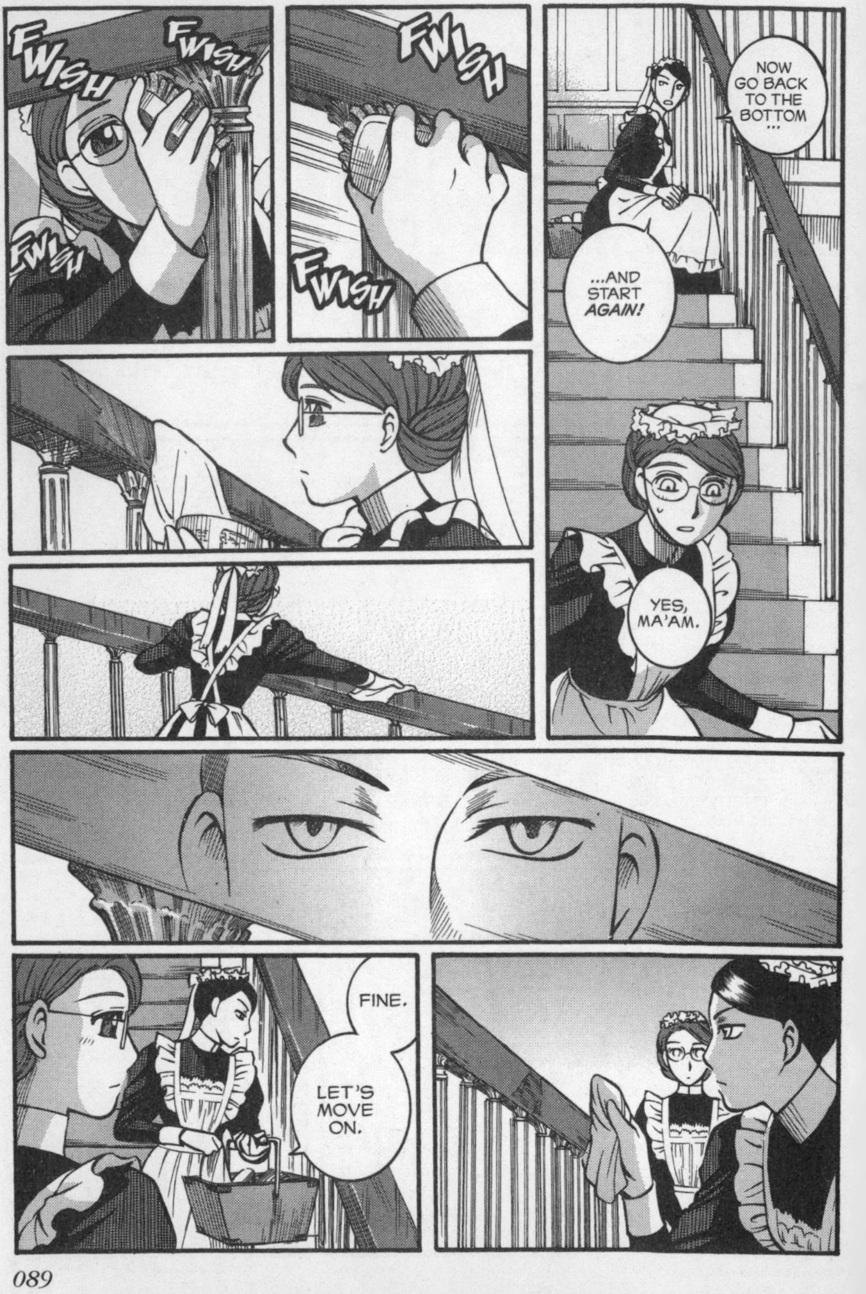
NOW GO BACK TO THE BOTTOM ...
...AND START AGAIN!
YES, MA'AM.
FWISH
FWISH
FWISH
FWISH
FWISH
FWISH
FINE.
LET'S MOVE ON.

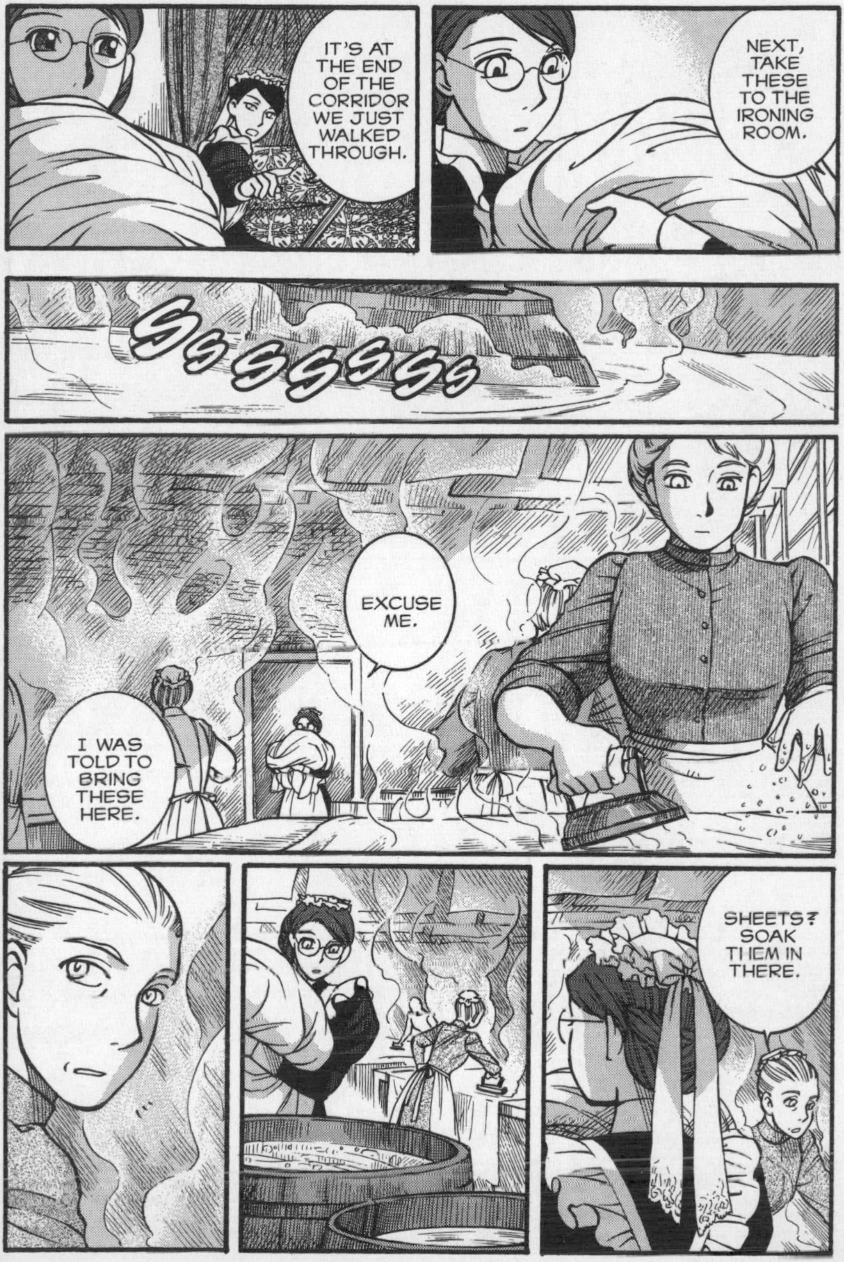
NEXT, TAKE THESE TO THE IRONING ROOM.
IT'S AT THE END OF THE CORRIDOR WE JUST WALKED THROUGH.
SSSSSSSSS
EXCUSE ME.
I WAS TOLD TO BRING THESE HERE.
SHEETS? SOAK THEM IN THERE.

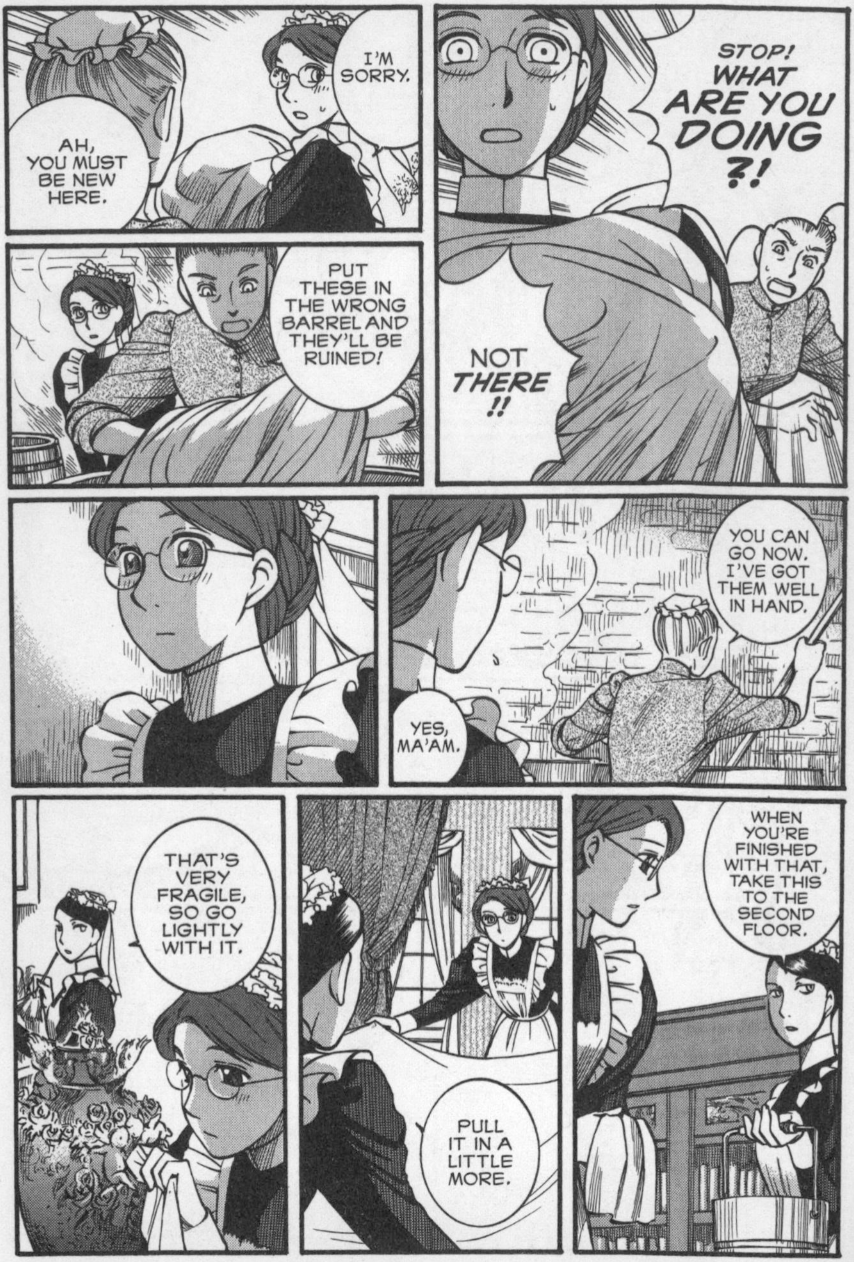
STOP! WHAT ARE YOU DOING ?!
NOT THERE !!
I'M SORRY.
AH, YOU MUST BE NEW HERE.
PUT THESE IN THE WRONG BARREL AND THEY'LL BE RUINED!
YOU CAN GO NOW. I'VE GOT THEM WELL IN HAND.
YES, MA'AM.
WHEN YOU'RE FINISHED WITH THAT, TAKE THIS TO THE SECOND FLOOR.
PULL IT IN A LITTLE MORE.
THAT'S VERY FRAGILE, SO GO LIGHTLY WITH IT.

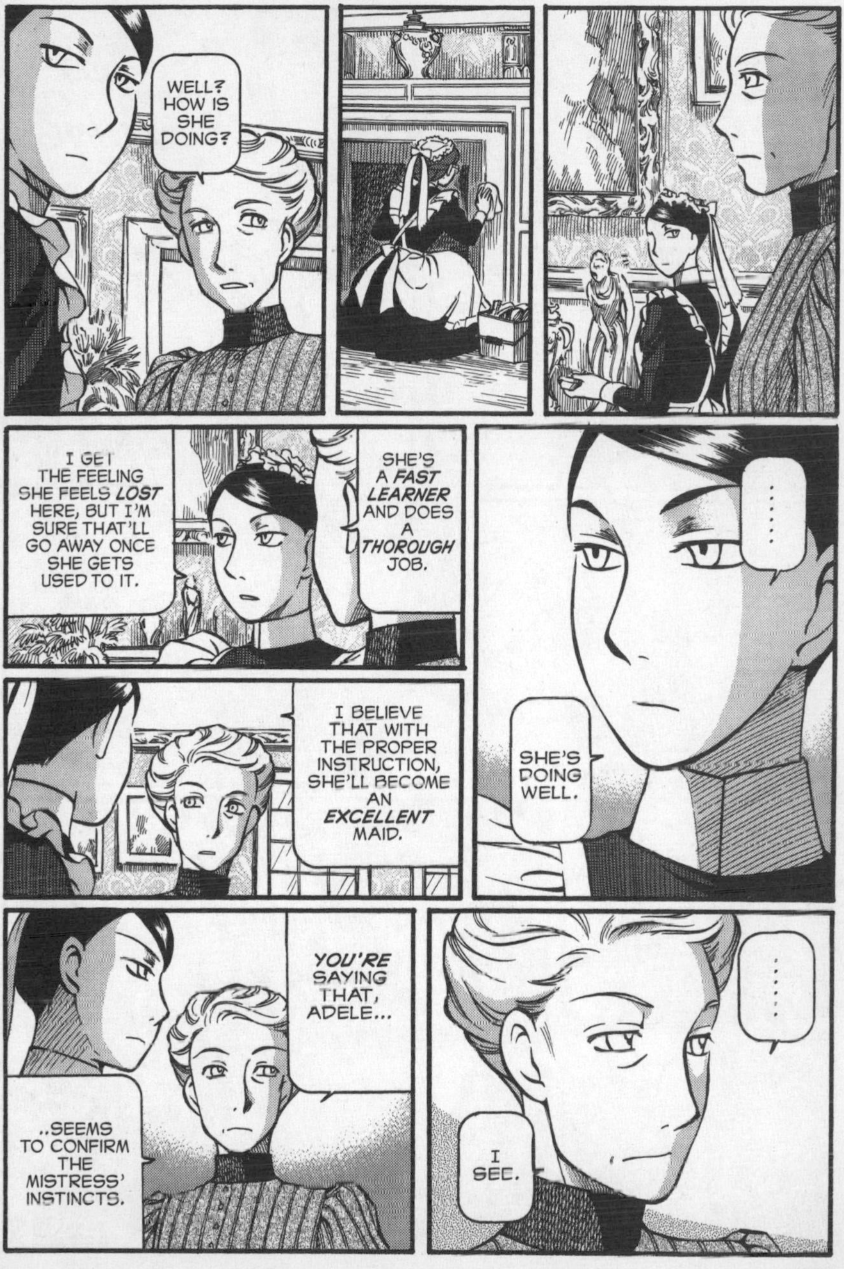
WELL? HOW IS SHE DOING?
......
SHE'S DOING WELL.
SHE'S A *FAST LEARNER* AND DOES A *THOROUGH* JOB.
I GET THE FEELING SHE FEELS *LOST* HERE, BUT I'M SURE THAT'LL GO AWAY ONCE SHE GETS USED TO IT.
I BELIEVE THAT WITH THE PROPER INSTRUCTION, SHE'LL BECOME AN *EXCELLENT* MAID.
......
I SEE.
YOU'RE SAYING THAT, ADELE...
..SEEMS TO CONFIRM THE MISTRESS' INSTINCTS.

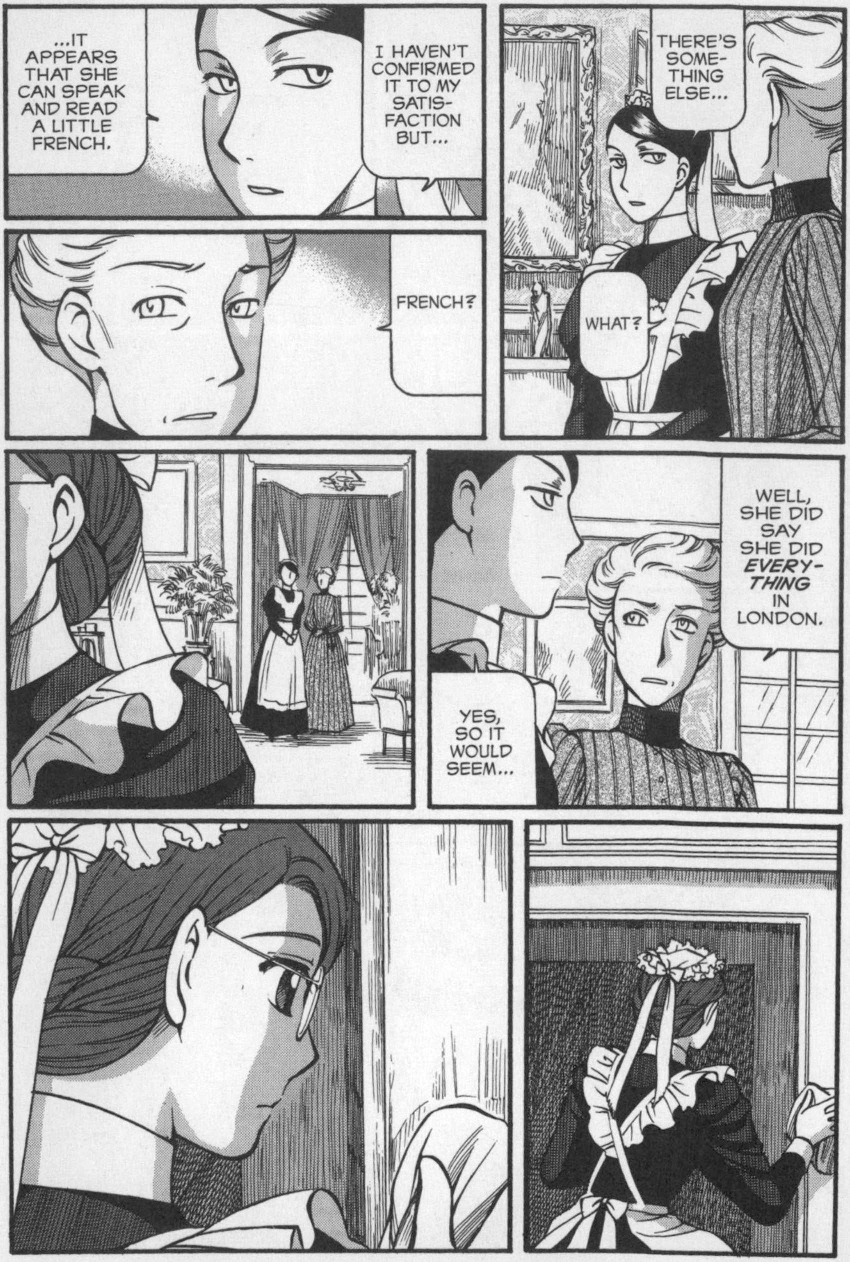
THERE'S SOME-THING ELSE...
WHAT?
I HAVEN'T CONFIRMED IT TO MY SATIS-FACTION BUT...
...IT APPEARS THAT SHE CAN SPEAK AND READ A LITTLE FRENCH.
FRENCH?
WELL, SHE DID SAY SHE DID *EVERY-THING* IN LONDON.
YES, SO IT WOULD SEEM...

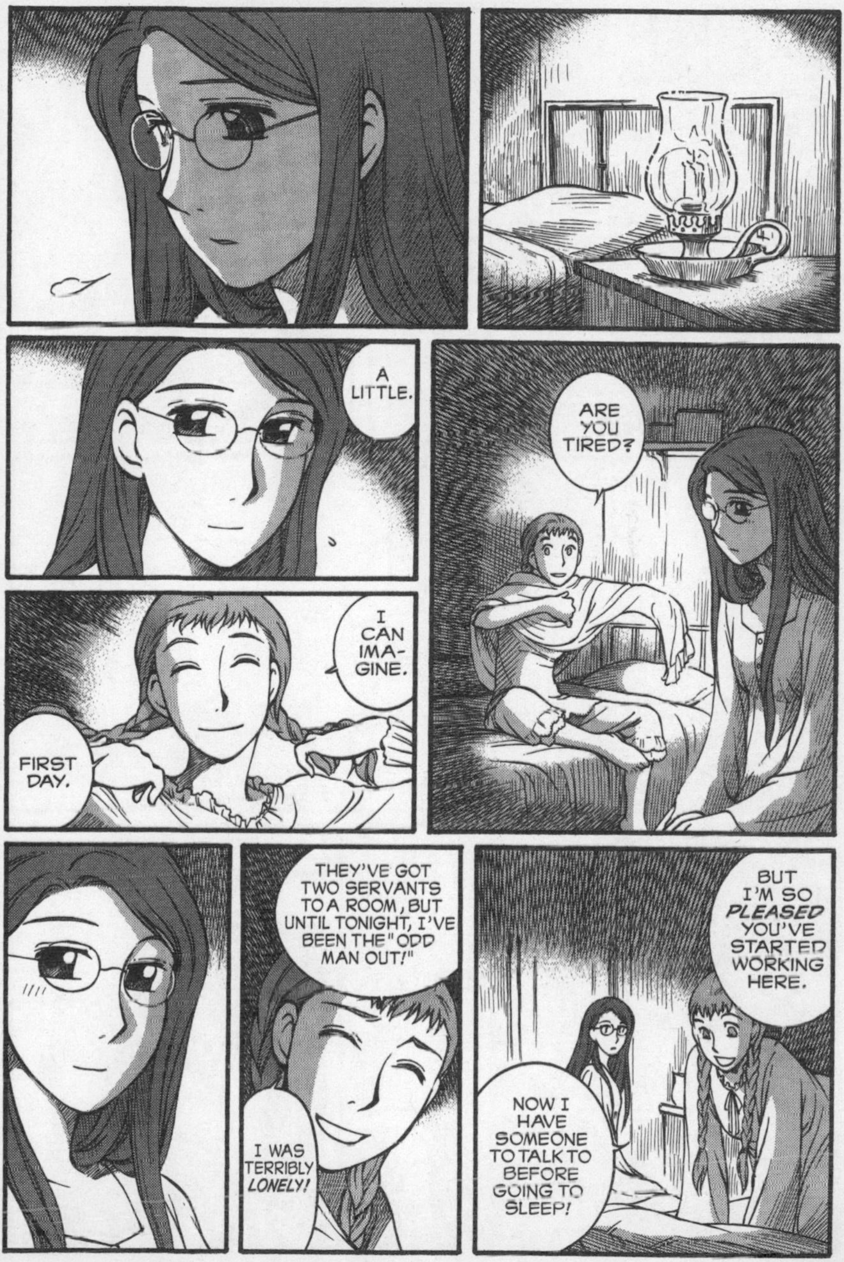
ARE YOU TIRED?
A LITTLE.
I CAN IMAGINE.
FIRST DAY.
BUT I'M SO *PLEASED* YOU'VE STARTED WORKING HERE.
NOW I HAVE SOMEONE TO TALK TO BEFORE GOING TO SLEEP!
THEY'VE GOT TWO SERVANTS TO A ROOM, BUT UNTIL TONIGHT, I'VE BEEN THE "ODD MAN OUT!"
I WAS TERRIBLY *LONELY!*

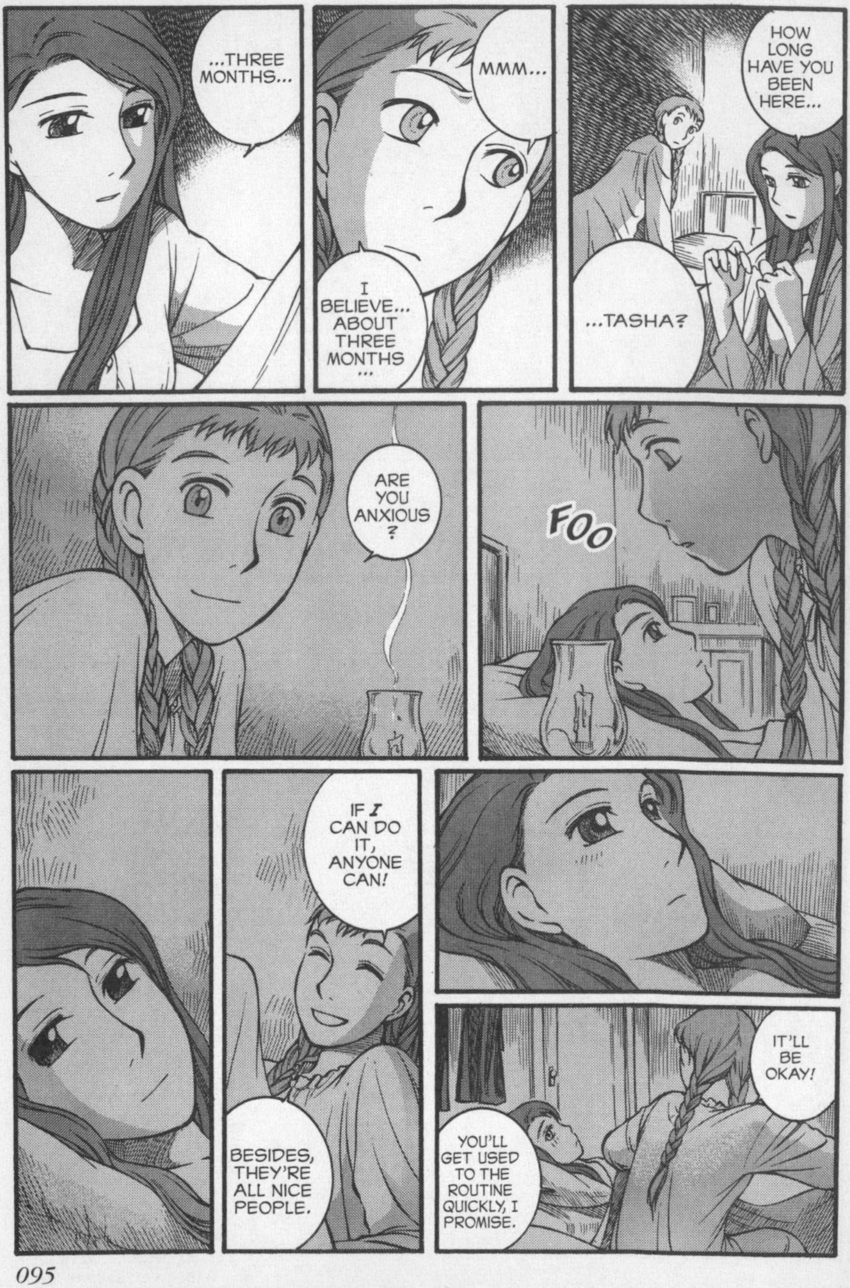

HOW LONG HAVE YOU BEEN HERE...
...TASHA?
MMM...
I BELIEVE... ABOUT THREE MONTHS...
...THREE MONTHS...
FOO
ARE YOU ANXIOUS?
IT'LL BE OKAY!
YOU'LL GET USED TO THE ROUTINE QUICKLY, I PROMISE.
IF *I* CAN DO IT, ANYONE CAN!
BESIDES, THEY'RE ALL NICE PEOPLE.

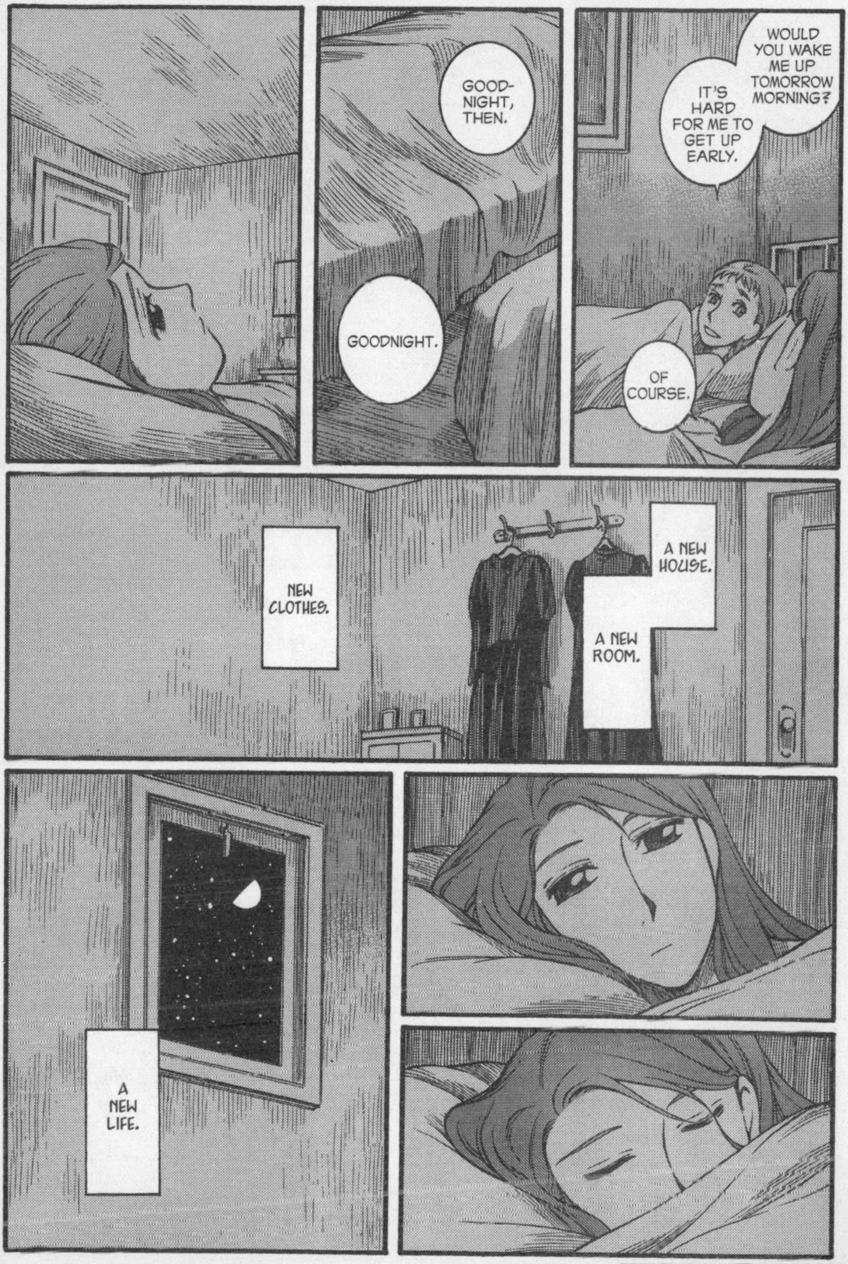
WOULD YOU WAKE ME UP TOMORROW MORNING?
IT'S HARD FOR ME TO GET UP EARLY.
OF COURSE.
GOOD-NIGHT, THEN.
GOODNIGHT.
A NEW HOUSE.
A NEW ROOM.
NEW CLOTHES.
A NEW LIFE.

Chapter Eighteen:
The End

EPILOGUE

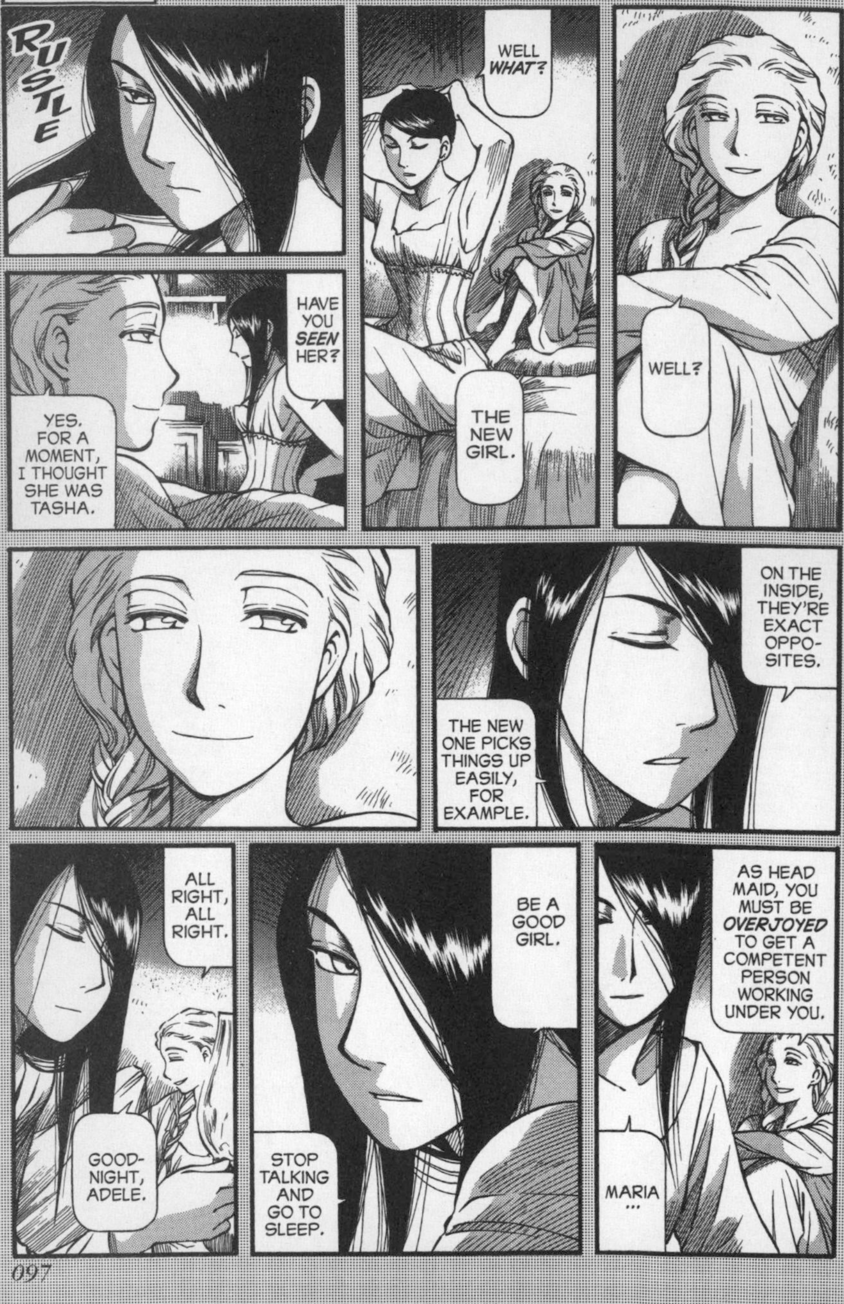
WELL?
WELL *WHAT*?
THE NEW GIRL.
RUSTLE
HAVE YOU *SEEN* HER?
YES. FOR A MOMENT, I THOUGHT SHE WAS TASHA.
ON THE INSIDE, THEY'RE EXACT OPPO-SITES.
THE NEW ONE PICKS THINGS UP EASILY, FOR EXAMPLE.
AS HEAD MAID, YOU MUST BE *OVERJOYED* TO GET A COMPETENT PERSON WORKING UNDER YOU.
MARIA...
BE A GOOD GIRL.
STOP TALKING AND GO TO SLEEP.
ALL RIGHT, ALL RIGHT.
GOOD-NIGHT, ADELE.

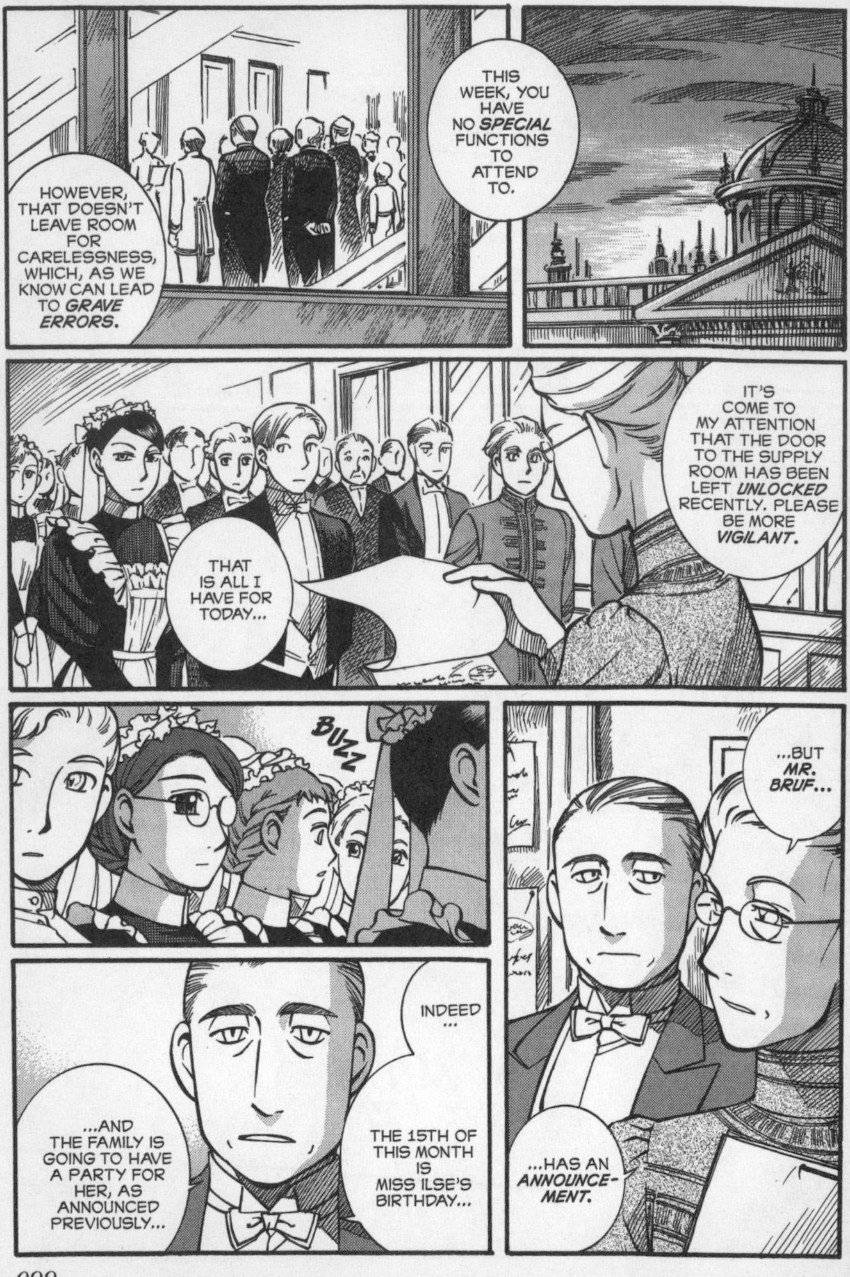
THIS WEEK, YOU HAVE NO SPECIAL FUNCTIONS TO ATTEND TO.
HOWEVER, THAT DOESN'T LEAVE ROOM FOR CARELESSNESS, WHICH, AS WE KNOW CAN LEAD TO GRAVE ERRORS.
IT'S COME TO MY ATTENTION THAT THE DOOR TO THE SUPPLY ROOM HAS BEEN LEFT UNLOCKED RECENTLY. PLEASE BE MORE VIGILANT.
THAT IS ALL I HAVE FOR TODAY...
...BUT MR. BRUF...
...HAS AN ANNOUNCEMENT.
BUZZ
INDEED...
THE 15TH OF THIS MONTH IS MISS ILSE'S BIRTHDAY...
...AND THE FAMILY IS GOING TO HAVE A PARTY FOR HER, AS ANNOUNCED PREVIOUSLY...

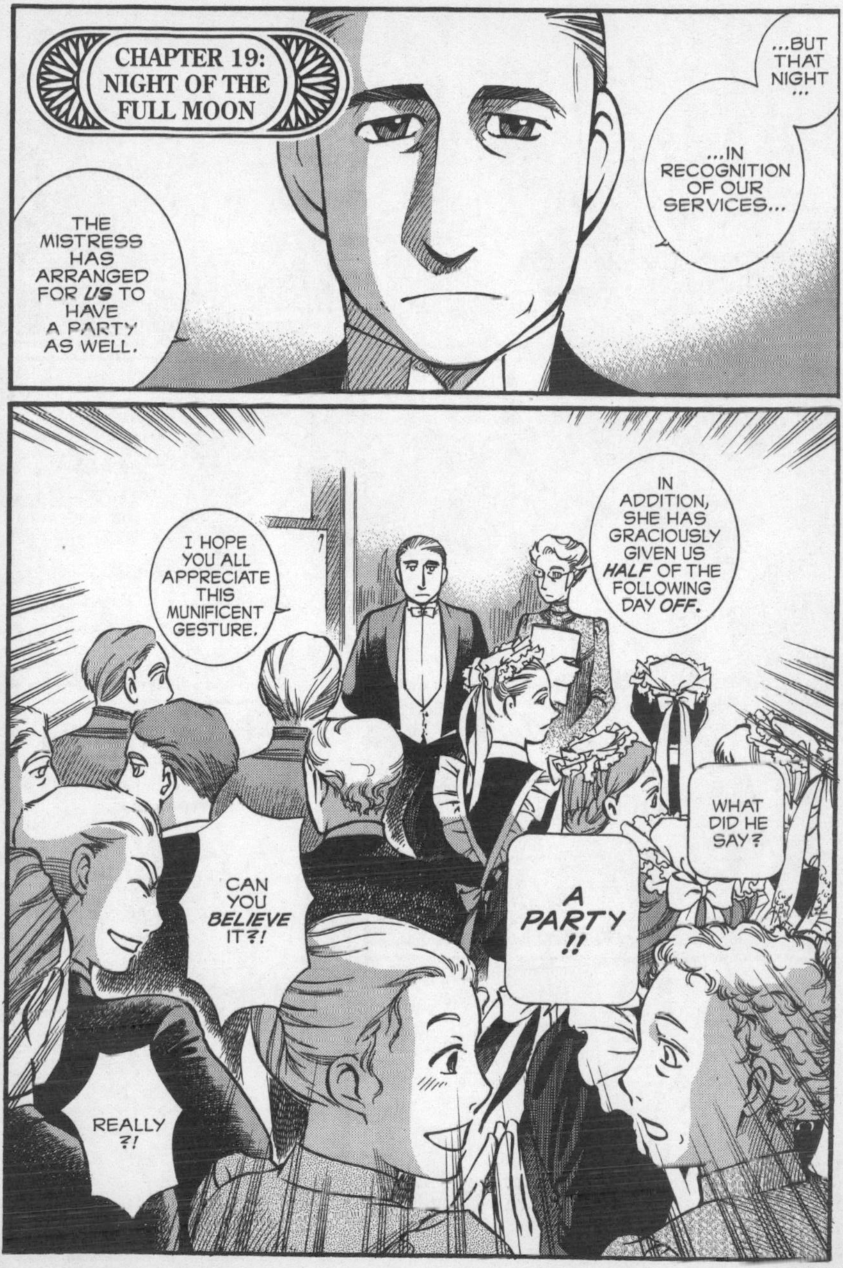
CHAPTER 19: NIGHT OF THE FULL MOON
...BUT THAT NIGHT...
...IN RECOGNITION OF OUR SERVICES...
THE MISTRESS HAS ARRANGED FOR *US* TO HAVE A PARTY AS WELL.
IN ADDITION, SHE HAS GRACIOUSLY GIVEN US *HALF* OF THE FOLLOWING DAY *OFF*.
I HOPE YOU ALL APPRECIATE THIS MUNIFICENT GESTURE.
WHAT DID HE SAY?
A PARTY!!
CAN YOU *BELIEVE* IT?!
REALLY?!

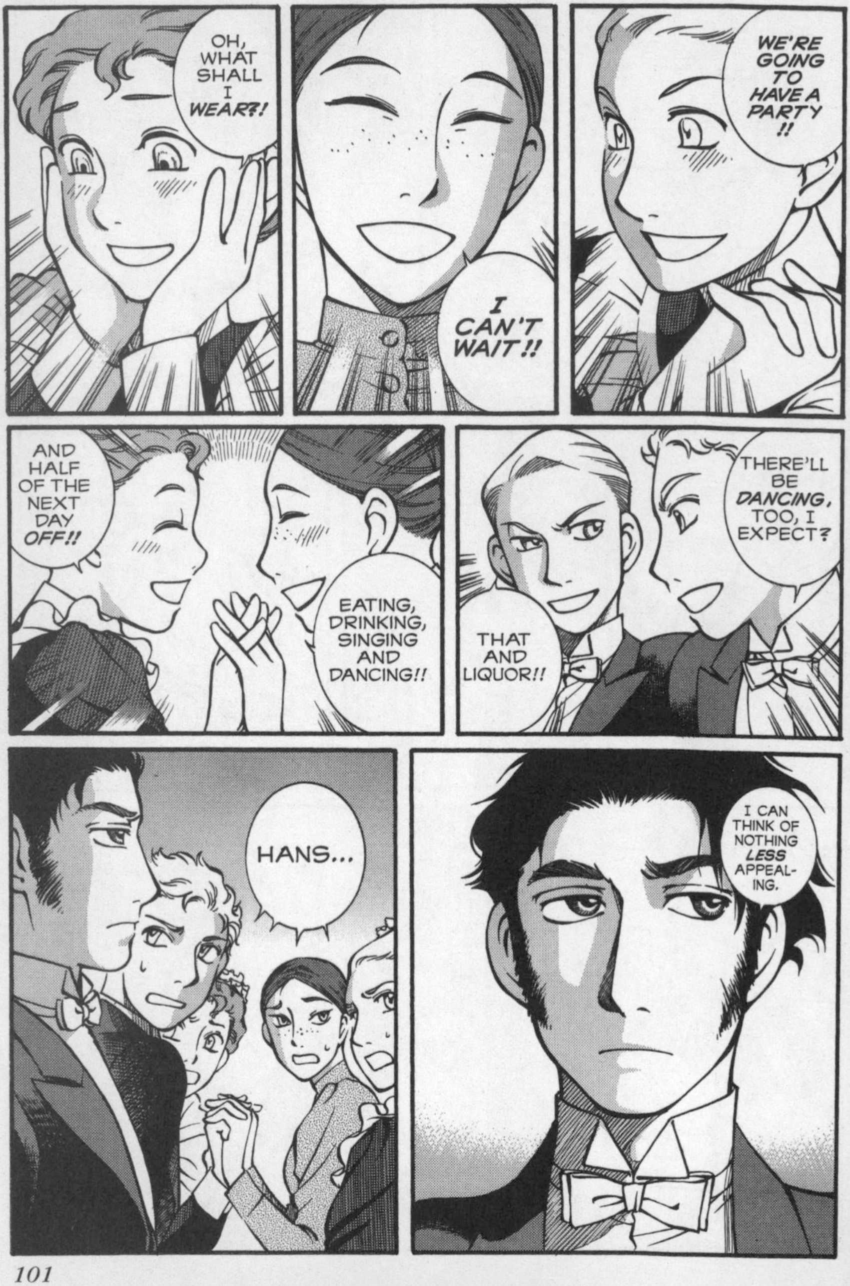
WE'RE GOING TO HAVE A PARTY!!
I CAN'T WAIT!!
OH, WHAT SHALL I WEAR?!
THERE'LL BE DANCING, TOO, I EXPECT?
THAT AND LIQUOR!!
EATING, DRINKING, SINGING AND DANCING!!
AND HALF OF THE NEXT DAY OFF!!
I CAN THINK OF NOTHING LESS APPEAL-ING.
HANS...

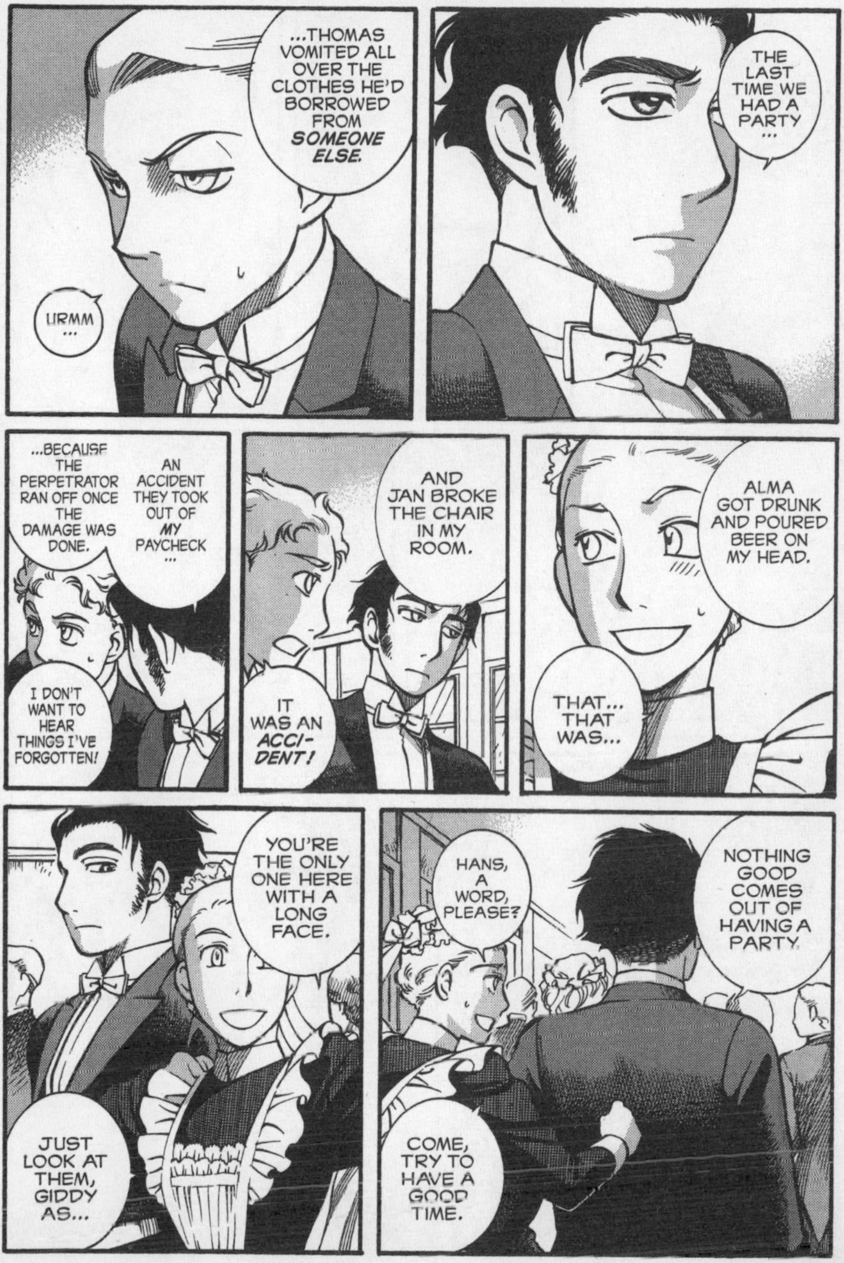
THE LAST TIME WE HAD A PARTY ...
...THOMAS VOMITED ALL OVER THE CLOTHES HE'D BORROWED FROM SOMEONE ELSE.
URMM ...
ALMA GOT DRUNK AND POURED BEER ON MY HEAD.
THAT... THAT WAS...
AND JAN BROKE THE CHAIR IN MY ROOM.
IT WAS AN ACCI-DENT!
AN ACCIDENT THEY TOOK OUT OF MY PAYCHECK ...
...BECAUSE THE PERPETRATOR RAN OFF ONCE THE DAMAGE WAS DONE.
I DON'T WANT TO HEAR THINGS I'VE FORGOTTEN!
NOTHING GOOD COMES OUT OF HAVING A PARTY.
HANS, A WORD, PLEASE?
COME, TRY TO HAVE A GOOD TIME.
YOU'RE THE ONLY ONE HERE WITH A LONG FACE.
JUST LOOK AT THEM, GIDDY AS...

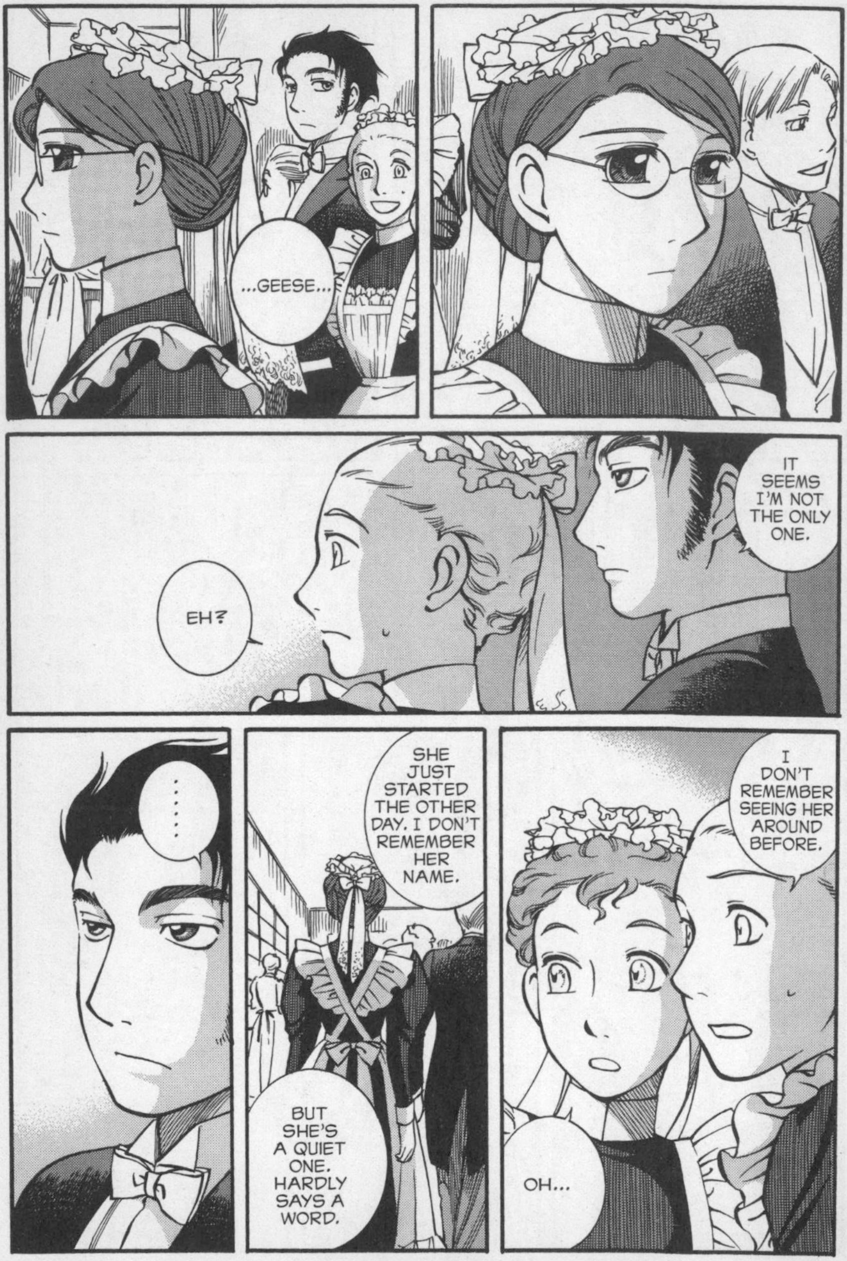
...GEESE...
IT SEEMS I'M NOT THE ONLY ONE.
EH?
I DON'T REMEMBER SEEING HER AROUND BEFORE.
OH...
SHE JUST STARTED THE OTHER DAY. I DON'T REMEMBER HER NAME.
BUT SHE'S A QUIET ONE. HARDLY SAYS A WORD.
......

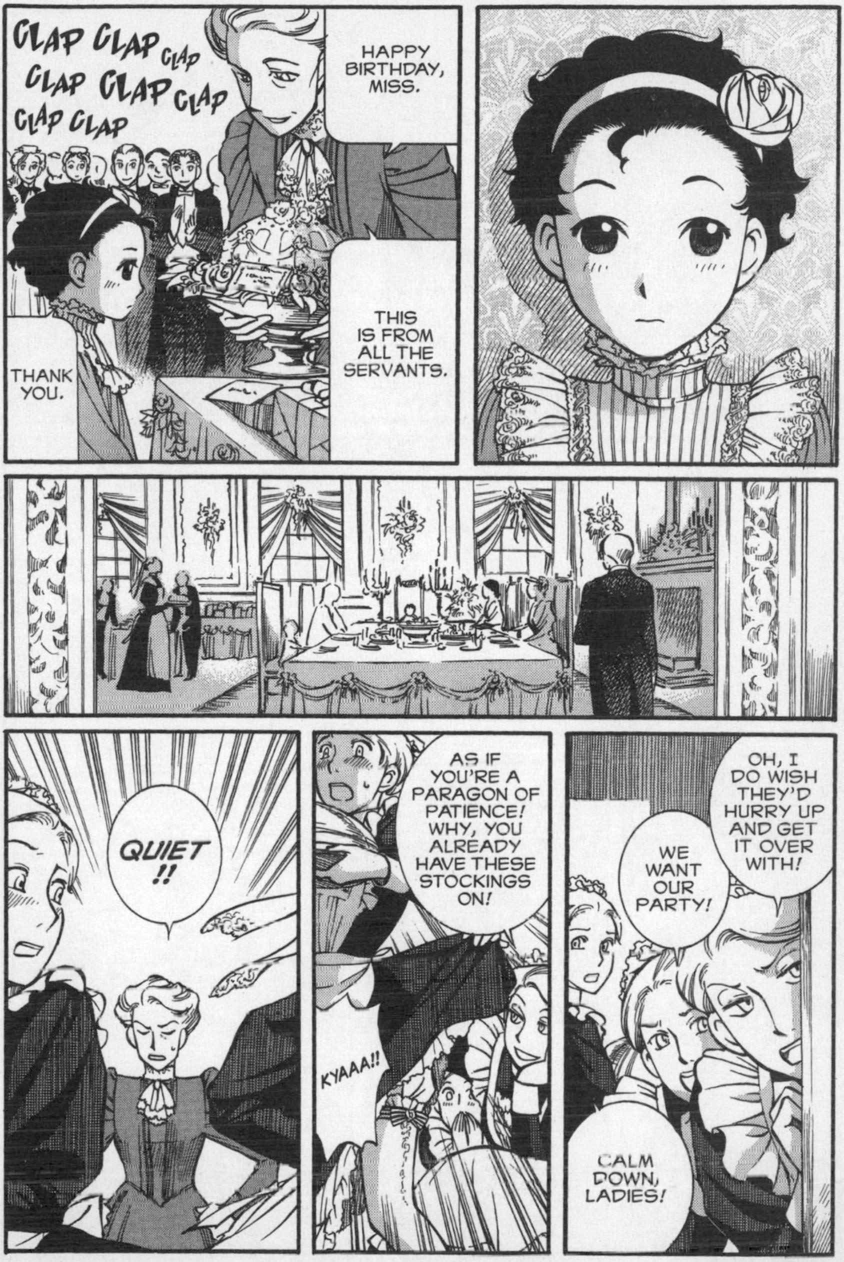
HAPPY BIRTHDAY, MISS.
CLAP CLAP CLAP CLAP CLAP CLAP CLAP CLAP
THIS IS FROM ALL THE SERVANTS.
THANK YOU.
OH, I DO WISH THEY'D HURRY UP AND GET IT OVER WITH!
WE WANT OUR PARTY!
CALM DOWN, LADIES!
AS IF YOU'RE A PARAGON OF PATIENCE! WHY, YOU ALREADY HAVE THESE STOCKINGS ON!
KYAAA!!
QUIET !!

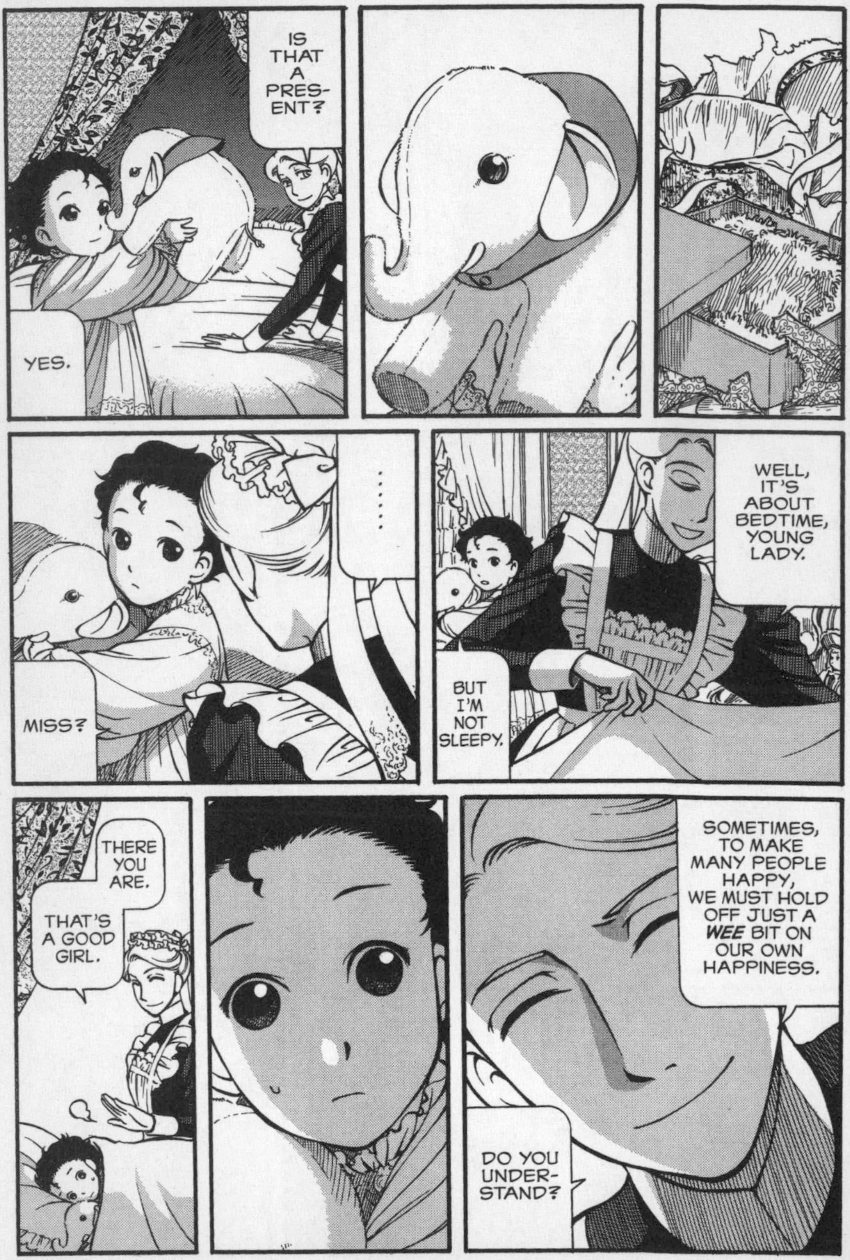
IS THAT A PRESENT?
YES.
WELL, IT'S ABOUT BEDTIME, YOUNG LADY.
BUT I'M NOT SLEEPY.
......
MISS?
SOMETIMES, TO MAKE MANY PEOPLE HAPPY, WE MUST HOLD OFF JUST A *WEE* BIT ON OUR OWN HAPPINESS.
DO YOU UNDERSTAND?
THERE YOU ARE.
THAT'S A GOOD GIRL.

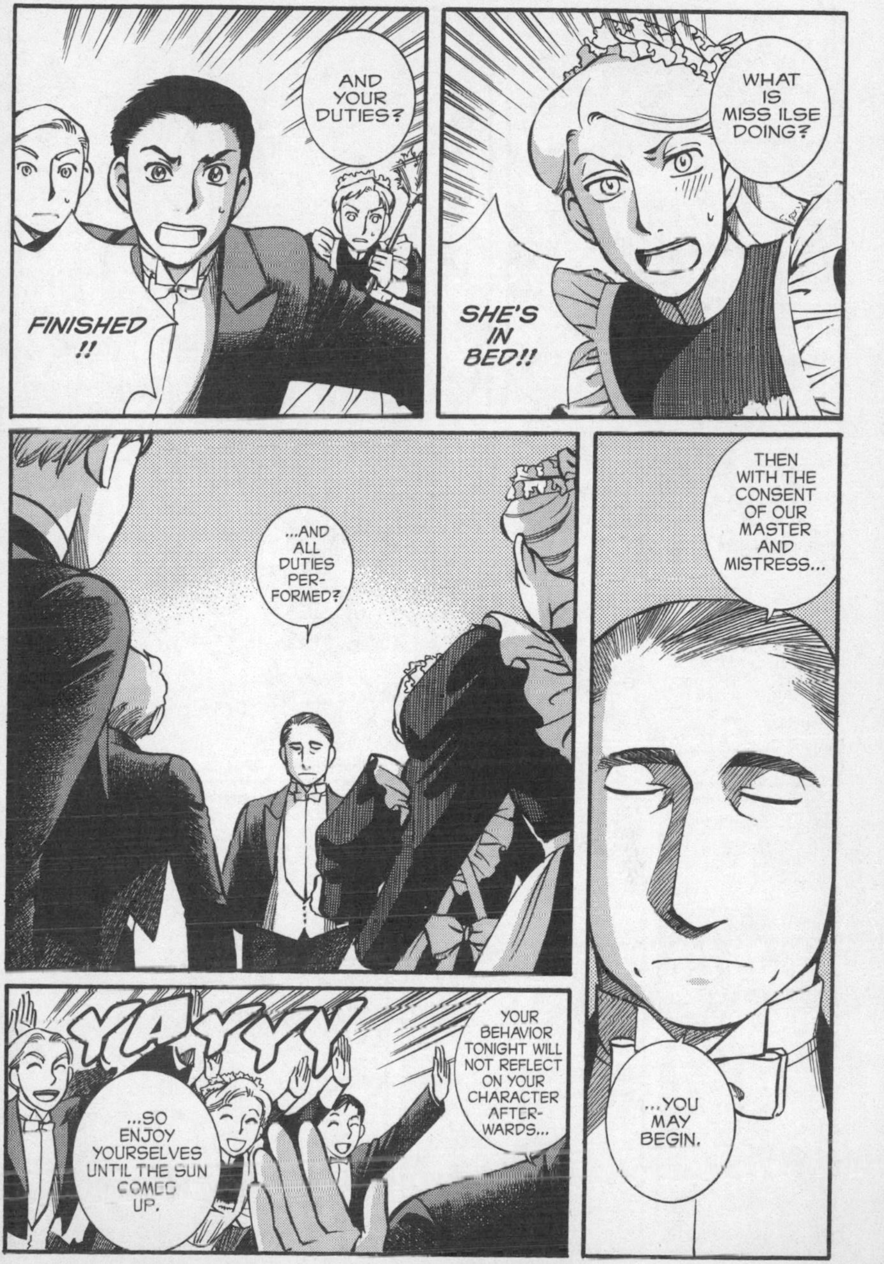
AND YOUR DUTIES?
FINISHED!!
WHAT IS MISS ILSE DOING?
SHE'S IN BED!!
...AND ALL DUTIES PERFORMED?
THEN WITH THE CONSENT OF OUR MASTER AND MISTRESS...
...YOU MAY BEGIN.
YOUR BEHAVIOR TONIGHT WILL NOT REFLECT ON YOUR CHARACTER AFTERWARDS...
...SO ENJOY YOURSELVES UNTIL THE SUN COMES UP.
YAYYY

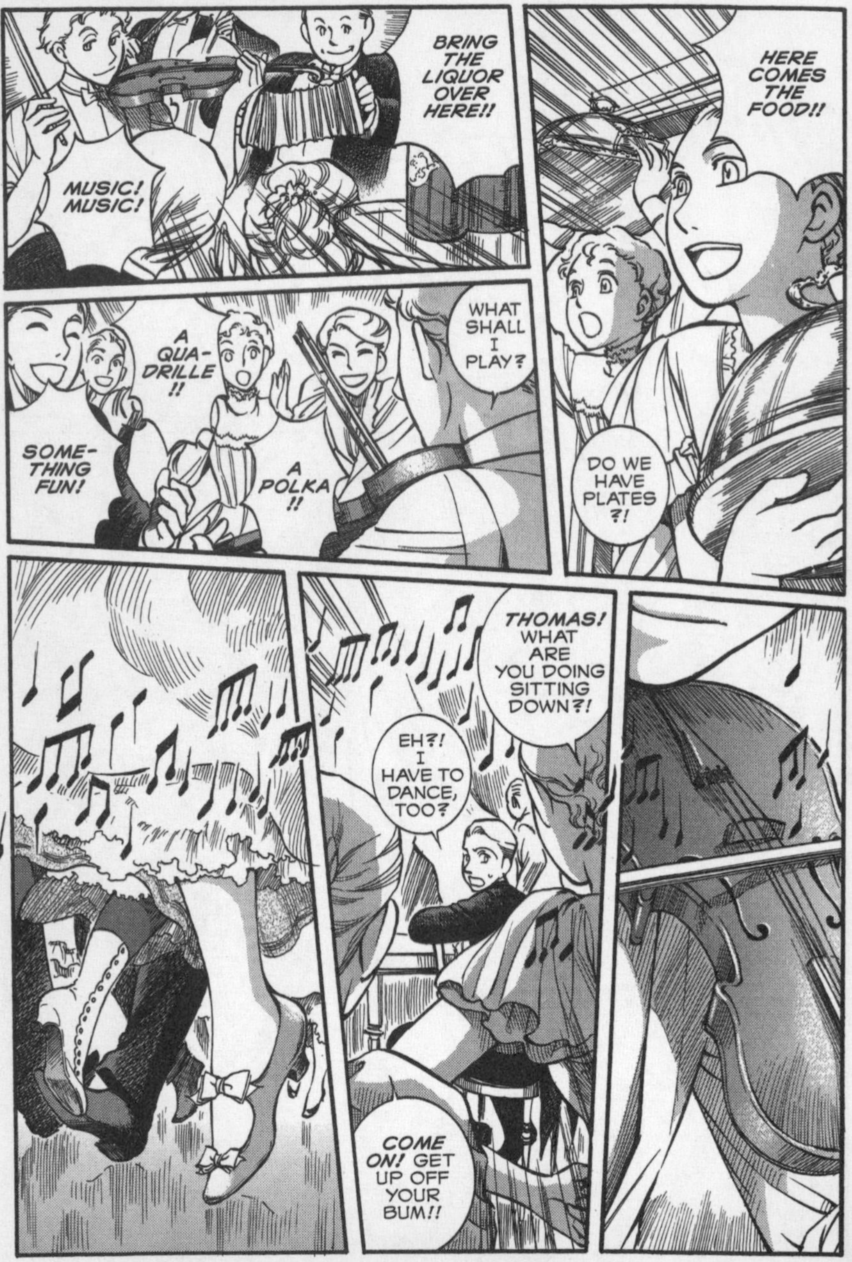
HERE COMES THE FOOD!!
DO WE HAVE PLATES?!
BRING THE LIQUOR OVER HERE!!
MUSIC! MUSIC!
WHAT SHALL I PLAY?
A QUADRILLE!!
A POLKA!!
SOMETHING FUN!
THOMAS! WHAT ARE YOU DOING SITTING DOWN?!
EH?! I HAVE TO DANCE, TOO?
COME ON! GET UP OFF YOUR BUM!!

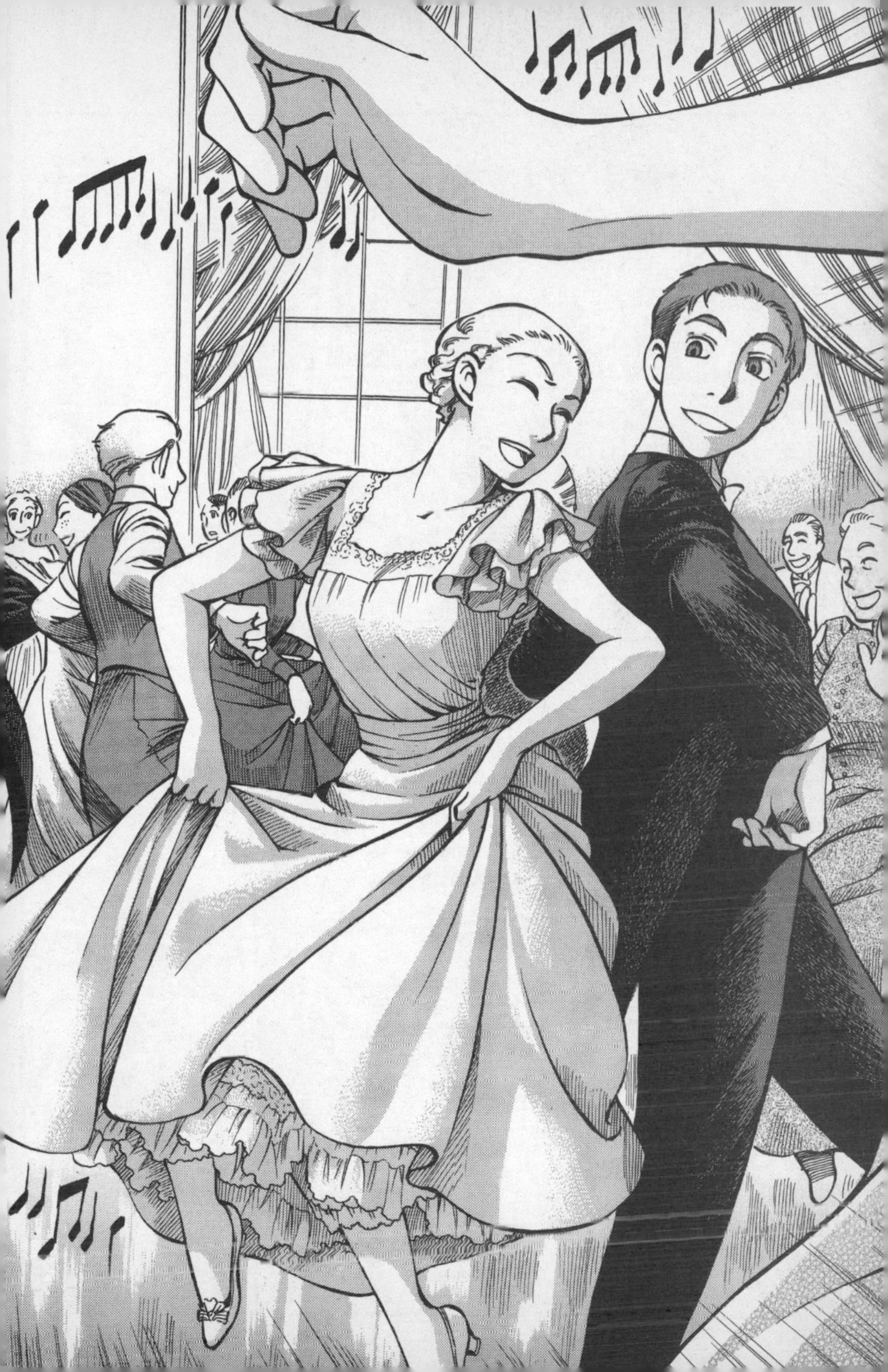

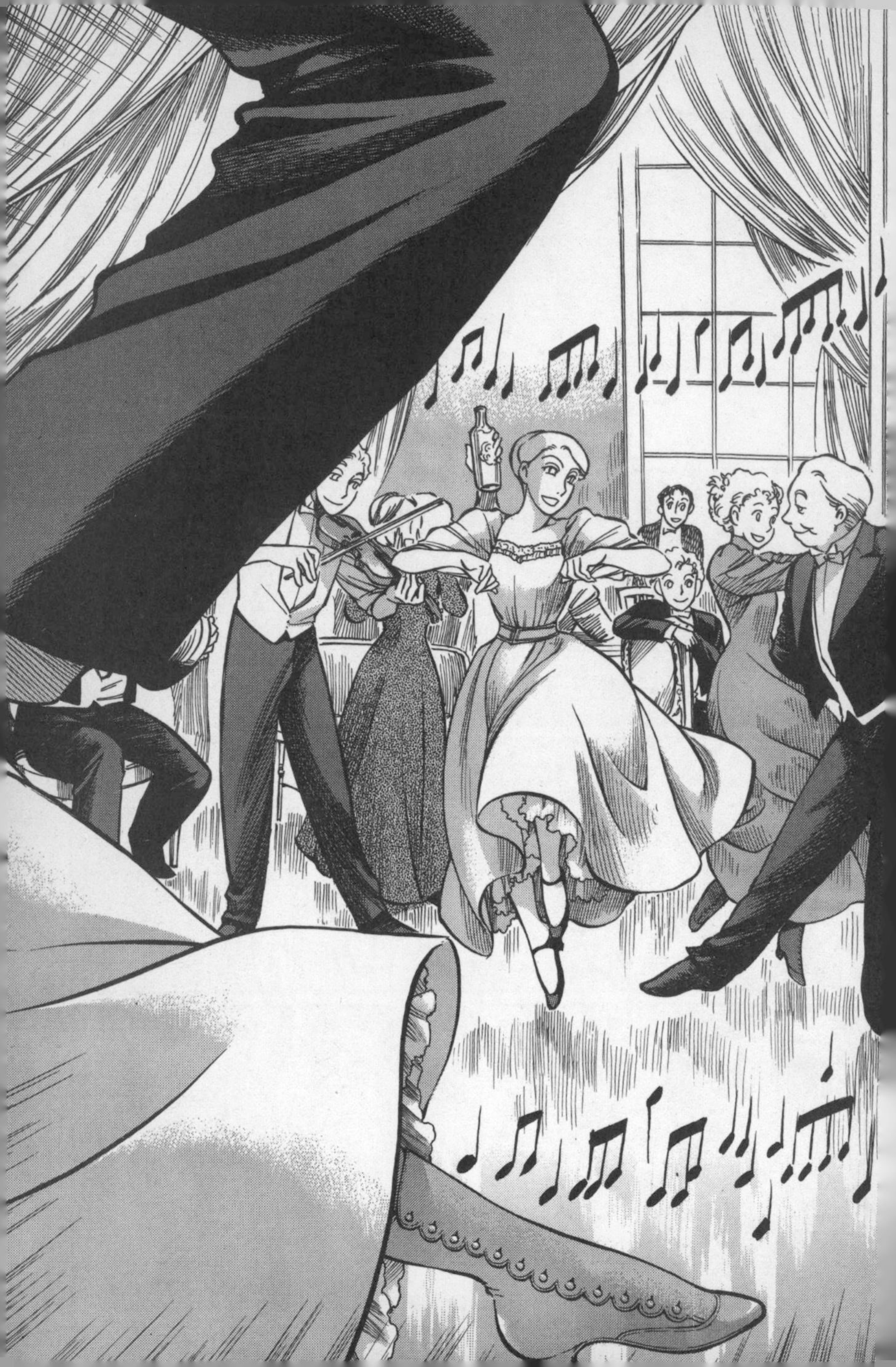

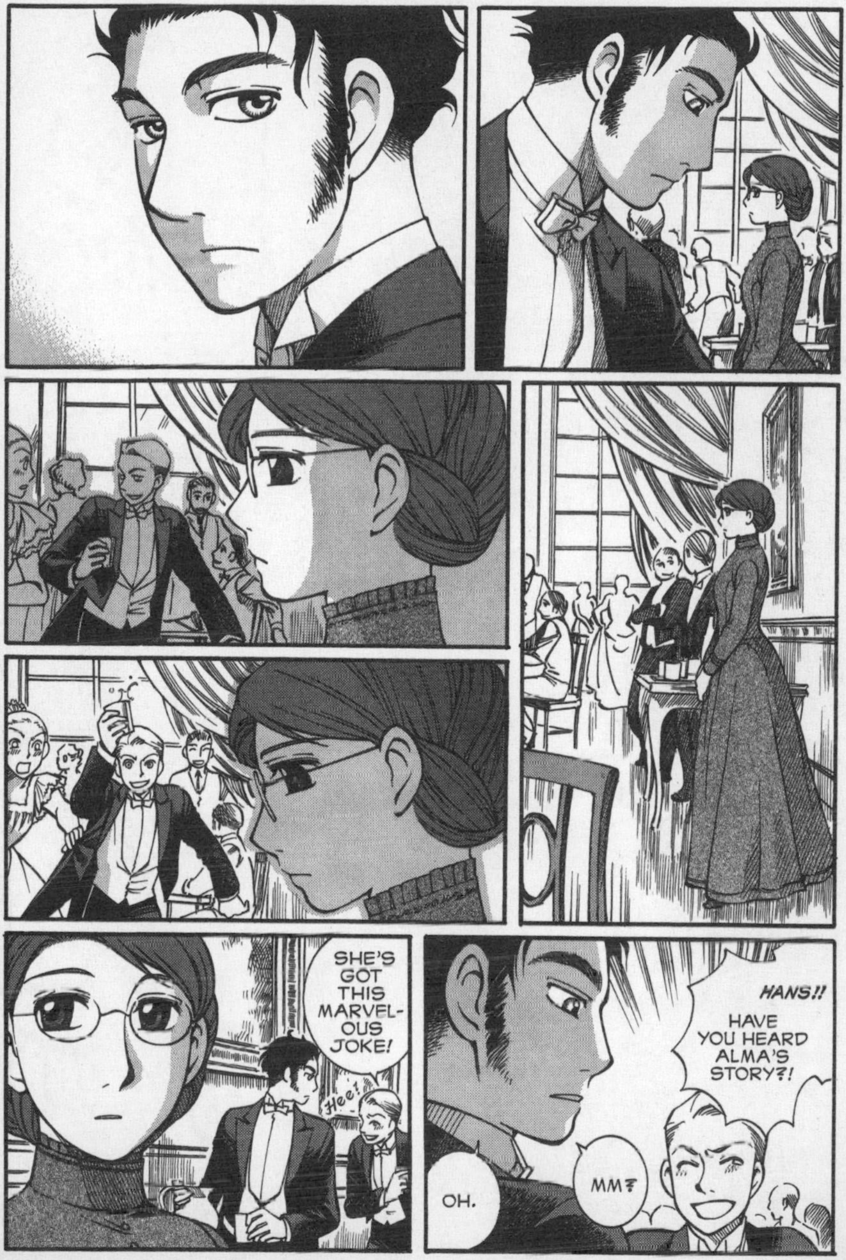
HANS!!
HAVE YOU HEARD ALMA'S STORY?!
MM?
OH.
SHE'S GOT THIS MARVEL-OUS JOKE!
Hee!

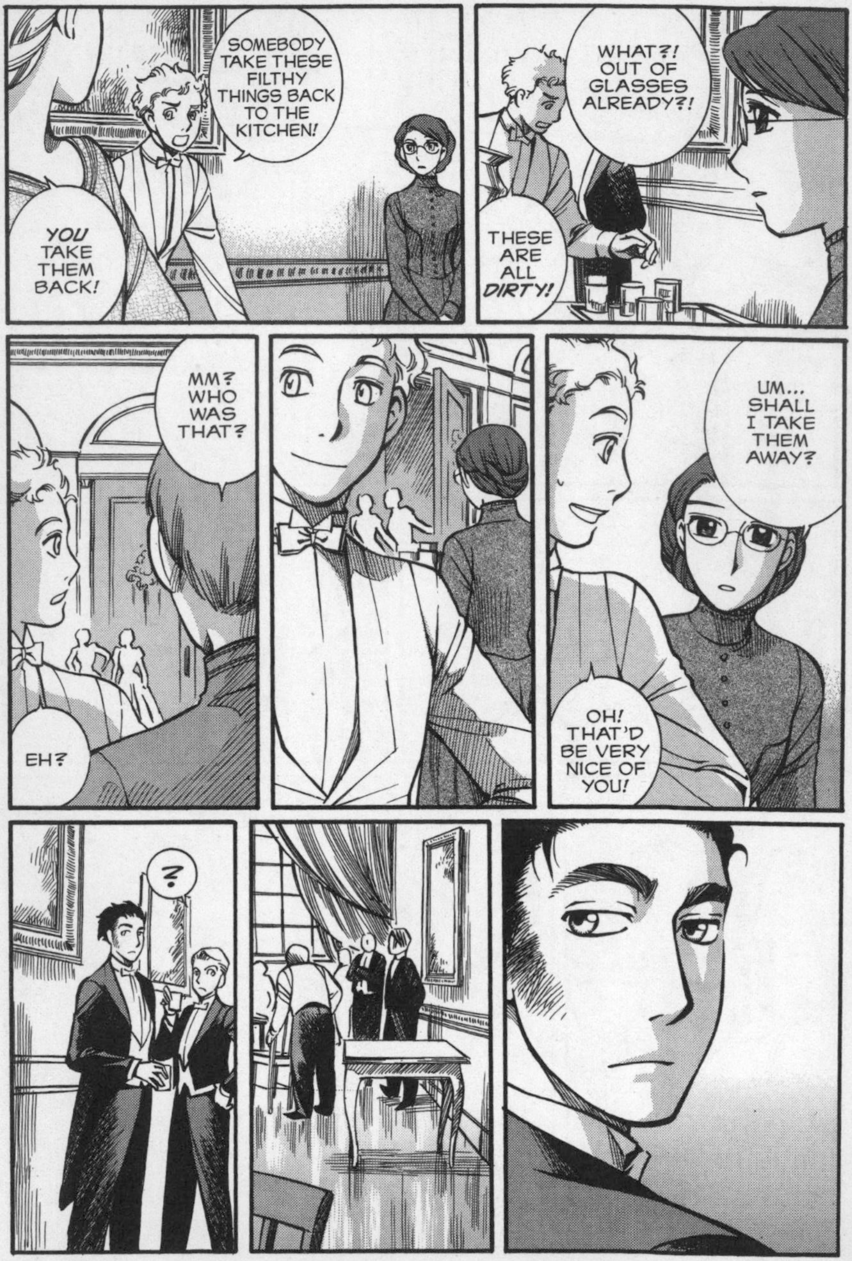
WHAT?! OUT OF GLASSES ALREADY?!
THESE ARE ALL *DIRTY!*
SOMEBODY TAKE THESE FILTHY THINGS BACK TO THE KITCHEN!
YOU TAKE THEM BACK!
UM... SHALL I TAKE THEM AWAY?
OH! THAT'D BE VERY NICE OF YOU!
MM? WHO WAS THAT?
EH?
?

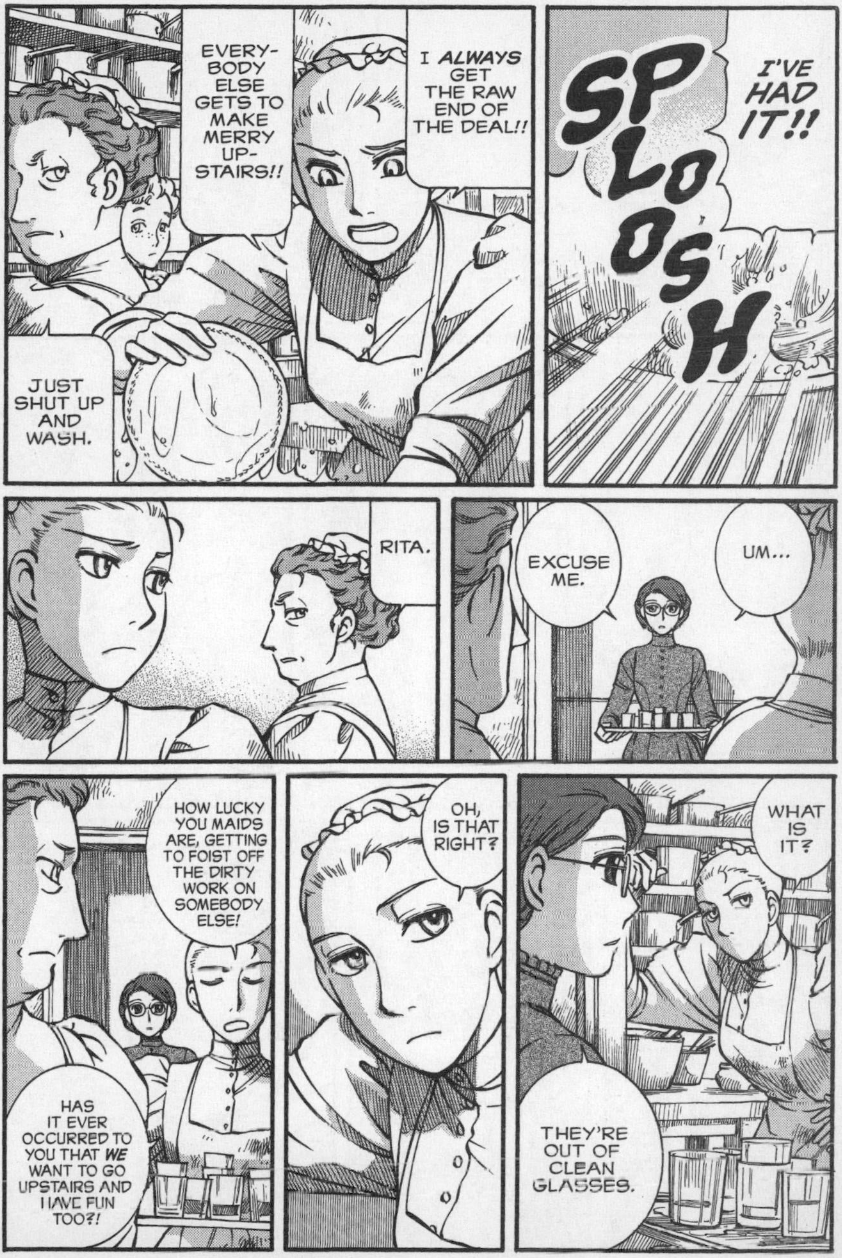
I'VE HAD IT!!
SPLOOSH
I *ALWAYS* GET THE RAW END OF THE DEAL!!
EVERYBODY ELSE GETS TO MAKE MERRY UPSTAIRS!!
JUST SHUT UP AND WASH.
UM...
EXCUSE ME.
RITA.
WHAT IS IT?
THEY'RE OUT OF CLEAN GLASSES.
OH, IS THAT RIGHT?
HOW LUCKY YOU MAIDS ARE, GETTING TO FOIST OFF THE DIRTY WORK ON SOMEBODY ELSE!
HAS IT EVER OCCURRED TO YOU THAT *WE* WANT TO GO UPSTAIRS AND HAVE FUN TOO?!

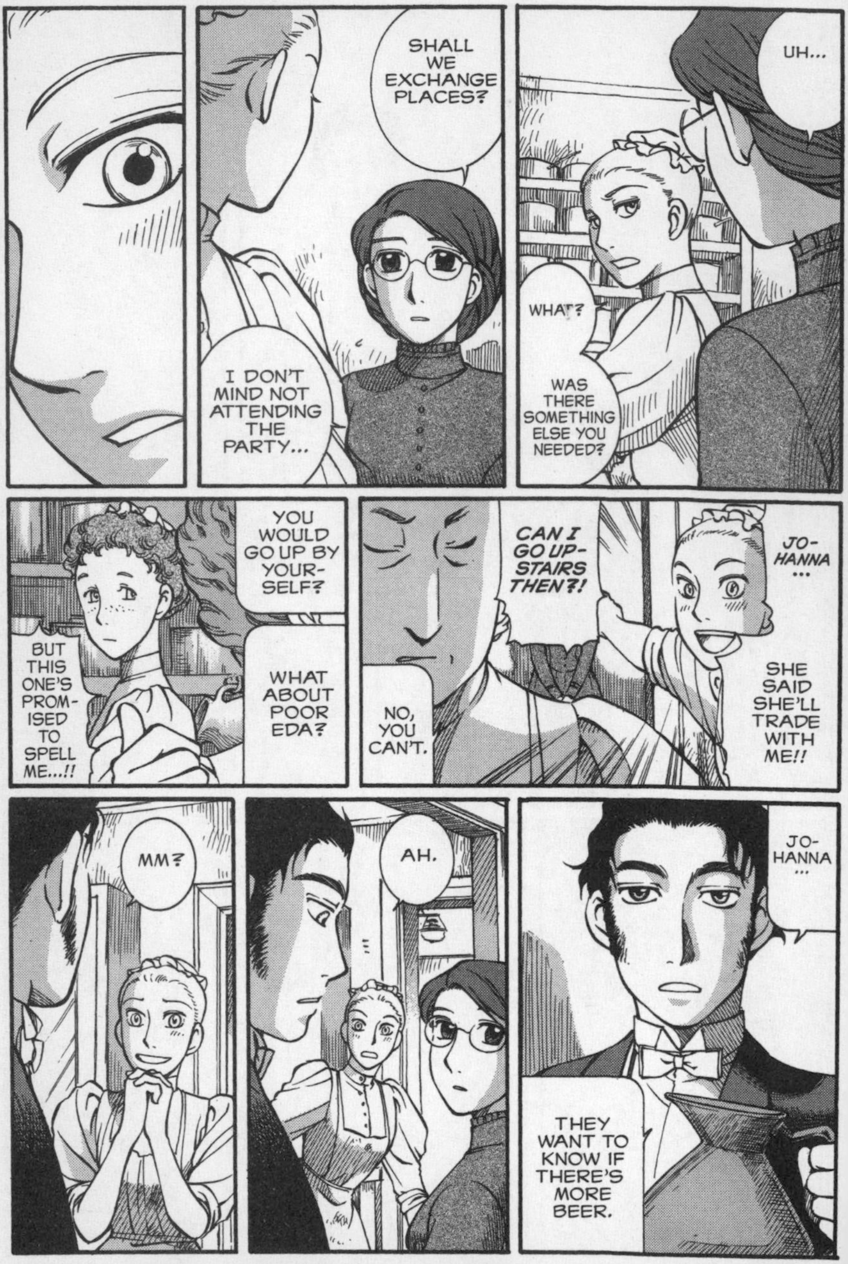
UH...
WHAT?
WAS THERE SOMETHING ELSE YOU NEEDED?
SHALL WE EXCHANGE PLACES?
I DON'T MIND NOT ATTENDING THE PARTY...
JO-HANNA...
CAN I GO UP-STAIRS THEN?!
SHE SAID SHE'LL TRADE WITH ME!!
NO, YOU CAN'T.
YOU WOULD GO UP BY YOUR-SELF?
WHAT ABOUT POOR EDA?
BUT THIS ONE'S PROM-ISED TO SPELL ME...!!
JO-HANNA...
THEY WANT TO KNOW IF THERE'S MORE BEER.
AH.
MM?

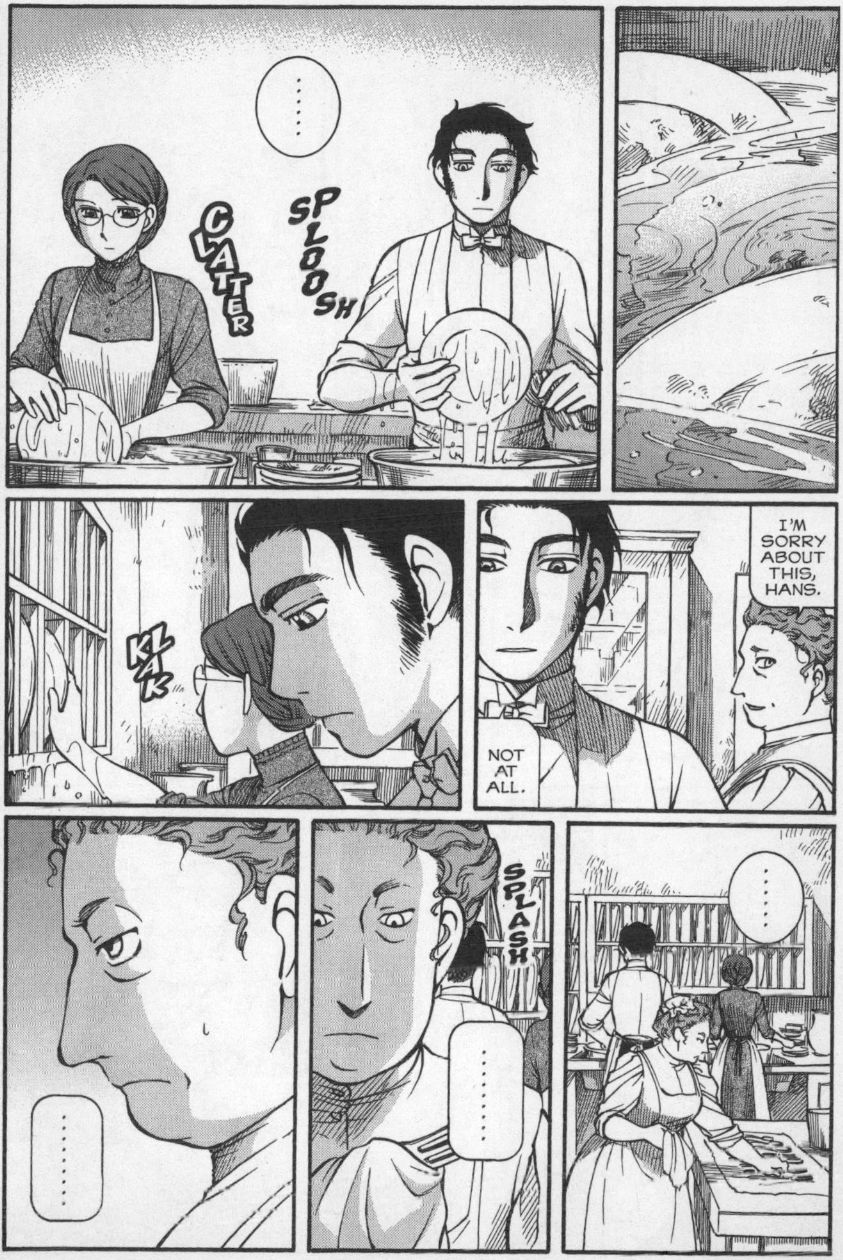
......
SPLOOSH
CLATTER
I'M SORRY ABOUT THIS, HANS.
NOT AT ALL.
KLAK
......
SPLASH
......
......

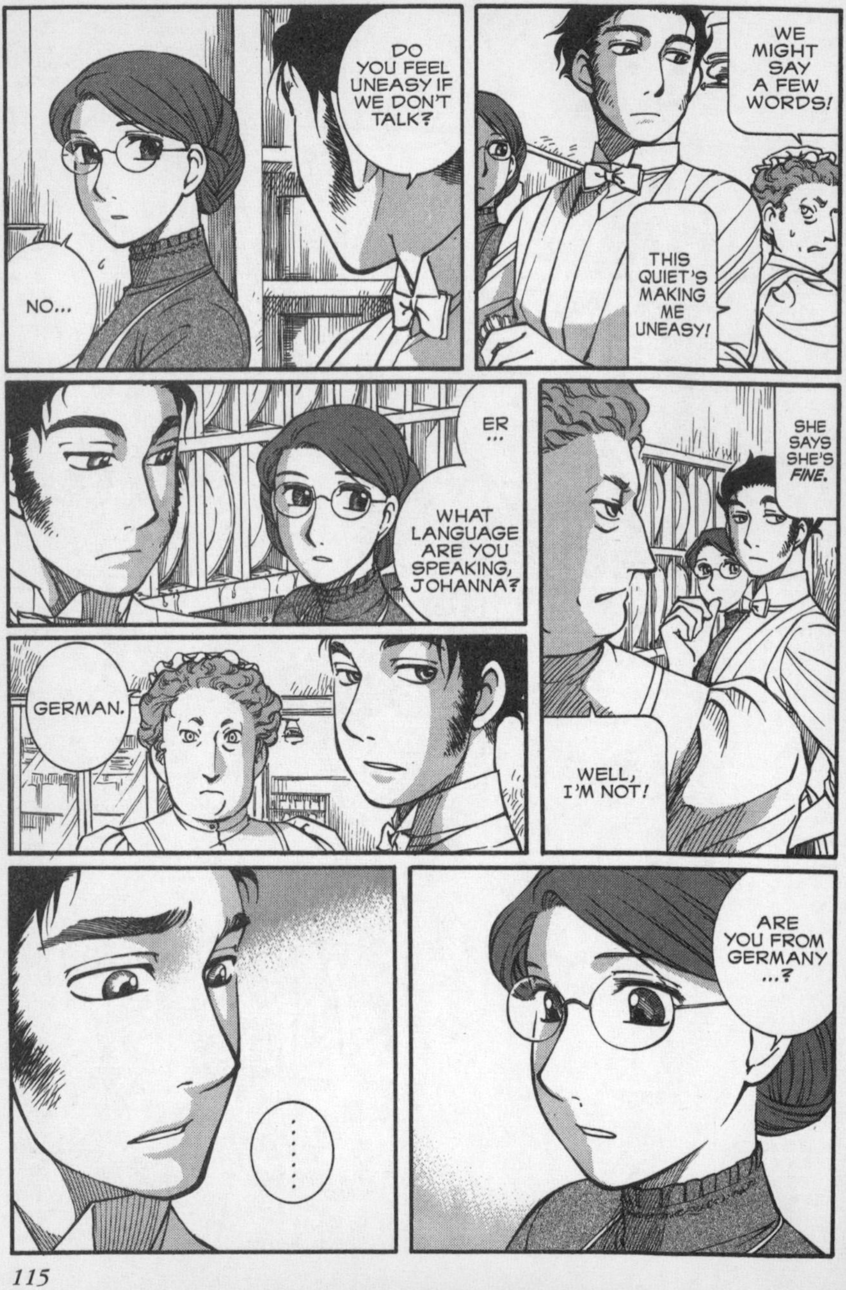
WE MIGHT SAY A FEW WORDS!
THIS QUIET'S MAKING ME UNEASY!
DO YOU FEEL UNEASY IF WE DON'T TALK?
NO...
SHE SAYS SHE'S *FINE.*
WELL, I'M NOT!
ER...
WHAT LANGUAGE ARE YOU SPEAKING, JOHANNA?
GERMAN.
ARE YOU FROM GERMANY...?
......

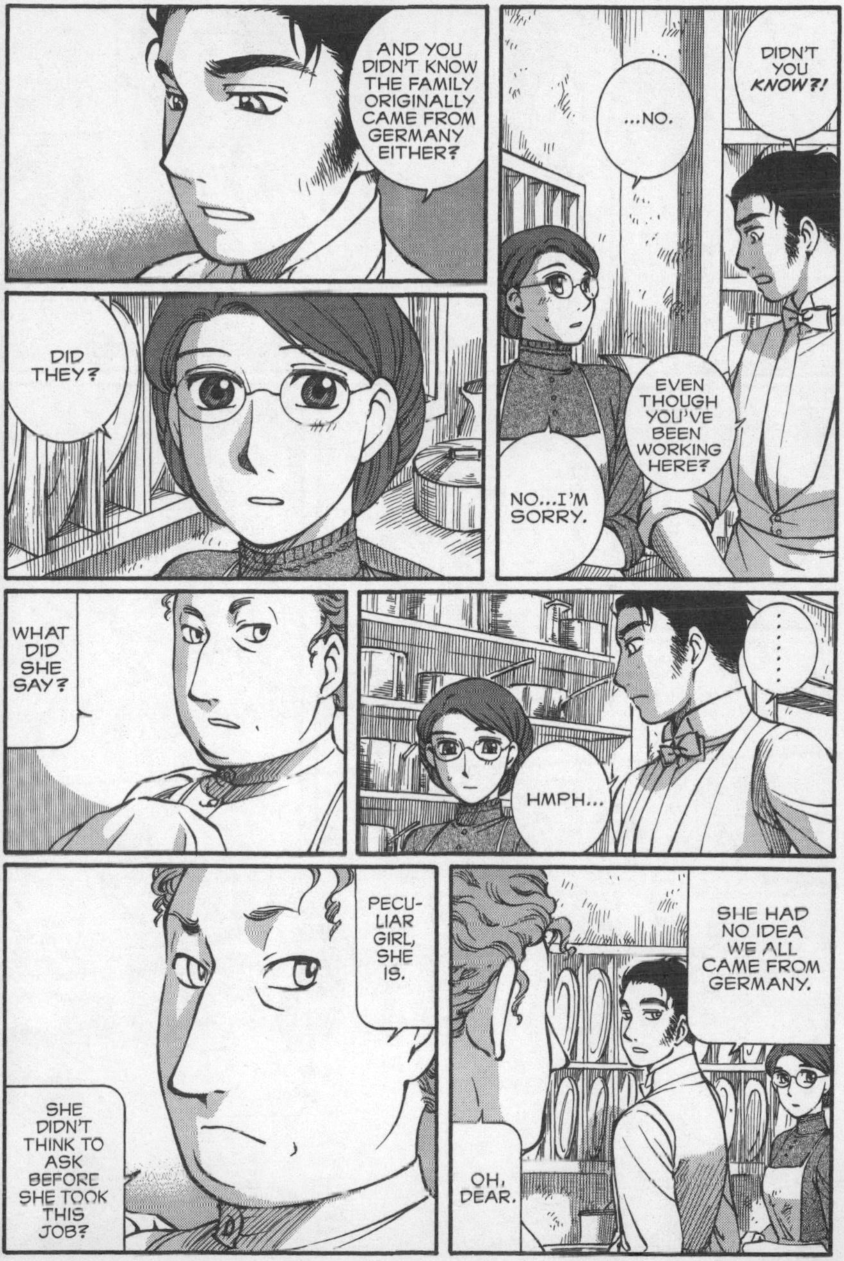
DIDN'T YOU *KNOW?!*
...NO.
EVEN THOUGH YOU'VE BEEN WORKING HERE?
NO...I'M SORRY.
AND YOU DIDN'T KNOW THE FAMILY ORIGINALLY CAME FROM GERMANY EITHER?
DID THEY?
......
HMPH...
WHAT DID SHE SAY?
SHE HAD NO IDEA WE ALL CAME FROM GERMANY.
OH, DEAR.
PECULIAR GIRL, SHE IS.
SHE DIDN'T THINK TO ASK BEFORE SHE TOOK THIS JOB?

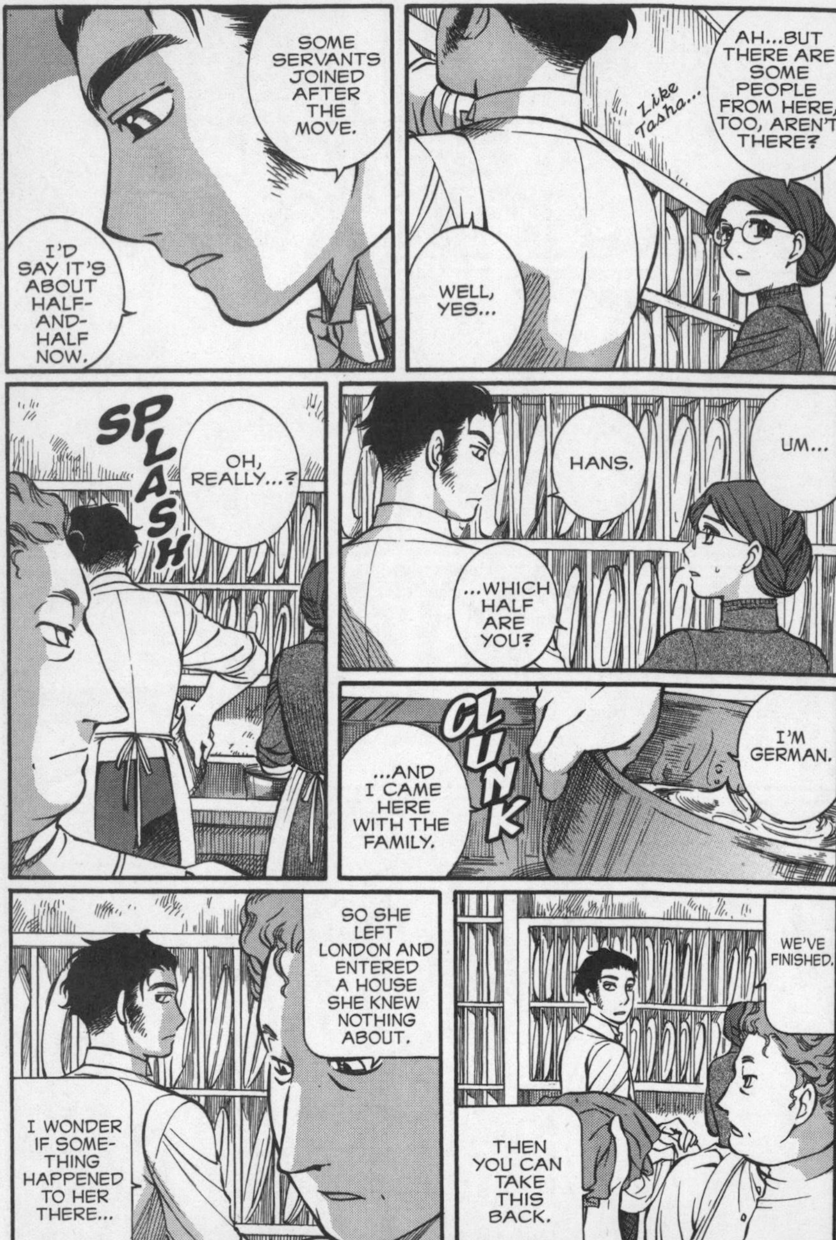
AH...BUT THERE ARE SOME PEOPLE FROM HERE, TOO, AREN'T THERE?
Like Tasha...
WELL, YES...
SOME SERVANTS JOINED AFTER THE MOVE.
I'D SAY IT'S ABOUT HALF-AND-HALF NOW.
UM...
HANS.
...WHICH HALF ARE YOU?
I'M GERMAN.
CLUNK
...AND I CAME HERE WITH THE FAMILY.
SPLASH
OH, REALLY...?
WE'VE FINISHED.
THEN YOU CAN TAKE THIS BACK.
SO SHE LEFT LONDON AND ENTERED A HOUSE SHE KNEW NOTHING ABOUT.
I WONDER IF SOME-THING HAPPENED TO HER THERE...

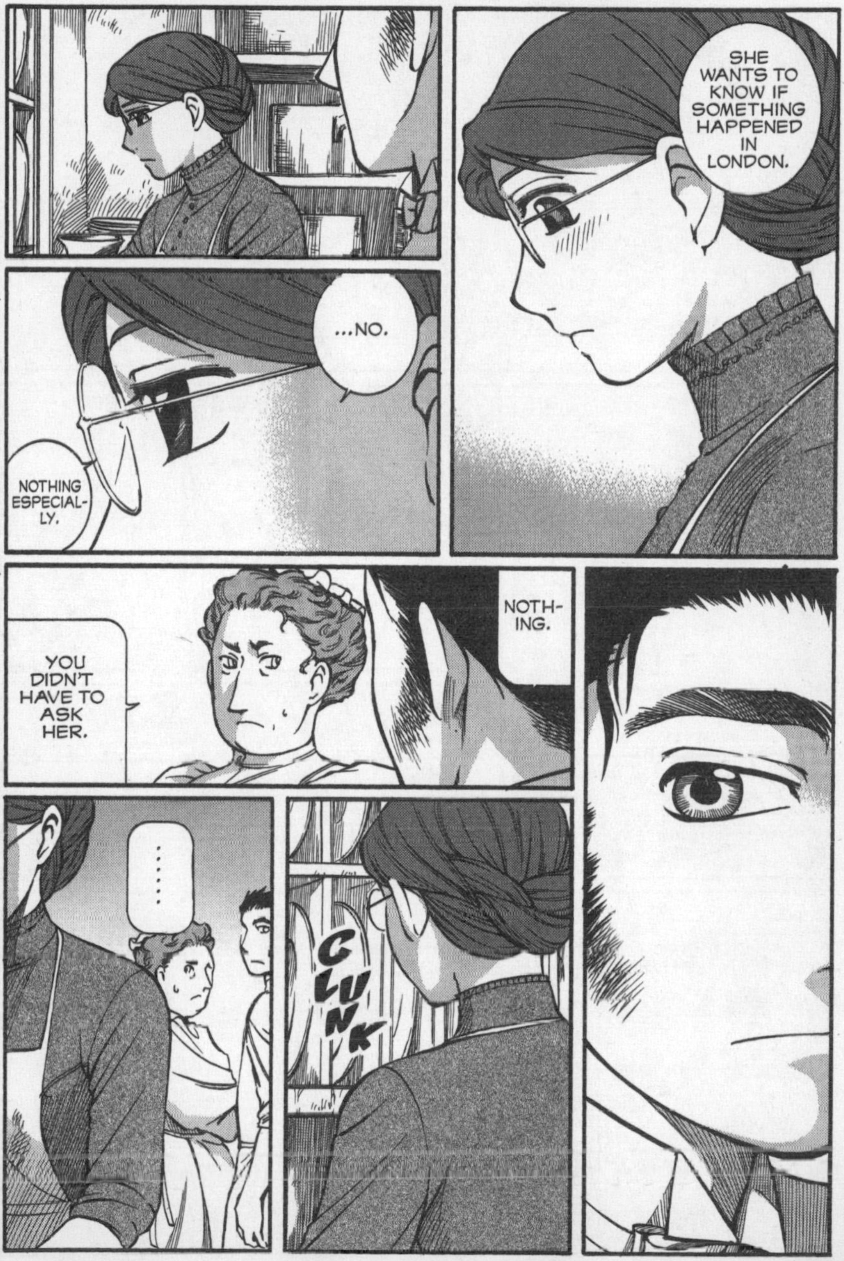
SHE WANTS TO KNOW IF SOMETHING HAPPENED IN LONDON.
...NO.
NOTHING ESPECIAL-LY.
NOTH-ING.
YOU DIDN'T HAVE TO ASK HER.
CLUNK
......

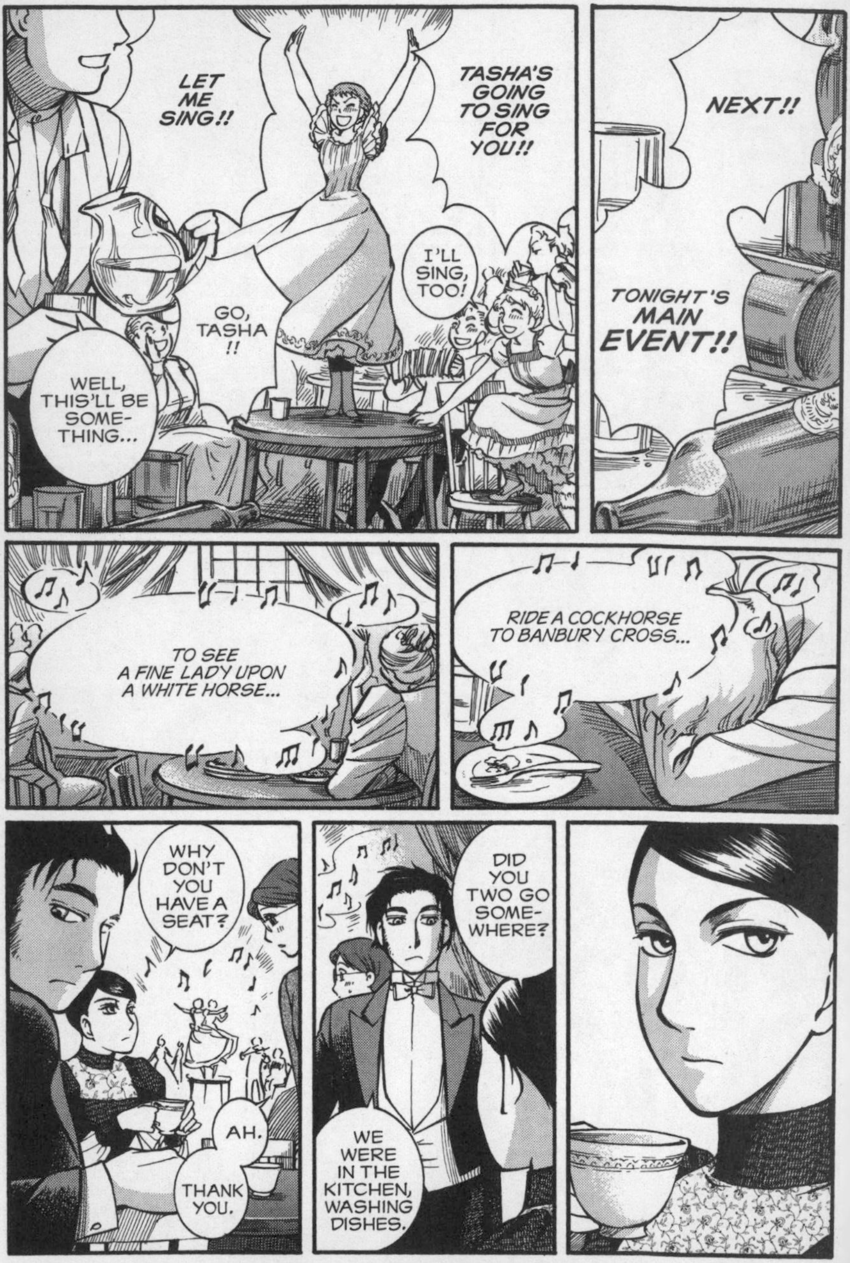
NEXT!!
TONIGHT'S MAIN EVENT!!
TASHA'S GOING TO SING FOR YOU!!
LET ME SING!!
I'LL SING, TOO!
GO, TASHA!!
WELL, THIS'LL BE SOME-THING...
RIDE A COCKHORSE TO BANBURY CROSS...
TO SEE A FINE LADY UPON A WHITE HORSE...
DID YOU TWO GO SOME-WHERE?
WE WERE IN THE KITCHEN, WASHING DISHES.
WHY DON'T YOU HAVE A SEAT?
AH.
THANK YOU.

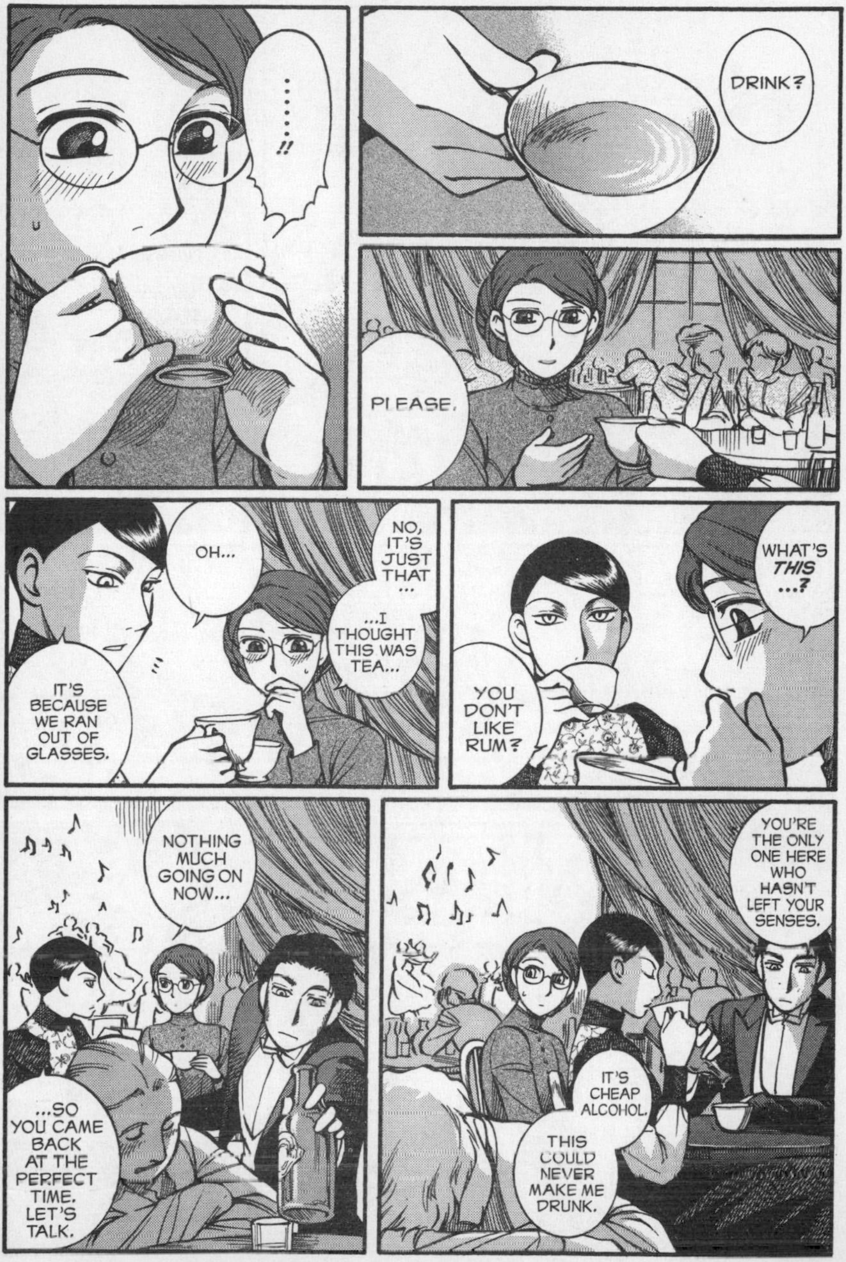
DRINK?
PLEASE.
......!!
WHAT'S *THIS* ...?
YOU DON'T LIKE RUM?
NO, IT'S JUST THAT ...
...I THOUGHT THIS WAS TEA...
OH...
IT'S BECAUSE WE RAN OUT OF GLASSES.
YOU'RE THE ONLY ONE HERE WHO HASN'T LEFT YOUR SENSES.
IT'S CHEAP ALCOHOL.
THIS COULD NEVER MAKE ME DRUNK.
NOTHING MUCH GOING ON NOW...
...SO YOU CAME BACK AT THE PERFECT TIME. LET'S TALK.

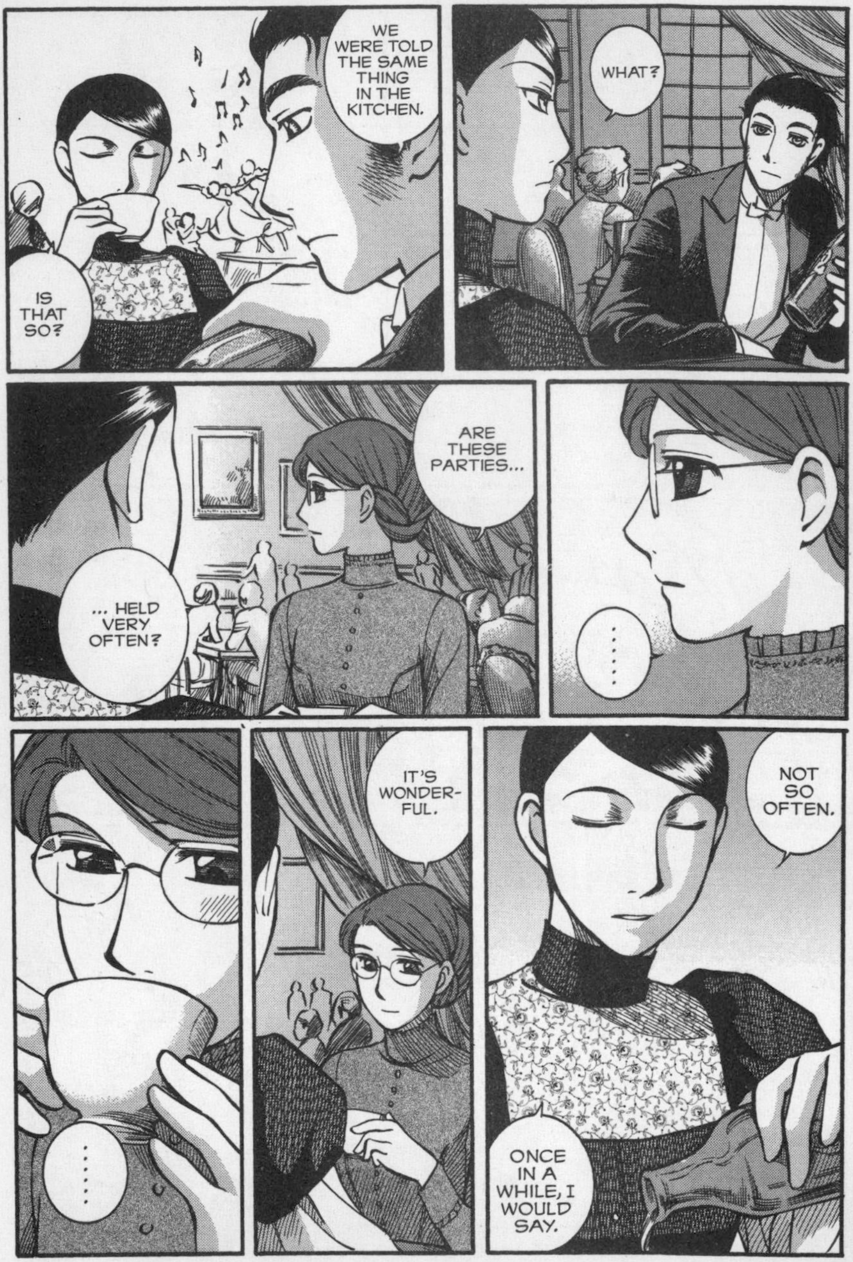
WHAT?
WE WERE TOLD THE SAME THING IN THE KITCHEN.
IS THAT SO?
......
ARE THESE PARTIES...
... HELD VERY OFTEN?
NOT SO OFTEN.
ONCE IN A WHILE, I WOULD SAY.
IT'S WONDERFUL.
......

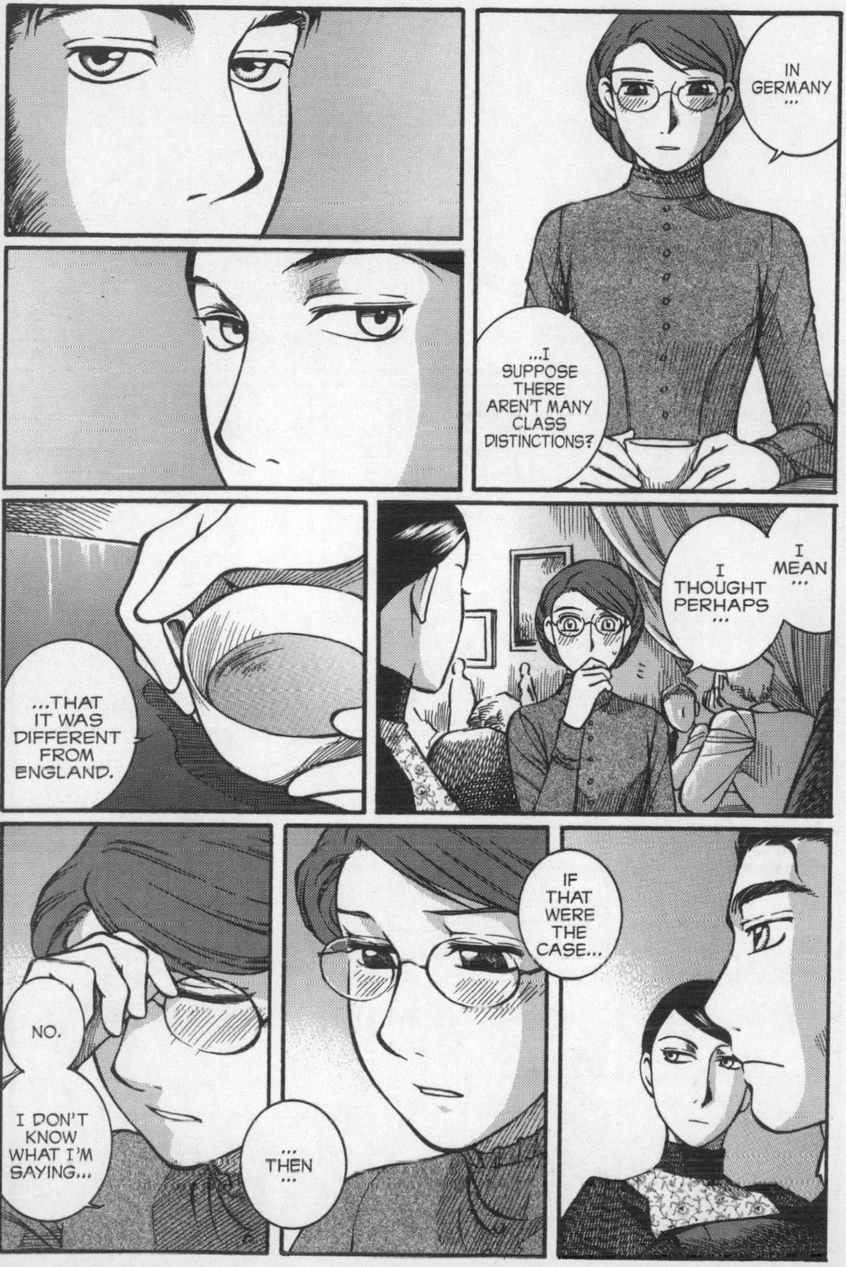
IN GERMANY ...
...I SUPPOSE THERE AREN'T MANY CLASS DISTINCTIONS?
I MEAN ...
I THOUGHT PERHAPS ...
...THAT IT WAS DIFFERENT FROM ENGLAND.
IF THAT WERE THE CASE...
... THEN ...
NO.
I DON'T KNOW WHAT I'M SAYING...

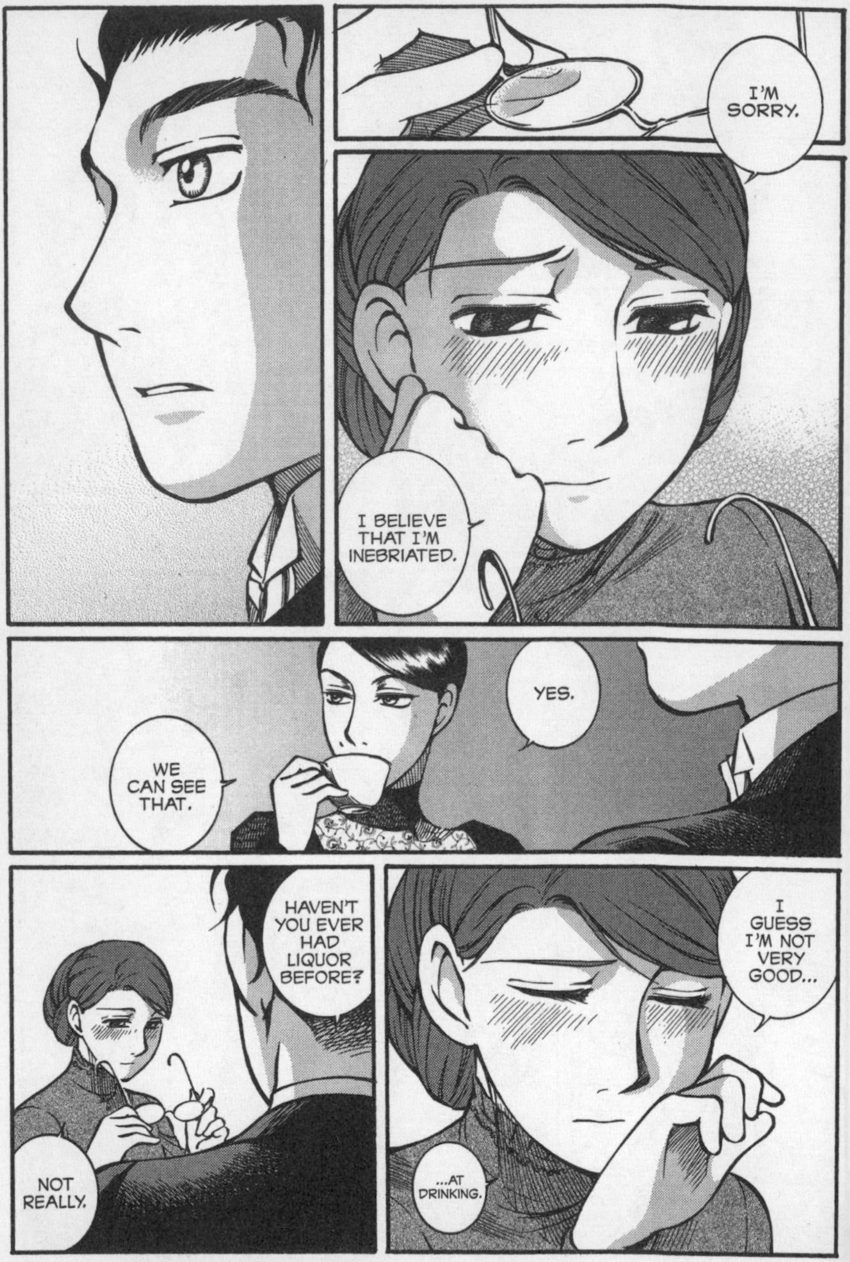
I'M SORRY.
I BELIEVE THAT I'M INEBRIATED.
YES.
WE CAN SEE THAT.
I GUESS I'M NOT VERY GOOD...
...AT DRINKING.
HAVEN'T YOU EVER HAD LIQUOR BEFORE?
NOT REALLY.

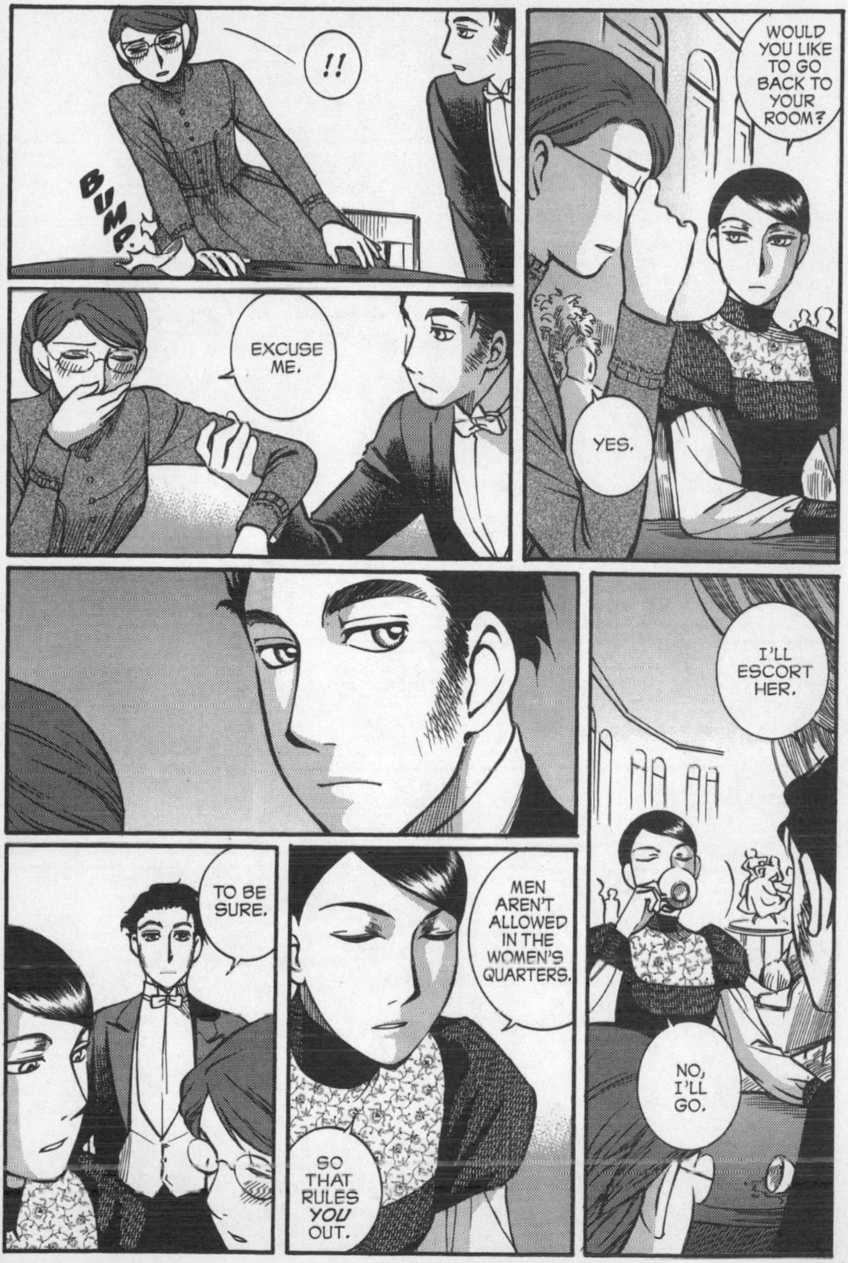
WOULD YOU LIKE TO GO BACK TO YOUR ROOM?
YES.
!!
BUMP
EXCUSE ME.
I'LL ESCORT HER.
NO, I'LL GO.
MEN AREN'T ALLOWED IN THE WOMEN'S QUARTERS.
SO THAT RULES *YOU* OUT.
TO BE SURE.

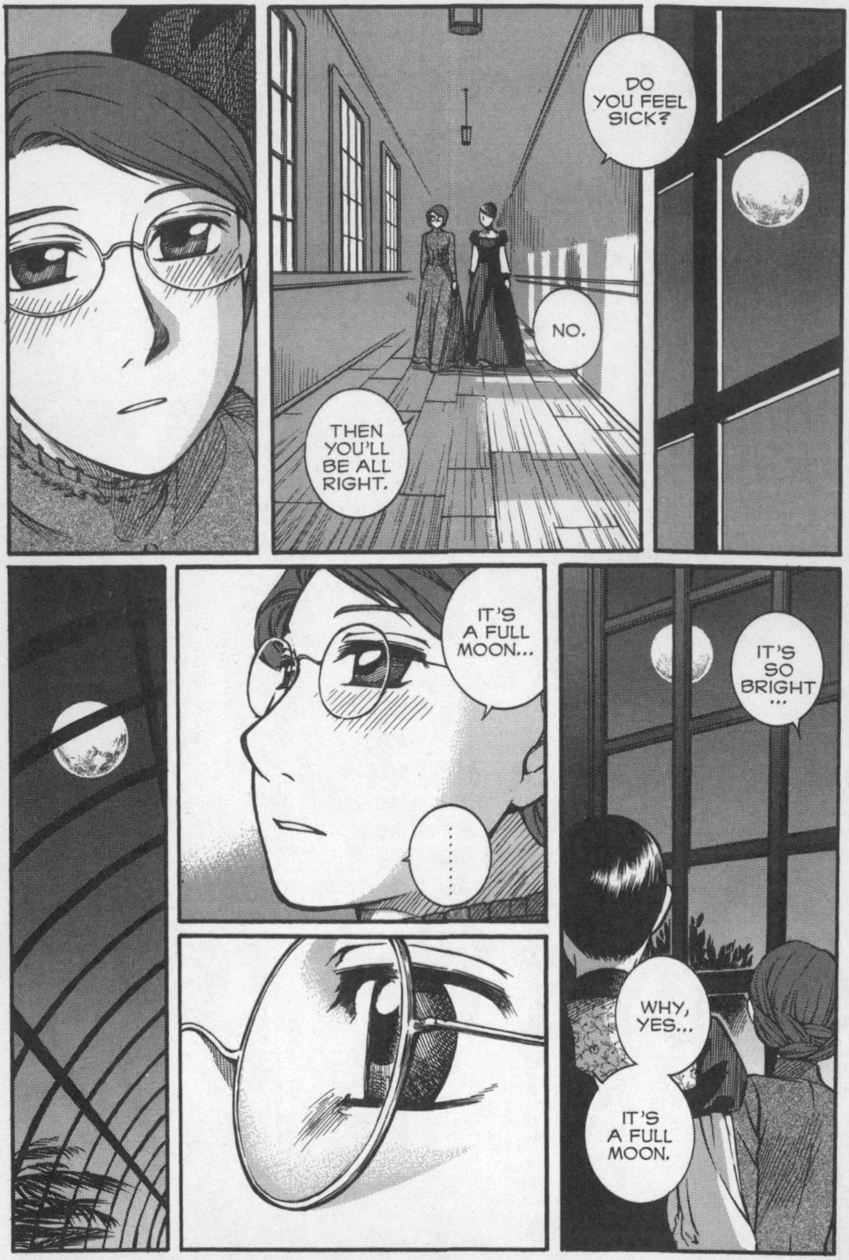
DO YOU FEEL SICK?
NO.
THEN YOU'LL BE ALL RIGHT.
IT'S SO BRIGHT...
WHY, YES...
IT'S A FULL MOON.
IT'S A FULL MOON...
......

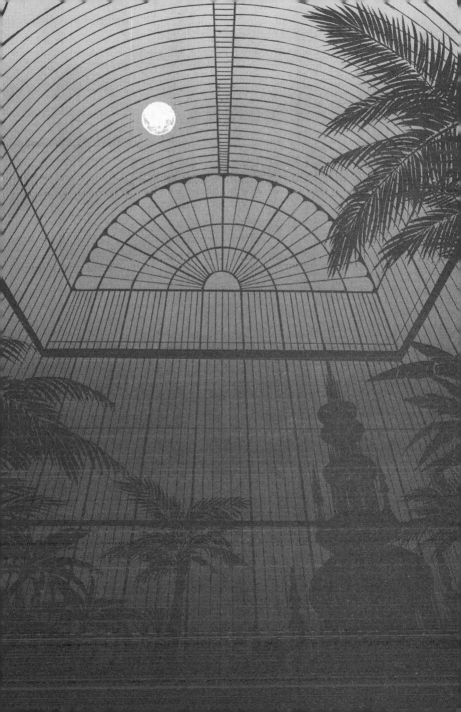

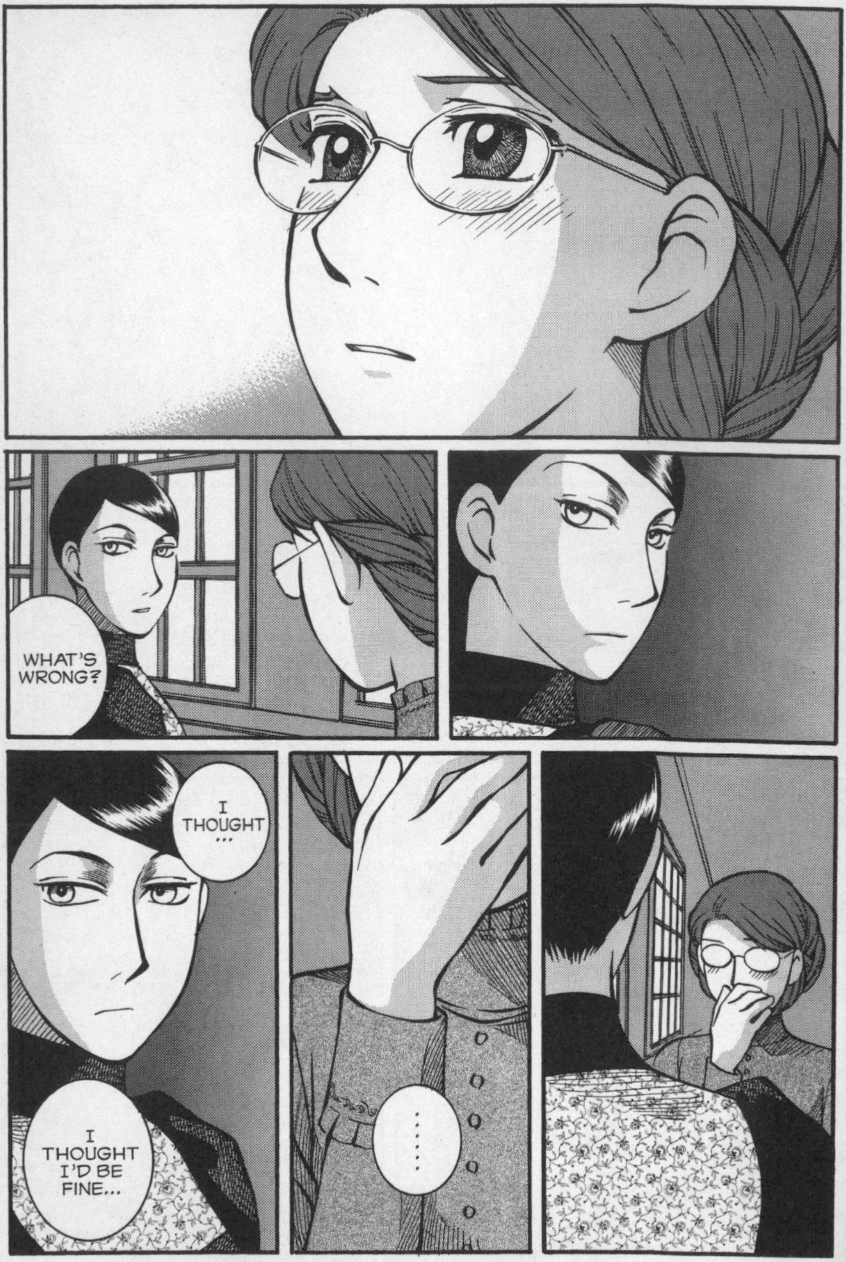
WHAT'S WRONG?
......
I THOUGHT...
I THOUGHT I'D BE FINE...

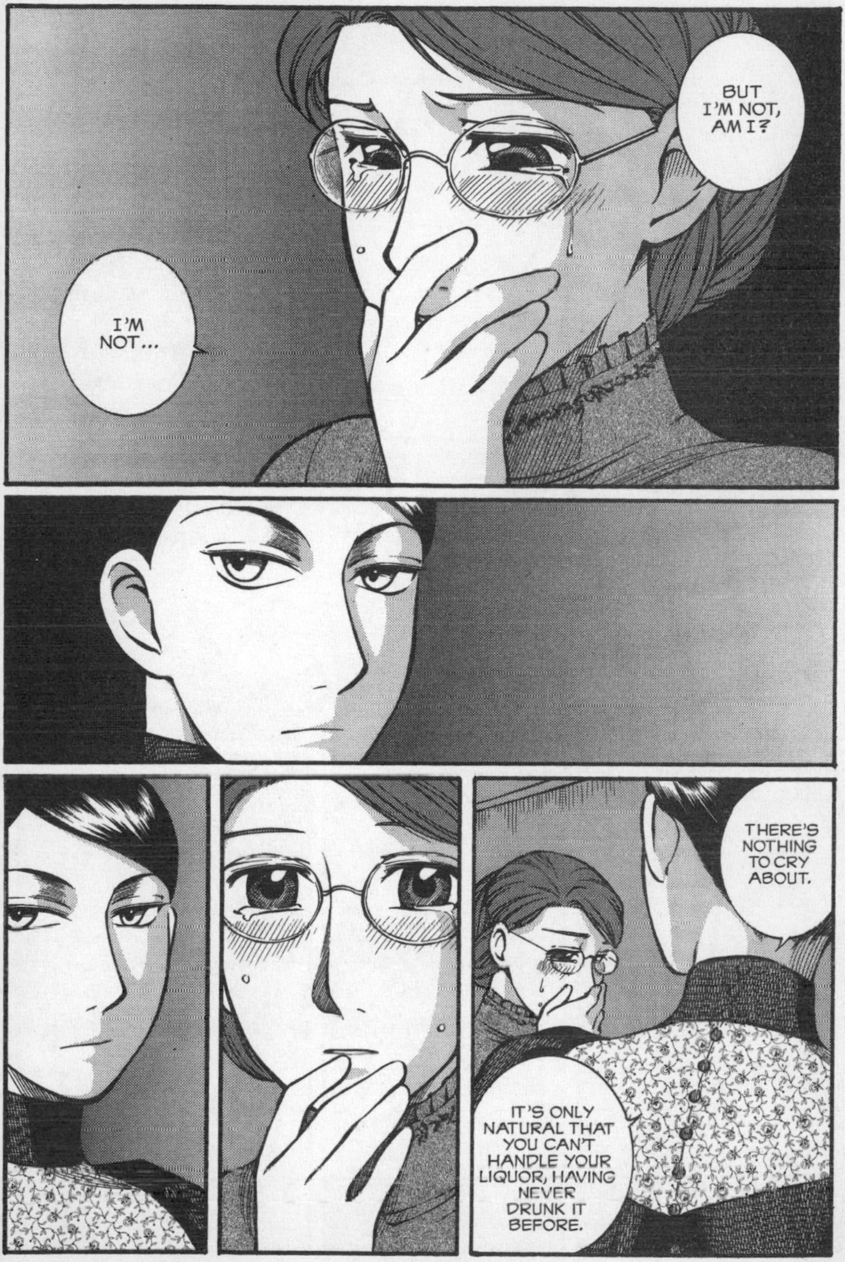
BUT I'M NOT, AM I?
I'M NOT...
THERE'S NOTHING TO CRY ABOUT.
IT'S ONLY NATURAL THAT YOU CAN'T HANDLE YOUR LIQUOR, HAVING NEVER DRUNK IT BEFORE.

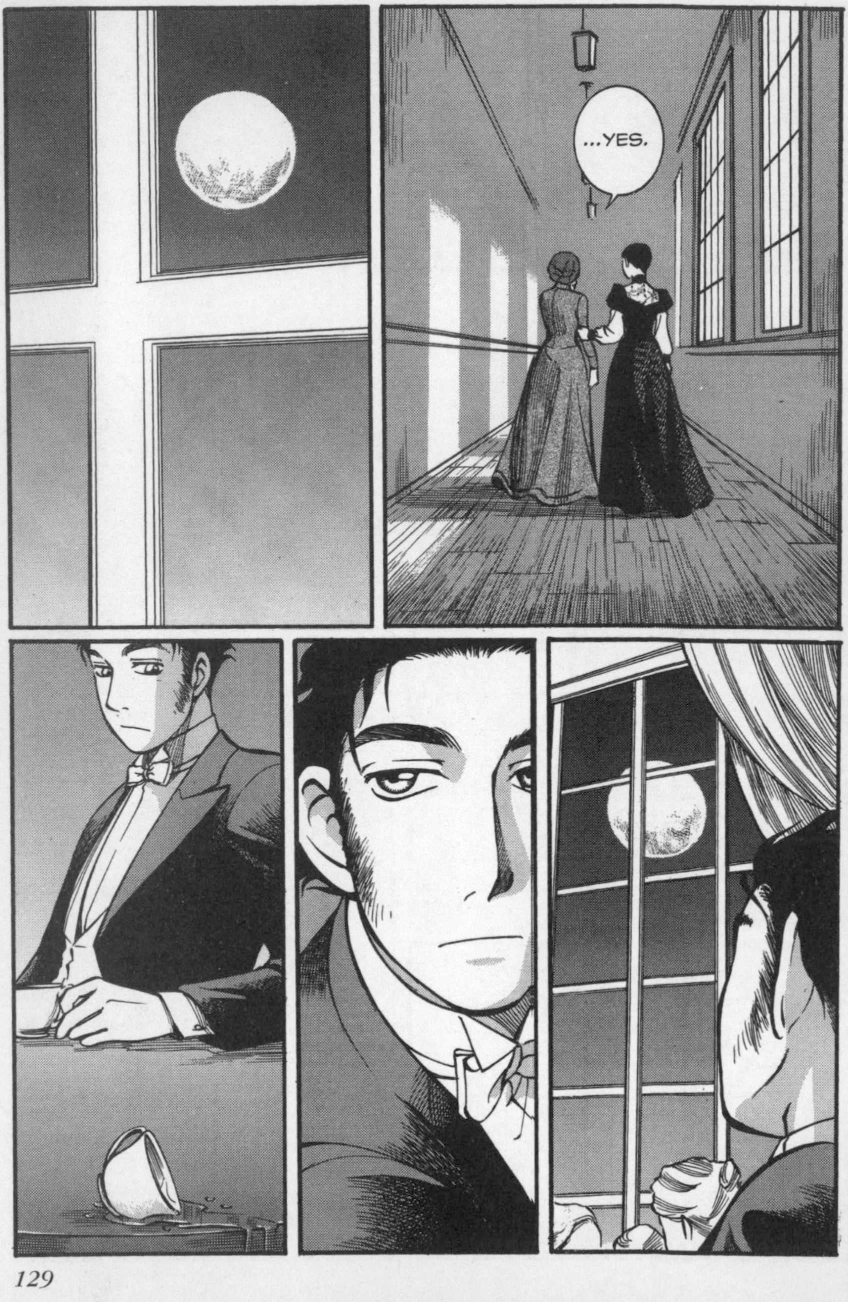
...YES.

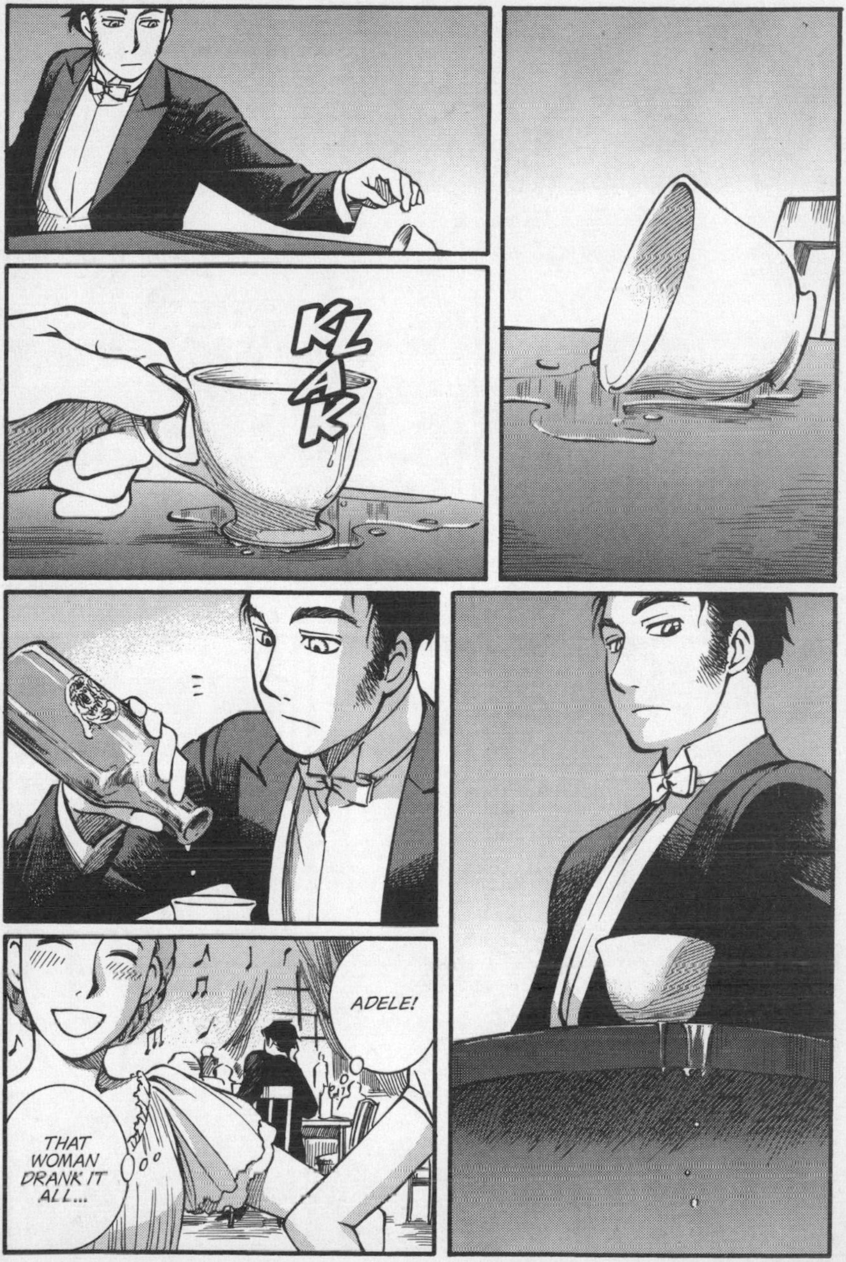
KLAK
ADELE!
THAT WOMAN DRANK IT ALL...

Chapter Nineteen: The End

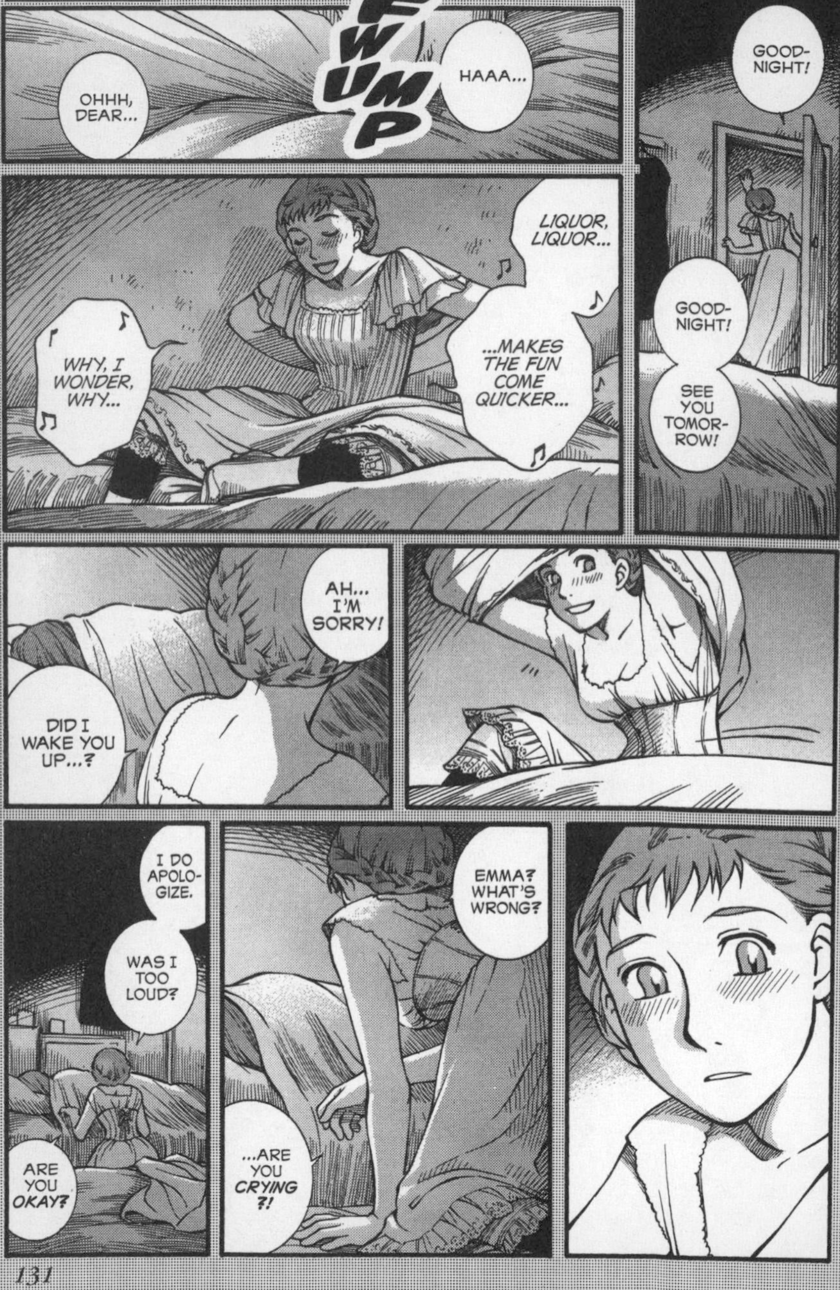
GOOD-NIGHT!
GOOD-NIGHT!
SEE YOU TOMORROW!
FWUMP
HAAA...
OHHH, DEAR...
LIQUOR, LIQUOR...
...MAKES THE FUN COME QUICKER...
WHY, I WONDER, WHY...
AH... I'M SORRY!
DID I WAKE YOU UP...?
EMMA? WHAT'S WRONG?
...ARE YOU CRYING?!
I DO APOLOGIZE.
WAS I TOO LOUD?
ARE YOU OKAY?

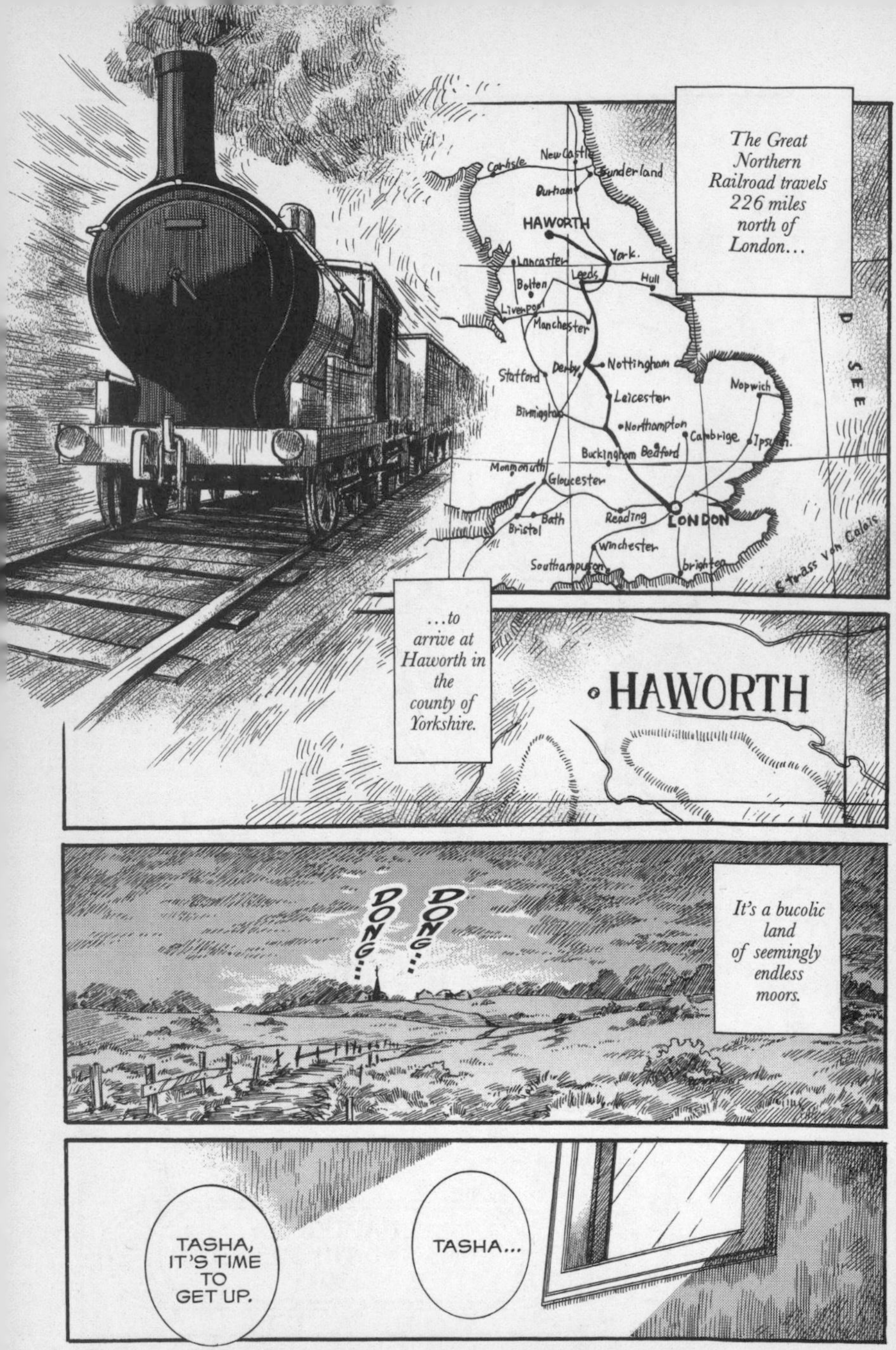
The Great Northern Railroad travels 226 miles north of London...
HAWORTH
York.
Leeds
Hull
Manchester
Liverpool
Nottingham
Leicester
Northampton
Birmingham
Gloucester
Bath
Bristol
Reading
LONDON
Winchester
...to arrive at Haworth in the county of Yorkshire.
HAWORTH
It's a bucolic land of seemingly endless moors.
DONG...
DONG...
TASHA...
TASHA, IT'S TIME TO GET UP.

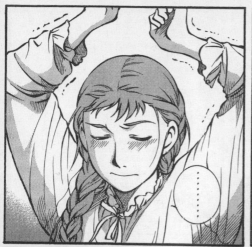

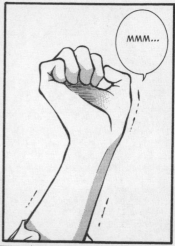

MMM...

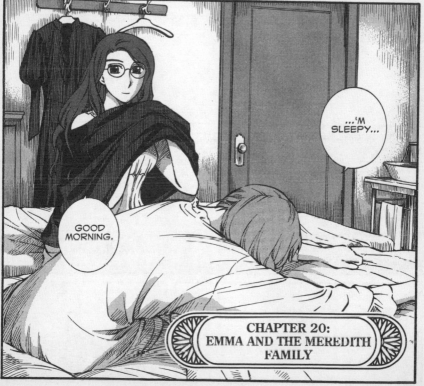

...'M SLEEPY...

GOOD MORNING.

CHAPTER 20:
EMMA AND THE MEREDITH FAMILY

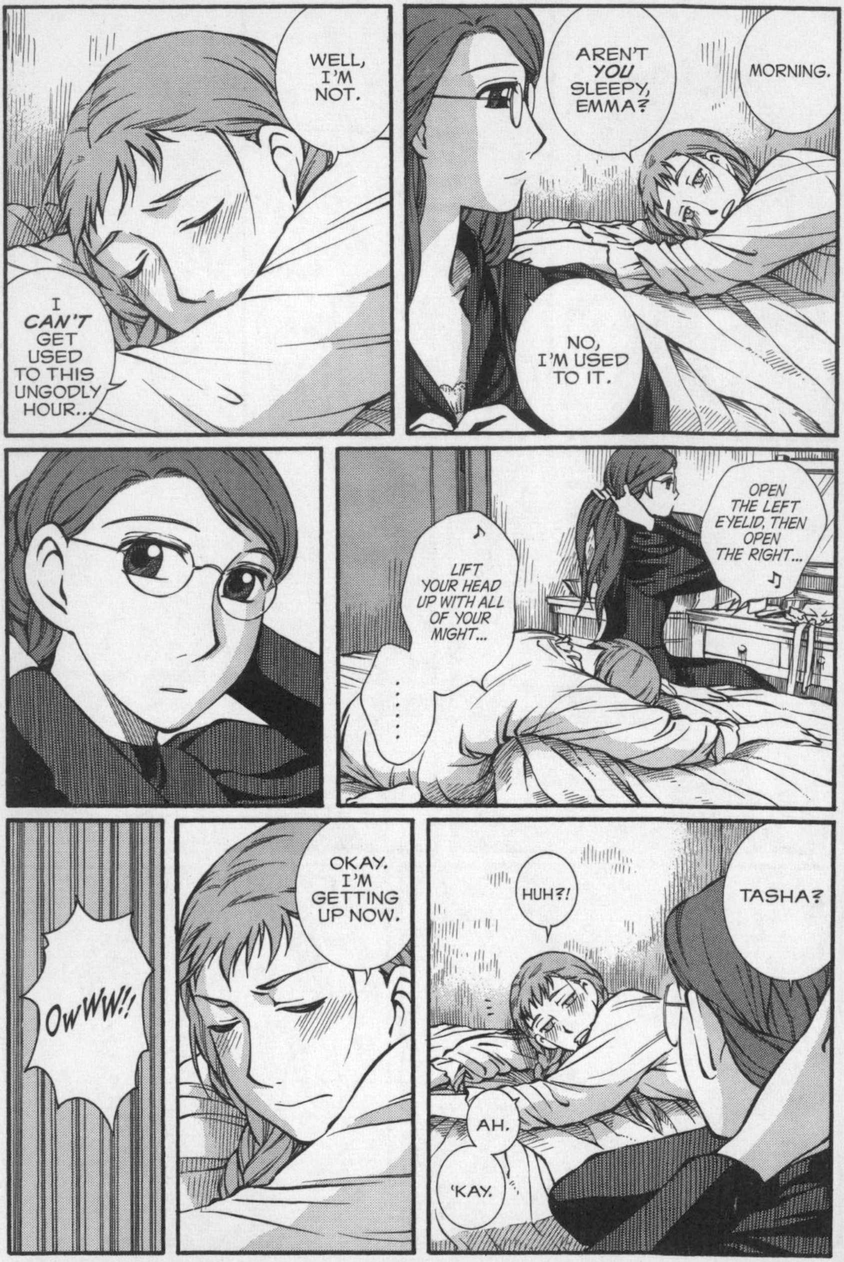

MORNING.
AREN'T *YOU* SLEEPY, EMMA?
NO, I'M USED TO IT.
WELL, I'M NOT.
I *CAN'T* GET USED TO THIS UNGODLY HOUR...
OPEN THE LEFT EYELID, THEN OPEN THE RIGHT... ♫
♪ LIFT YOUR HEAD UP WITH ALL OF YOUR MIGHT...
......
TASHA?
HUH?!
AH.
'KAY.
OKAY. I'M GETTING UP NOW.
OwWW!!

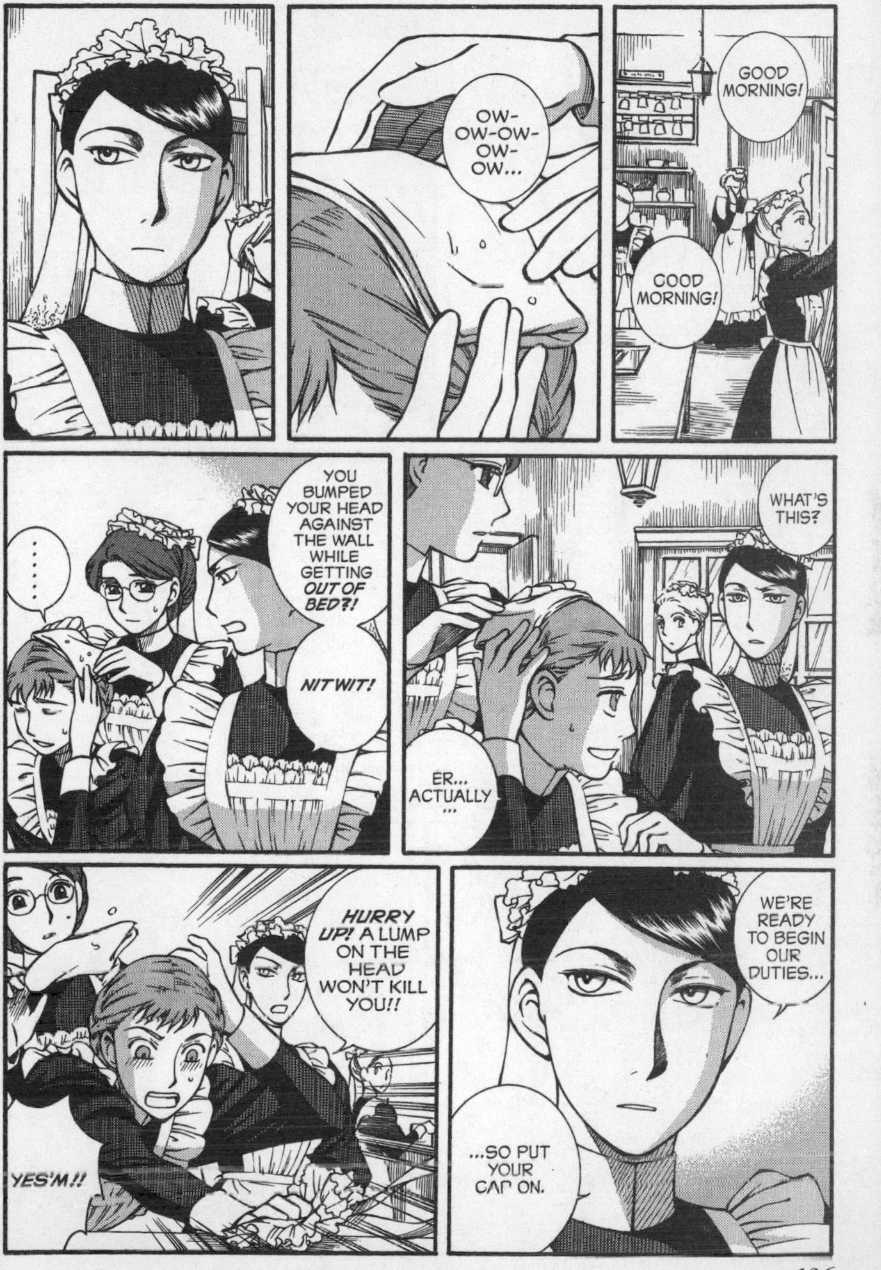
GOOD MORNING!
GOOD MORNING!
OW-OW-OW-OW-OW...
WHAT'S THIS?
ER... ACTUALLY...
YOU BUMPED YOUR HEAD AGAINST THE WALL WHILE GETTING OUT OF BED?!
NITWIT!
......
WE'RE READY TO BEGIN OUR DUTIES...
...SO PUT YOUR CAP ON.
HURRY UP! A LUMP ON THE HEAD WON'T KILL YOU!!
YES'M!!

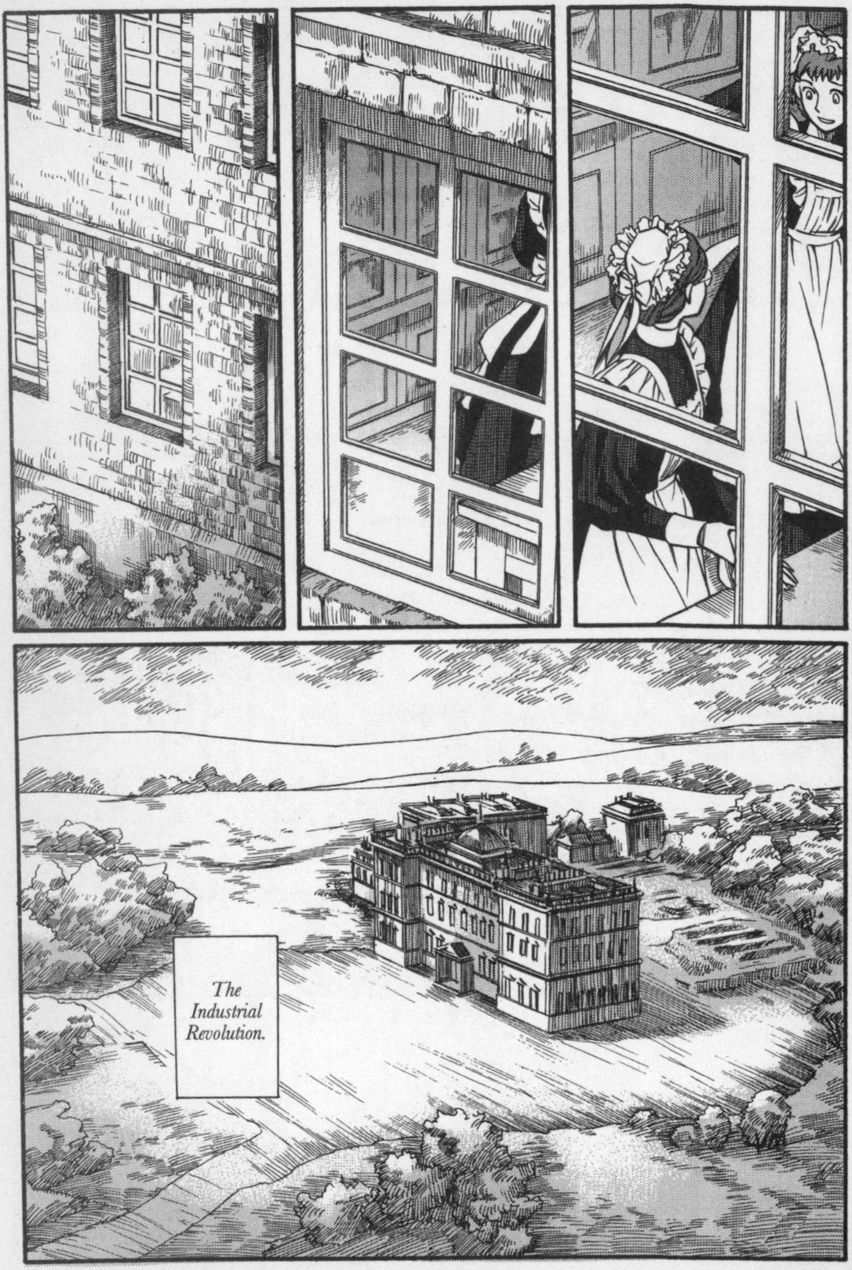
The Industrial Revolution.

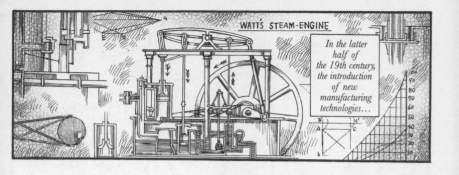

WATT'S STEAM-ENGINE
In the latter half of the 19th century, the introduction of new manufacturing technologies...

... changed **everything.**

Merchants rose to prominence.

The overall quality of life improved.

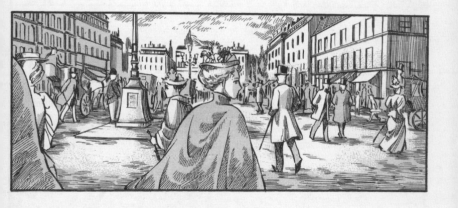

Society, economics, wisdom and customs evolved.

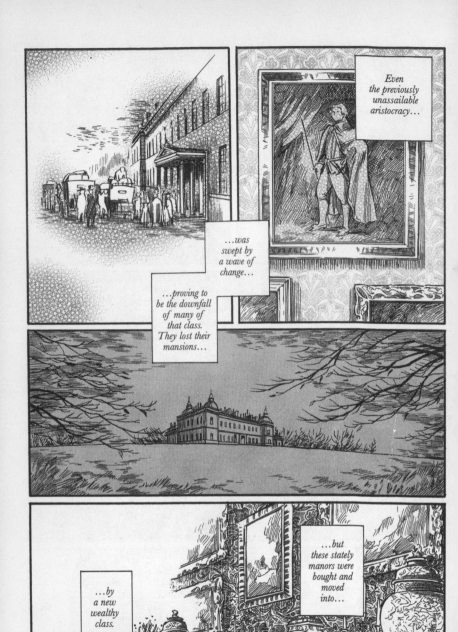

Even the previously unassailable aristocracy...

...was swept by a wave of change...

...proving to be the downfall of many of that class. They lost their mansions...

...but these stately manors were bought and moved into...

...by a new wealthy class.

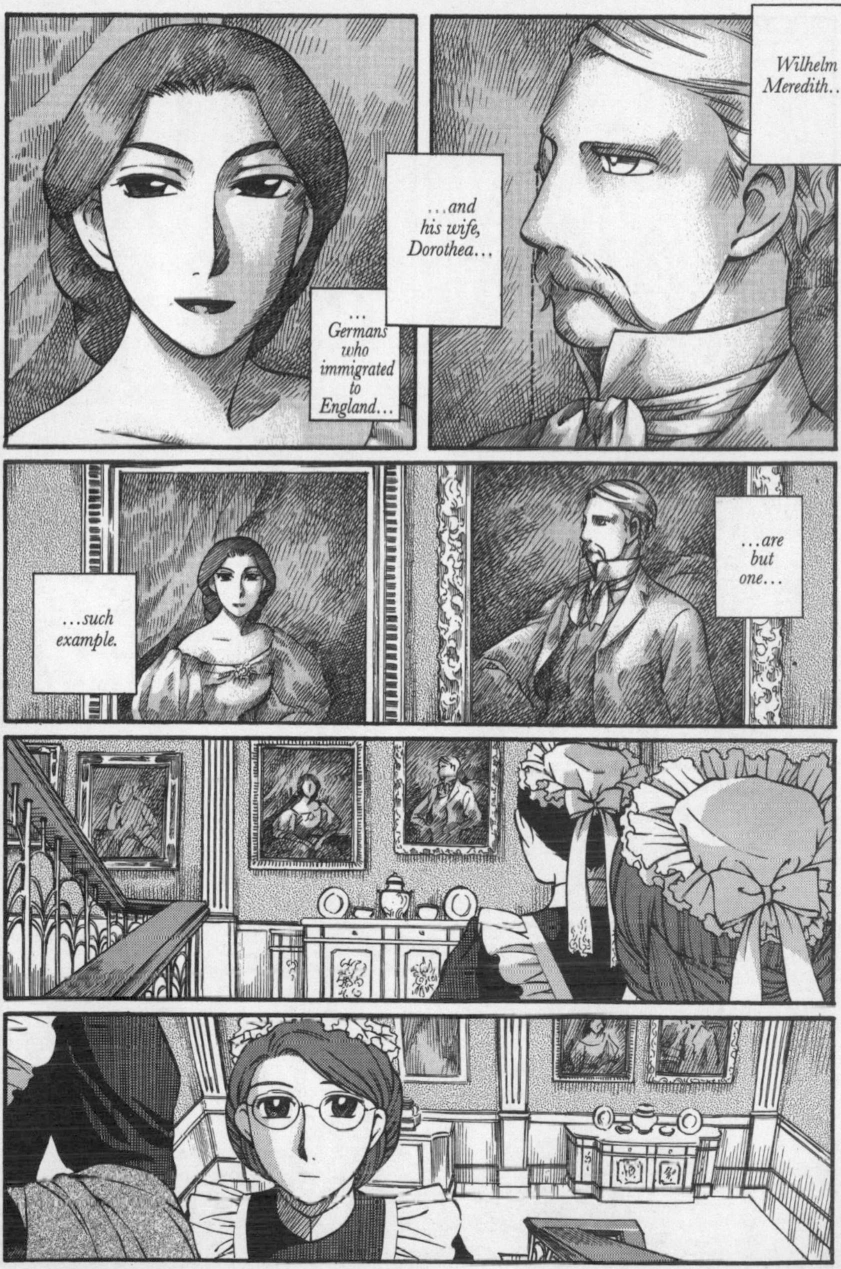
Wilhelm Meredith…
…and his wife, Dorothea…
…Germans who immigrated to England…
…are but one…
…such example.

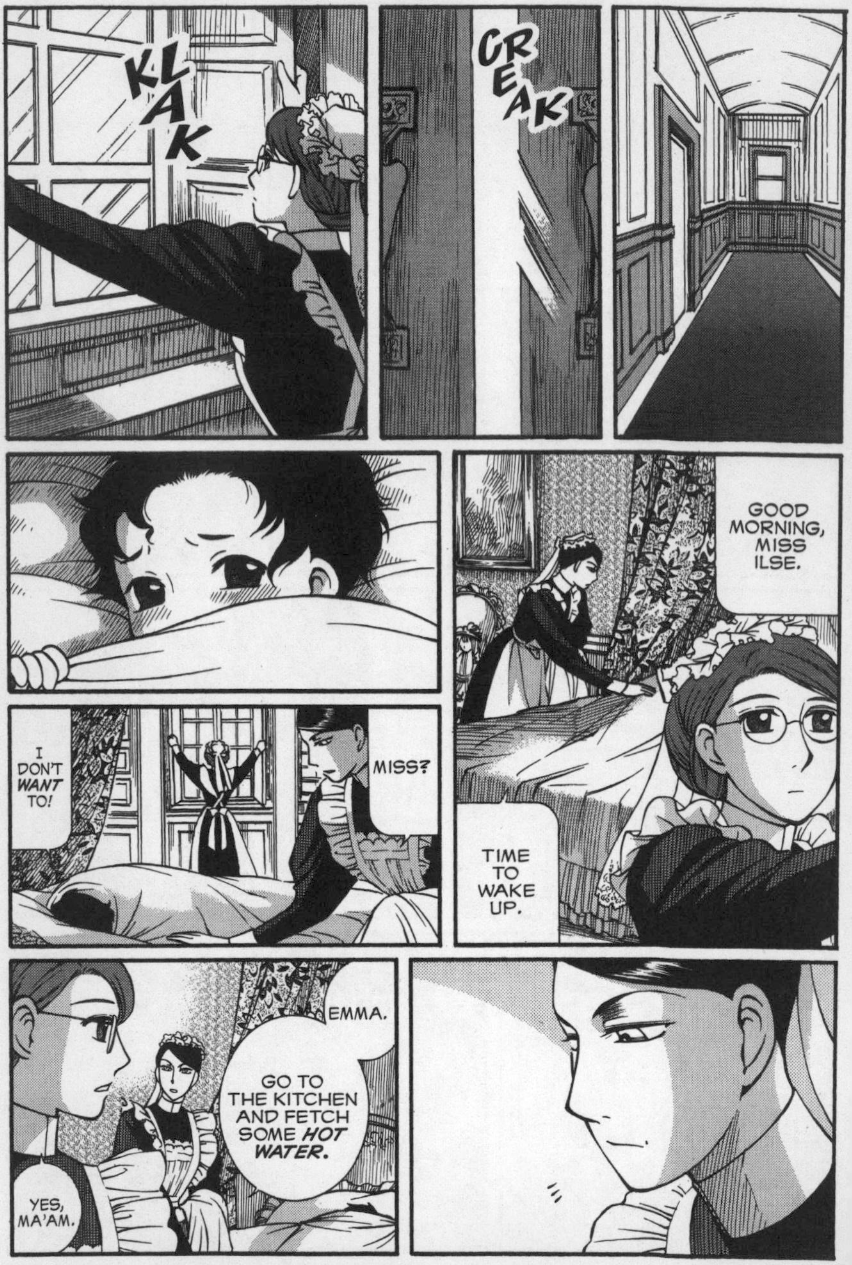
CREAK
KLAK
GOOD MORNING, MISS ILSE.
TIME TO WAKE UP.
MISS?
I DON'T *WANT* TO!
EMMA.
GO TO THE KITCHEN AND FETCH SOME *HOT WATER*.
YES, MA'AM.

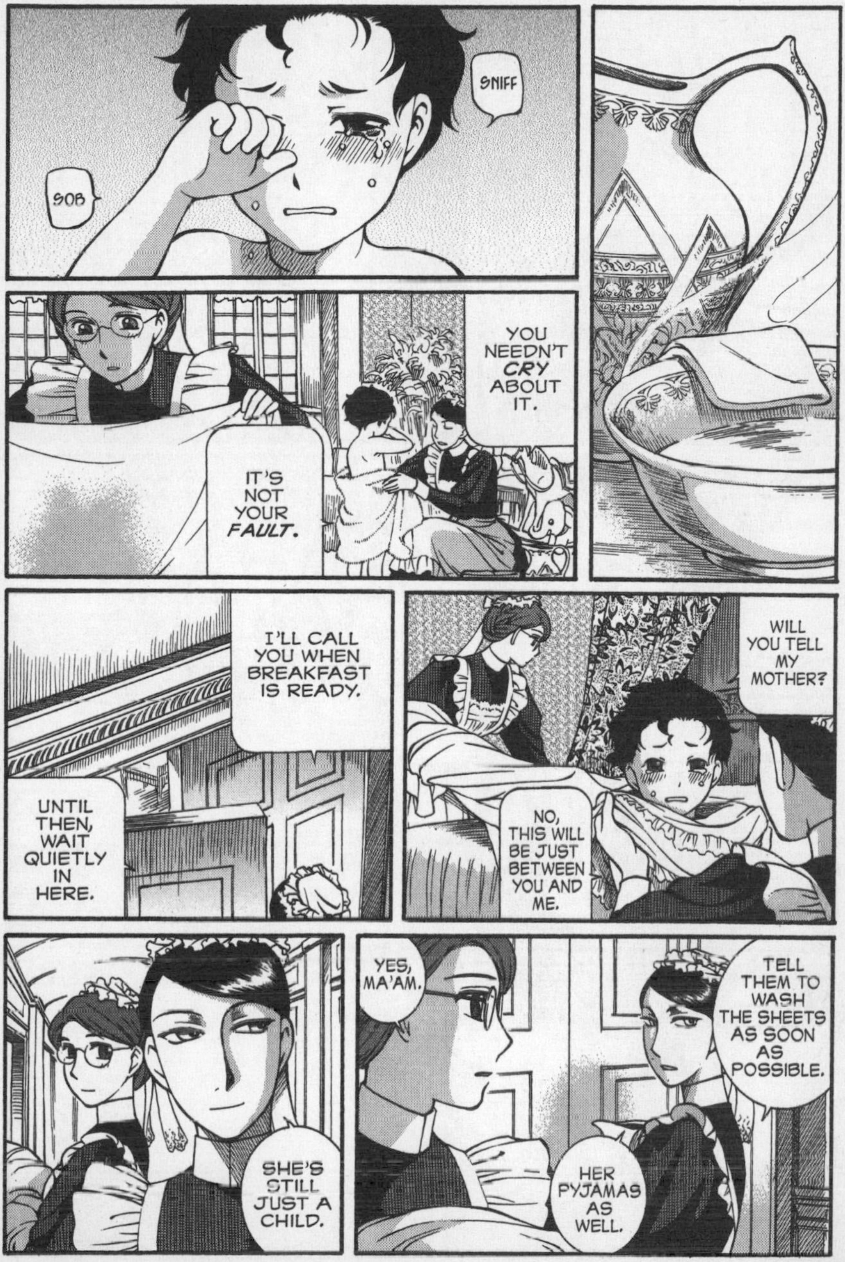
SNIFF
SOB
YOU NEEDN'T CRY ABOUT IT.
IT'S NOT YOUR FAULT.
WILL YOU TELL MY MOTHER?
NO, THIS WILL BE JUST BETWEEN YOU AND ME.
I'LL CALL YOU WHEN BREAKFAST IS READY.
UNTIL THEN, WAIT QUIETLY IN HERE.
TELL THEM TO WASH THE SHEETS AS SOON AS POSSIBLE.
YES, MA'AM.
HER PYJAMAS AS WELL.
SHE'S STILL JUST A CHILD.

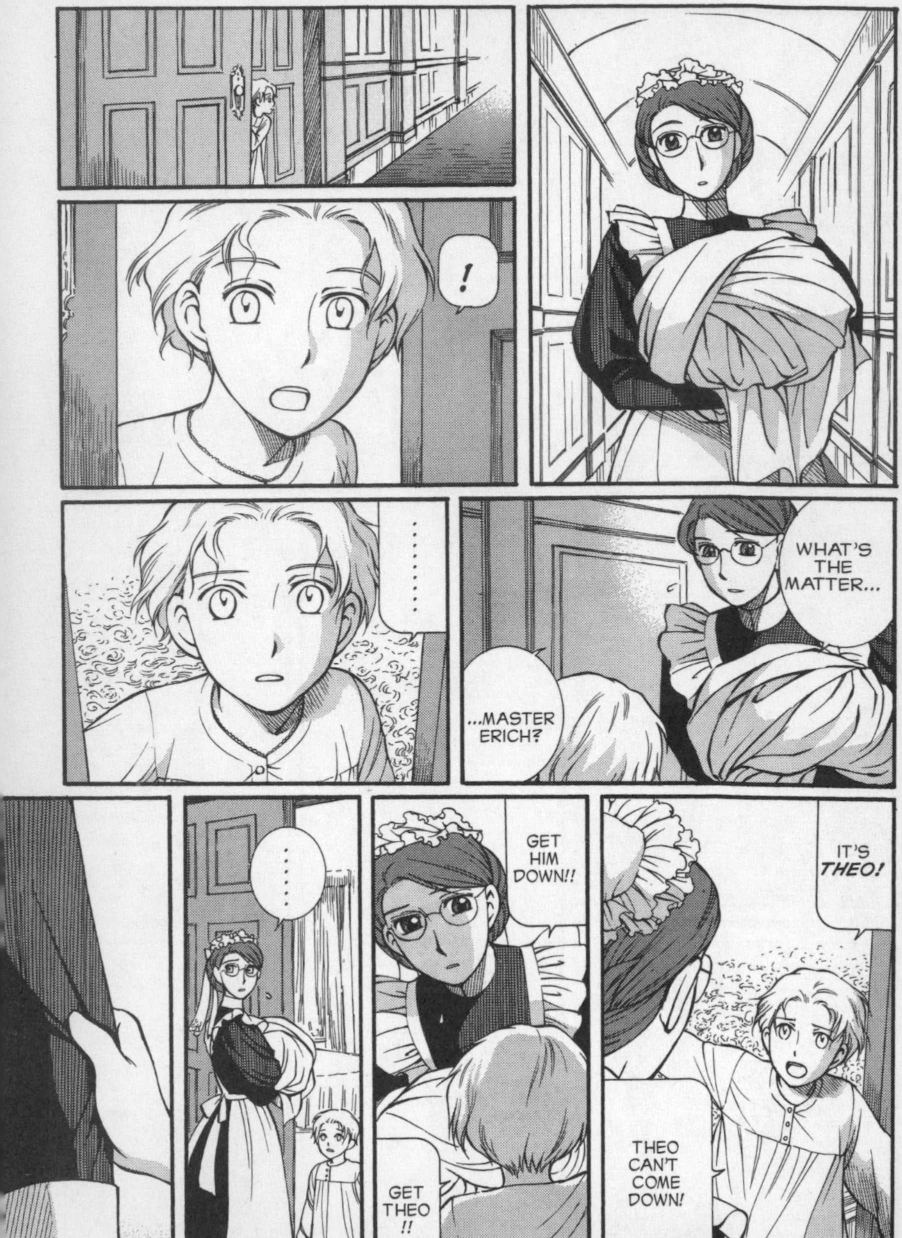
!
WHAT'S THE MATTER...
...MASTER ERICH?
......
IT'S *THEO!*
THEO CAN'T COME DOWN!
GET HIM DOWN!!
GET THEO!!
......

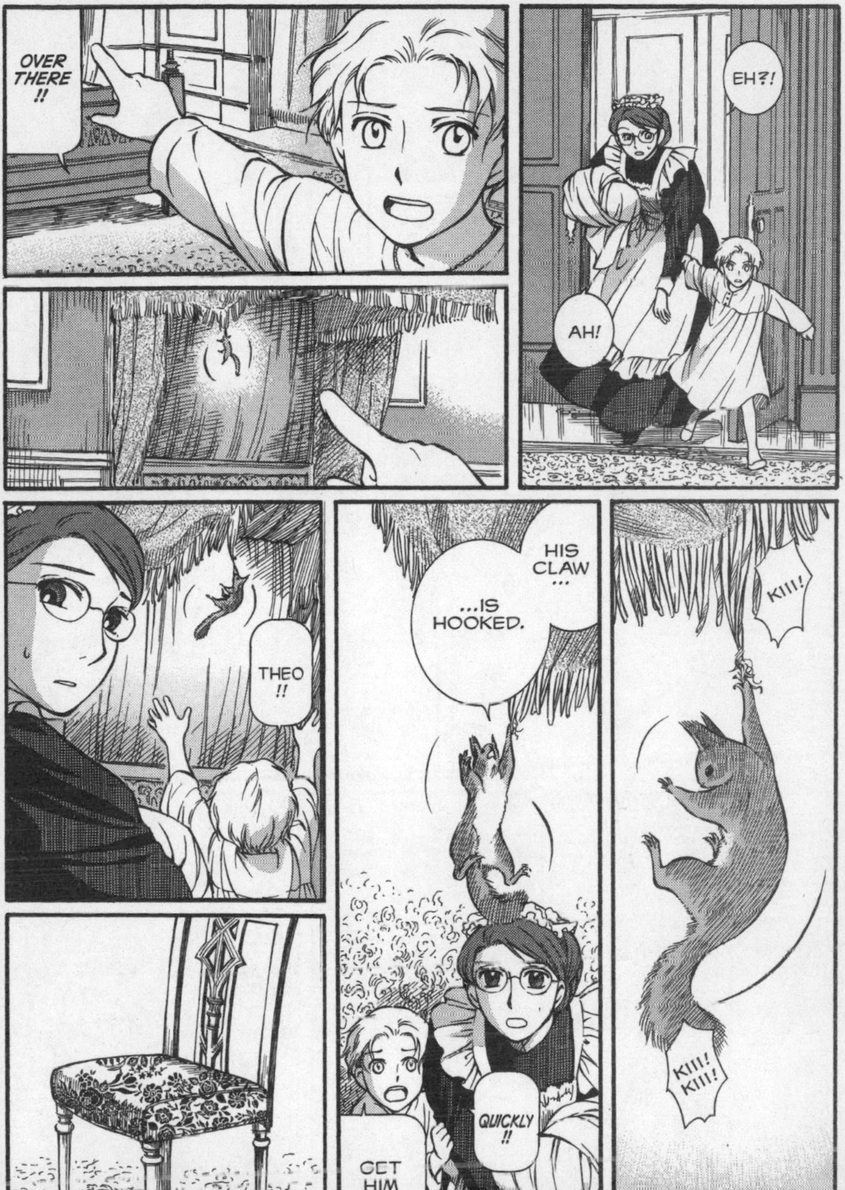
EH?!
AH!
OVER THERE !!
KIII!
KIII! KIII!
HIS CLAW ...
...IS HOOKED.
QUICKLY !!
GET HIM DOWN !!
THEO !!

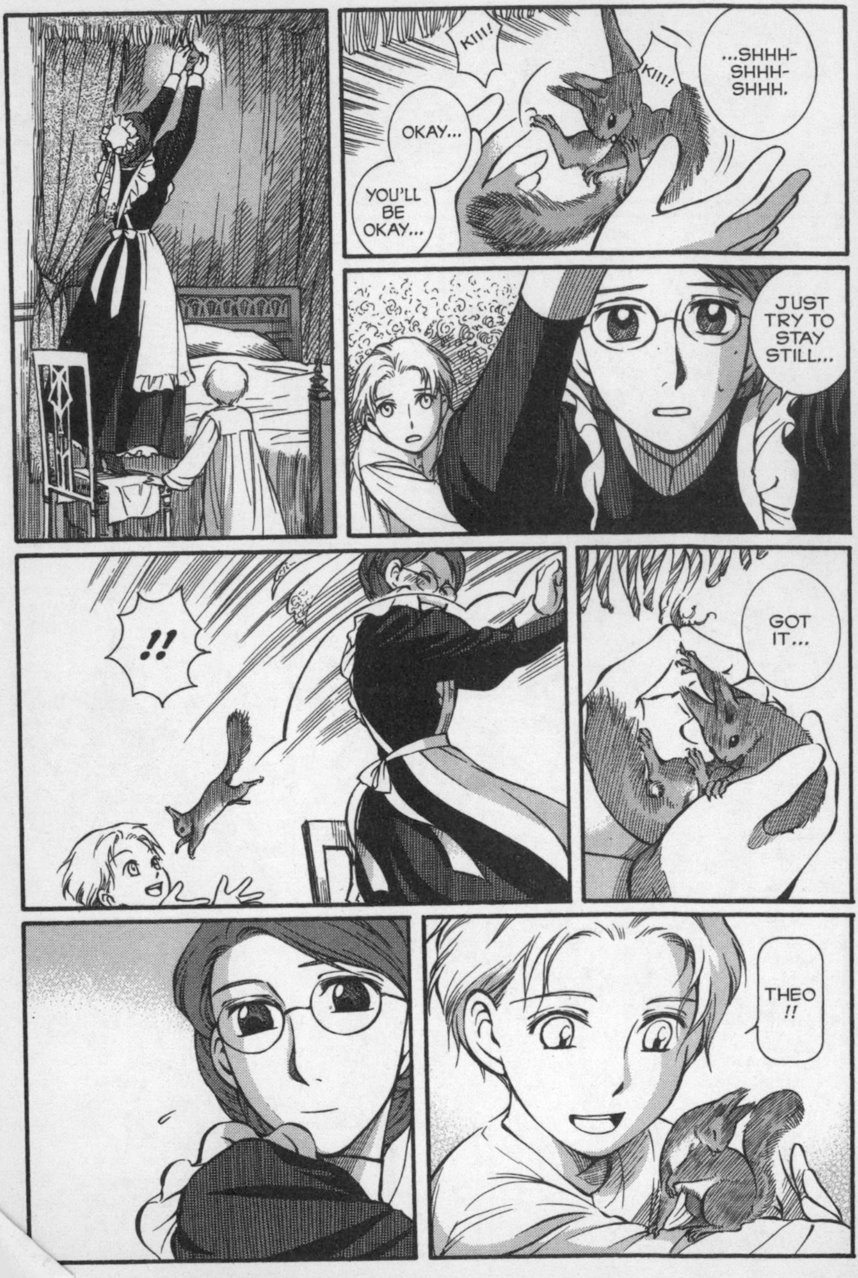
...SHHH-SHHH-SHHH.
KIII!
KIII!
OKAY...
YOU'LL BE OKAY...
JUST TRY TO STAY STILL...
GOT IT...
!!
THEO !!

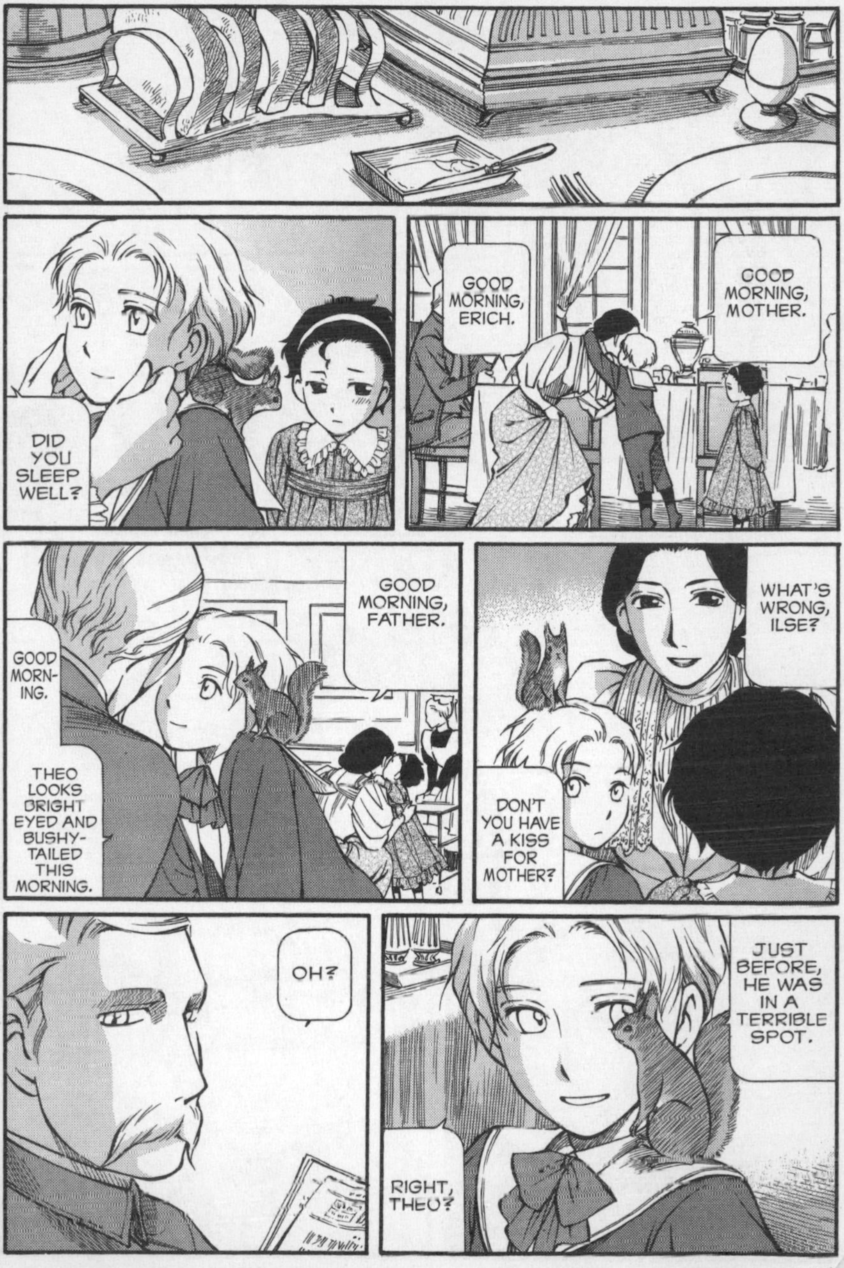
GOOD MORNING, MOTHER.
GOOD MORNING, ERICH.
DID YOU SLEEP WELL?
WHAT'S WRONG, ILSE?
DON'T YOU HAVE A KISS FOR MOTHER?
GOOD MORNING, FATHER.
GOOD MORN-ING.
THEO LOOKS BRIGHT EYED AND BUSHY-TAILED THIS MORNING.
JUST BEFORE, HE WAS IN A TERRIBLE SPOT.
RIGHT, THEO?
OH?

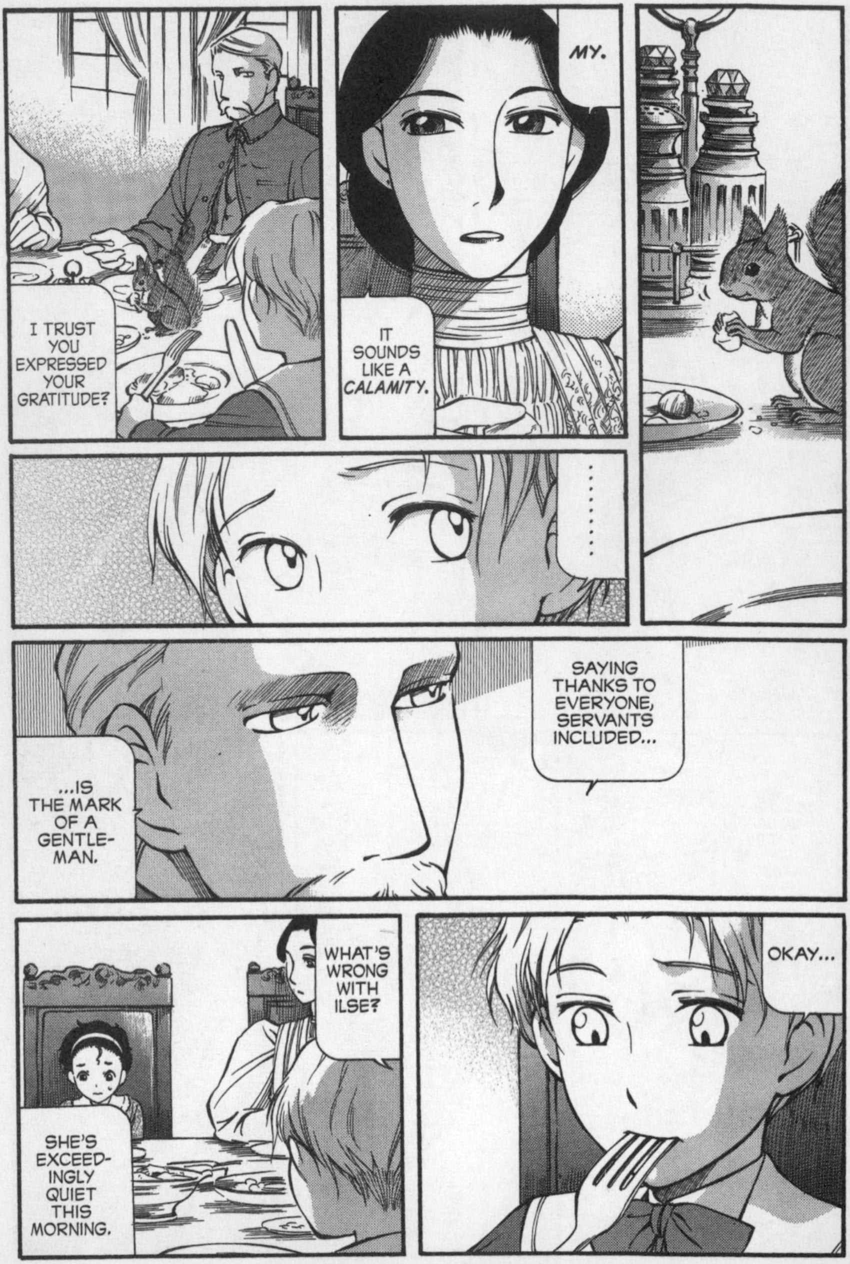
MY.
IT SOUNDS LIKE A *CALAMITY*.
I TRUST YOU EXPRESSED YOUR GRATITUDE?
......
SAYING THANKS TO EVERYONE, SERVANTS INCLUDED...
...IS THE MARK OF A GENTLE-MAN.
OKAY...
WHAT'S WRONG WITH ILSE?
SHE'S EXCEED-INGLY QUIET THIS MORNING.

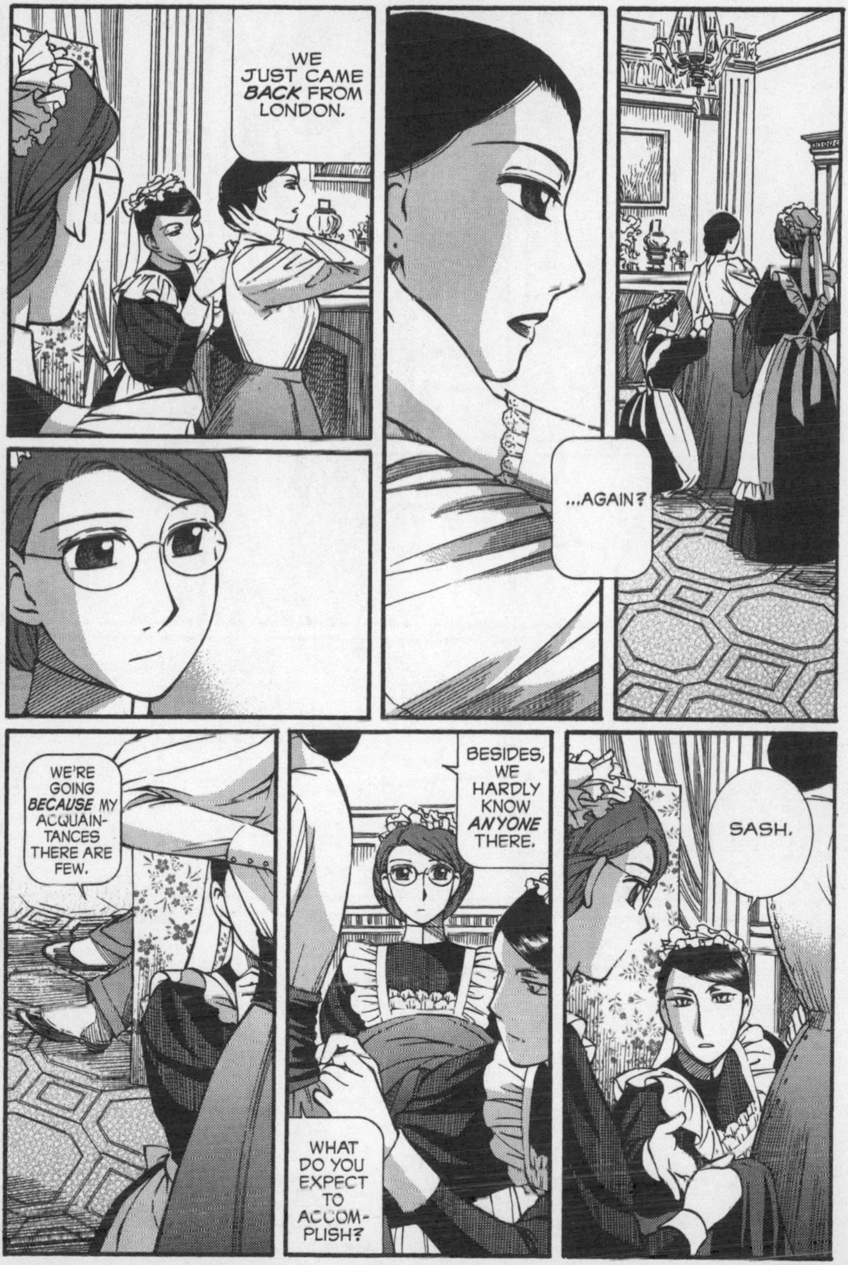
...AGAIN?
WE JUST CAME BACK FROM LONDON.
SASH.
BESIDES, WE HARDLY KNOW ANYONE THERE.
WHAT DO YOU EXPECT TO ACCOMPLISH?
WE'RE GOING BECAUSE MY ACQUAINTANCES THERE ARE FEW.

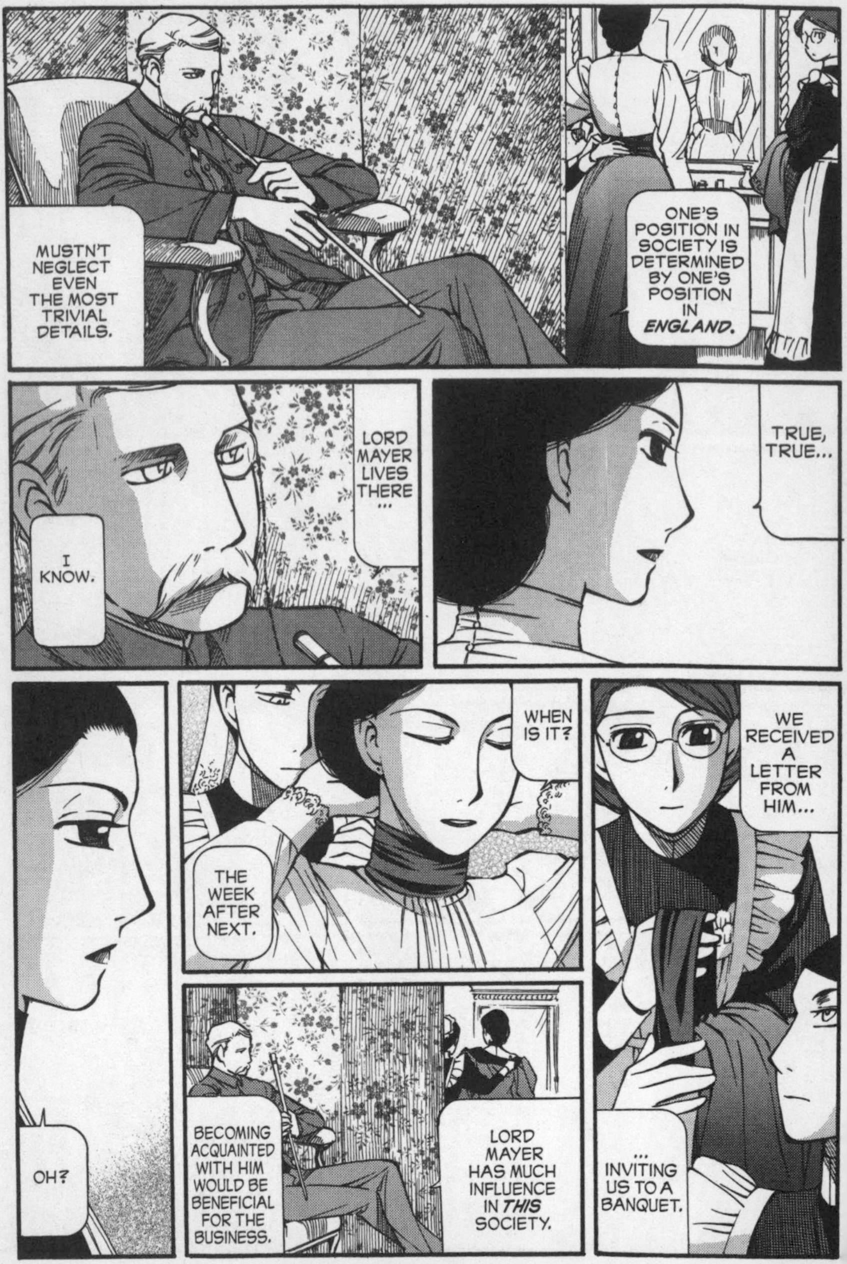
ONE'S POSITION IN SOCIETY IS DETERMINED BY ONE'S POSITION IN *ENGLAND*.
MUSTN'T NEGLECT EVEN THE MOST TRIVIAL DETAILS.
TRUE, TRUE...
LORD MAYER LIVES THERE...
I KNOW.
WE RECEIVED A LETTER FROM HIM...
...INVITING US TO A BANQUET.
WHEN IS IT?
THE WEEK AFTER NEXT.
LORD MAYER HAS MUCH INFLUENCE IN *THIS* SOCIETY.
BECOMING ACQUAINTED WITH HIM WOULD BE BENEFICIAL FOR THE BUSINESS.
OH?

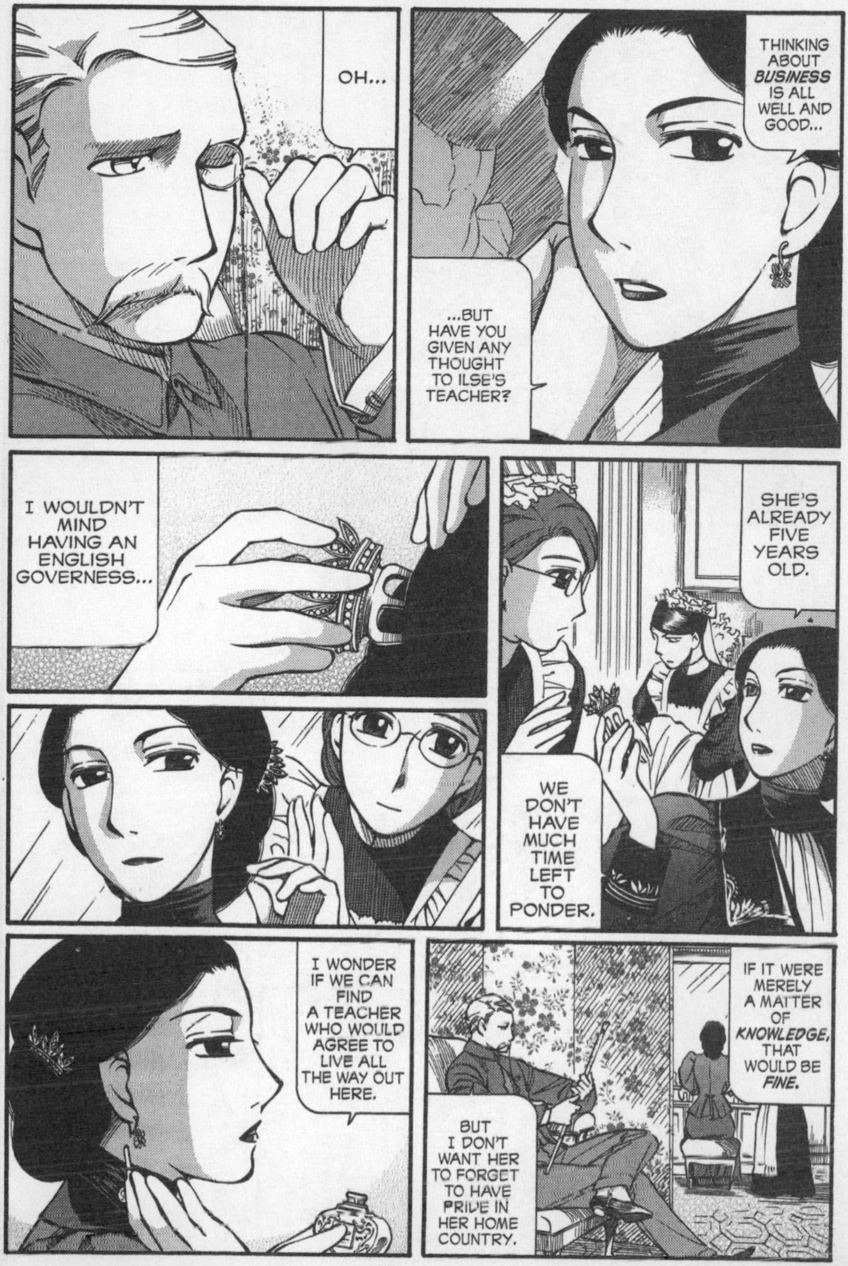
THINKING ABOUT BUSINESS IS ALL WELL AND GOOD...
...BUT HAVE YOU GIVEN ANY THOUGHT TO ILSE'S TEACHER?
OH...
SHE'S ALREADY FIVE YEARS OLD.
WE DON'T HAVE MUCH TIME LEFT TO PONDER.
I WOULDN'T MIND HAVING AN ENGLISH GOVERNESS...
IF IT WERE MERELY A MATTER OF KNOWLEDGE, THAT WOULD BE FINE.
BUT I DON'T WANT HER TO FORGET TO HAVE PRIDE IN HER HOME COUNTRY.
I WONDER IF WE CAN FIND A TEACHER WHO WOULD AGREE TO LIVE ALL THE WAY OUT HERE.

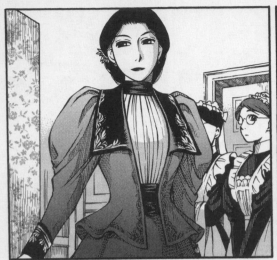
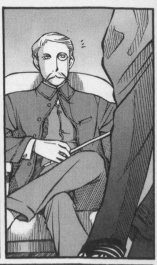
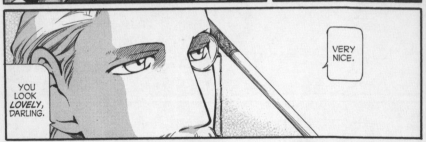

VERY NICE.

YOU LOOK *LOVELY,* DARLING.

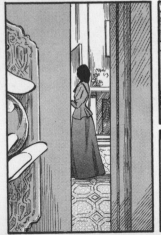
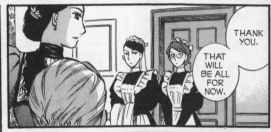

THANK YOU.

THAT WILL BE ALL FOR NOW.

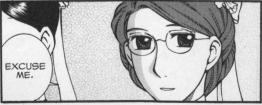

EXCUSE ME.

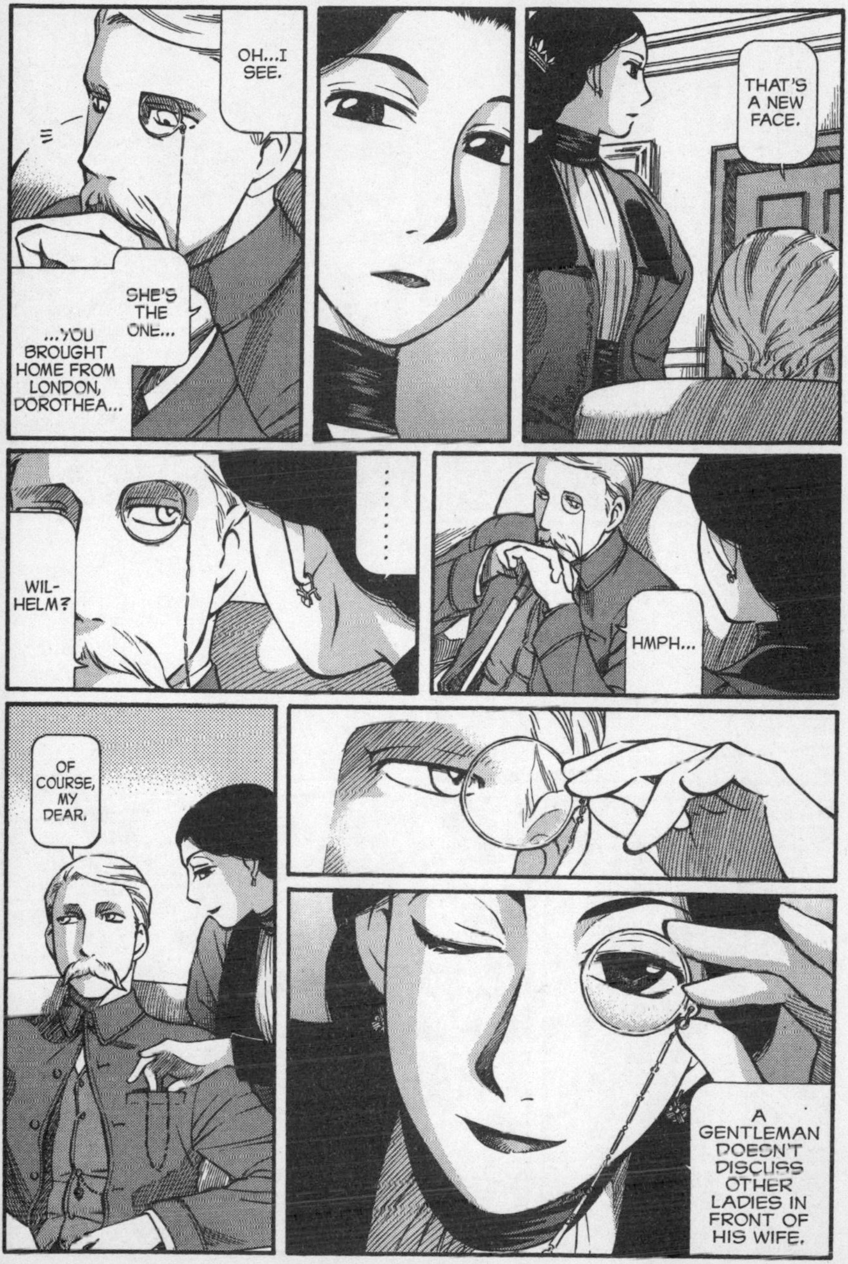
THAT'S A NEW FACE.
OH...I SEE.
SHE'S THE ONE...
...YOU BROUGHT HOME FROM LONDON, DOROTHEA...
HMPH...
......
WIL-HELM?
A GENTLEMAN DOESN'T DISCUSS OTHER LADIES IN FRONT OF HIS WIFE.
OF COURSE, MY DEAR.

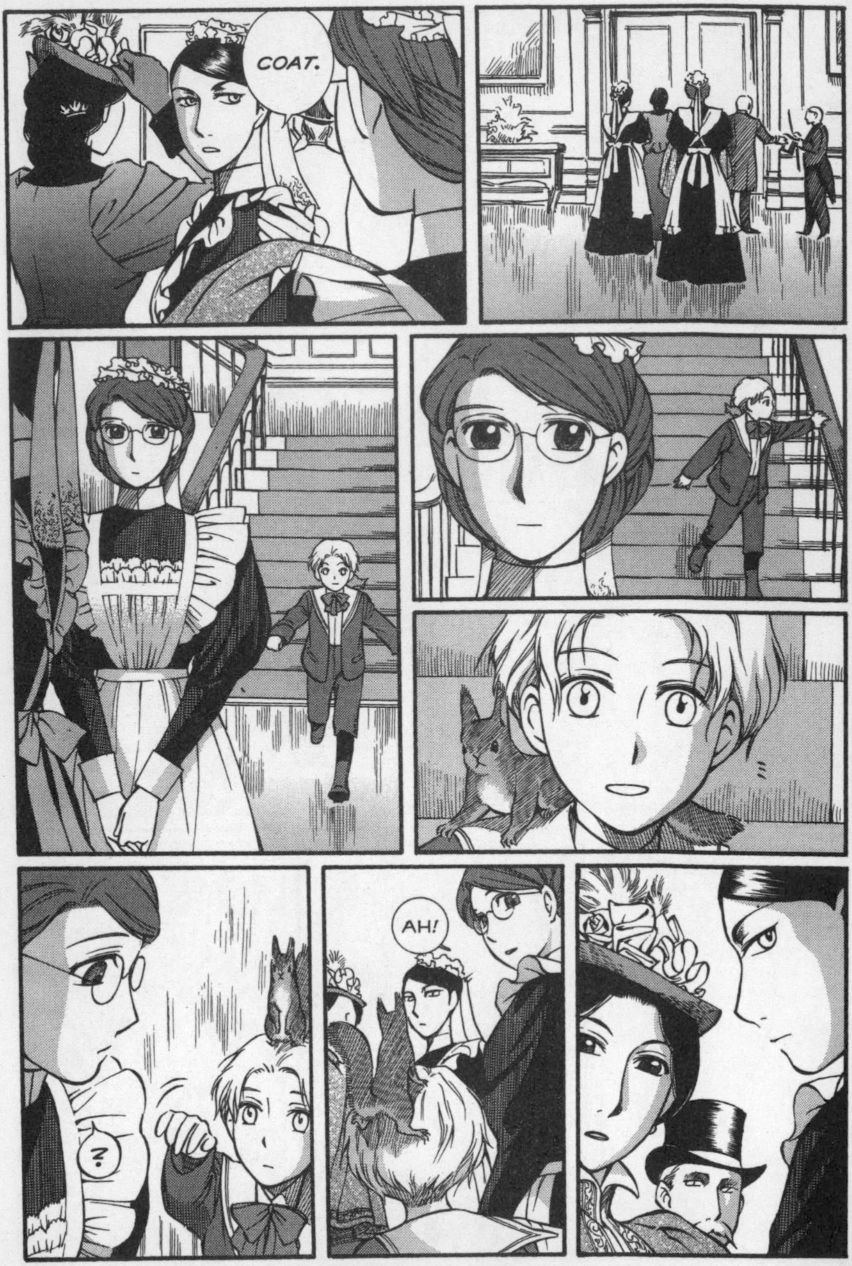
COAT.
AH!
?

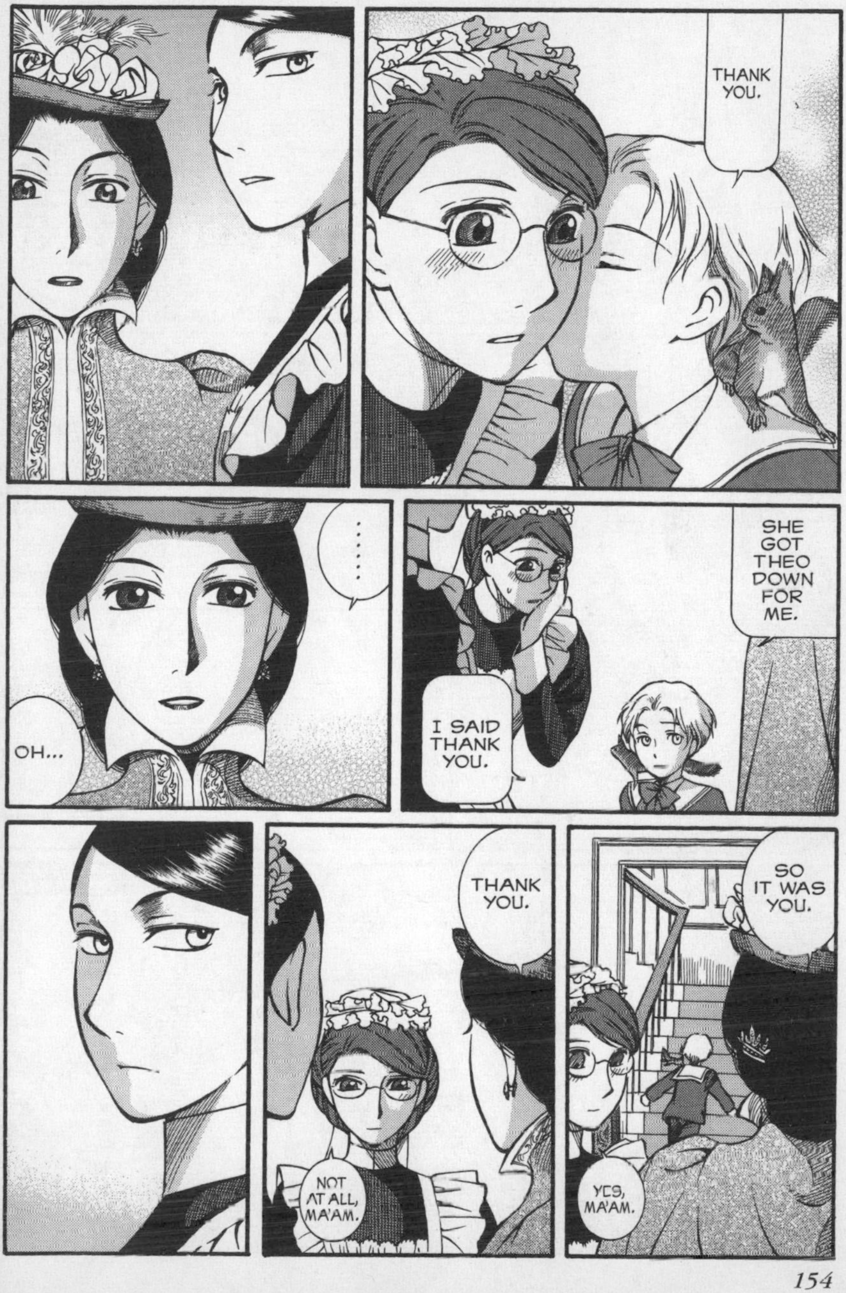
THANK YOU.
SHE GOT THEO DOWN FOR ME.
I SAID THANK YOU.
......
OH...
SO IT WAS YOU.
YES, MA'AM.
THANK YOU.
NOT AT ALL, MA'AM.

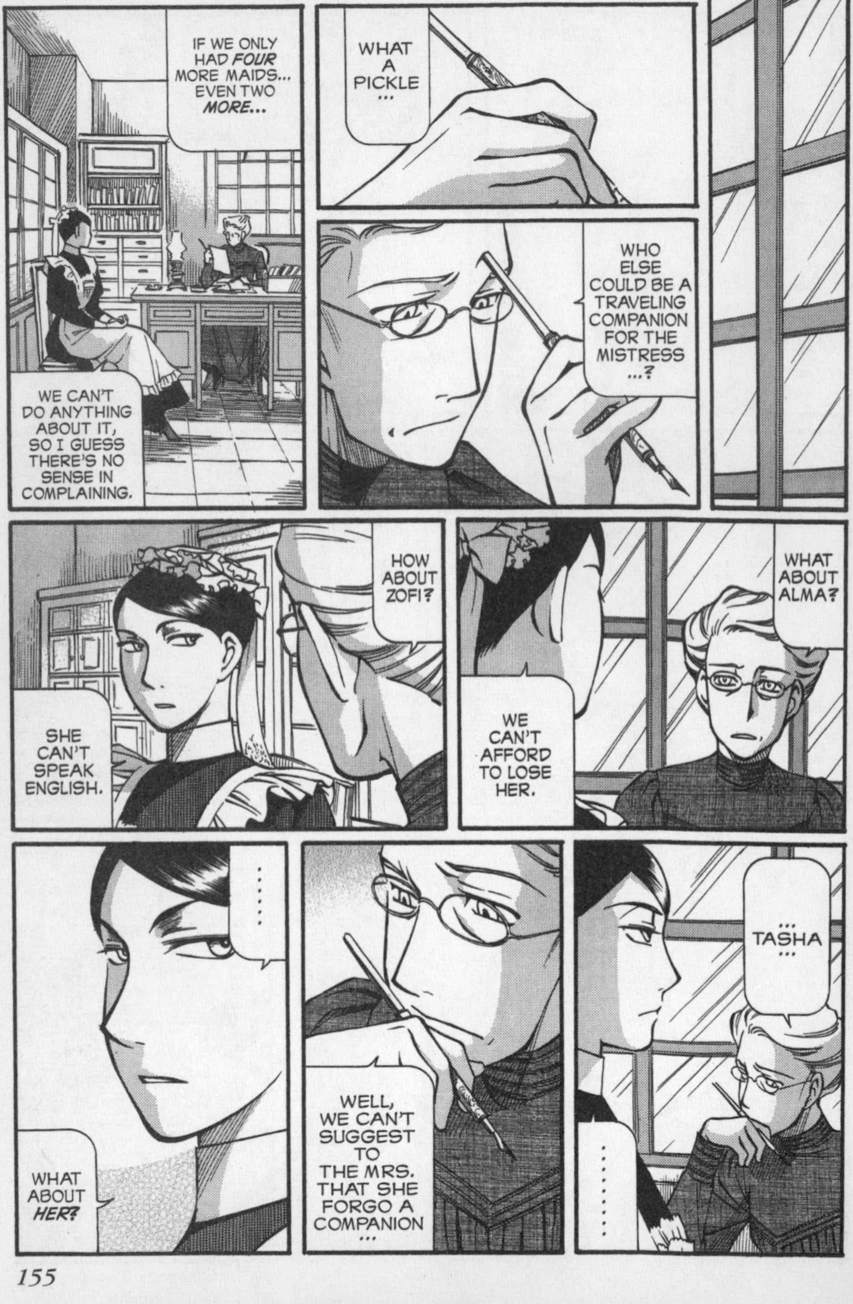
WHAT A PICKLE...
WHO ELSE COULD BE A TRAVELING COMPANION FOR THE MISTRESS...?
IF WE ONLY HAD *FOUR* MORE MAIDS... EVEN TWO *MORE...*
WE CAN'T DO ANYTHING ABOUT IT, SO I GUESS THERE'S NO SENSE IN COMPLAINING.
WHAT ABOUT ALMA?
WE CAN'T AFFORD TO LOSE HER.
HOW ABOUT ZOFI?
SHE CAN'T SPEAK ENGLISH.
...TASHA...
......
WELL, WE CAN'T SUGGEST TO THE MRS. THAT SHE FORGO A COMPANION...
......
WHAT ABOUT *HER?*

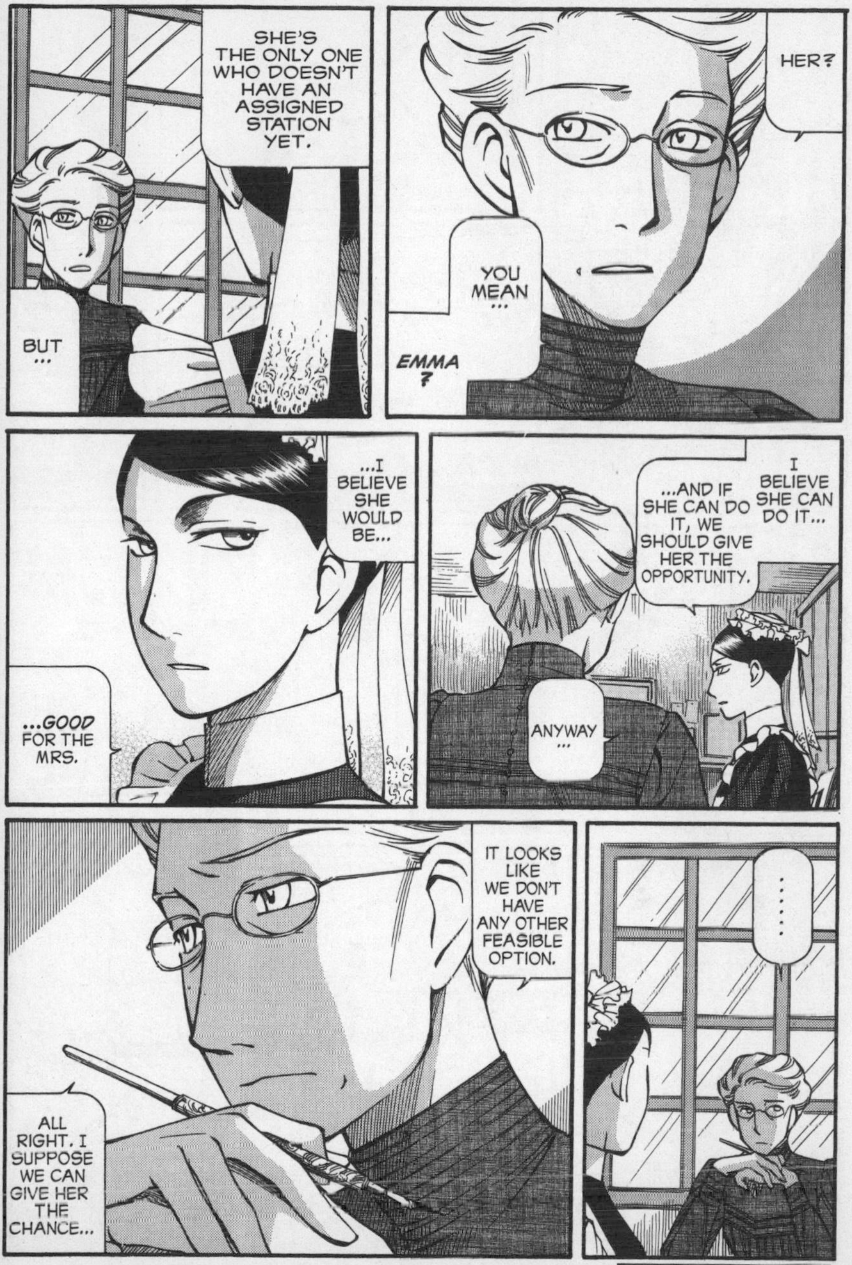
HER?
YOU MEAN...
EMMA?
SHE'S THE ONLY ONE WHO DOESN'T HAVE AN ASSIGNED STATION YET.
BUT...
I BELIEVE SHE CAN DO IT...
...AND IF SHE CAN DO IT, WE SHOULD GIVE HER THE OPPORTUNITY.
ANYWAY...
...I BELIEVE SHE WOULD BE...
...GOOD FOR THE MRS.
......
IT LOOKS LIKE WE DON'T HAVE ANY OTHER FEASIBLE OPTION.
ALL RIGHT. I SUPPOSE WE CAN GIVE HER THE CHANCE...

Chapter Twenty: The End

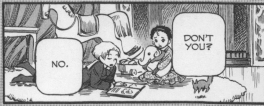

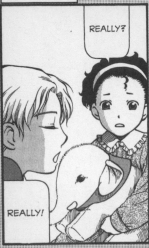

REALLY?

REALLY!

NO.

DON'T YOU?

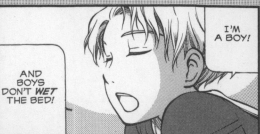

I'M A BOY!

AND BOYS DON'T *WET* THE BED!

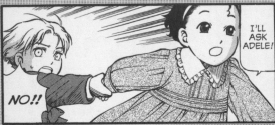

I'LL ASK ADELE!

NO!!

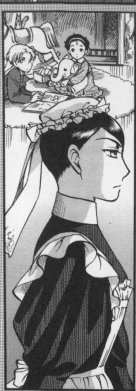

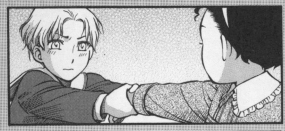

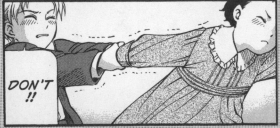

DON'T !!

157

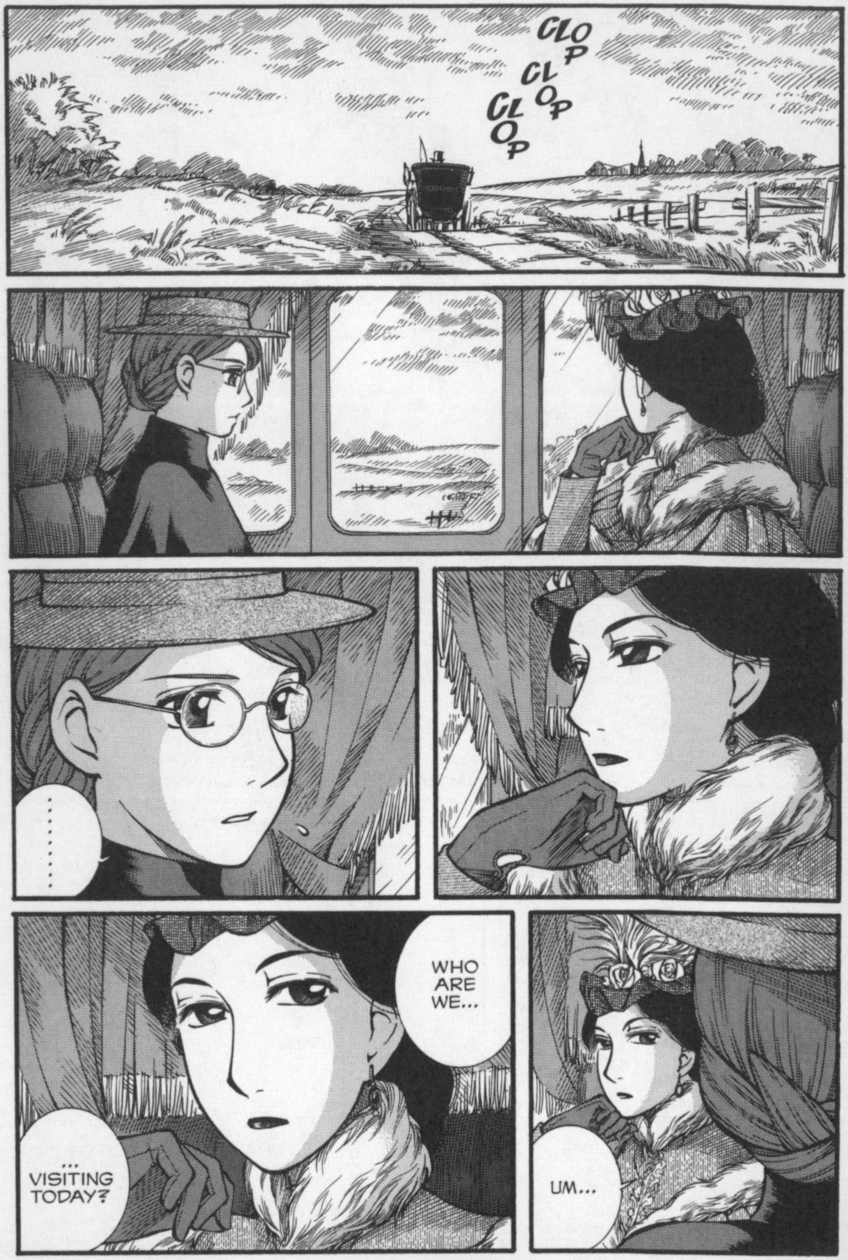
CLOP
CLOP
CLOP
......
UM...
WHO ARE WE...
...VISITING TODAY?

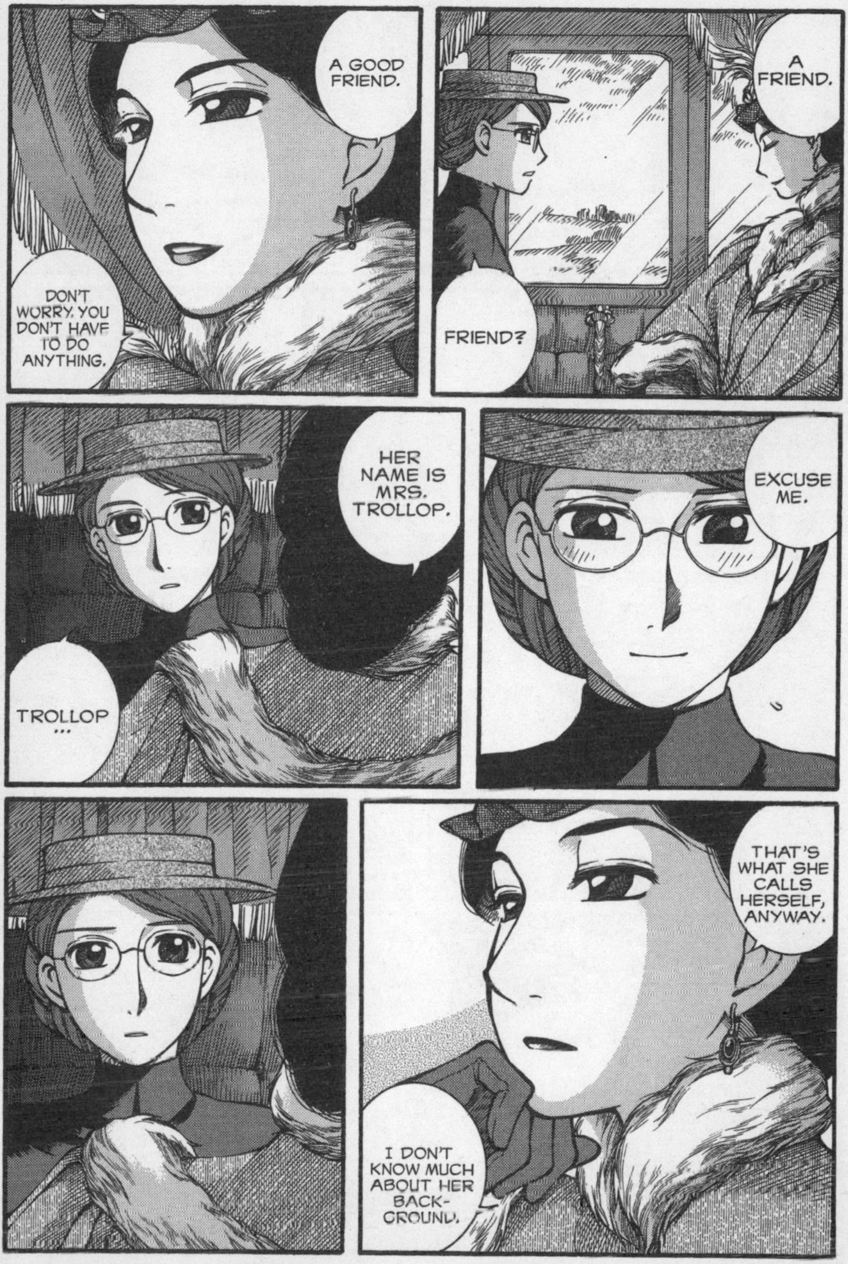
A FRIEND.
FRIEND?
A GOOD FRIEND.
DON'T WORRY. YOU DON'T HAVE TO DO ANYTHING.
EXCUSE ME.
HER NAME IS MRS. TROLLOP.
TROLLOP...
THAT'S WHAT SHE CALLS HERSELF, ANYWAY.
I DON'T KNOW MUCH ABOUT HER BACK-GROUND.

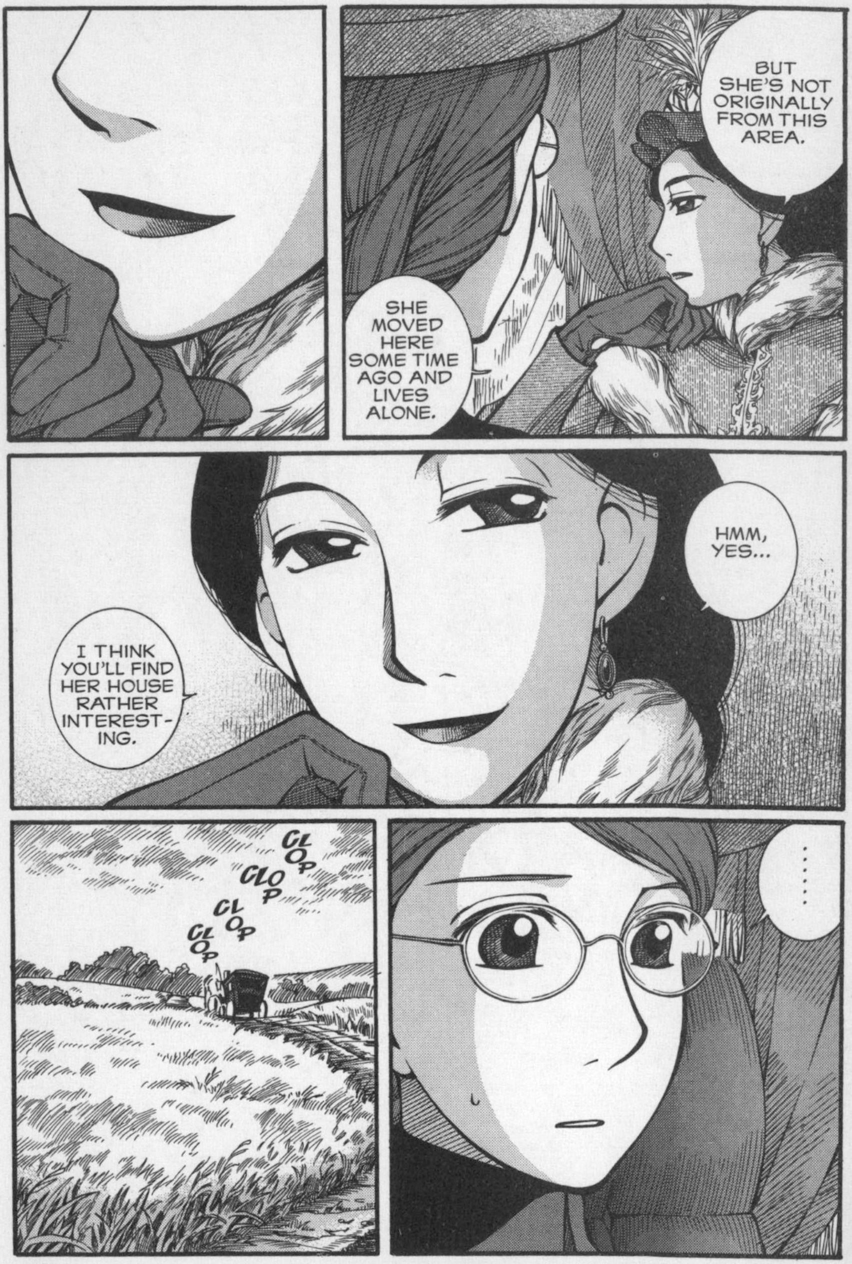
BUT SHE'S NOT ORIGINALLY FROM THIS AREA.
SHE MOVED HERE SOME TIME AGO AND LIVES ALONE.
HMM, YES...
I THINK YOU'LL FIND HER HOUSE RATHER INTEREST-ING.
......
CLOP CLOP CLOP CLOP

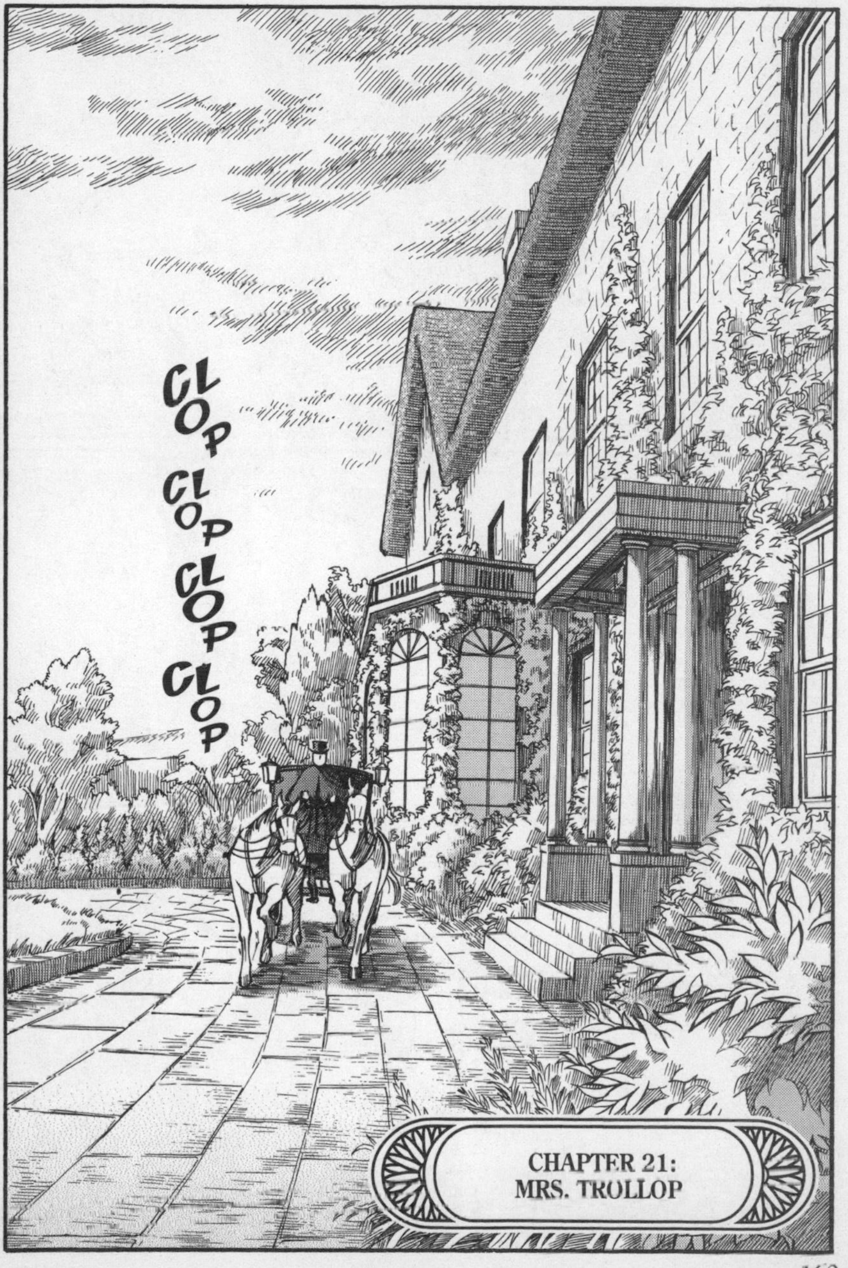
CLOP
CLOP
CLOP
CLOP
CHAPTER 21:
MRS. TROLLOP

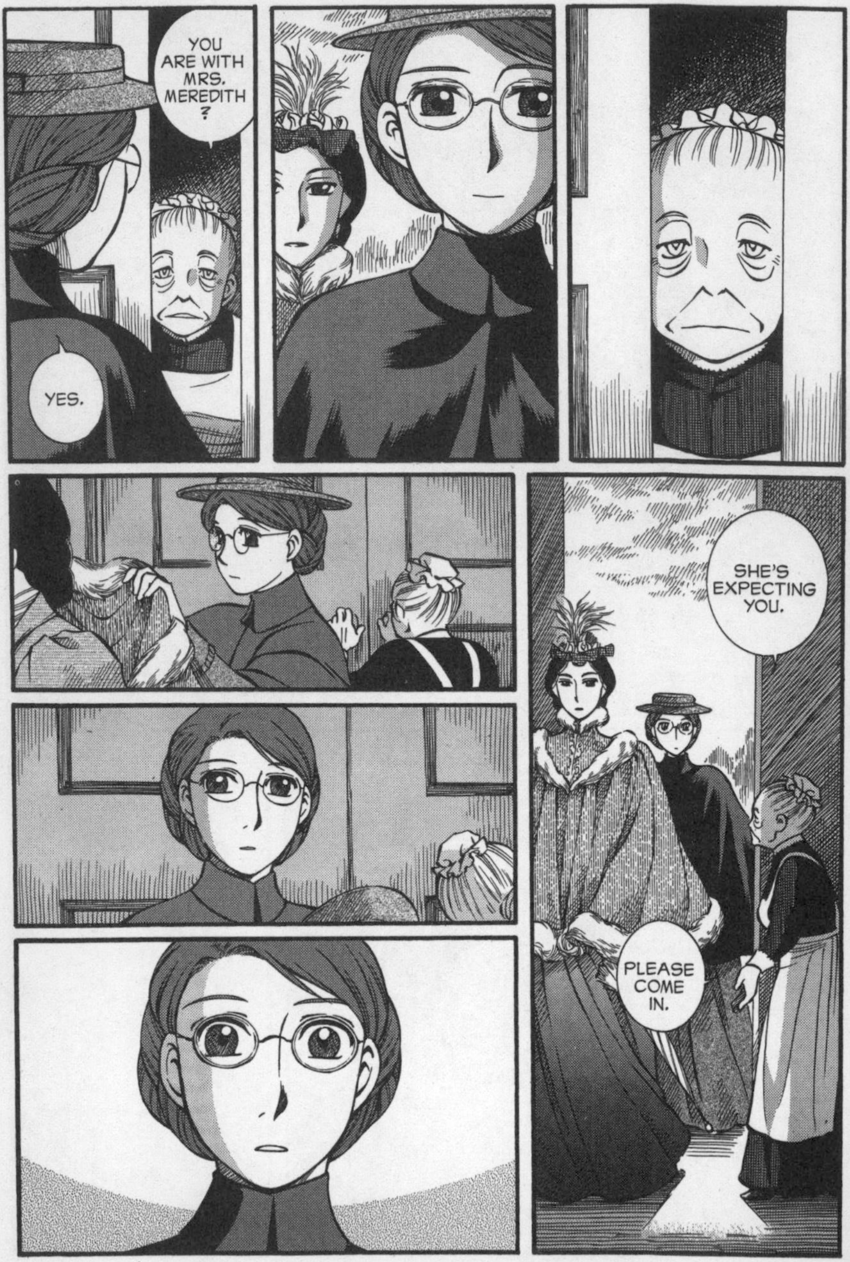
YOU ARE WITH MRS. MEREDITH?
YES.
SHE'S EXPECTING YOU.
PLEASE COME IN.

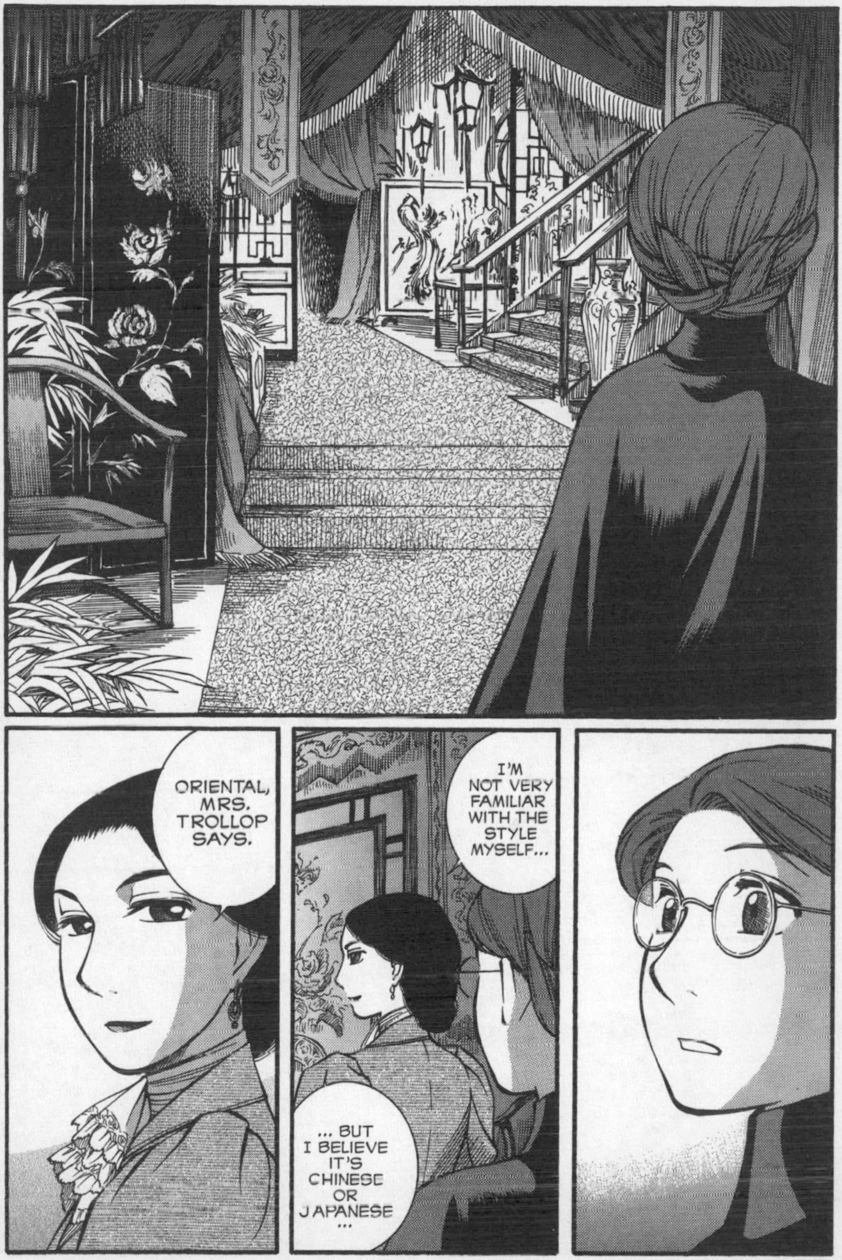
I'M NOT VERY FAMILIAR WITH THE STYLE MYSELF...
... BUT I BELIEVE IT'S CHINESE OR JAPANESE ...
ORIENTAL, MRS. TROLLOP SAYS.

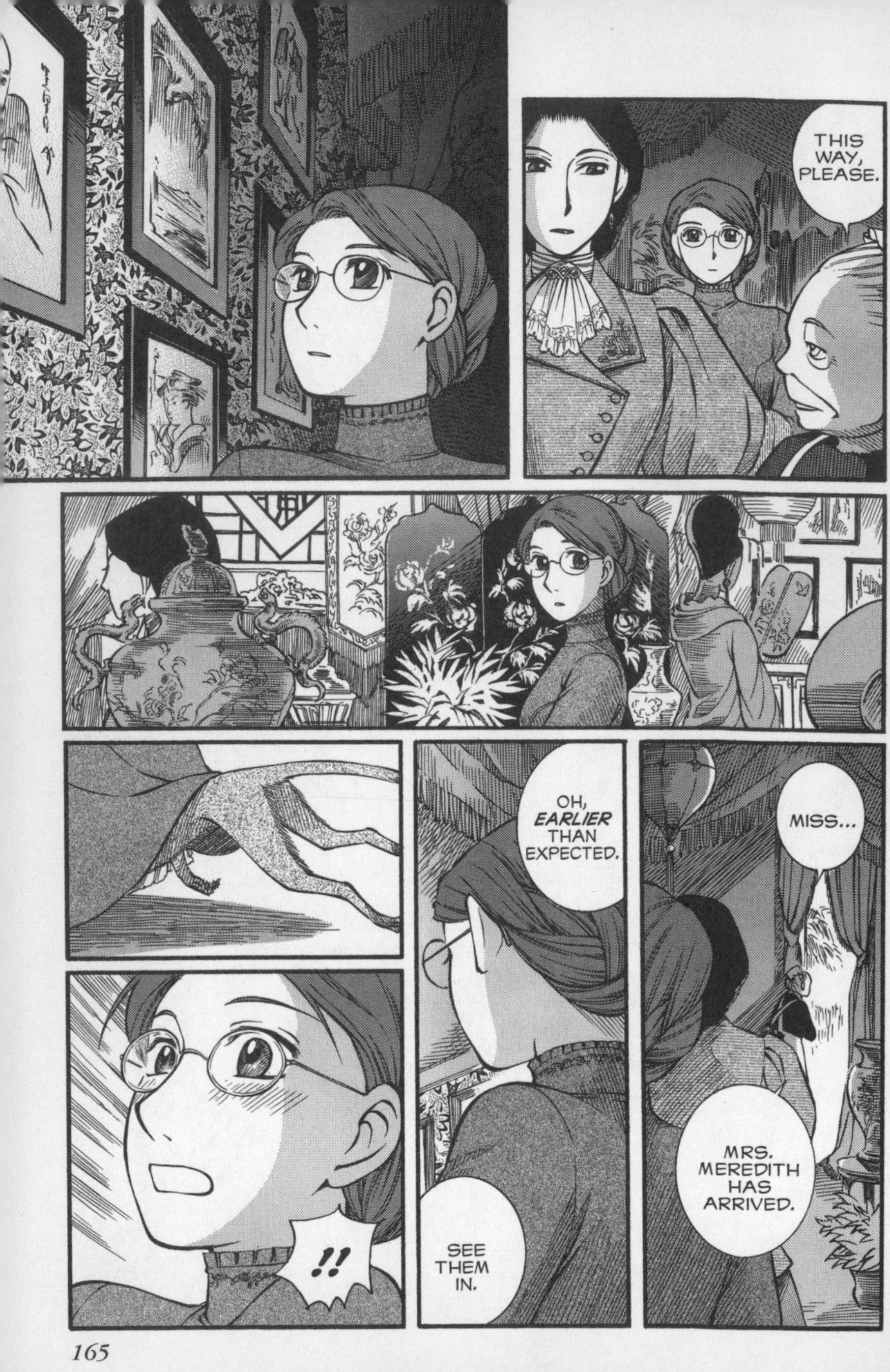
THIS WAY, PLEASE.
MISS...
MRS. MEREDITH HAS ARRIVED.
OH, *EARLIER* THAN EXPECTED.
SEE THEM IN.
!!

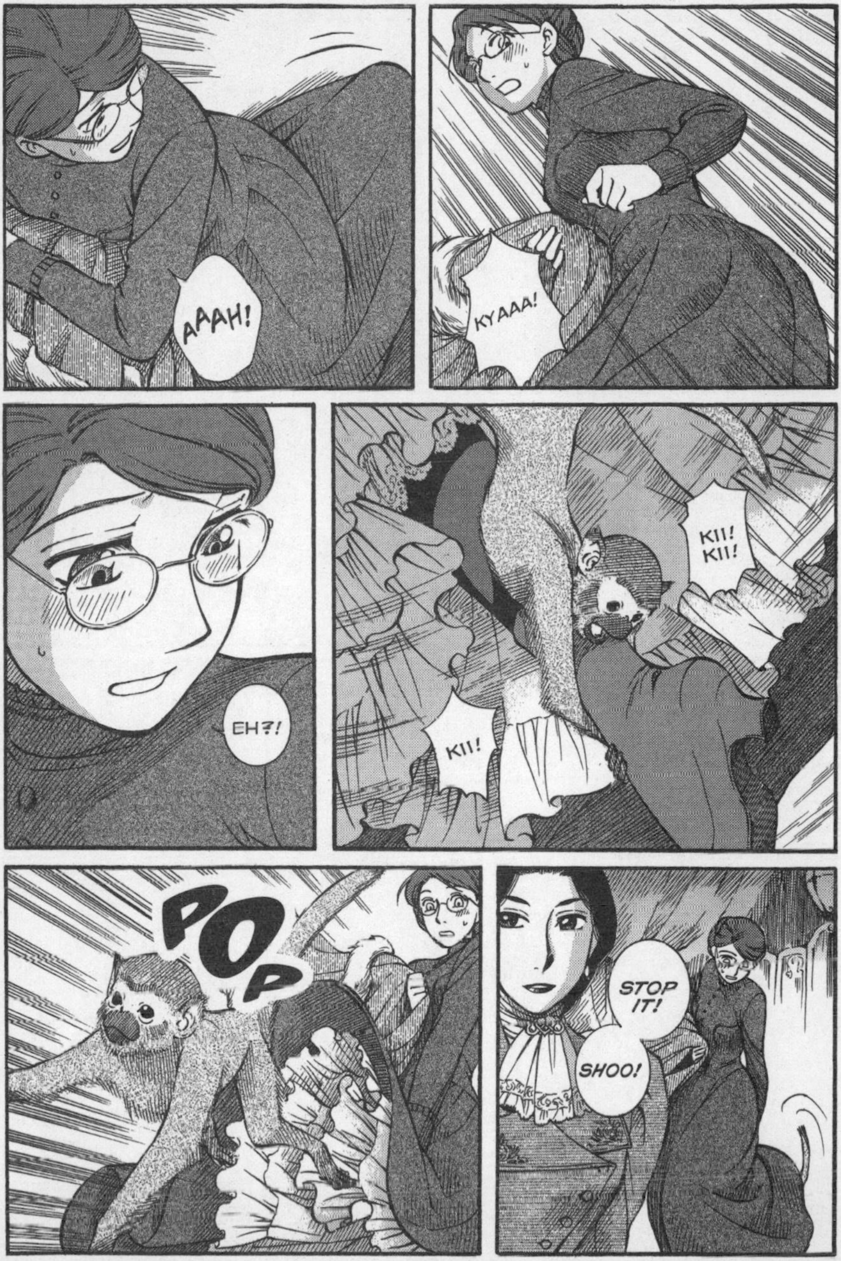
KYAAA!
AAAH!
KII! KII!
KII!
EH?!
STOP IT!
SHOO!
POP

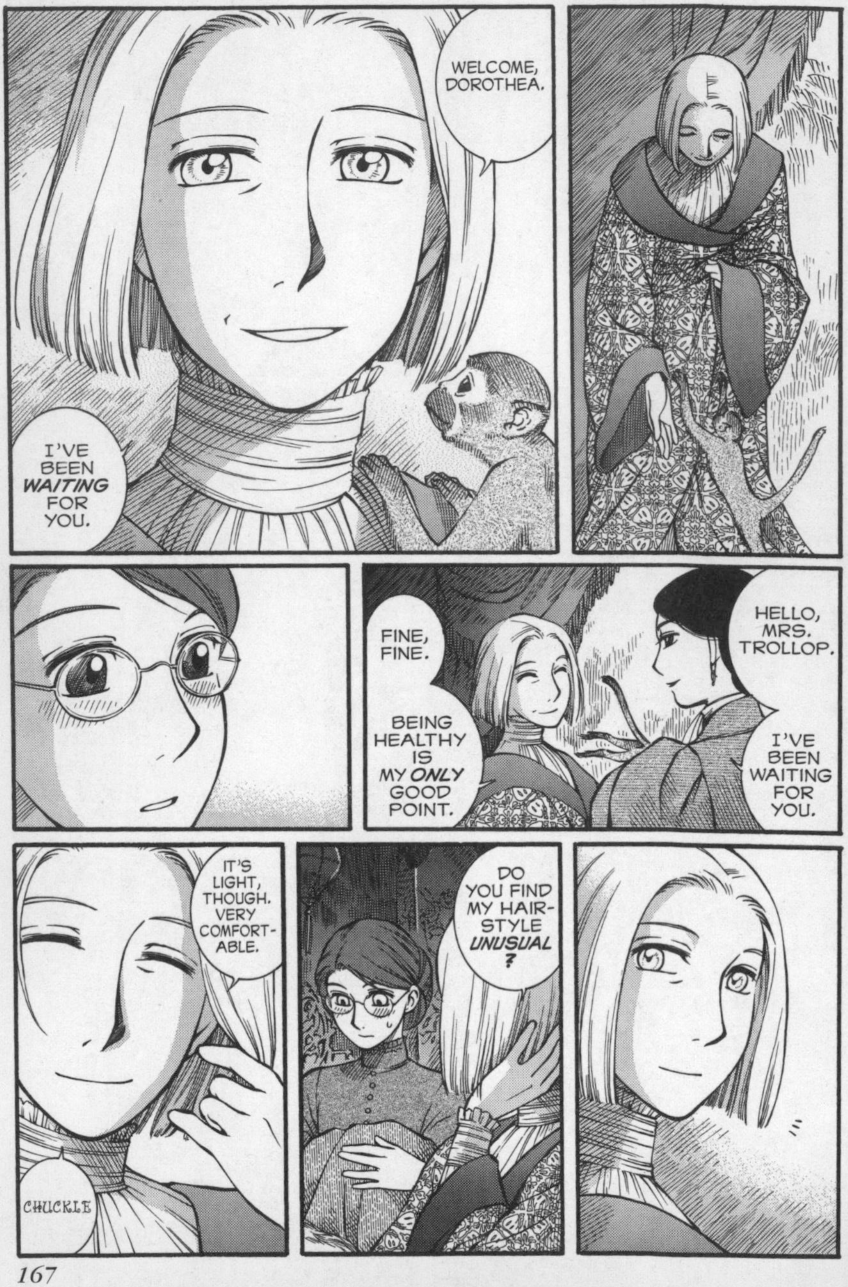
WELCOME, DOROTHEA.
I'VE BEEN *WAITING* FOR YOU.
HELLO, MRS. TROLLOP.
I'VE BEEN WAITING FOR YOU.
FINE, FINE.
BEING HEALTHY IS MY *ONLY* GOOD POINT.
DO YOU FIND MY HAIR-STYLE *UNUSUAL*?
IT'S LIGHT, THOUGH. VERY COMFORT-ABLE.
CHUCKLE

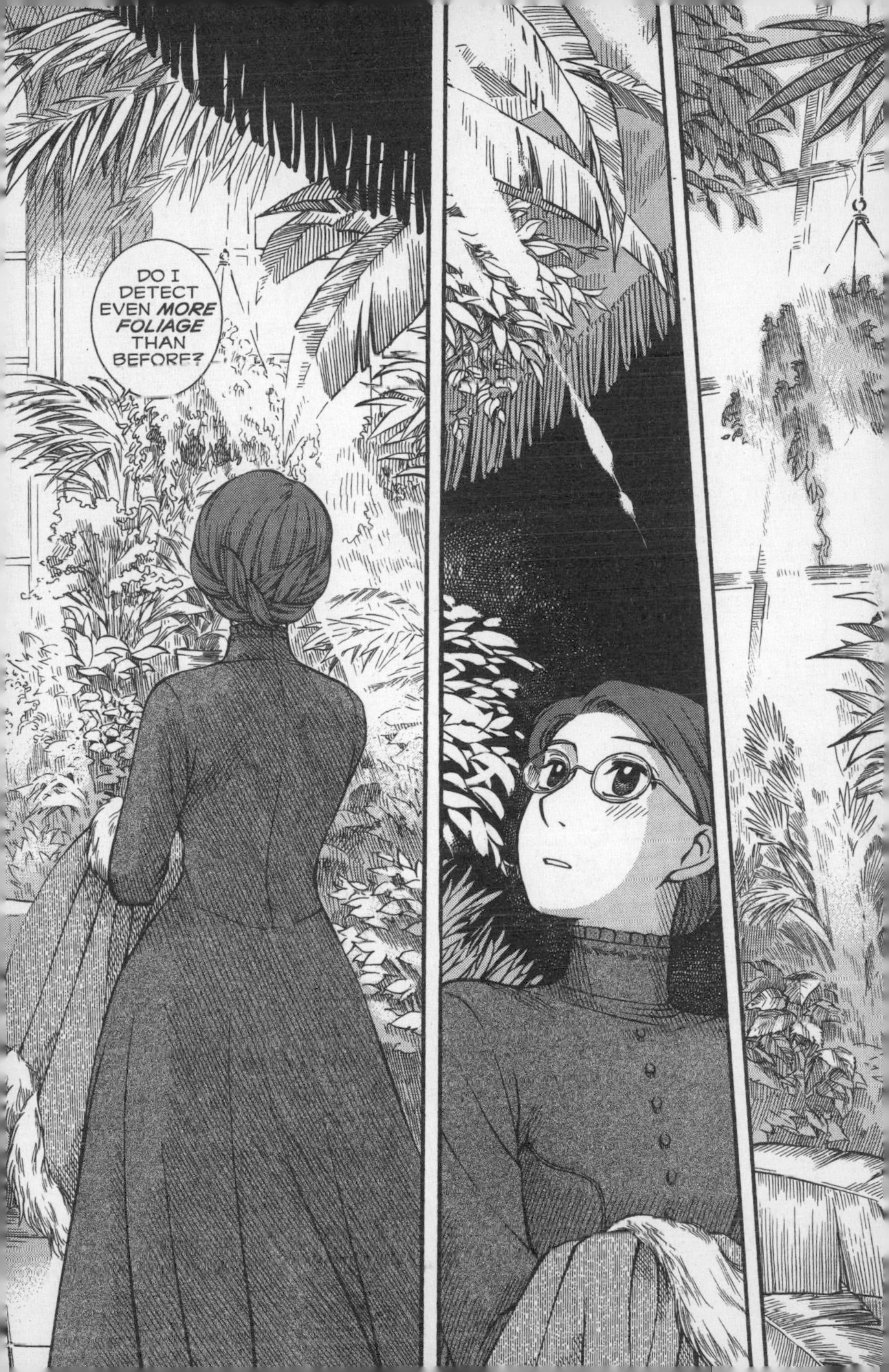
DO I DETECT EVEN *MORE FOLIAGE* THAN BEFORE?

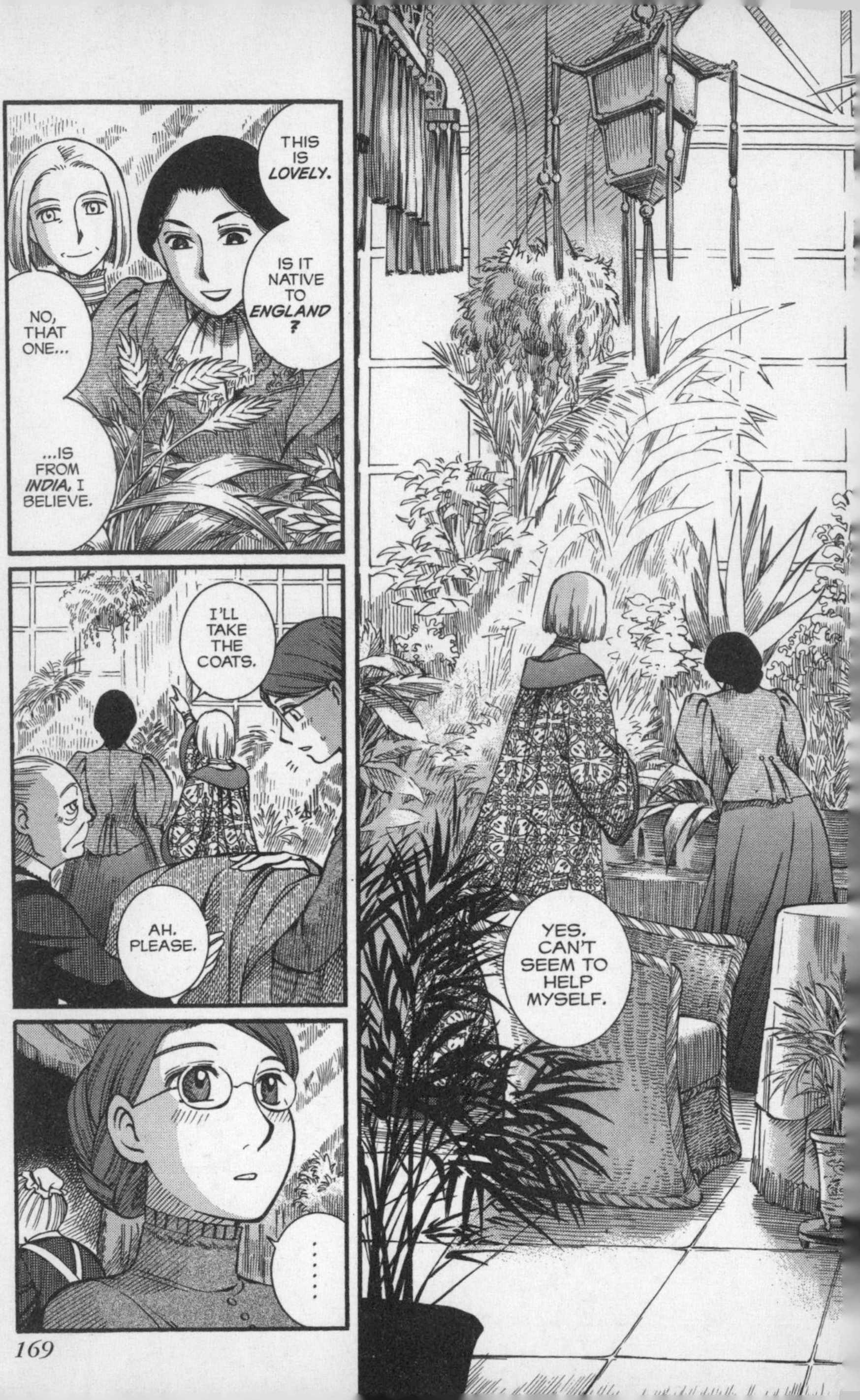
YES. CAN'T SEEM TO HELP MYSELF.
THIS IS *LOVELY*.
IS IT NATIVE TO *ENGLAND*?
NO, THAT ONE...
...IS FROM *INDIA*, I BELIEVE.
I'LL TAKE THE COATS.
AH. PLEASE.
......

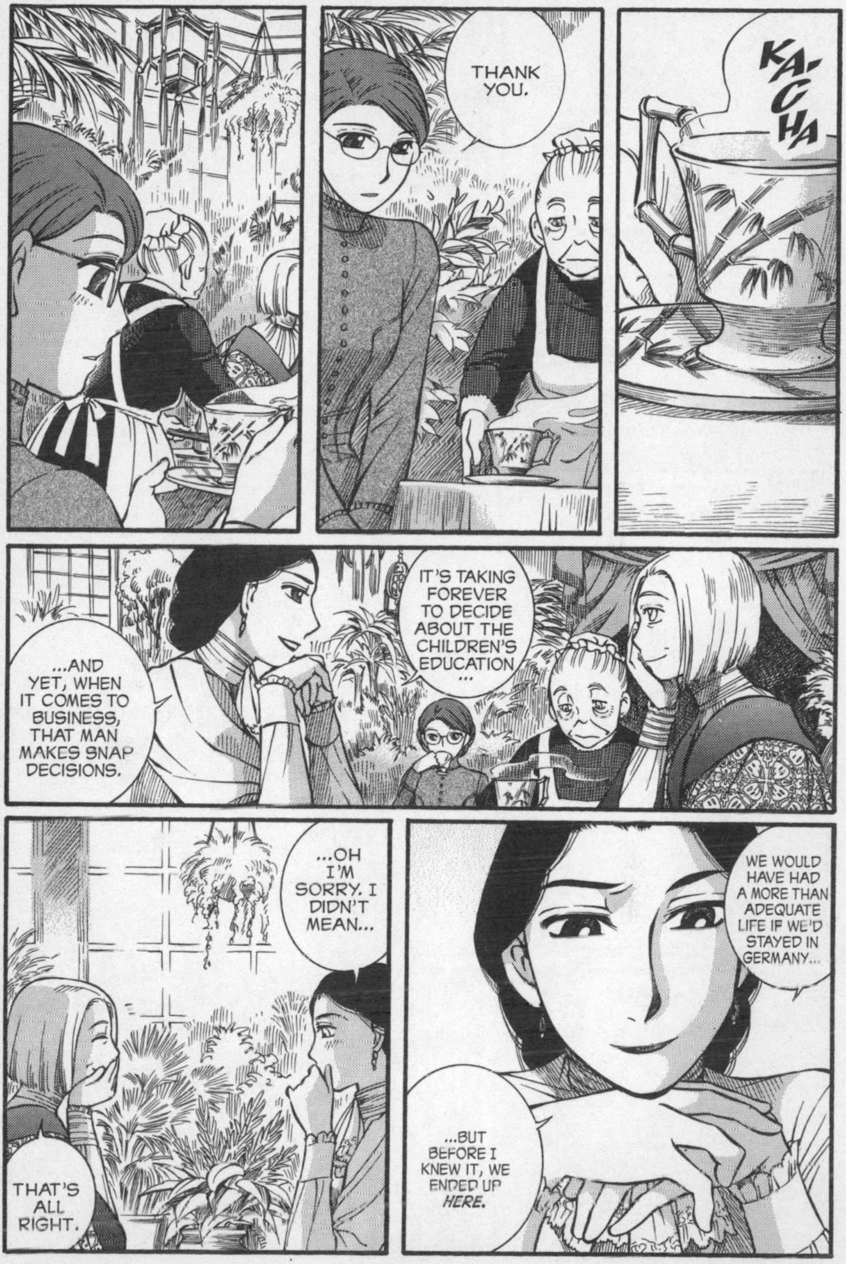
KA-CHA
THANK YOU.
IT'S TAKING FOREVER TO DECIDE ABOUT THE CHILDREN'S EDUCATION ...
...AND YET, WHEN IT COMES TO BUSINESS, THAT MAN MAKES SNAP DECISIONS.
WE WOULD HAVE HAD A MORE THAN ADEQUATE LIFE IF WE'D STAYED IN GERMANY...
...BUT BEFORE I KNEW IT, WE ENDED UP *HERE*.
...OH I'M SORRY. I DIDN'T MEAN...
THAT'S ALL RIGHT.

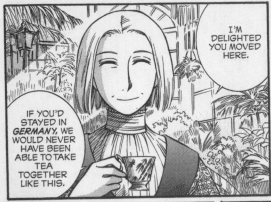

I'M DELIGHTED YOU MOVED HERE.

IF YOU'D STAYED IN *GERMANY*, WE WOULD HAVE NEVER BEEN ABLE TO TAKE TEA TOGETHER LIKE THIS.

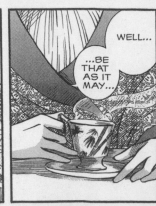

WELL...

...BE THAT AS IT MAY...

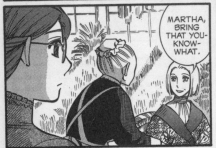

MARTHA, BRING THAT YOU-KNOW-WHAT.

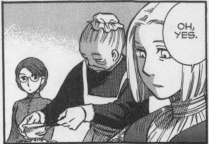

OH, YES.

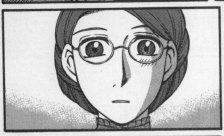

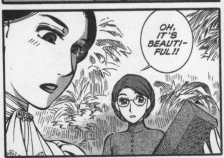

OH, IT'S BEAUTI-FUL!!

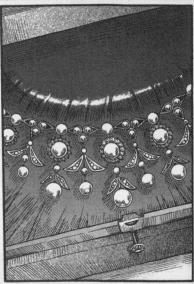

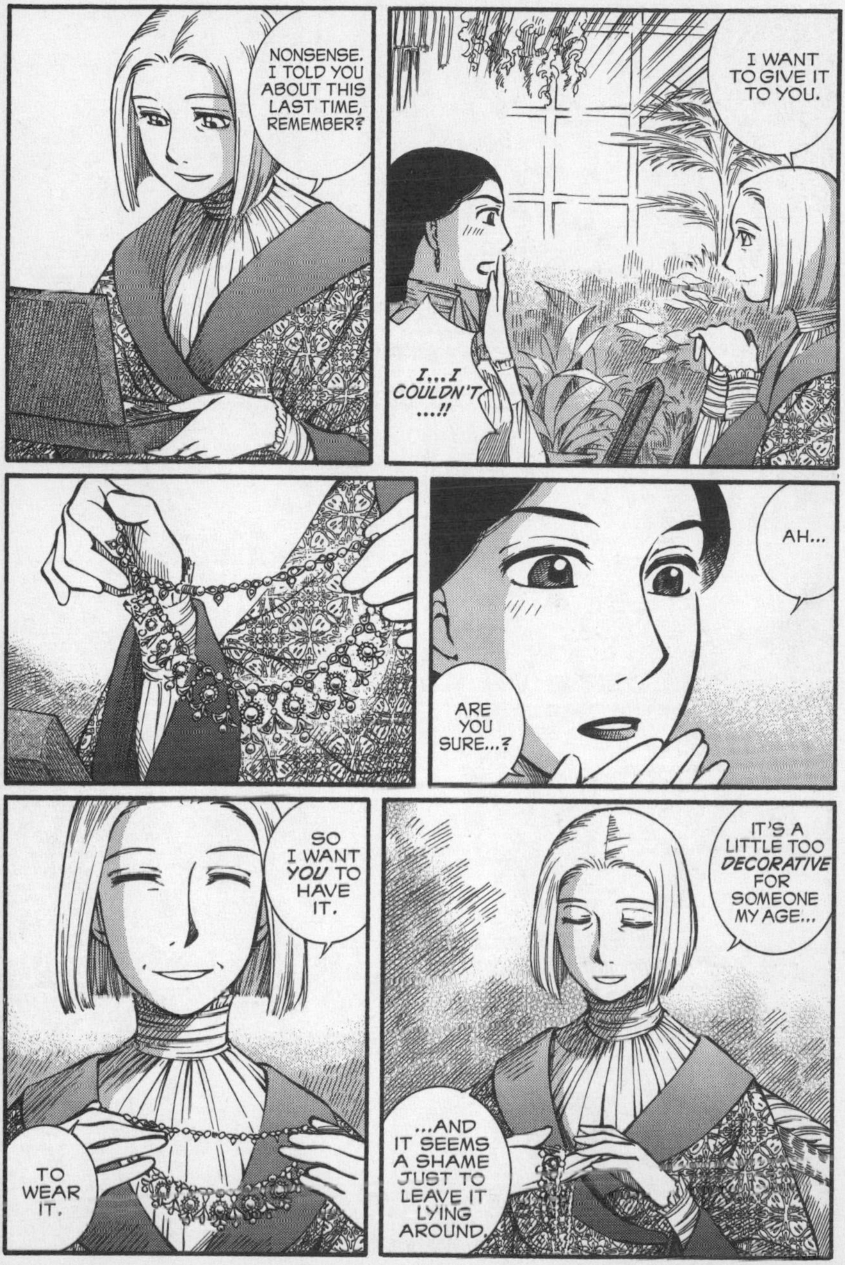
I WANT TO GIVE IT TO YOU.
I...I COULDN'T ...!!
NONSENSE. I TOLD YOU ABOUT THIS LAST TIME, REMEMBER?
AH...
ARE YOU SURE...?
IT'S A LITTLE TOO *DECORATIVE* FOR SOMEONE MY AGE...
...AND IT SEEMS A SHAME JUST TO LEAVE IT LYING AROUND.
SO I WANT *YOU* TO HAVE IT.
TO WEAR IT.

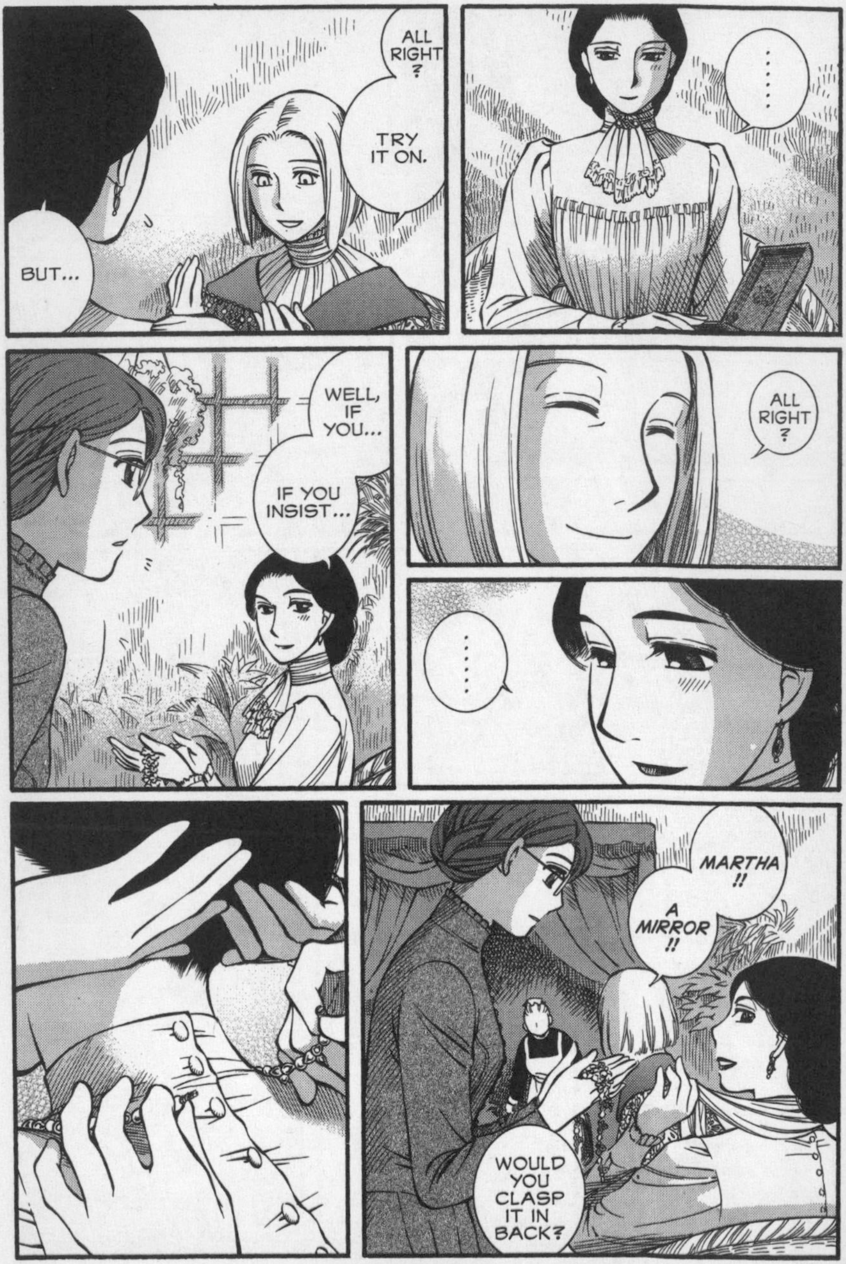

……
ALL RIGHT?
TRY IT ON.
BUT...
ALL RIGHT?
……
WELL, IF YOU...
IF YOU INSIST...
MARTHA!!
A MIRROR!!
WOULD YOU CLASP IT IN BACK?

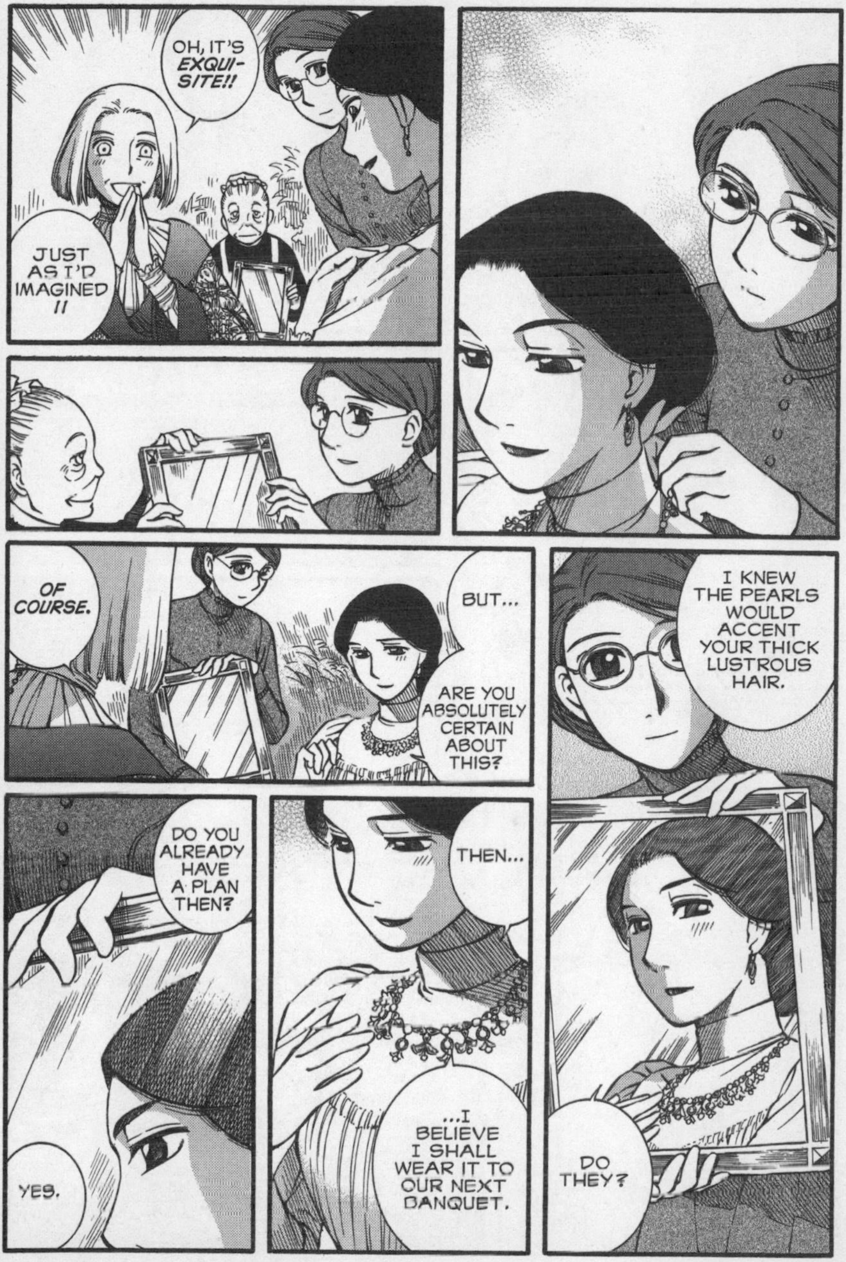
OH, IT'S *EXQUISITE!!*
JUST AS I'D IMAGINED !!
I KNEW THE PEARLS WOULD ACCENT YOUR THICK LUSTROUS HAIR.
DO THEY?
BUT...
ARE YOU ABSOLUTELY CERTAIN ABOUT THIS?
OF COURSE.
THEN...
...I BELIEVE I SHALL WEAR IT TO OUR NEXT BANQUET.
DO YOU ALREADY HAVE A PLAN THEN?
YES.

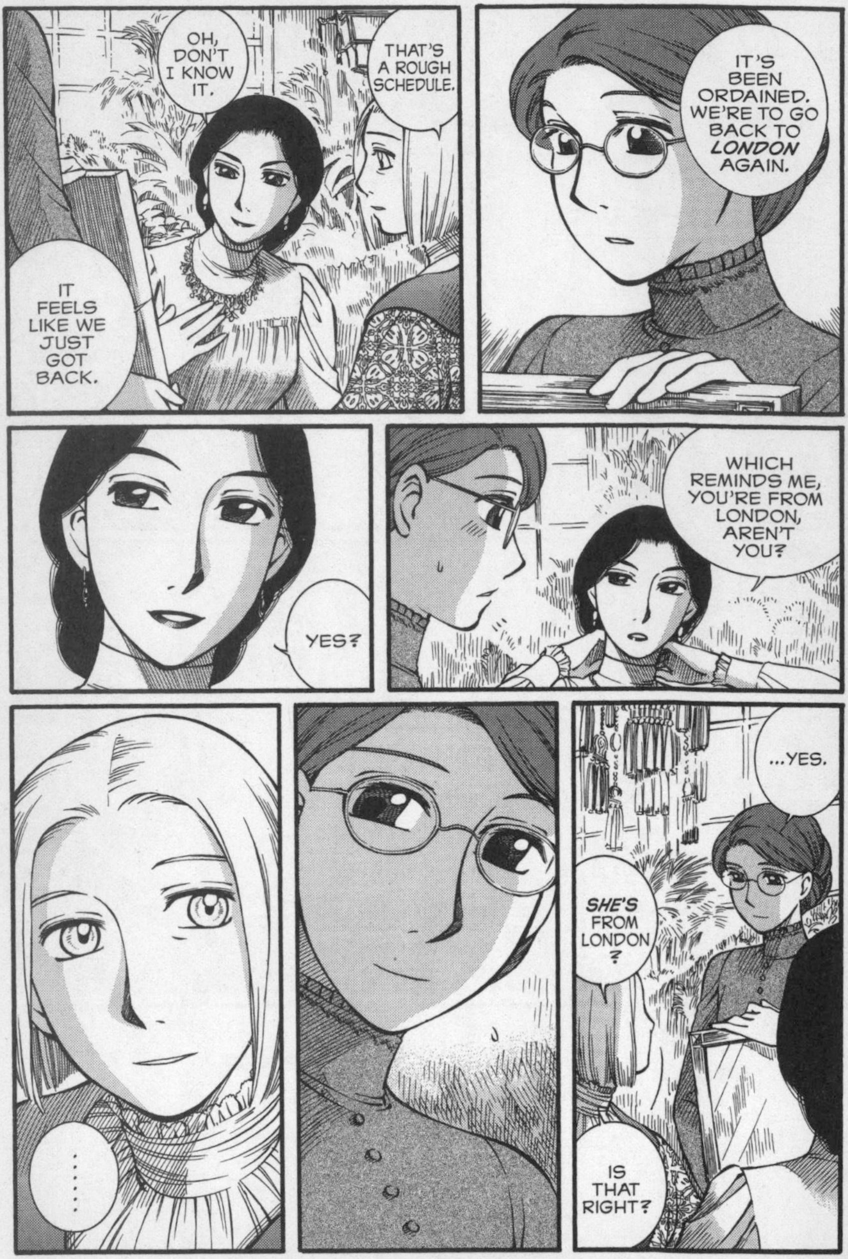
IT'S BEEN ORDAINED. WE'RE TO GO BACK TO *LONDON* AGAIN.
THAT'S A ROUGH SCHEDULE.
OH, DON'T I KNOW IT.
IT FEELS LIKE WE JUST GOT BACK.
WHICH REMINDS ME, YOU'RE FROM LONDON, AREN'T YOU?
YES?
...YES.
SHE'S FROM LONDON?
IS THAT RIGHT?
......

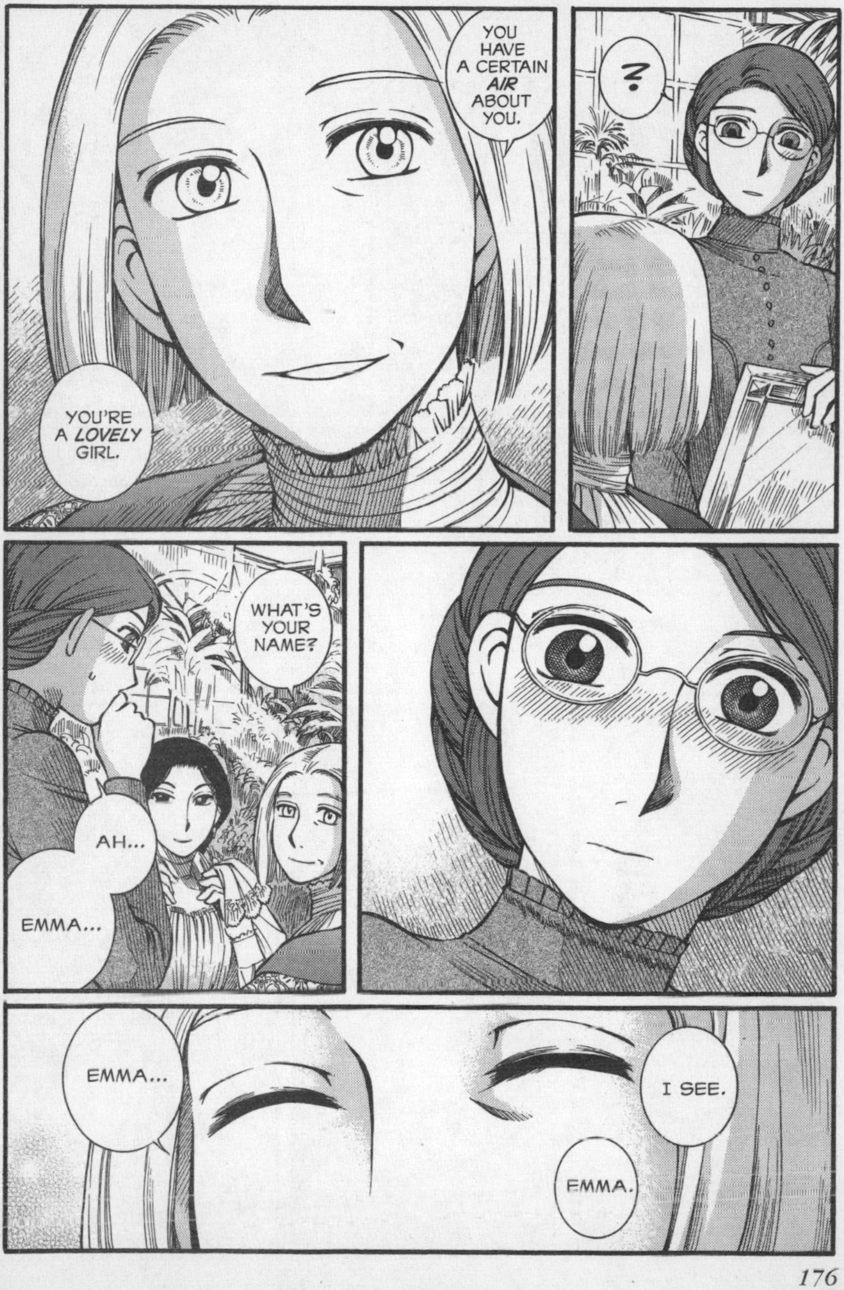
?
YOU HAVE A CERTAIN AIR ABOUT YOU.
YOU'RE A LOVELY GIRL.
WHAT'S YOUR NAME?
AH...
EMMA...
EMMA...
I SEE.
EMMA.

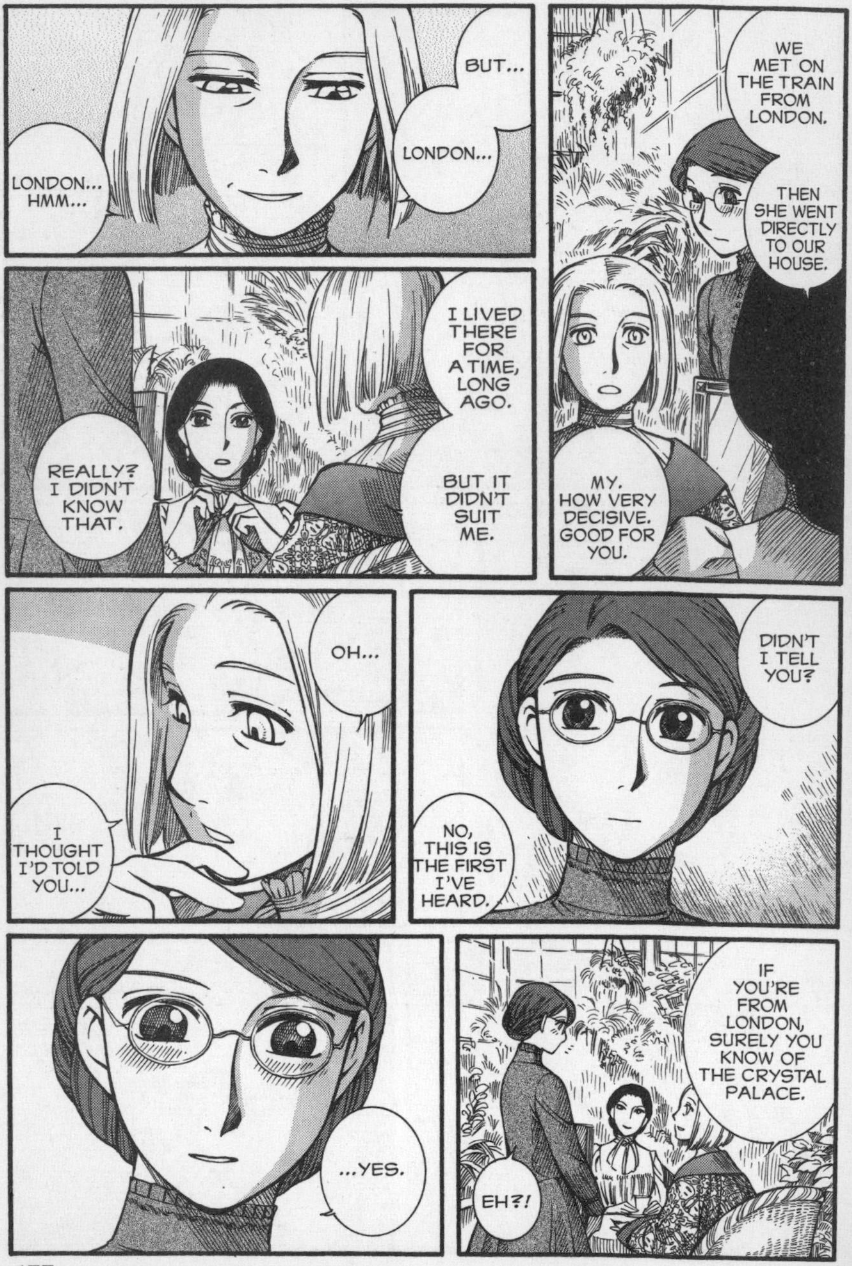
WE MET ON THE TRAIN FROM LONDON.
THEN SHE WENT DIRECTLY TO OUR HOUSE.
MY. HOW VERY DECISIVE. GOOD FOR YOU.
BUT...
LONDON...
LONDON... HMM...
I LIVED THERE FOR A TIME, LONG AGO.
BUT IT DIDN'T SUIT ME.
REALLY? I DIDN'T KNOW THAT.
DIDN'T I TELL YOU?
NO, THIS IS THE FIRST I'VE HEARD.
OH...
I THOUGHT I'D TOLD YOU...
IF YOU'RE FROM LONDON, SURELY YOU KNOW OF THE CRYSTAL PALACE.
EH?!
...YES.

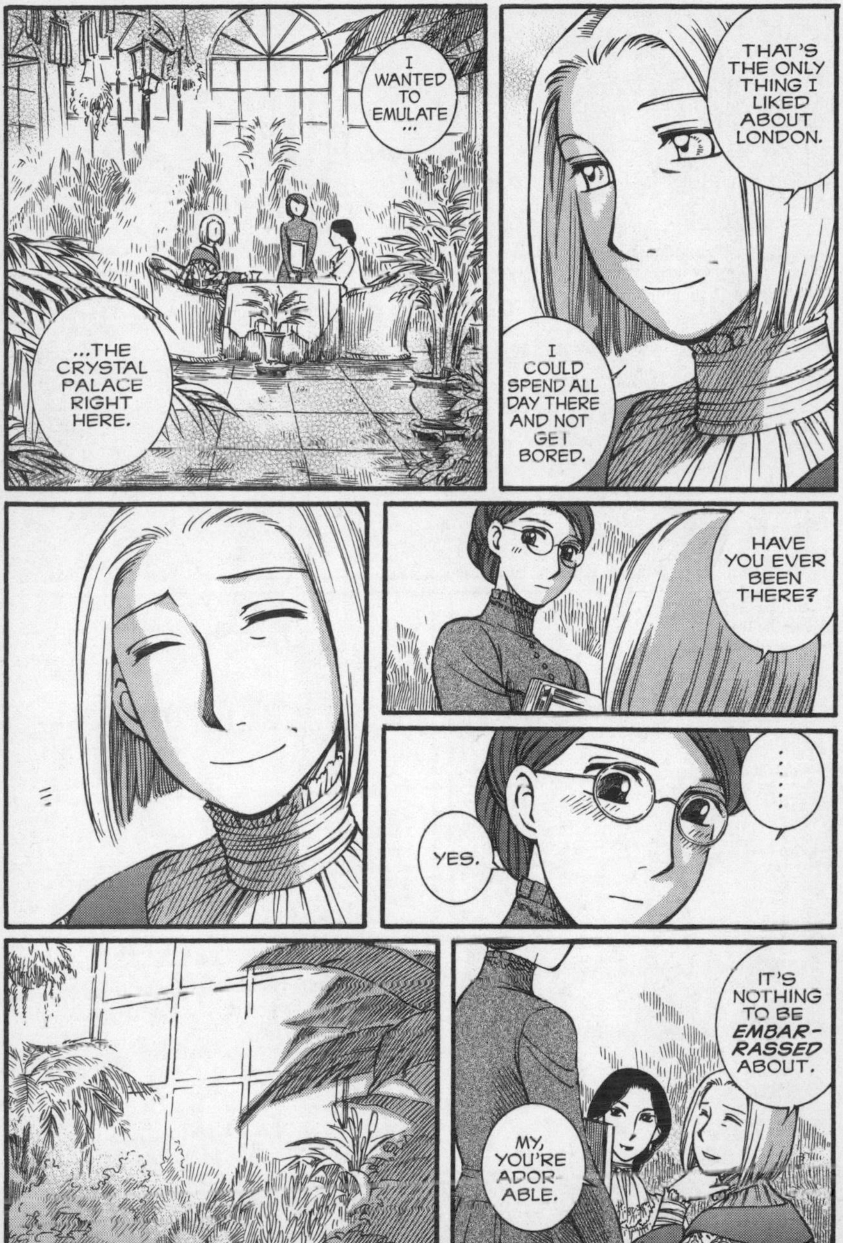
THAT'S THE ONLY THING I LIKED ABOUT LONDON.
I COULD SPEND ALL DAY THERE AND NOT GET BORED.
I WANTED TO EMULATE ...
...THE CRYSTAL PALACE RIGHT HERE.
HAVE YOU EVER BEEN THERE?
......
YES.
IT'S NOTHING TO BE *EMBARRASSED* ABOUT.
MY, YOU'RE ADORABLE.

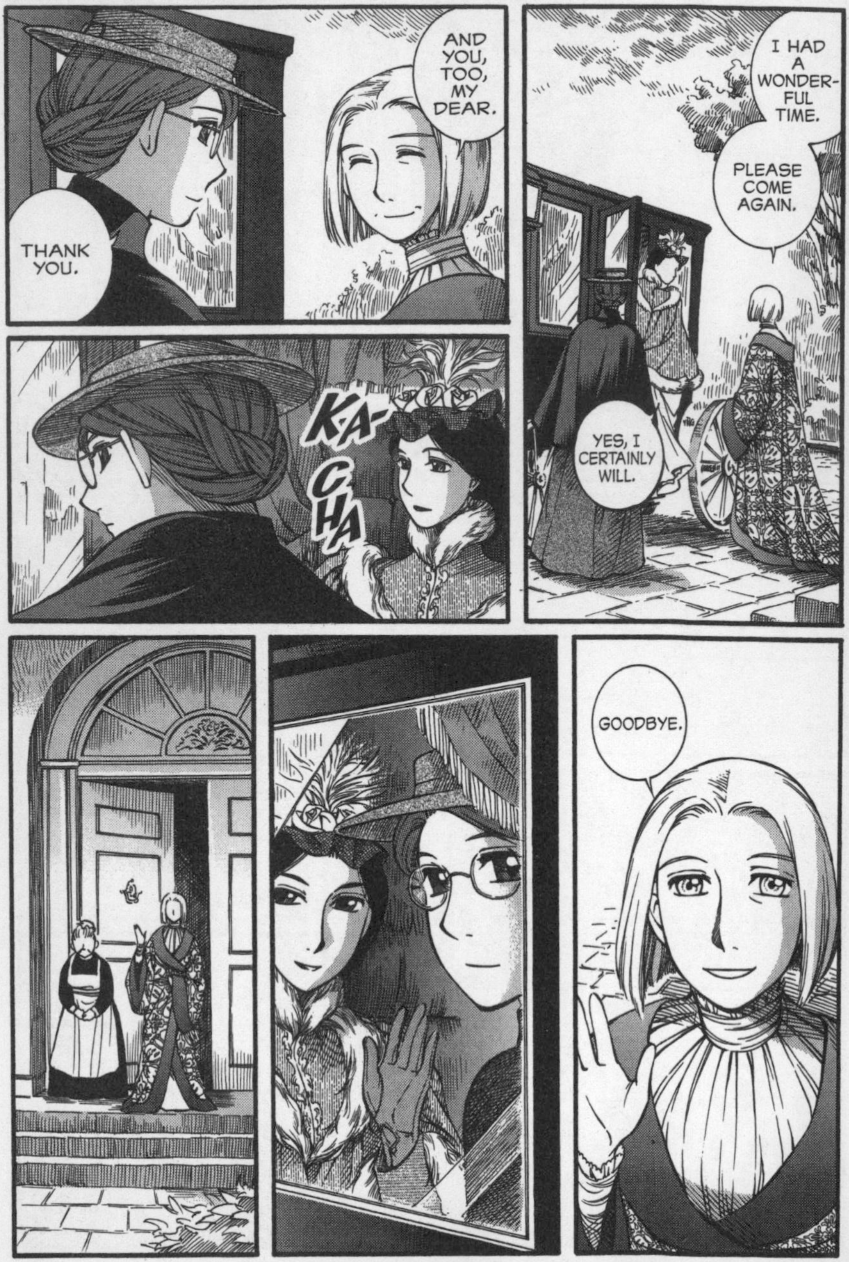
I HAD A WONDERFUL TIME.
PLEASE COME AGAIN.
YES, I CERTAINLY WILL.
AND YOU, TOO, MY DEAR.
THANK YOU.
KA-CHA
GOODBYE.

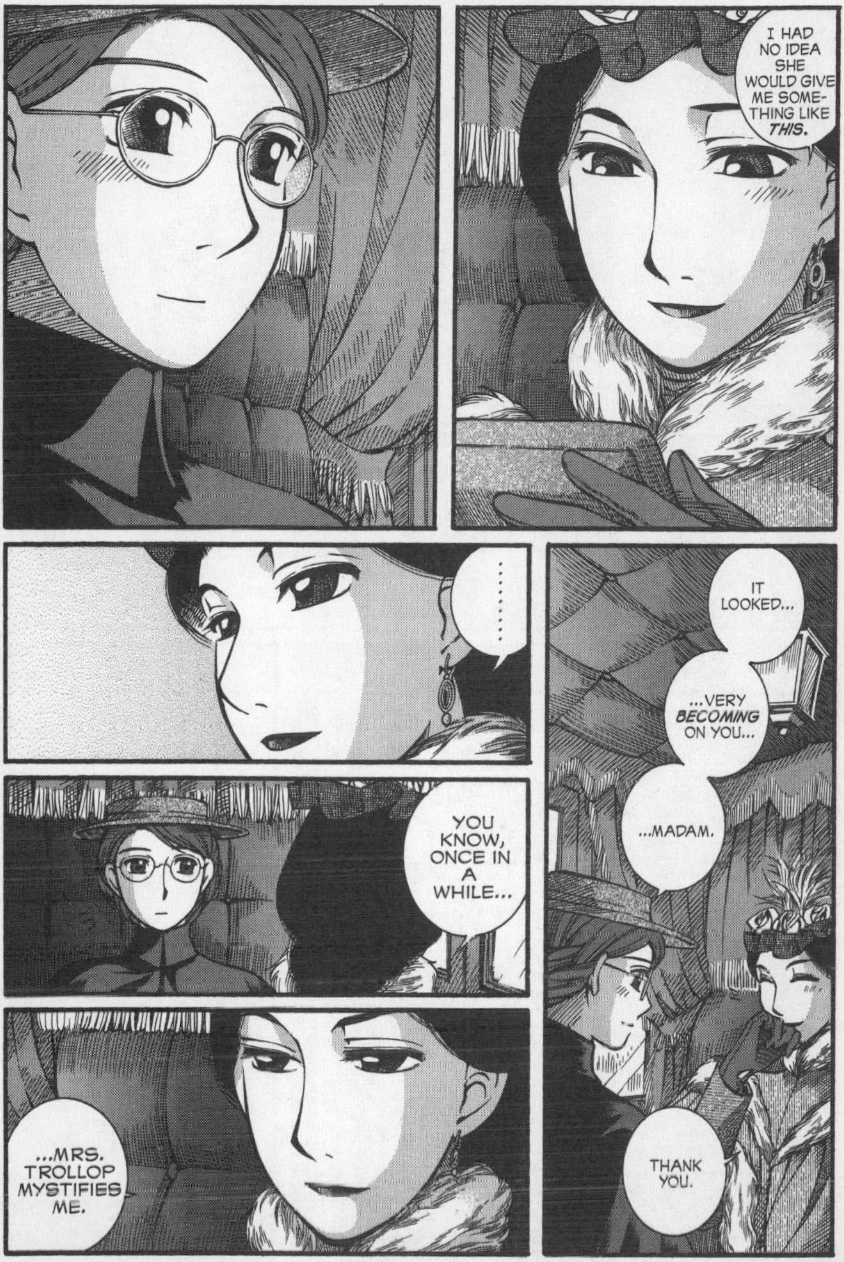
I HAD NO IDEA SHE WOULD GIVE ME SOME-THING LIKE *THIS*.
IT LOOKED...
...VERY *BECOMING* ON YOU...
...MADAM.
THANK YOU.
......
YOU KNOW, ONCE IN A WHILE...
...MRS. TROLLOP MYSTIFIES ME.

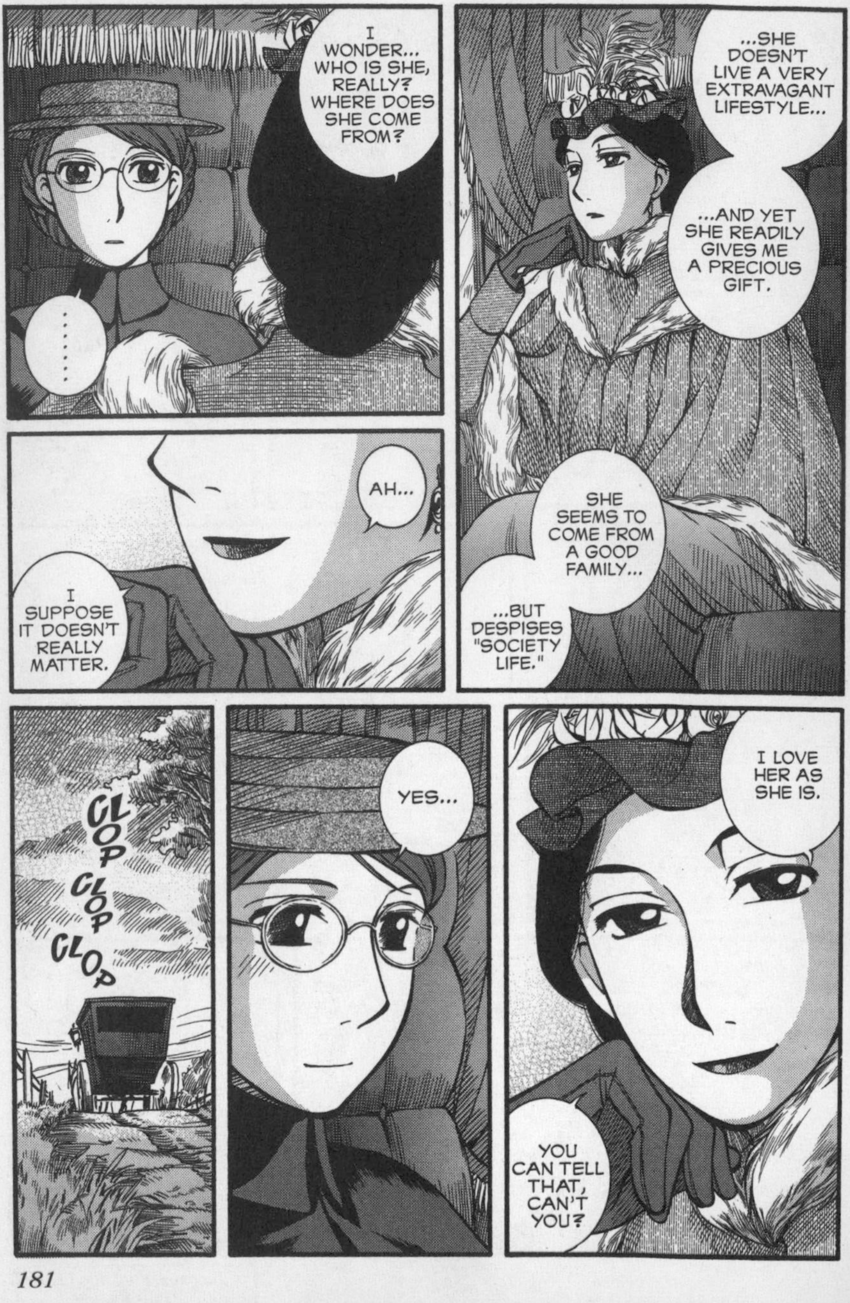
...SHE DOESN'T LIVE A VERY EXTRAVAGANT LIFESTYLE...
...AND YET SHE READILY GIVES ME A PRECIOUS GIFT.
SHE SEEMS TO COME FROM A GOOD FAMILY...
...BUT DESPISES "SOCIETY LIFE."
I WONDER... WHO IS SHE, REALLY? WHERE DOES SHE COME FROM?
......
AH...
I SUPPOSE IT DOESN'T REALLY MATTER.
I LOVE HER AS SHE IS.
YOU CAN TELL THAT, CAN'T YOU?
YES...
CLOP
CLOP
CLOP

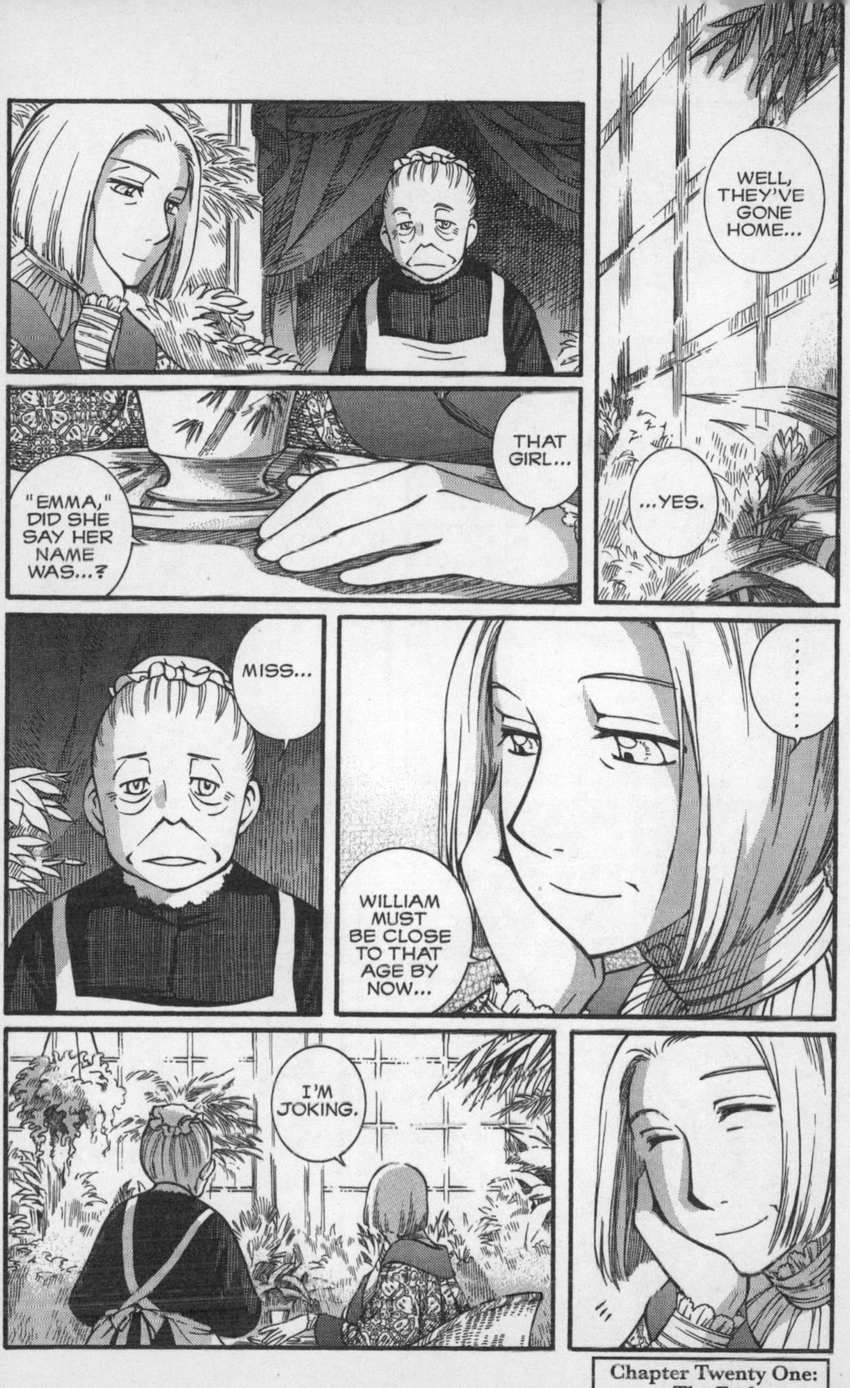
WELL, THEY'VE GONE HOME...
...YES.
THAT GIRL...
"EMMA," DID SHE SAY HER NAME WAS...?
......
WILLIAM MUST BE CLOSE TO THAT AGE BY NOW...
MISS...
I'M JOKING.

Chapter Twenty One: The End

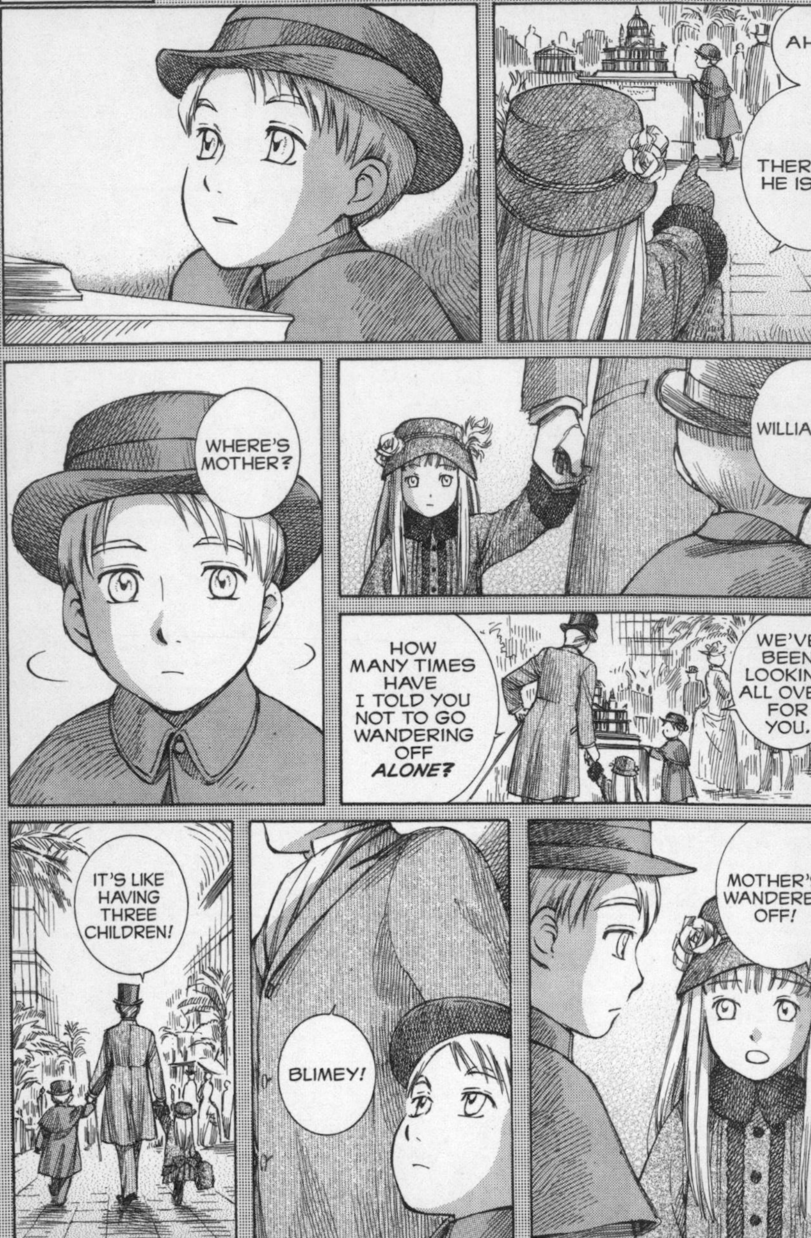
AH!
THERE HE IS!
WILLIAM.
WE'VE BEEN LOOKING ALL OVER FOR YOU.
HOW MANY TIMES HAVE I TOLD YOU NOT TO GO WANDERING OFF *ALONE?*
WHERE'S MOTHER?
MOTHER'S WANDERED OFF!
BLIMEY!
IT'S LIKE HAVING THREE CHILDREN!

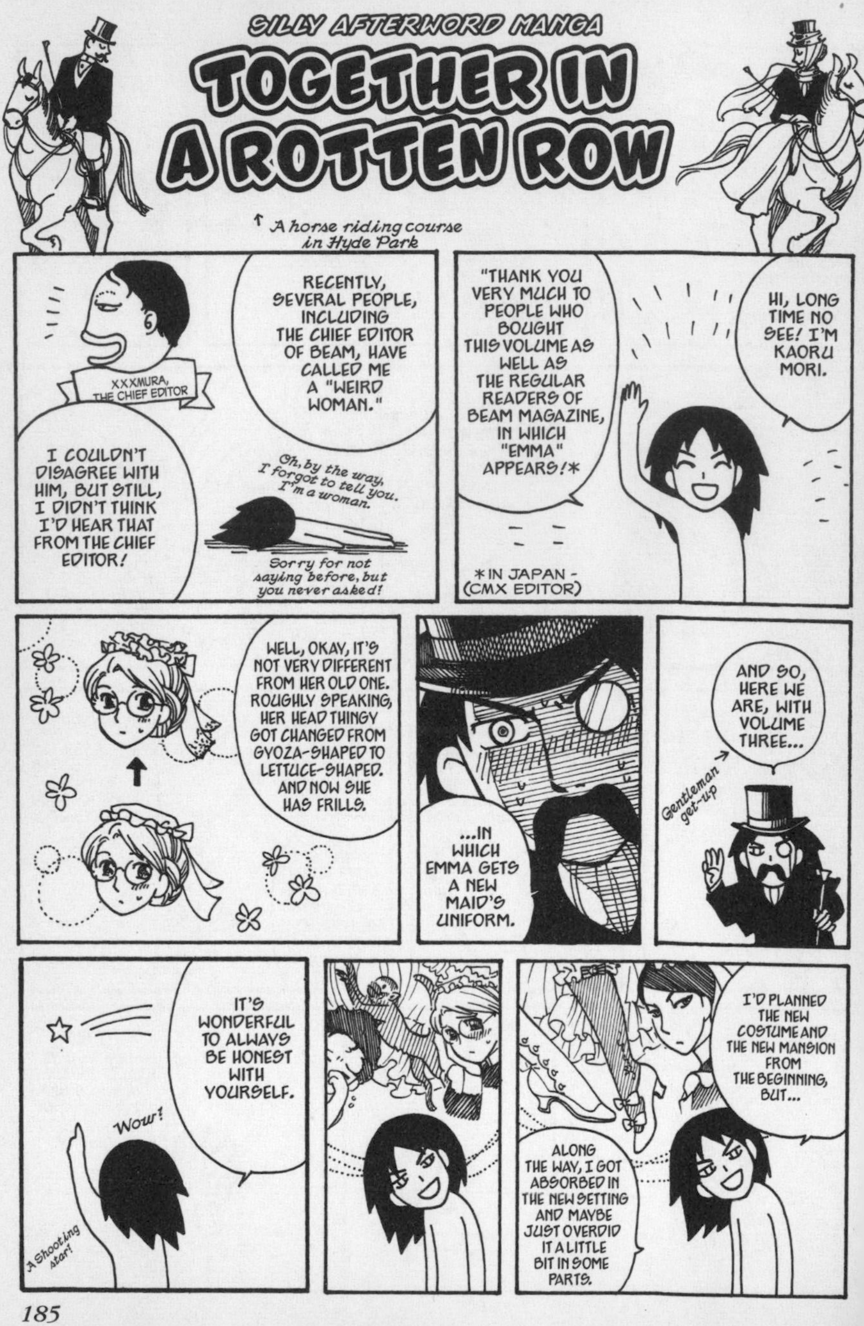

SILLY AFTERWORD MANGA
TOGETHER IN A ROTTEN ROW
A horse riding course in Hyde Park
HI, LONG TIME NO SEE! I'M KAORU MORI.
"THANK YOU VERY MUCH TO PEOPLE WHO BOUGHT THIS VOLUME AS WELL AS THE REGULAR READERS OF BEAM MAGAZINE, IN WHICH "EMMA" APPEARS!*
*IN JAPAN - (CMX EDITOR)
RECENTLY, SEVERAL PEOPLE, INCLUDING THE CHIEF EDITOR OF BEAM, HAVE CALLED ME A "WEIRD WOMAN."
XXXMURA, THE CHIEF EDITOR
I COULDN'T DISAGREE WITH HIM, BUT STILL, I DIDN'T THINK I'D HEAR THAT FROM THE CHIEF EDITOR!
Oh, by the way, I forgot to tell you. I'm a woman.
Sorry for not saying before, but you never asked!
AND SO, HERE WE ARE, WITH VOLUME THREE...
Gentleman get-up
...IN WHICH EMMA GETS A NEW MAID'S UNIFORM.
WELL, OKAY, IT'S NOT VERY DIFFERENT FROM HER OLD ONE. ROUGHLY SPEAKING, HER HEAD THINGY GOT CHANGED FROM GYOZA-SHAPED TO LETTUCE-SHAPED. AND NOW SHE HAS FRILLS.
I'D PLANNED THE NEW COSTUME AND THE NEW MANSION FROM THE BEGINNING, BUT...
ALONG THE WAY, I GOT ABSORBED IN THE NEW SETTING AND MAYBE JUST OVERDID IT A LITTLE BIT IN SOME PARTS.
IT'S WONDERFUL TO ALWAYS BE HONEST WITH YOURSELF.
Wow!
A Shooting star!

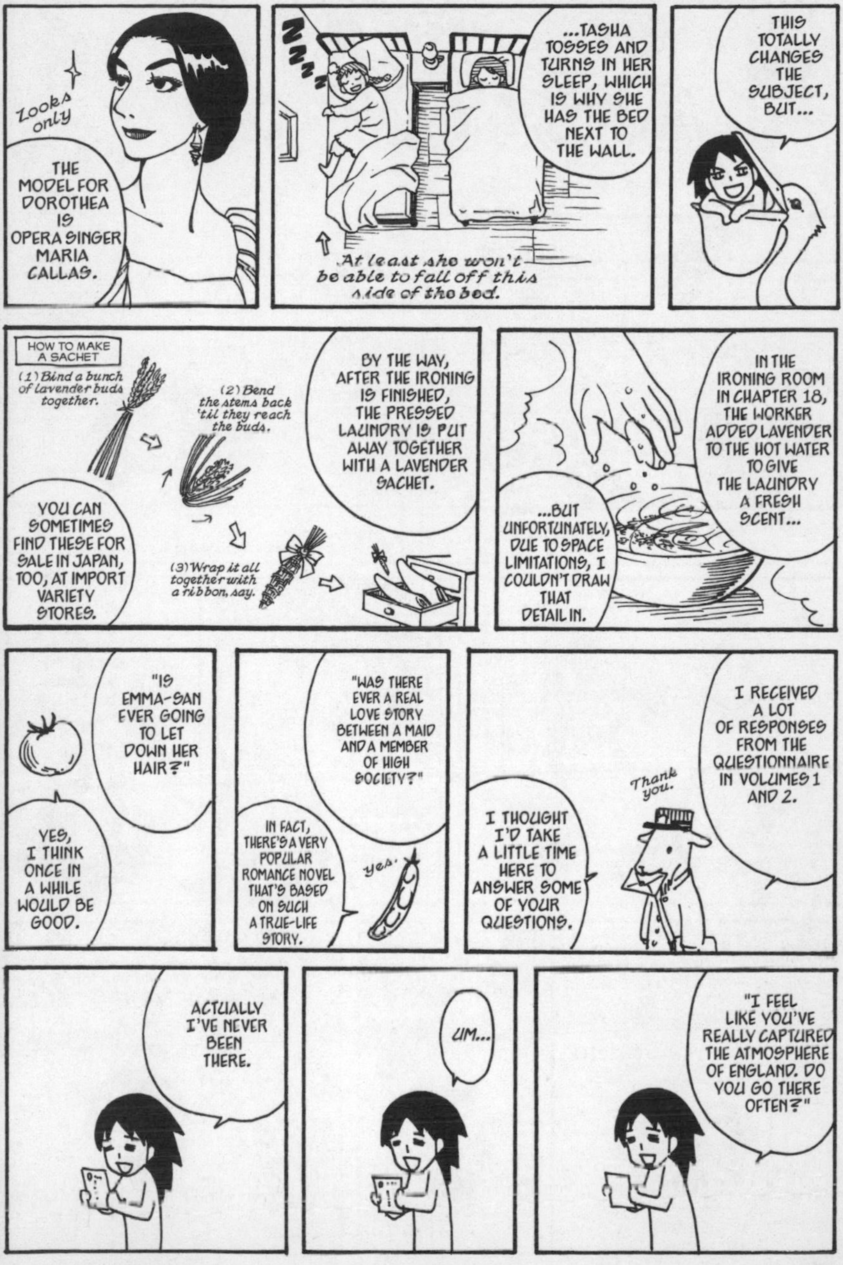
THIS TOTALLY CHANGES THE SUBJECT, BUT...
...TASHA TOSSES AND TURNS IN HER SLEEP, WHICH IS WHY SHE HAS THE BED NEXT TO THE WALL.
ZZZZ
At least she won't be able to fall off this side of the bed.
Looks only
THE MODEL FOR DOROTHEA IS OPERA SINGER MARIA CALLAS.
IN THE IRONING ROOM IN CHAPTER 18, THE WORKER ADDED LAVENDER TO THE HOT WATER TO GIVE THE LAUNDRY A FRESH SCENT...
...BUT UNFORTUNATELY, DUE TO SPACE LIMITATIONS, I COULDN'T DRAW THAT DETAIL IN.
BY THE WAY, AFTER THE IRONING IS FINISHED, THE PRESSED LAUNDRY IS PUT AWAY TOGETHER WITH A LAVENDER SACHET.
HOW TO MAKE A SACHET
(1) Bind a bunch of lavender buds together.
(2) Bend the stems back 'til they reach the buds.
(3) Wrap it all together with a ribbon, say.
YOU CAN SOMETIMES FIND THESE FOR SALE IN JAPAN, TOO, AT IMPORT VARIETY STORES.
I RECEIVED A LOT OF RESPONSES FROM THE QUESTIONNAIRE IN VOLUMES 1 AND 2.
Thank you.
I THOUGHT I'D TAKE A LITTLE TIME HERE TO ANSWER SOME OF YOUR QUESTIONS.
"WAS THERE EVER A REAL LOVE STORY BETWEEN A MAID AND A MEMBER OF HIGH SOCIETY?"
yes.
IN FACT, THERE'S A VERY POPULAR ROMANCE NOVEL THAT'S BASED ON SUCH A TRUE-LIFE STORY.
"IS EMMA-SAN EVER GOING TO LET DOWN HER HAIR?"
YES, I THINK ONCE IN A WHILE WOULD BE GOOD.
"I FEEL LIKE YOU'VE REALLY CAPTURED THE ATMOSPHERE OF ENGLAND. DO YOU GO THERE OFTEN?"
UM...
ACTUALLY I'VE NEVER BEEN THERE.

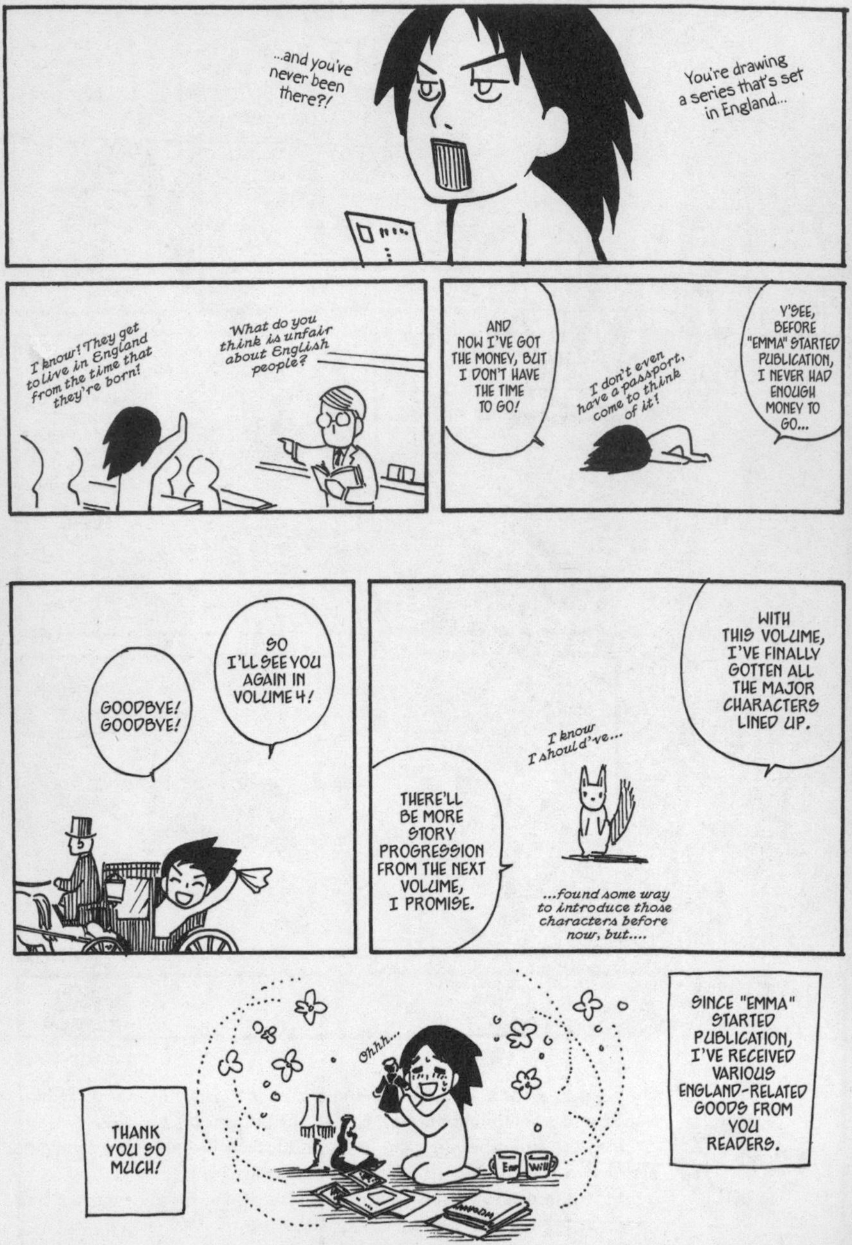
You're drawing a series that's set in England...
...and you've never been there?!
Y'SEE, BEFORE "EMMA" STARTED PUBLICATION, I NEVER HAD ENOUGH MONEY TO GO...
I don't even have a passport, come to think of it!
AND NOW I'VE GOT THE MONEY, BUT I DON'T HAVE THE TIME TO GO!
What do you think is unfair about English people?
I know! They get to live in England from the time that they're born!
WITH THIS VOLUME, I'VE FINALLY GOTTEN ALL THE MAJOR CHARACTERS LINED UP.
I know I should've...
...found some way to introduce those characters before now, but....
THERE'LL BE MORE STORY PROGRESSION FROM THE NEXT VOLUME, I PROMISE.
SO I'LL SEE YOU AGAIN IN VOLUME 4!
GOODBYE! GOODBYE!
SINCE "EMMA" STARTED PUBLICATION, I'VE RECEIVED VARIOUS ENGLAND-RELATED GOODS FROM YOU READERS.
Ohhh...
THANK YOU SO MUCH!

HAS WILLIAM MOVED ON?
FIND OUT IN JUNE!

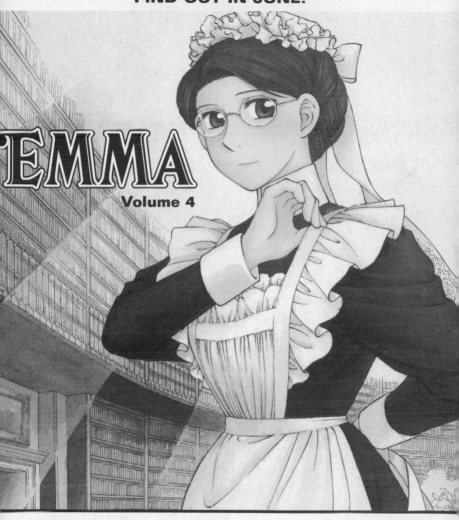

EMMA

Volume 4

By Kaoru Mori. William's trying his best to be the aristocrat his father and society expect him to be, but behind closed doors, he's circling the drain because he still can't forget Emma. After William's sister Grace suddenly gets feverish, he ends up taking her place by going to the opera with Eleanor. But by act two, Eleanor shows him how she feels about him in no uncertain terms. Will she make William forget about Emma?!

EMMA Vol. 4 © 2004 Kaoru Mori/PUBLISHED BY ENTERBRAIN, INC.

IF YOU LIKE *EMMA*, YOU'LL LOVE THESE SERIES, TOO!

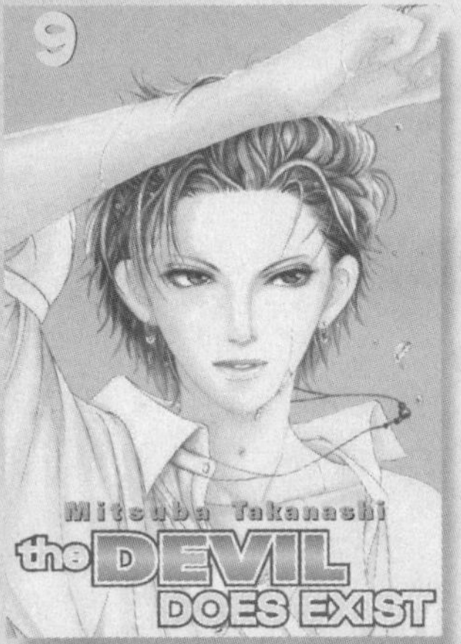

9
Mitsuba Takanashi
the DEVIL DOES EXIST

By Mitsuba Takanashi
9 Volumes Available

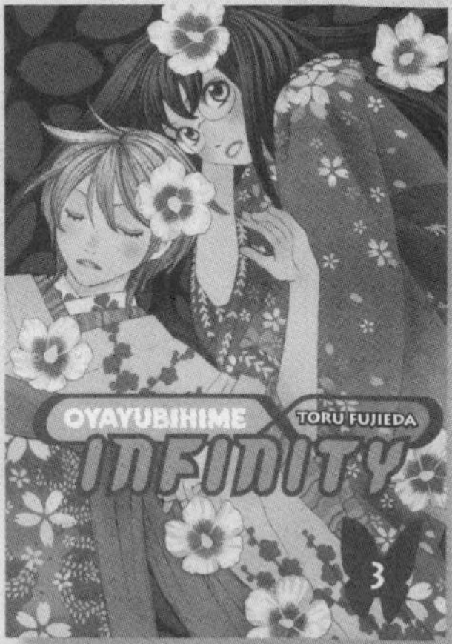

OYAYUBIHIME
TORU FUJIEDA
INFINITY
3

By Toru Fujieda
3 Volumes Available

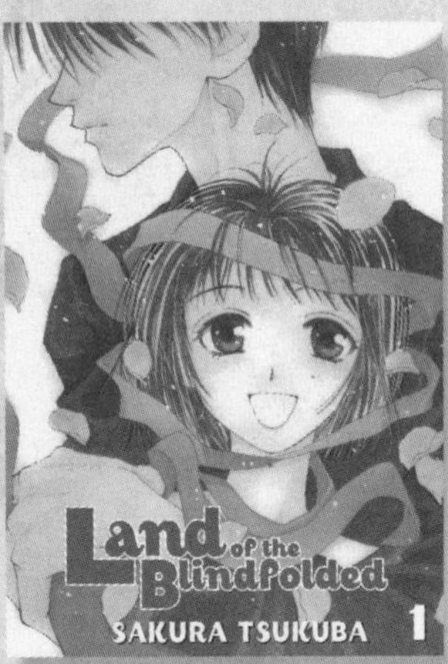

Land of the Blindfolded
SAKURA TSUKUBA
1

By Sakura Tsukuba
Entire Series Available!

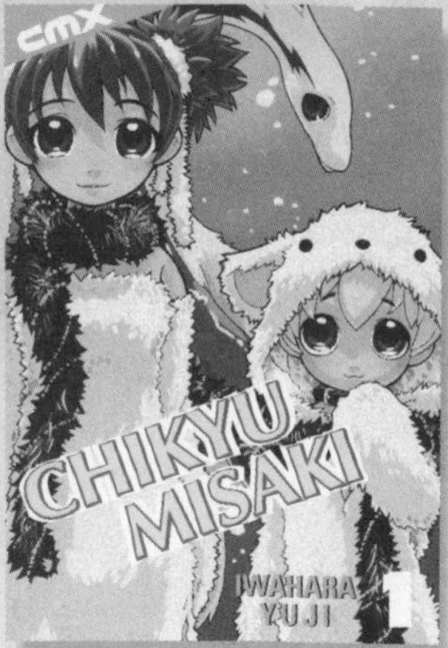

cmx
CHIKYU MISAKI
IWAHARA YUJI
1

By Iwahara Yuji
Entire Series Available!

For more information and sneak previews, visit cmxmanga.com. Call 1-800-COMIC BOOK for the nearest comics shop or head to your local book store.

Cover art and design may not be final.

CHECK OUT MORE OF OUR CMX TITLES!

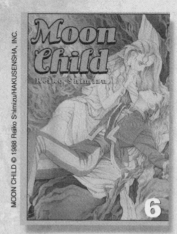

MOON CHILD © 1988 Reiko Shimizu/HAKUSENSHA, INC.

By Reiko Shimizu
6 Volumes Available

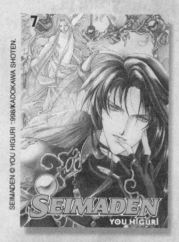

SEIMADEN © YOU HIGURI ·998/KADOKAWA SHOTEN.

By You Higuri
7 Volumes Available

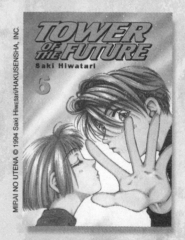

MIRAI NO UTENA © 1994 Saki Hiwatari/HAKUSENSHA, INC.

By Saki Hiwatari
6 Volumes Available

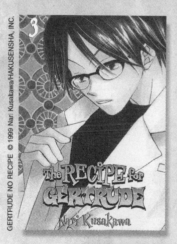

GERTRUDE NO RECIPE © 1999 Nari Kusakawa/HAKUSENSHA, INC.

By Nari Kusakawa
3 Volumes Available

For more information and sneak previews, visit cmxmanga.com.
Call 1-800-COMIC BOOK for the nearest comics shop or head
to your local book store.

Cover art and design may not be final.

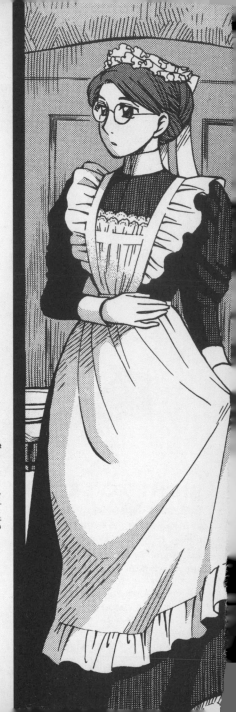

EMMA Vol. 3 © 2003 Kaoru Mori. All Rights Reserved. First
published in Japan in 2003 by ENTERBRAIN, INC.

EMMA Volume 3, published by WildStorm Productions, an
imprint of DC Comics, 888 Prospect St. #240, La Jolla, CA
92037. English Translation © 2007. All Rights Reserved.
English translation rights in U.S.A. and Canada arranged by
ENTERBRAIN, INC. through Tuttle-Mori Agency, Inc., Tokyo.
The stories, characters, and incidents mentioned in this
magazine are entirely fictional. Printed on recyclable paper.
WildStorm does not read or accept unsolicited submissions
of ideas, stories or artwork. Printed in Canada.

DC Comics, a Warner Bros. Entertainment Company.

Sheldon Drzka – Translation and Adaptation
Janice Chiang – Lettering
Larry Berry – Design
Jim Chadwick – Editor

ISBN:1-4012-1134-8
ISBN-13: 978-1-4012-1134-9

All the pages in this book were created—and are printed here—in Japanese RIGHT-to-LEFT format. No artwork has been reversed or altered, so you can read the stories the way the creators meant for them to be read.

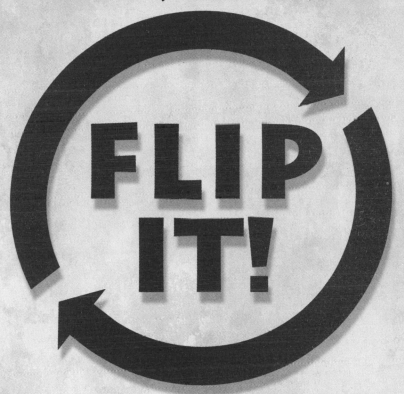

RIGHT TO LEFT?!

Traditional Japanese manga starts at the upper right-hand corner, and moves right-to-left as it goes down the page. Follow this guide for an easy understanding.

For more information and sneak previews, visit cmxmanga.com. Call 1-800-COMIC BOOK for the nearest comics shop or head to your local book store.

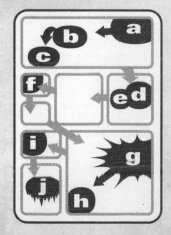